S0-DQB-385

Garden Gate®

The YEAR IN GARDENING

— VOLUME 13 —

AUGUST HOME
PUBLISHING COMPANY

SPECIAL PUBLICATIONS

The butterfly counts not months
but moments,
and has time enough.
— *Rabindranath Tagore*

Garden Gate®

Please contact us to find out about other *Garden Gate* products and services:

By Phone:	1-800-341-4769
By Mail:	2200 Grand Avenue, Des Moines IA 50312
By E-mail:	GardenGate@GardenGateMagazine.com

OR VISIT OUR
Web Sites: www.GardenGateMagazine.com
or www.GardenGateStore.com
or www.GardenGateSpecials.com

Copyright 2007 August Home Publishing Co.

All gardeners live in beautiful places
because they make them so.

— Joseph Joubert

Welcome

You hold in your hands a wealth of information from the pages of *Garden Gate* magazine 2007. Each year the editors bring you great stories about the plants you love, design ideas for your garden and basic how-to information from our test garden, along with tips and questions from our readers, before and after gardens and plans straight from our drawing board. We're here to help you create a beautiful place of your own!

In this new book, not only are all of the year's stories at your fingertips, but we've organized them in an easy-to-access format. Whether you're looking for inspiration from gardens we've photographed or how to plant and care for daylilies, you'll be able to find the information quickly and easily. It's like having the editors of *Garden Gate* in your own back yard.

Each section has its own contents and in the back of the book you'll find an index for the entire book along with zone maps.

So sit back with a cup of coffee and enjoy a full year of gardening!

Steven

Garden Gate®
The Illustrated Guide to Home Gardening and Design®

PUBLISHER Donald B. Peschke

EDITOR Steven M. Nordmeyer

MANAGING EDITOR Kristin Beane Sullivan

ART DIRECTOR Eric Flynn

SENIOR EDITOR Stephanie Polsley Bruner

ASSOCIATE EDITORS Jim Childs, Deborah Gruca

ASSISTANT EDITOR Sherri Ribbey

SENIOR GRAPHIC DESIGNERS Monte Hammond, Kevin Venhaus

ILLUSTRATOR Carlie Hamilton

SENIOR PHOTOGRAPHER David C. McClure

CORPORATE GARDENER Marcia Leeper

VIDEOGRAPHERS Mark A. Hayes, Jr., Craig Ruegsegger

ELECTRONIC IMAGE SPECIALIST Troy Clark

EDITORIAL INTERN Myra Gottl

Garden Gate® (ISBN 978-0-9798873-3-8) Garden Gate® is a registered trademark of August Home Publishing Co., 2200 Grand Avenue, Des Moines, IA 50312. © Copyright 2007, August Home Publishing Company. All rights reserved. PRINTED IN CHINA.

TO ORDER ADDITIONAL COPIES OF THIS BOOK VISIT, WRITE OR CALL

www.GardenGateStore.com

Customer Service
P.O. Box 842, Des Moines, IA 50304-9961

800-341-4769
(Weekdays 8 a.m. to 5 p.m. CT)

To learn more about *Garden Gate* magazine visit

www.GardenGateMagazine.com

Garden Gate®
contents

The YEAR IN GARDENING VOLUME 13

great plants *for* your garden

A BIT OF FRIENDLY ADVICE never hurts when it comes to getting your favorite flowers to grow better or coaxing a never-tried-before perennial into bloom for the first time. That experience is just what you'll find here. Learn growing tips, variety recommendations and even some great companion ideas in the pages that follow.

They're not just for fall anymore!

Extraordinary Asters

Botanical Names

Aster *Aster* spp.
Baby's breath
  Gypsophila paniculata
Bergenia
  Bergenia spp.
Lamb's ear
  Stachys byzantina
Mum
  Chrysanthemum hybrid
Sedum *Sedum* spp.

Gardens go out with a bang. Well, they do if you're growing asters. In the past few years, late-blooming asters have rivaled mums as plants you can pick up at your local garden shop. They're in pots, already blooming, so you can take them home and quickly freshen up your containers and gardens. But if those are the only members of the aster family you know, stay tuned. I have some unusual, and frankly extraordinary, ones to share that you may not be familiar with — and I know you'll want them in your garden next year.

But before I share all my aster family secrets with you, let's talk about the many ways you can use these flowers in your garden. All asters bloom with rounded daisy-shaped flowers. That makes them perfect companions to plants with spiky or narrow foliage or flowers. One of my favorite pairings, especially for the late-season cultivars, is asters and ornamental grasses. Surprisingly, that combo is also how you find many of the native asters — growing wild in a grassy meadow. But don't stop there.

Since several of the aster species have a delicate, almost airy look — kind of like a large-flowered baby's breath — pair them with plants that have coarse flowers and foliage. Low or short asters, like the spring- and summer-blooming species, contrast nicely with the large leaves of bergenia or lamb's ear. Taller asters can be planted next to tall sedum, such as dark-foliaged 'Black Jack', for both color and texture contrast.

Many of the taller asters are also good weavers, tying a grouping of plants together. To achieve this effect, don't pinch or cut back your asters to make them more compact — you want them to grow tall and be a bit on the floppy side. But do plant them between perennials that are almost as tall as they are so they can lean on their neighbors.

Asters fit lots of spots in most any garden. Let's take a closer look at some of the lesser-known, but beautiful, family members. We'll start with spring blooms and continue into late autumn. □

— Jim Childs

PHOTO: © Joseph G. Strauch Jr.

Size 10 to 12 in. tall by 10 to 12 in. wide

Bloom time Spring

Color Pink, white, blue and violet

Soil Well-drained

Light Full sun

Hardiness
Cold: USDA zones 3 to 8
Heat: AHS zones 8 to 1

Source
Busse Gardens
www.bussegardens.com
800-544-3192

SPRING FLOWERS

Alpine aster *Aster alpinus*

Have you ever noticed that every family has a few members who always show up early for an event? These asters bloom in late spring, usually May into June, and they're great in the front of the border. Each flower is on a single stem, perfect for small spring bouquets. 'Happy End', to the right, is a lovely pink, but you'll also find white, blue and deep violet shades. Alpine asters do best in lean, well-drained to dry conditions, like rock gardens. Plus, they're easily grown from seed, often flowering the first year. And don't deadhead: Alpine asters may even reseed in your garden if they like the spot.

SUMMER FLOWERS FOR BOUQUETS

East Indies aster *Aster tongolensis*

The 3-in.-diameter flowers of these asters would get noticed in any family. Each thick, unbranched stem supports a single flower, just like 'Wartburgstern' (Wartburg Star), the cultivar in this photo. That makes them stand straight in the garden, as well as in a vase. To get the sturdiest stems, plant in well-drained to moist, compost-enriched soil. There are several other cultivars of this early summer-blooming perennial, and almost all of them are in shades of violet and lavender. Grow East Indies asters near the front of the border. After the flowers are finished, the low mounds of foliage stay fresh-looking the rest of the season.

Size	16 in. tall by 15 in. wide
Bloom time	Summer
Color	Shades of violet
Soil	Well-drained to moist
Light	Full sun
Hardiness	Cold: USDA zones 4 to 8 Heat: AHS zones 8 to 1
Source	Forestfarm www.forestfarm.com 541-846-7269

Size	20 in. tall by 12 in. wide
Soil	Well-drained to dry
Bloom time	Late summer
Color	Golden yellow
Light	Full sun
Hardiness	Cold: USDA zones 4 to 8 Heat: AHS zones 8 to 1
Source	Specialty Perennials www.hardyplants.com 952-432-8673

BRIGHT YELLOW FLOWERS

Goldilocks *Aster linosyris*

Do you have distant cousins you rarely see? Goldilocks is from the European branch of the aster family and can be a bit hard to locate. But because it's one of the few yellow asters, it's worth looking for. In the photo at left you'll notice each flower doesn't have the usual skirt of flat petals. Instead, the gold center of each flower is shaggy with narrow, twisted petals, giving the plant a charming, casual look. Native to dry, sunny slopes in Europe, it's a good choice if you garden in sandy or sharply drained soils. Let the lanky stems weave in among ornamental grasses or other tall perennials for a colorful and informal autumn combination.

PHOTO: © Donna & Tom Krischan (East Indies aster, Goldilocks); © Jerry Pavia (calico aster)

Size   20 in. tall by 15 in. wide

**Bloom
time**   Late summer

Color   Pale pink to white

Soil   Moist to dry

Light   Full sun

Hardiness
   Cold: USDA zones 4 to 8
   Heat: AHS zones 8 to 1

Source
   Bluestone Perennials
   www.bluestoneperennials.com
   800-852-5243

GROWS ALMOST ANYWHERE

Calico aster *Aster lateriflorus*

One of the North American natives, calico aster can make itself at home in just about any sunny spot. While it grows best in well-drained garden soil, it'll perform quite beautifully even in clay. The one in the photo is 'Lovely'. If calico aster has one drawback, it's that it tends to lose its lower leaves to powdery mildew or drought. But then so do several of its cousins. Usually that happens about the time the flowers start to open. But it's not a problem if you remember to plant a slightly shorter plant in front of it. Bare knees on asters are a minor consideration when you're presented with billows of late-summer flowers.

CLASSIC ASTERS

New England asters, like 'Purple Dome' in this photo, and New York asters are often the ones you'll find in containers, ready to plant in fall. They're hardy cultivars you can plant in your garden and keep growing from year to year. But have you noticed that the second year some plants grow much taller and the flowers are smaller? Why is that?

First, the blooming asters you picked up in pots were pinched or clipped to make them compact and well-branched. Second, even though your garden soil may be rich, it can't compare with the constant fertilizing at a greenhouse to grow lush foliage and large flowers. And finally, most greenhouses use growth regulators that keep the plants short and stocky. These chemicals keep the stems from stretching to their full height. The next year, the chemical is gone from the plant, allowing it to grow to its normal size.

KEEPING THEM OVER If you like the compact, flower-covered look of the asters in the pots, simply buy them each fall. But if you want to keep them, pop the asters out of their pots and transfer them into your garden soil. Make sure they have a couple of weeks to establish roots out into the surrounding soil before the ground freezes. Add a layer of straw or crisp leaves over the crown and odds are your plants will make it through the winter. And next fall you'll have asters in the colors you like, only taller with a more casual, open look.

'Purple Dome' maintains a full, compact habit on its own. But many other asters need pinching or pruning to keep them from growing leggy.

COVER THE GROUND
Prostrate heath aster
Aster ericoides prostratus

Believe it or not, this family member comes to gardens by way of dry areas like roadside ditches. Some early ancestors grew quite tall. But over the years, some were bred to stay short. Check out 'Snow Flurry' in the photo. It's a low-spreading heath aster that's perfect as a ground cover, bed edging or a specimen cascading down a wall. Heath asters are rarely affected by mildew, a disease that disfigures the lower leaves of many asters. Another plus: Heath asters don't need pinching to grow clouds of flowers like this; they'll do it all on their own.

Size 4 to 6 in. tall by 18 in. wide

Bloom time Midautumn

Color White

Soil Well-drained to dry

Light Full sun

Hardiness
Cold: USDA zones 4 to 9
Heat: AHS zones 9 to 1

Source
High Country Gardens
www.highcountry
gardens.com
800-925-9387

LATEST BLOOMS
Tatarian aster *Aster tataricus*

Wow! This family member is tall — it can grow to 6 ft. or more — and doesn't require pinching or staking! 'Jindai', to the left, a compact cultivar, is usually not over 4 ft. tall. However, I think Tatarian aster's real claim to fame is its late bloom — often not until October, even after frost. Unlike many of its more delicate-looking relatives, this aster has stout stems and large, almost tobaccolike, leaves that really stand out in the autumn garden. This is another aster with almost no mildew problems. But in moist soil, its favorite spot, the species has a tendency to spread aggressively. 'Jindai' has better manners. It's still a good idea to divide Tatarian asters every three or four years to keep them in bounds.

Size 4 to 6 ft. tall by 2 ft. wide

Bloom time Late autumn

Color Lavender

Soil Moist to wet

Light Full sun

Hardiness
Cold: USDA zones 4 to 8
Heat: AHS zones 8 to 1

Source
Niche Gardens
www.nichegardens.com
919-967-0078

3 TIPS FOR GREAT ASTERS

Pinching and pruning

The most common method to make asters more compact is to simply pinch out the tip of each stem to force more side branching. You'll need to start in late spring and pinch every couple of weeks to get really bushy plants. New England, New York, calico and goldilocks asters can be pruned or pinched. But Tatarian, East Indies, alpine and prostrate heath asters really don't need it.

AN ALTERNATIVE TECHNIQUE Rather than pinching, simply cut the entire aster back in midsummer. Wait until the plant is half to two-thirds its full size and cut off one-third to half of its current height. As the aster resumes growing, it'll branch out, giving you more flowers on a compact plant.

Figure that most asters will stay about a third shorter than normal if you cut them back like this. Be sure to stop pruning asters by mid-July so the plants have time to set flower buds.

One note: Cutting back asters may delay the flowers a week or two. You can use this to your advantage and extend their bloom time. Check out the illustrations to the right to learn more about keeping the color going.

Pinch or prune asters near the front for later blooms.

Leave the asters behind to grow to full height and bloom earlier.

You won't see these 20-in.-tall stakes when this 30-in.-tall aster matures and begins to flower.

The pruned asters will cover the cut stems of the earlier flowers.

When the taller plants in back are done blooming, cut them back.

Stake asters right after you cut them back in midsummer.

Staking

If you haven't grown asters for years because they flop over, I've shown you a few that do fine without staking. But unfortunately, some, such as New England, New York, goldilocks and calico asters, often do need a bit of support to look their best. The key to staking is to get the supports in early, before they're really needed. I do mine shortly after I cut the plants back or do my last pinching, usually late June or early July. That's just before asters make a fast growth spurt in the heat of summer.

KEEP IT SIMPLE The easiest support technique is to place several thin bamboo stakes several inches from the edge of the crown and weave light twine or string between them. Make sure that when the stakes are firmly stuck in the soil they're about two-thirds the ultimate height of the aster. That way they'll still support the stems but are less likely to show when the aster is in flower.

Dividing

You'll have fuller, healthier plants if you divide your asters occasionally. So when the center looks woody, with new growth in a circle around it, like the illustration at right, it's time to lift, split and share.

Most asters have shallow roots that are easy to dig and split apart. In fact, many, like calico asters, simply fall apart when you shake the soil off. If you encounter a woody base, such as you'll find on a heath aster, you may need to pull and twist the roots apart.

THE BEST TIME TO DIVIDE Divide summer- to late-fall-blooming asters in spring, as soon as you see new leaves sprouting. Spring-blooming asters should be divided right after they flower. That'll give each type enough time to re-establish before it sends up flowers.

After replanting, keep the divisions moist (even asters that like it dry) for a week or two until they get growing again. Then adjust your watering to fit individual needs.

Divide asters when you spot a woody center with new sprouts in a ring around it.

Purple Beautyberry

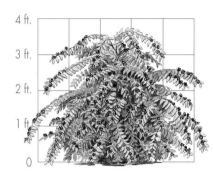

Callicarpa dichotoma

Size   3 to 4 ft. tall,
         4 to 5 ft. wide

Bloom   Small pink summer blooms,
         purple or white berries in fall

Type   Shrub

Soil   Moist, well-drained

Light   Full sun to part shade

Pests   None serious

Hardiness   Cold: USDA zones 5 to 8
             Heat: AHS zones 8 to 1

Mail-order sources

Fairweather Gardens
www.fairweathergardens.com
856-451-6261. *Catalog $5/2 years*

Forestfarm
www.forestfarm.com
541-846-7269. *Catalog free in U.S.,
$5 in Canada*

Your garden has only a few more weeks until winter, so dress it up for fall in bright colors. These glossy, almost metallic purple berries are some of the showiest around.

Beautyberry reaches 3 to 4 feet tall and a little wider. Paired medium-green leaves create a fine-textured, "fish-bone" look. Pink summer flowers aren't too showy, but the berries follow in early fall, changing from green to pink to rich purple. The leaves may stay green until they drop, or they may change to a pale yellow-green, as you see in the inset photo at right. After the leaves fall, the berries stay on the plant into early winter unless hungry birds pick them off.

Although you usually find the species for sale, there are a few cultivars with slight differences available. 'Early Amethyst' sets fruit earlier than others. 'Issai' is about 3 feet tall and wide and bears fruit even on very young plants. And *C. dichotoma albifructa* has glossy white berries, instead of purple.

GROWING BEAUTIFUL BEAUTYBERRY This shrub tolerates part shade and dry soil. But for the healthiest plants and best fruit display, plant it in full sun, in soil that stays consistently moist.

In USDA zone 5 or colder, beautyberry can die back in a harsh winter, sometimes almost to the ground. This won't kill the plant, but you'll need to prune in early spring to get rid of dead areas. Some gardeners like to cut beautyberry back to 6 inches tall every spring, whether it dies back or not, for a fuller, more compact plant.

GREAT DESIGN IDEAS Tuck beautyberry behind other late-season bloomers, like you see in "A fall bouquet" below. It'll form a soft backdrop during the summer. But make sure it's close enough to the front of the garden so you can appreciate the berries in fall.

Because beautyberry has a loose, open growing habit, group two or three plants together. That way, they'll form a nice, full cluster. They'll also cross-pollinate, so you'll have more fruit.

This shrub's berries will add "beauty" to your fall garden! □

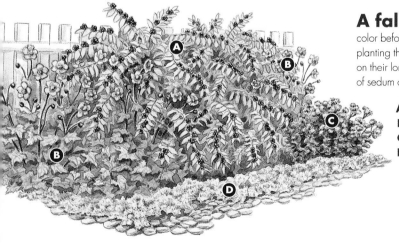

A fall bouquet Let your garden enjoy one last burst of color before winter closes in. Two beautyberries are at the center of this planting that's at its best in early to midfall. Japanese anemone's flowers, on their long stems, weave up through the beautyberry, while two kinds of sedum create a colorful border in front.

A   Purple beautyberry *Callicarpa dichotoma*
B   Japanese anemone *Anemone xhybrida* 'Robustissima'
C   Sedum *Sedum* 'Purple Emperor'
D   Creeping sedum *Sedum rupestre* 'Angelina'

Fancy-leafed *and* foolproof!

Angelwing Begonia

ANGELWING BEGONIA
Begonia coccinea

2 to 4 ft. tall,
   1 ft. wide
*White, pink, orange or red
   flowers in spring to fall*
Part shade
Well-drained soil
No serious pests or diseases
*Cold-hardy in
   USDA zones 10 to 11*
*Heat-tolerant in
   AHS zones 12 to 1*

Mail-order sources

Logee's Greenhouse
www.logees.com
888-330-8038. *Catalog free*

Avant Gardens
www.avantgardensne.com
508-998-8819. *Catalog $3*

Looking for a plant with fantastic foliage? You can't go wrong with angelwing begonias. A glance at these photos just begins to tell the story of all the leaf shapes and patterns they offer. And believe it or not, gorgeous leaves are just the tip of the iceberg for this plant.

Angelwing begonias are ridiculously easy to grow, and clusters of colorful flowers shine among the leaves all summer long. You can even bring your plants indoors at the end of the season, so you can keep on enjoying the show!

USING YOUR WINGS Growing in either an upright or an arching habit, angelwings have stems that remind me of bamboo. Some, like 'Cracklin' Rosie' in the inset at right, can reach 4 feet or taller in the ground, a little smaller if you grow it in a pot. After a few years, the plant can get a bit leggy. Cut it back hard to keep it to a manageable size and encourage branching. I'll talk about that in "Cutting back older plants" below.

Other cultivars, such as 'Orange Angels' in the other inset, have more spreading habits, perfect for smaller containers indoors or hanging baskets. Outside, the front of the border is my favorite spot to use them, especially along a path or sidewalk where you can enjoy the flowers.

GROWING WINGS For such dramatic-looking plants, angelwing begonias are actually very easy to grow. I planted two young 'Sinbad' starts in this part-shade pot last spring and they quickly filled it and bloomed all summer. The pink polka-dot plants and ivies make great container companions. Indoors, a bright east or west window will give you the best leaf color and the most flowers. Whether you grow them indoors or out, let the surface of the soil dry out between waterings.

Feed your angelwings once a month in spring and summer with a half-strength 20-20-20 fertilizer. Mine bloom from early summer right into fall, when temperatures drop to about 50 degrees at night. That's when I bring the plants inside. Or if you'd rather, take some cuttings to overwinter. When you bring in the pot, don't be in a hurry to move your plants to a larger container. Angelwings bloom best when their roots are just a bit crowded in the pot. I've had some in the same pot for three years, and they're still going strong.

Whether you grow angelwing begonias for the fancy leaves or their clusters of brightly colored flowers, being surrounded by this kind of beauty is pretty close to paradise! □

— *Deborah Gruca*

Cutting back older plants

Cut back older, lanky angelwings. Since they don't branch on their own, cut back all but one or two stems to three to four leaf nodes in late winter to early spring.

Eight weeks later the plant will have lots of leafy, branched stems and be flowering again.

PHOTO: Deborah Gruca (lead)

'Cracklin'
Rosie'

'Orange
Angels'

'Sinbad' has bicolored pink blooms
all summer long. Give the plant late
afternoon shade to keep the leaves
from scorching.

'Oranges and Lemons' Blanket Flower

24 in.

18 in.

12 in.

6 in.

0

Gaillardia '**Oranges and Lemons**'

Size	18 to 24 in. tall, 15 to 20 in. wide
Habit	Upright
Bloom	Early summer to frost; deadhead for best rebloom
Soil	Lean, well-drained
Light	Full sun
Pests	None serious
Hardiness	Cold: USDA zones 4 to 9 Heat: AHS zones 9 to 1

Daisy-shaped flowers always look happy. Add a burst of bright orange, and this blanket flower will put a smile on any gardener's face!

You've probably seen blanket flower around. In fact, it would be hard *not* to notice it, because most cultivars are bright red and yellow. 'Oranges and Lemons', a new-comer to the family, has orange flowers that are still showy but a bit more subtle. Unlike other blanket flowers, which often sprawl, this one tends to stay more upright.

But 'Oranges and Lemons' does share the best trait of all blanket flowers. It blooms practically nonstop from early summer until frost. A little deadheading as flowers fade will keep the plant looking tidy and blooming its best. Snip the long stems below the foliage, or you'll end up with lots of dry, twiggy stems.

Try 'Oranges and Lemons' in a container planting; it won't wimp out by midsummer. It's great with other dry-soil plants, like the ones in "Sunny skies" below. And be sure to include it in your but-terfly garden!

STAND BACK AND LET IT GROW This is one of the easiest perennials you can grow. Blanket flower not only toler-ates drought, it actually prefers poor, dry soil and hot sun. In moist, rich soil or too much shade, it may flop over.

Like many plants that bloom prolifically, blanket flower can be short-lived. But you can keep it going longer by dividing it. Every three or four years, dig the plant and split it — these new divisions will be more vigorous. Blanket flower can also heave out of the ground in winter, so dividing it is a chance to reset the plants to the right depth. You could also just buy a few new plants now and then — they grow quickly and usually flower the first year.

'Oranges and Lemons' may be a new twist on an old favorite, but it's still a plant you can turn to when the gardening gets tough. □

Sunny skies Blue and sun-orange — a classic color combination for a hot, dry spot. Soft-orange yarrow begins the show in early summer. (Cut it back and it'll rebloom.) Blanket flower and hyssop bloom in early to mid-summer and keep on going until frost. Plumbago sports bright-blue flowers in late summer and red foliage in fall. Tufts of blue fescue keep the garden interesting all season.

A Blanket flower *Gaillardia* 'Oranges and Lemons'
B Hyssop *Agastache* 'Blue Fortune'
C Yarrow *Achillea millefolium* 'Terracotta'
D Blue fescue *Festuca glauca* 'Boulder Blue'
E Plumbago *Ceratostigma plumbaginoides*

Mail-order sources

Garden Crossings LLC
www.gardencrossings.com
616-875-6355. *Online catalog only*

Busse Gardens
www.bussegardens.com
800-544-3192. *Catalog $3*

(1) Even in shade, coleus offers exuberant color. Ferns' calmer color helps temper the vibrant display.

Coleus

Color in the shade — no flowers required!

Question: What's red and green and grows in the shade? Oh yes, and also yellow and chartreuse and burgundy and cream and…I think you get the idea. The answer: Coleus, of course! You can see a small sample of what I'm talking about in the photo at left.

Coleus has been around since Victorian days and there are lots of reasons why it's as popular today as it was back then. For one thing, the leaves come in dozens of colors, patterns, shapes and sizes. They can be tiny, spotted, marbled and striped to giant, toothed, lobed or deeply divided, in almost every color but blue. In addition, the plants have a range of different habits and sizes, but I'll talk more about that on the next pages. Thinking about all that variety is enough to make your head spin. It's almost a relief that most coleus don't have showy flowers. That just might be too much!

GROWING COLEUS Although coleus is technically a tender perennial, even a hint of frost makes mush out of the sturdiest one. In spring, the soil warms up slower in garden beds than in containers. So fight the urge to rush out and set young plants in the garden too soon — the cold can stunt or even kill them. Once soil temperatures stay above 55 degrees, or about the time you set out tomato plants, it's OK to plant.

But aside from being frost-sensitive, coleus is a "no-brainer" to grow. Just give it part sun and warm, well-drained soil. Morning sun with afternoon shade is a good rule of thumb for just about any coleus. And though most coleus do well in all but dense shade, breeders have been introducing lots of sun coleus that can handle more light than many older hybrids. Some, but not all, have the word "sun" or "solar" in their

names. In general, leaves of brighter reds or greens look most vivid in sunnier locations. (Sometimes coleus with variegated leaves of white, yellow or cream will "green" up in too much sun.) If your plant is in a container, try it in different amounts of sun to see what it likes best.

MOISTURE MATTERS While coleus prefers even moisture, when grown in shade it'll tolerate dryer soil much better than it will soil that's too wet. If you garden where summers are very hot, be sure to give any coleus growing in sun plenty of water. Though it sometimes wilts in heat, it recovers quickly when you give it a drink. A couple inches of mulch around your plant will help keep the soil moist, too.

It might surprise you that despite all the color it provides, coleus doesn't need a lot of feeding. In fact, you get the best leaf color with just one dose of a balanced, 10-10-10 water-soluble plant food early in the spring with one or two applications more during the season. Even without fertilizer, coleus grows quickly. When the plant is small, pinch the stems back by about a third, if you want to keep the plant compact. And deadhead any flowers you see to keep the plant going strong.

COLEUS INDOORS When you grow coleus outdoors, it's pretty pest-free. If you overwinter plants indoors, keep an eye out for an occasional mealybug, spider mite or aphid. A couple sprays of Safer® soap should take care of the problem.

Want more of your favorite coleus? Let me show you an easy way to get 3-in. cuttings off to a fast start at right. Then turn the page to see some of the ways you can use this great plant in your garden — you may be surprised!

COLEUS
Solenostemon
hybrids

*6 in. to 5 ft. tall,
1 to 3 ft. wide*

*Colorful foliage with
purple spikes of flowers
(many people pinch
them off)*

Sun to part shade

Moist, well-drained soil

No serious pests or diseases

*Cold-hardy in
USDA zones 10 to 12*

*Heat-tolerant in
AHS zones 12 to 1*

*After a few days,
your cuttings
should form roots.
Pot them up
before the roots
are more than
½ in. long. Longer
water roots won't
make the
transition well
into soil.*

*If you let the
roots go too
long, it's OK,
too. Wait until
spring and take
a fresh
cutting from
this stem.*

(2) **Large-leafed coleus** makes a great accent plant, especially when you repeat it as a solitary plant in a unique container.

Botanical Names

Geranium
Pelargonium hybrid
New Guinea
impatiens
Impatiens hybrid
Oakleaf hydrangea
Hydrangea quercifolia
Purple heart
Tradescantia pallida
Rex begonia
Begonia rex
Tiarella
Tiarella hybrid

PHOTO: John Holtorf (3)

(3) **Use delicate, fine-textured foliage,** such as that of 'Inky Fingers', to create a soft background for the larger leaves and brighter colored flowers of impatiens and geraniums.

DESIGNING
WITH COLEUS

With all those leaf shapes, colors and patterns, coleus is a dream to design with. And with sizes that range from low-growing trailers to some that reach 5 feet tall or more, it's at home in lots of different situations.

CONTAINER CLASSIC Coleus grows happily in pots and makes great portable color for those midsummer blooming lulls anywhere in your garden. In photo 2, a single Kong™ Rose fills each pot. If you plant this variety in a container, you'll need to give it plenty of room. Each of these pots is 12 inches in diameter, so you can see that if it were growing with other plants, you'd need an even larger pot. Coleus also works great when you let it cozy up to other companions or trail lazily down the side of the pot. The burgundy centers of the 'Inky Fingers' leaves in photo 3 echo the color of the container.

Many coleus have a contrasting color on the undersides of the leaves. Take advantage of this. Why not match the top-of–the-leaf color of a coleus with the flower of one neighbor and the bottom-of-the-leaf color with the flower of another neighbor? The slightest breeze will reveal a whole new color combination!

Because it's fast-growing, coleus makes a great plant to train as a standard. See "High standards" below for cultivars that work especially well for this.

MASS APPEAL For an eye-popping effect, plant several different coleus together. It's like daubing paint on a canvas with a palette of coleus colors. Mix single-colored plants with ones with patterned leaves, so you don't leave visitors feeling woozy. Also, see how the chartreuse coleus at right are planted around the darker ones? The bright color helps the darker ones show up, and the burgundy/chartreuse combination really injects color into this shady bed. At the same time, the deeper hues keep the combination from looking too garish.

Space plants about a foot apart (a little more for taller cultivars). They'll fill in the space, knit together and crowd out any weeds in the process. And since all the coleus like the same conditions, maintenance is a breeze.

GREAT IN GARDENS Coleus also plays well with other plants in mixed beds. But you *do* need to watch what you plant around it. Because it's such a vigorous grower, it can easily overtake less-energetic companions. Of course, you can always pinch or cut back the stems of any bullies to keep them in check. But don't throw the stems away — tuck them into bare spots elsewhere in your beds. Coleus stem cuttings start easily in moist, well-drained soil, if you give them a little protection from harsh midday sun until they're established.

Another thing to think about when you choose garden partners for coleus: Pick ones that like the same growing conditions. Rex begonias or purple heart or even shrubs, such as oakleaf hydrangeas, make great neighbors. Large-leafed coleus (whether in containers or the garden) look especially beautiful when contrasted with plants with finer foliage, like shade-loving tiarellas and ferns.

(4) Coleus is perfect planted in mass. Use cultivars of different heights together to create a colorful, undulating effect.

HIGH STANDARDS

Making standards from traditionally used plants often takes years. But coleus grows quickly and is easy to train in as little as six months. You can use taller cultivars like 'Sunset' or 'Saturn', shown here, that top out around 5 ft. But shorter ones will give you the same effect, too.

WEB extra
Check out our *video* to create your own coleus standard.

A PALETTE OF COLEUS

Because the profusion of coleus can seem a bit mind-boggling, I've shared some of my favorites for you here. It's nice to know that they all basically boil down to two types: Annual and perennial.

Annual coleus grow quickly, flower, set seeds and then start to decline. Annuals are most often started by seed. These less-expensive coleus varieties are the ones sold in six-packs at garden centers.

Perennials (cold-hardy in USDA zones 10 to 12) flower later, if at all. Nurseries and garden centers tend to sell them in larger containers. Most coleus mail-order sources sell named annuals or perennials, but not all garden center coleus are identified. Unless you want to keep your coleus in a container for more than a year, either type will work fine.

There can sometimes be confusion about cultivar names, so it's often a challenge to find a specific one. But there are so many plants to choose from and they're so easy to grow, simply pick whichever one catches your eye. No matter what you call it, coleus is just plain fun. So get one — or two, or a dozen — and color your world with coleus! □

— *Deborah Gruca*

Mail-order sources

Color Farm
www.colorfarm.com

Rosy Dawn Gardens
www.rosydawngardens.com

www.coleusfinder.org
You can't order plants here, but you can identify hundreds of different coleus cultivars and find out where to buy them.

CRAZY NAMES What's in a name? Pretty bizarre things if the names of some coleus are any indication!

'Religious Radish' (in photo) Deep red with prominent deep-purple centers; 30 in. tall

'Murder Suspect' Cream and green spattered with deep red; 30 in. tall

'Rumpled Pink Skin' Crinkled, burgundy splotched with cream and pink markings; 18 in. tall

UNUSUAL LEAVES From tiny to frilly and everything in between — coleus has a huge array of leaf shapes.

'Swallowtail' (in photo) Green with bright-yellow frilly edges; 18 in. tall

'Tilt-a-Whirl' Twisting, round red, yellow and green with yellow jagged edges; 18 in. tall

'Tiny Toes' Diminutive, ¼-in.-wide oval red with chartreuse bands; 8 in. tall

BEST IN SUN If you have a spot that's sunny most of the day, these will perform best in your garden.

'JoDonna' (in photo) Burgundy centers surrounded by lime green; 30 in. tall

'Pineapple' Bright lime gold with burgundy stems; 18 in. tall

'Solar Eclipse' Black-marked, cherry-red toothed; 24 in. tall

'Solar Flare' Wide light-green with red centers and yellow edges; 24 in. tall

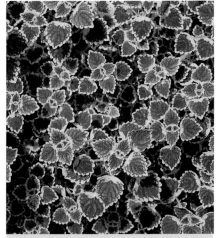

TRAILING OR SHORT These are 12 in. high or less and are perfect for spilling out of a container or at the front of any border.

'Red Trailing Queen' (in photo) Green-rimmed red; 12 in. tall

'Thumbellina' Tiny, 1-in., round green and burgundy; 6 in. tall

'Trailing Salamander' Black with green edges; 12 in. tall

GIANT LEAVES The only thing better than a beautiful, brightly colored leaf is a jumbo-sized, beautiful, brightly colored leaf. The leaves of these are all larger than 5 in. across.

'Atlas' (in photo) Large, cupped leaves; 18 in. tall

'Large Marge' Giant yellow and red with white veins; 24 in. tall

'Mocha Mint' Large, striking chartreuse and deep purple; 24 in. tall

FUNKY COLORS If you're looking for outlandish color combinations, try one or two of these.

'Gold Brocade' (in photo) Gold speckled with red-purple; 18 in. tall

'Bipolar By Golly' Pale lavender with centers speckled with red and yellow; 28 in. tall

'Kaleidoscope' Lemon yellow with crazy deep red streaks and centers of bright green; 30 in. tall

BEST IN SHADE Most coleus will tolerate some sun, but some colors look their best in shade. Deep colors like black and brown will look most intense, while whites and creams will stay brighter.

'Diablo' (in photo) Long red-ruffled with black centers; 34 in. tall

'Black Magic' Purple-brown with green-scalloped edges; 12 in. tall

'Butter Cream' Heavily ruffled green with pale cream center; 18 in. tall

JUMBO-SIZED At more than 24 in., these work well in the back of the border or in extra large containers.

'Saw Grass' (in photo) Deeply divided, green and gold; 24 to 30 in. tall

'Candy Store' Raspberry-pink, light green, and magenta; 28 in. tall

'Japanese Giant' Pink, violet and burgundy; 36 in. tall

'Mariposa' Crimson and pink; 36 in. tall

OUR READER NAMED THIS COLEUS!

Coleus breeders love coleus. And it shows every year when they introduce new ones with creative, descriptive (and sometimes, downright wacky) names. That's why we thought it would be fun to give *Garden Gate* readers a chance to share their coleus-naming skills with the world!

We had a huge response — more than 4,000 entries! And although it was tough, the folks from Color Farm, who provided this plant, chose 'Pinata' from reader Norma Dellorto of Bethlehem, Pennsylvania.

KEY FACTS Ruffled red leaves edged and splashed with chartreuse spots; 18 to 24 in. tall

SOURCE Color Farm, www.colorfarm.com

'Pinata'

PHOTOS: Deborah Gruca ('Saw Grass'); Courtesy Color Farm ('Pinata')

'Cheerfulness'

'Mount Hood'

'Pipit'

'Erlicheer'

'Mary Gay Lirette'

'Ceylon'

'Golden Bells'

Find out which ones do best in your region.

Daffodil Favorites

When it comes to spring bulbs, nothing packs as much "flower power" as daffodils. Why? Well, first, there's a wide array of species and cultivars with a huge range of hardiness zones. Because of that, unlike other spring bulbs, there's a daffodil for almost every part of the country — including *your* garden.

I've divided the United States and southern Canada into four areas and I'll share some specific growing tips for each. In "And the winners are..." at right, I've put together a list to help you find the best ones. (Check out our Web extra for a list of daffodil mail-order sources.)

NORTHEAST Depending on your USDA zone, daffodils from almost every division (there are 12 official categories based on plant characteristics) grow here. About the only ones that don't do well are the less-hardy tazettas and bulbocodiums. (And even these will grow along the coast where winters are milder.)

In zones 3 to 6, if your autumn is dry, water the bulbs after planting to get the roots growing. For extra protection, put down a layer of chopped leaves or evergreen boughs once the soil freezes. Then pull the mulch away from the plants in early spring.

SOUTHEAST Since winters don't get as cold here, plant bulbs about twice the bulb's height, instead of the normal three times. Heavy summer rain and humidity can rot bulbs, so it's best to plant them in raised or bermed beds with sharp drainage. Or you may need to lift and store them in a dry area over summer and replant them in the fall. To protect the planted bulbs from intense summer heat, place them where they'll get part shade as the weather warms.

In zones 8 and warmer, where spring is very brief, plant prechilled early and late-blooming cultivars as soon as you get them in fall. Water them in well, and give them a few good drinks through the winter if it's dry.

SOUTHWEST You might be surprised to find that you can grow daffodils even in the hot, dry weather of the southernmost parts of this region. Jonquilla and tazetta cultivars actually prefer the summer heat, but you'll probably need to water them through fall and again in spring. Also try triandrus and cyclamineus cultivars in this area.

NORTHWEST Almost every type of daffodil will grow in the area west of the Rockies. Plant bulbs in the fall before the rainy season starts, but don't water them or they'll be more likely to rot before the weather cools down.

If you regularly get more than 5 inches of rain per month in summer, lift the bulbs (except for tazettas, which tolerate some summer moisture) as I described for the Southeast.

Daffodils offer you easy-to-grow, long-lived color that you can enjoy every spring. And with so many to choose from, you'll never run out of new ones to try! □

— *Deborah Gruca*

AND THE WINNERS ARE...

- ▲ Northeast
- ■ Southeast
- ● Southwest
- ◆ Northwest

 WEB **extra**

Our list of daffodil mail-order **sources**.

NORTHEAST

Cultivar Name (Division)	Color of Petals/ Trumpet	Height	USDA Cold Zones	Bloom Time*	Also Thrives In	Comments
'Actaea' (poeticus)	White/yellow	15 to 17 in.	3-7	Mid- to late	■ ◆	Long-blooming; red band on cup; naturalizes well
'Beryl' (cyclamineus)	Yellow/orange	7 to 9 in.	4-9	Mid	● ◆	Short, banded cup; heirloom narcissus
'Ceylon' (large cup)	Deep yellow/orange-red	14 to 16 in.	4-8	Early to mid	■ ◆	Long-lasting up-facing flowers; naturalizes well
'Cherry Spot' (small cup)	White/bright orange	14 to 17 in.	4-8	Mid- to late	◆	Flat orange cup; forces well indoors
'Dutch Master' (trumpet)	All yellow	18 to 20 in.	4-8	Early to mid	◆	Upward-facing cup; forces well indoors
'Tahiti' (double)	Yellow/dark orange	16 to 18 in.	4-8	Mid	◆	Striking, very double blooms
'Mount Hood' (trumpet)	White/cream	15 to 17 in.	4-8	Mid	◆	Cream cup ages to white
'Mary Gay Lirette' (split corona)	White/salmon collar	14 to 16 in.	3-8	Early to mid	◆	Large, ruffled cups start yellow, age to salmon
'Sweetness' (jonquilla)	All yellow	12 to 14 in.	4-9	Mid	■ ● ◆	Very fragrant; forces well indoors
'Tete-a-Tete' (miniature)	Yellow/dark yellow	5 to 6 in.	4-9	Early	◆	Great for containers; forces well indoors

Trumpet, large-cup, small-cup, cyclamineus, poeticus, split-corona and miniature daffodils perform well in the Northeast.

SOUTHEAST

Cultivar Name (Division)	Color of Petals/ Trumpet	Height	USDA Cold Zones	Bloom Time*	Also Thrives In	Comments
'Avalanche' (tazetta)	White/yellow	16 to 18 in.	6-9	Mid- to late	● ◆	Clusters of up to 20 flowers; sweet fragrance
'Waterperry' (jonquilla)	White/yellow	8 to 10 in.	5-9	Mid	● ◆	Upward-facing yellow cups age to pink
'Pink Angel' (jonquilla)	White/white	12 to 14 in.	4-8	Mid- to late	● ◆	Cup has pink rim; fragrant; three flowers per stem
'Geranium' (tazetta)	White/red-orange	15 to 17 in.	5-9	Late	● ◆	Very fragrant; four to six flowers per stem
'Grand Soleil d'Or' (tazetta)	Yellow/orange	12 to 14 in.	8-11	Early	● ◆	Fruity fragrance; forces well indoors
'Ice Follies' (large cup)	Cream/light yellow	16 to 18 in.	4-8	Early to mid	◆	Very popular; long-lasting; naturalizes well
'Pipit' (jonquilla)	Yellow/white	14 to 16 in.	4-9	Mid	● ◆	Long bloomer; three to four flowers on each stem
'St. Keverne' (large cup)	All yellow	16 to 18 in.	4-8	Early	● ◆	Showy flower; forces well indoors
'Sailboat' (jonquilla)	Cream/yellow	10 to 12 in.	4-9	Late	● ◆	Fragrant, dainty white flowers with swept-back petals

Jonquilla, tazetta, species and some large-cup cultivars work well in the Southeast.

SOUTHWEST

Cultivar Name (Division)	Color of Petals/ Trumpet	Height	USDA Cold Zones	Bloom Time*	Also Thrives In	Comments
'Chinese Sacred Lily' (tazetta)	White/yellow	10 to 14 in.	8-11	Early	■ ◆	May need staking; fragrant; forces well without chilling
'Katie Heath' (triandrus)	White/pink	12 to 14 in.	4-9	Mid	◆	Multiple fragrant, pendant blooms
'Erlicheer' (tazetta)	Double white/ivory	12 to 14 in.	6-9	Early to mid	▲ ■ ◆	Very fragrant; protect from wind; forces well indoors
'Jetfire' (cyclamineus)	Red-orange/yellow	12 to 14 in.	4-9	Mid	▲ ◆	Eye-catching in large drifts; naturalizes well
'Peeping Tom' (cyclamineus)	All yellow	6 to 14 in.	4-8	Early to mid	▲ ◆	Long-lasting flowers with petals that curve backwards
'Sweet Love' (jonquilla)	White/yellow	12 to 16 in.	4-9	Mid	■ ◆	Sweet fragrance; lots of flowers on each stem
'Rapture' (cyclamineus)	All yellow	8 to 10 in.	4-8	Early	▲ ◆	Petals flare back from long trumpet-shaped cup
'Thalia' (triandrus)	All white	12 to 14 in.	4-9	Mid- to late	◆	Petite, very fragrant flowers; naturalizes well

Triandrus, cyclamineus, jonquilla and tazetta are good choices for the Southwest.

NORTHWEST

Cultivar Name (Division)	Color of Petals/ Trumpet	Height	USDA Cold Zones	Bloom Time*	Also Thrives In	Comments
'Baby Moon' (miniature)	Yellow/gold	4 to 8 in.	5-9	Late	■ ●	Sweet fragrance; many flowers on each stem
'Barrett Browning' (small cup)	White/orange-red	14 to 16 in.	4-8	Early	▲	Forces and naturalizes well
'Cheerfulness' (double)	White/light yellow	14 to 16 in.	4-9	Late	▲	Fragrant, long-lasting blooms; naturalizes well
'Falconet' (tazetta)	Gold/orange	12 to 14 in.	5-9	Mid	■	Musky, sweet scent; up to eight flowers on each stem
'Felindre' (poeticus)	White/yellow	16 to 18 in.	3-7	Late	■	Star-shaped petals; cup has red rim, green eye
'Fragrant Rose' (large cup)	White/pink	16 to 18 in.	4-8	Late	▲	Rose-scented; pink-purple cup has green-white eye
'Golden Bells' (hoop petticoat)	All yellow	7 to 8 in.	5-9	Mid	▲	Megaphone-shaped cup, narrow petals
'Ice Wings' (triandrus)	All ivory-white	10 to 12 in.	4-9	Early to mid	●	Fragrant, long-lasting, nodding flowers
'Marieke' (trumpet)	All yellow	20 to 24 in.	4-8	Early	▲	Long-lasting, upward-facing cut flower
'Mondragon' (split corona)	Gold/orange collar	13 to 17 in.	4-8	Mid	▲	Spectacular showy flowers with strong apple scent
'Surfside' (cyclamineus)	Ivory/white	12 to 14 in.	4-9	Mid	▲ ●	Large, showy, ruffled ivory cup

Most daffodil types thrive in the Northwest.

* Bloom time varies by area and elevation. For example, early cultivars may open in February in the Southeast and in April in the Northeast.

'Scura'

'Crystal Beauty'

'Christmas Star'

Light up your late-summer garden.

Dahlias

'Park Princess'

DAHLIA
Dahlia hybrid

*12 to 72 in. tall,
  12 to 36 in. wide*
Blooms late summer into fall
Sun to part shade
Moist, well-drained soil
No serious pests or diseases
*Cold-hardy in
  USDA zones 8 to 12*
*Heat-tolerant in
  AHS zones 12 to 1*

There's always such a rush to get everything in the ground in spring. Wouldn't it be nice if some plants could wait just a bit? Dahlias can. They need warmth to grow — rush to get them into cold spring soil and they'll just sit. Or worse yet, rot. So, after you see how easy dahlias are to grow, you'll still have time to order a few for your garden this year.

When you start shopping, you'll discover there are lots of cultivars to consider. Color usually attracts me first. With dahlias, there's a virtual rainbow to choose from. Next comes flower size and shape, and again there's a huge variety. Just look at the range in the photos below — this is just a fraction of what you can find. And finally, you need to know how tall the plant will grow. You'll find everything from dwarf cultivars to towering giants.

Many gardeners only focus on the dahlia flowers. And that's fine if you're just growing them for cutting. But if you want to plant a few into containers or flower borders, you need more information. For example, giant dinner-plate dahlias look so stunning on the package photos. But when I've grown them, they usually don't produce many blooms, and sometimes they look like giant space aliens in my garden, dwarfing the other flowers. In the end, I've always been happier with dahlias that produce smaller blossoms (about 4 inches in diameter, like 'Tasagore' in the lead photo). They have a more graceful branching habit and set more flowers.

I like to buy from a specialty retailer, like the ones at right. The folks there can share information on flower size and plant habit and plenty of other tips on specific varieties to help you make the best choices.

If you've always thought dahlias were hard to work into your garden, I'll share some design ideas next. Later, I have tips on the best way to grow, store and make sure you keep getting more of them.

Mail-order sources

Swan Island Dahlias
www.swanislanddahlias.com
503-266-7711. *Catalog $4*

Old House Gardens
www.oldhousegardens.com
734-995-1486. *Catalog $2*

'Ms. Kennedy'

'Nita'

'Forty Niner'

BIRDHOUSE DESIGN: Matt Vanderwerff

DESIGNING WITH DAHLIAS

PHOTO: © Charles Mann (1)

Botanical Names

Baby's breath
 Gypsophila paniculata
Columbine *Aquilegia* spp.
Crocosmia *Crocosmia* spp.
Dahlia *Dahlia* hybrid
Leopard's bane
 Doronicum spp.
Oriental poppy
 Papaver orientale
Zinnia *Zinnia* hybrid

Because of the variables you've just read about, dahlias are extremely versatile when it comes to design. If you're growing them for cutting, it's probably best to plant them in beds of their own. That way you don't have to worry about ruining your landscape when you cut a few blooms to bring indoors. But let me show you how to make them welcome additions in the rest of your garden, too.

CONTRAST FLOWER SHAPES The bold, round shaped blooms of dahlias comple-ment smaller flowers, making them great companions in a flower border. The cactus-flowered dahlia in photo 1 is a great foil for the arching spikes of this crocosmia.

Before you tuck dahlias into your perennial beds, you need to consider a few things. First of all, they need some room. A dahlia that grows 4 to 5 feet tall will need a space about 3 feet wide. That can leave a big hole in your border for much of the early summer. One way you can remedy this is to grow perennials nearby that peak early and fade. If Oriental poppies were sharing space with the dahlias in photo 1, they'd bloom in spring and be long gone by the time the later-blooming dahlias and crocosmias hit their stride. Other good early blooming companions include columbine, baby's breath and leopard's bane.

CONSIDER FLOWER SIZE Smaller-flowered dahlias, like the pink-flowered ones in photo 2, are great planted in mass. When choosing dahlias for the middle or near the front of a border like this, I prefer cultivars that have blooms less than 4 inches in diameter. They tend to be better neighbors, not stealing the show from flowers and foliage around them. You'll find compact forms to grow near the edge like these, or tall cultivars with small blossoms for further back in the border.

However, if you want a show-stopping focal point, don't shy away from the tall, 10- to 12-inch-diameter dahlias. The flowers will all be near the top so you'll want to plant tall perennials in front of them to cover their bare legs.

(1) Contrast rounded dahlia flowers with nearby plants that have different shapes, like this spiky crocosmia, for a stimulating and energizing combination.

(2) **Dark foliage** ties a color blend of dahlias together in this border of annuals. It also provides a backdrop for these vivid 'Profusion Fire' zinnias.

LET THEM RELAX You always read that dahlias have to be staked. The ones in photos 1 and 2 are, but take a look at photo 3. These look just fine tumbling over a low wall. I think this is a really unusual and innovative way to show off the beautiful flowers without trying to change the plant's naturally loose habit.

PLANT THEM IN CONTAINERS At around 12 inches tall, dwarf dahlias are wonderful container partners. You can usually purchase them in spring as started plants at your local garden center. One thing to keep in mind as you pot up dwarf dahlias: They may not grow much taller than they are when you bring them home. Surrounding plants will swallow them up if you're not careful. I think they're ideal at the edge of a pot or narrow window box where they're less likely to be squeezed out by close neighbors.

Because they look so perfect, you might think dahlias are hard to grow, but they're not. On the next pages I'll show you how to have spectacular blooms this summer.

(3) **You don't *have* to stake dahlias.** If you have one that's around 3 ft. tall, let it cascade gracefully over the edge of a low wall.

LOCATION: Sunken Gardens, Lincoln, NE (2)

GROW STUNNING DAHLIAS

The first time you mail-order a dahlia, you may be surprised at what arrives. I know I was. I didn't expect a single tuber about the size of my thumb. After a quick phone call, I was assured I would have beautiful flowers from this puny thing. Sure enough, by late summer I had a 5-foot-tall plant loaded with flowers. I'll show you how to get the same results I got in "What great dahlias need" to the right.

WATER AND FEED YOUR DAHLIAS After planting, don't water your newly planted tuber until you see sprouts, or it may rot. (If it rains, don't worry, that's OK.) Once the tuber is up and growing, it'll need about an inch of water a week. And a couple of inches of mulch will help keep an even supply of moisture for the roots. A low-nitrogen fertilizer, such as a 5-10-10, will give you strong dahlias. Too much of the first number and you'll get lots of foliage, weak flower stems and fewer flowers.

THE BEST WAY TO DIG If you don't grow dahlias because you can't find a good spot to store them, don't let that stop you — simply replace the tubers each spring. But if you grow a favorite cultivar, or are frugal like I am, you can dig and store the tubers. Wait until the leaves have been blackened by frost and then cut the stems off. Leave the tubers in the ground for another week, then dig them and gently wash off the soil. Lay them in the shade for a day or two to dry. You can store the entire cluster of tubers and separate it in spring or divide in fall when the tubers are still plump and the buds are easier to spot. I'll show you how in "Where to cut" below.

STORE THE TUBERS Before you store your tubers, soak them in a solution of 1 cup chlorine bleach and 3 gallons of water for 15 minutes. This will head off disease and insect problems. Let them

dry for a day and place them in large resealable plastic bags. Add 2 or 3 cups of damp sphagnum peat or vermiculite to each bag before zipping it shut. Store the bags in a dark spot that stays 40 to 45 degrees F. Check the bags once a month. If there's lots of condensation on the plastic, or you spot mold on the tubers, open the bag for a few days to let out excess moisture. But if the tubers are starting to shrivel, add a tiny bit of water. Throw out any tubers that are rotting before the problem spreads.

Next spring, the tubers will be firm and moist. You may find they've shriveled a bit, but they'll feel heavy for their size. If they're dry and light, they won't grow.

Spring is just around the corner. You still have time to check out our sources on p. 31, order a few tubers and get them in the ground for a spectacular late-summer show. □

— *Jim Childs*

WHERE TO CUT

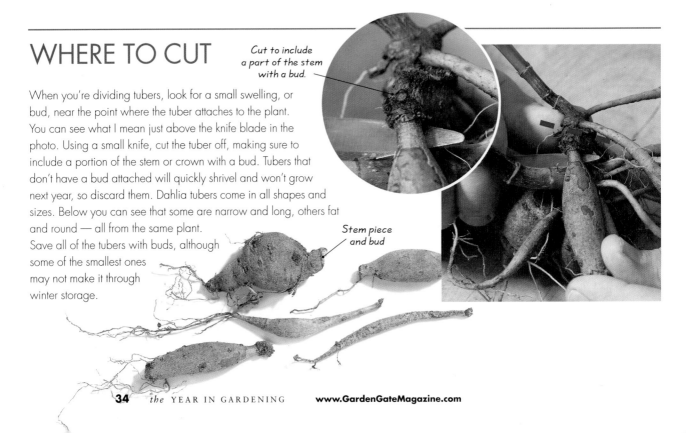

Cut to include a part of the stem with a bud.

When you're dividing tubers, look for a small swelling, or bud, near the point where the tuber attaches to the plant. You can see what I mean just above the knife blade in the photo. Using a small knife, cut the tuber off, making sure to include a portion of the stem or crown with a bud. Tubers that don't have a bud attached will quickly shrivel and won't grow next year, so discard them. Dahlia tubers come in all shapes and sizes. Below you can see that some are narrow and long, others fat and round — all from the same plant.

Save all of the tubers with buds, although some of the smallest ones may not make it through winter storage.

Stem piece and bud

WHAT GREAT DAHLIAS NEED

In this illustration, you'll learn how to plant and grow dahlias to perfection. But don't be in a hurry to get them in the ground in spring. The soil needs to be at least 60 degrees F or the tuber will rot. Plan to plant dahlias about the same time you set out tomato plants.

Dahlias need well-drained soil; they don't like wet feet. And a pH around 6 is ideal. Meet these requirements and follow the simple tips you see here and you'll be rewarded with beautiful dahlias by late summer.

PINCH FOR MORE BRANCHES. When you see two or three sets of leaves on your dahlia plant, pinch out the growing tip, as you see above. That'll stimulate more branching so you get more flowers later on. If you're growing giant flowers, don't pinch. You want the energy to go into fewer, but bigger, flowers.

GET THE TUBER IN THE GROUND. Dig a hole 12 in. deep. Mix in a shovelful of well-rotted compost and bring the level back up to about 6 in. Lay the tuber on its side and cover it with 2 in. of soil. As the sprout grows, add soil until the area is level. This keeps the tuber warmer and helps it grow faster.

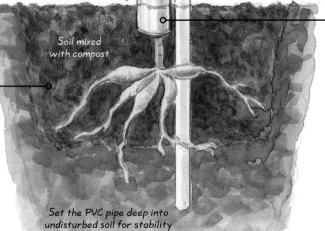

Soil mixed with compost

Set the PVC pipe deep into undisturbed soil for stability

KEEP THE FLOWERS COMING. Cut or snap the spent flower heads off so the plant won't waste energy trying to produce seeds. Or if you prefer, cut flowers at their peak for bouquets. Cutting in the early morning will help your flowers last longer in the vase, often much longer than ones cut in the heat of the day.

TIE THEM TO THE STAKE. Dahlia stems are hollow and brittle, so don't tie them too tightly. Make a figure-8 loop as you see here. Or wrap the fabric strip or twine around the stake a couple of times before you bring the stem up to it. Otherwise the stem will rub on the stake and be damaged, opening the plant to infection.

HELP THE STEMS STAND TALL. Dahlias over 3 ft. tall will need to be staked. But until the plant grows, who wants to look at a bare stake sticking up in the garden? When planting, insert a 2-ft. piece of ½-in.-diameter PVC pipe at the bud end of the tuber. When the stem needs support, insert a section of steel rerod into the pipe and tie the stem to it.

PEST PROTECTION. This is a mostly trouble-free flower. However, slugs and cutworms can quickly destroy young plants. To keep cutworms away, set a small can as a collar around the sprout as it pokes through the soil. And a band of diatomaceous earth sprinkled on the soil after each rain will help prevent slug damage.

DATURA
Datura spp.

*12 to 48 in. tall,
18 to 60 in. wide*

*White, yellow or purple
flowers in mid- to
late summer*

Full sun

Well-drained soil

No serious pests or diseases

*Cold-hardy in
USDA zones 5 to 10
(varies by species)*

*Heat-tolerant in
AHS zones 12 to 1*

___

Botanical Names

Brugmansia
Brugmansia hybrids
Hollyhock
Alcea hybrids
Maiden grass
Miscanthus spp.

Exotic, fragrant and easy to grow

Datura

There's nothing shy about datura! Huge, 6- to 8-inch-long flowers that open in late afternoon and evening, bold foliage and fragrance that can fill a yard make this plant stand out anywhere.

You'll find lots of common names: thorn apple, angel's trumpet, or devil's trumpet. (This last name refers to the plants being quite poisonous, so don't eat them!) Unfortunately, lots of species share those common names, so to tell them apart, we've used botanical names here.

Some plants are big and spreading, like the purple-tinged white datura (*D. wrightii*) in the photo. But others are more compact, with white, purple or yellow flowers that can be single, double or triple. There are many species, but *D. metel*, a tender perennial hardy in USDA zone 10, is the one you'll usually find for sale. The two in the small photos are *D. metel* cultivars. Datura flowers face upward, which distinguishes them from brugmansia, a related species with woody stems and dangling flowers.

USING DATURA IN THE GARDEN Big, bold plants like this can be hard to work into a planting. But datura adds an exotic touch to any garden in the heat of summer when other plants aren't looking their best.

Hollyhocks are great partners — see how their height and bright color balance the bulkier datura in the photo? Maiden grass is another good companion, as it's not overwhelmed by datura's spreading growth. And its fine texture contrasts with datura's coarser leaves.

But if you don't have much room, grow datura in containers. It'll stay smaller, and one in a pot will scent your patio every evening with a sweet, lemony fragrance.

EASY TO GROW Datura needs full sun. It'll bloom best with regular watering, but it needs well-drained soil. A little compost is all the fertilizer most datura plants want, though you might add a handful of slow-release fertilizer to the soil if you're growing one in a container.

You can treat datura as a summer annual, or keep *D. metel* hybrids over the winter indoors. Other species, like *D. wrightii* and *D. inoxia*, can make it through a mild winter outdoors as far north as USDA zone 5. Check out "The seed scene" at left for more info on growing them from seeds.

This plant doesn't have a lot of pests, but you may see big green tobacco hornworms munching on it. They're 3 or 4 inches long, so you'll be able to find them and pick them off the plants if necessary.

Want exotic charm in a low-maintenance package? Take a look at datura. □

— *Stephanie Polsley Bruner*

THE SEED SCENE

Datura's spiky seed pods, at left, look great in winter, but many species reseed. So deadhead the plant to keep seedlings in check if necessary

If you want a specific cultivar and you can't purchase small plants, you can start them from seed in soil that's about 68 degrees. Start seeds indoors six to eight weeks before the last frost date, and don't transplant until there's no chance of a freeze.

PHOTOS: © Charles Mann (lead);
© Donna & Tom Krischan ('Ballerina Purple')

'Ballerina Purple'

'Ballerina Yellow'

Mail-order sources

Thompson & Morgan
www.thompson-morgan.com
800-274-7333. *Catalog free*

Select Seeds
www.selectseeds.com
800-684-0395. *Catalog free*

'Baja'

DAYLILY
Hemerocallis hybrid

*1 to 3 ft. tall,
   9 to 24 in. wide*

*Red, pink, orange
   yellow, purple or cream
   flowers in early summer
   through fall*

Full sun to part shade

Well-drained soil

*Daylily rust is an
   occasional problem*

*Cold-hardy in
   USDA zones 3 to 9*

*Heat-tolerant in
   AHS zones 9 to 1*

There's nothing easier to grow
Daylilies

Looking for a cheery flower for a cottage garden? Try a daylily. Prefer something elegant for a formal garden? Try a daylily. Or maybe you want an easy perennial for just about anywhere? You guessed it…try a daylily. These versatile flowers fit any garden. And for plants with a lot of flower power, they don't need much care.

Sometimes people think that daylilies are just orange, like the ones at right. But the photo below should change your mind — daylilies come in yellow, pink, red, purple, cream and white.

Now, I admit I have a soft spot for those common-as-dirt orange "ditch lilies." They're tough as nails and great for stabilizing a slope. But they can get out of hand, and they're just not very interesting. However, there are daylilies out there that will knock your socks off! (And they won't spread like crazy, either.) In addition to all those colors, you'll find ruffled edges, double flowers, colorful eye zones and more.

On the next pages, I'll help you find just the right daylilies for *your* garden.

(1) A massed planting of **daylilies** can offer blossoms from early summer until fall if you choose cultivars with overlapping bloom times.

Daylilies hybridize easily, so you might not find a cultivar just like this one. But with so many to choose from, you'll find one that's pretty similar.

REBLOOMING DAYLILIES

Botanical Names

Foxtail lily *Eremurus* hybrid
Garden phlox *Phlox* hybrid

You just can't have too much of a good thing. And a daylily that reblooms is definitely a good thing.

There's some debate in gardening circles about how to classify these plants. Most plants that rebloom have a flush of flowers, then a rest period, then another flush. Some reblooming daylilies do that, but many of them just keep going for several months instead of three or four weeks. (That's often called "extended bloom.") How they act in your garden depends on the temperature and the amount of water and sun they get, so it can be a little hard to tell the difference between reblooming and extended bloom. But whatever you call it, most gardeners aren't going to complain!

One thing you'll notice about many reblooming daylilies is that they're compact, with small flowers and slender foliage, like 'Black Eyed Stella' in photo 2. This helps them stand up better to wind and rain than some taller daylilies, so they'll give you a neater look in the garden.

'Stella de Oro', in the inset at left, is the "original" rebloomer. It flowers all summer and it's tough as nails, but that yellow-orange isn't everyone's favorite color. Don't despair — you'll find pink and red rebloomers for sale too, like pink 'Rosy Returns' and red 'Pardon Me' on the next page. In "Keep them blooming" at right, I'll share more reliable rebloomers and extended bloomers, as well as some tips about how to keep them going strong.

DESIGNING WITH REBLOOMERS A massed planting of reblooming daylilies is a great way to fill in a spot where you need lots of color quickly. After all, these plants can even stand the conditions around parking lots, so imagine how great they'll look in your garden with just a little basic care.

Or mix rebloomers into a perennial border. With their long bloom time, they'll add a lot of color, and since many of them are less than 18 inches tall, they're great front-of-the-border plants. Plus, reblooming daylilies, especially the smaller ones, tend to stay in neat, upright clumps that don't fall open in the center. So you won't have a ratty looking plant taking up space in the front of your planting. That tidy habit also makes them great for edging a sidewalk or pathway.

Rebloom isn't all that daylilies have to offer. Keep reading to learn about ruffles, eye zones and other colorful features!

'Stella de Oro'

(2) Many reblooming daylilies are small, compact plants. That's why this 'Black Eyed Stella' is great in front of this taller foxtail lily and clump of garden phlox.

(3) Some rebloomers, like 'Rosy Returns', actually flower from summer until fall without any "down time."

(4) Small daylilies like 'Pardon Me' make great, long-blooming container plants.

KEEP THEM BLOOMING

Like all daylilies, rebloomers are easy to have around. But a little extra care in deadheading will keep them looking their very best. Snap off the spent blooms every day or two. When all the blooms on a stalk are done, snip the entire stalk off. In the illustration at right, see how we're snipping the stalk as close to the ground as possible? Your plant will be able to put all its energy into setting more flowers, and you won't have to look at brown stalks poking up out of the middle of the plant.

Seven great rebloomers
'Apricot Sparkles' Apricot, "diamond-dusted," 24 in. tall, 4-in. blooms
'Black Eyed Stella' Yellow, burgundy-red eye; 22 in. tall; 3-in. blooms
'Happy Returns' Lemon-yellow; 18 in. tall; 3-in. blooms
'Joan Senior' White with pale-yellow throat; 18-24 in. tall; 5-in. blooms; semi-evergreen
'Pardon Me' Red with yellow-green throat; 18 in. tall; 2½-in. blooms
'Rosy Returns' Rose-pink, darker pink eye zone; 15 in. tall; 4-in. blooms
'Stella de Oro' Yellow-orange; 12 in. tall; 2-in. blooms

Snip spent stalks off at the base for a tidier plant.

PHOTOS: © Mary Howell Williams (2); © Image Botanica (3); © Jerry Pavia (4)
ILLUSTRATIONS: Mavis Augustine Torke; LOCATION: Sandra M. Branam, West Des Moines, IA (2)

PICK YOUR FAVORITES

I told you earlier that not all daylilies are orange — let me show you just how true that is. We've talked about the rebloomers; now let's meet the rest of the family. (Although some of the daylilies on these two pages have long bloom times, too.) Ruffles, double flowers, frilled edges, two-toned blooms and more…there's truly something to appeal to every gardener.

Below, you'll find some examples of different daylily looks, plus a list of others that share those characteristics. But as you're flipping through catalogs looking at daylilies, you'll notice a few terms that aren't quite as obvious from a photograph.

First, you might see the words *tetraploid* or *diploid* in a description. This has to do with how many chromosomes the plant has, which can affect hardiness, vigor and "extra" looks like ruffles. But since you're probably just buying them because you like how they look, don't worry too much about how many chromosomes a plant has!

RUFFLED PETALS Some daylilies, like 'My Pet', have softly ruffled petals, while others have tightly crimped edges.

'My Pet' (above) Apricot with rounded petals; midseason; 20 in. tall; 3- to 4-in. flowers

'Fairy Tale Pink' Diamond-dusted peach-pink with pale green throat; midseason; 24 in. tall; 5-in. blooms; long-blooming

'Gordon Biggs' Raspberry-pink; early to midseason; each flower lasts up to 16 hours; 24 in. tall; 4-in. blooms

'Grace, Peace and Love' Soft peach with yellow crimped edges; late season; 26 in. tall; 6-in. blooms; slightly fragrant

'Spacecoast Starburst' Lavender-pink with yellow crimped edges; early to midseason; 24 in. tall; 6-in. blooms; evergreen foliage

DOUBLE FLOWERS Want to make the neighbors talk? Plant double daylilies — they're a unique look in any garden. You're most likely to find them in yellow or apricot, but more are becoming available in other colors.

'Siloam Double Classic' (above) Clear pink with green throat; midseason; 16 to 24 in. tall; 4-in. blooms; fragrant; rust-resistant

'Chicago Firecracker' Bright red with yellow throat; blooms may be single or double; early to midseason; 26 in. tall; 5-in. blooms

'Jean Swann' Creamy white; midseason; 32 in. tall; 6-in. blooms

'Longfield's Twins' Rust-red with yellow highlights; midseason; 26 in. tall; 6-in. blooms; slightly fragrant

'Siloam Peony Display' Apricot with darker orange throat; mid- to late season; 18 in. tall; 5-in. blooms

COLORFUL THROATS Most daylilies have a slightly different color deep down in the "throat" of the flower, but on dark-colored daylilies, it's a striking color difference that really stands out.

'Malaysian Monarch' (above) Purple with yellow-green throat; color doesn't fade in full sun; midseason; 32 in. tall; 5-in. blooms

'Barbara Mitchell' Pale-pink with yellow-green throat; midseason; 32 in. tall; 5-in. blooms; long bloom time; rust-resistant

'Bela Lugosi' Dark burgundy-purple with yellow throat; midseason; 32 in. tall; 6-in. blooms; semi-evergreen foliage

'Night Beacon' Dark red with very large bright-yellow throat; early to midseason; 24 in. tall; 4-in. blooms

'Prairie Blue Eyes' Lavender-pink with pale yellow throat; midseason; 26 in. tall; 5-in. blooms

Another term you'll see is "diamond-dusted." Diamond-dusted petals, usually found on lighter colors, are covered with tiny, iridescent dots, making the flower surface seem to sparkle. Expect to see more of these in the future.

In the gallery below, I've mentioned whether each daylily is an early, midseason or late bloomer, so you can choose a few that will keep your garden flowering all summer long. Turn the page to find out some design tips for your favorite daylilies.

The evergreen myth?

Simply put, *evergreen* daylilies have foliage that stays green all winter, and *dormant* daylilies have foliage that dies back completely. But it's not quite that easy.

How a daylily behaves depends on your climate and the kind of winter you're having. Evergreen daylilies are truly evergreen only in warmer climates. In Northern winters, a daylily that might be evergreen farther south will die back. This won't hurt the plant, but it'll keep trying to grow, which may mean you'll end up looking at brown, damaged leaf tips instead of evergreen foliage.

EYE ZONES
Some daylilies show off a prominent "eye zone," or mark in the center of the petals. Flowers with this kind of marking are usually light-colored with darker eye zones.

'El Desperado' (above) Buff yellow with dark purple "picotee" edge and eye zone; late season; 30 in. tall; 4-in. blooms

'Awesome Blossom' Dusty rose with plum-purple eye zone; early to midseason; 24 in. tall; 5-in. blooms; evergreen foliage

'Cherry Valentine' Pink flowers with red eye zone, variable red picotee edge; early season; 24 in. tall; 4-in. blooms; evergreen foliage

'Raspberry Candy' Cream-white with raspberry-red eye zone; early season; 22 in. tall; 4-in. blooms

'Siloam Merle Kent' Lavender-pink with purple eye zone; midseason; 18 in. tall; 4-in. blooms

SPIDER FLOWERS
A "spider" daylily is one whose petals are at least four times as long as they are wide. Most spider daylilies have red or yellow petals that can be gently curved or crazy and twisted.

'Red Ribbons' (above) Bright red with large yellow-green throat; midseason; 42 in. tall; 8-in. blooms

'Easy Ned' Chartreuse-yellow; early to midseason; 40 in. tall; 6-in. blooms; semi-evergreen foliage

'Judge Roy Bean' Soft red with yellow throat; midseason; 39 in. tall; 9-in. blooms

'Kindly Light' Clear yellow; mid- to late season; 28 in. tall; 6-in. blooms

'Scorpio' Golden-orange; mid- to late season; 36 in. tall; 7-in. blooms; semi-evergreen

DAYLILY RUST

You may have heard about the growing threat of daylily rust. This disease is serious, but certainly no reason to stop growing daylilies! Rust doesn't kill plants, but it causes spots and streaking on the leaves, and infected leaves turn brown and die. If you see suspicious spots, rub a tissue along leaves — rust will leave an orange smear.

I've noted some resistant cultivars at left, but even those aren't bullet-proof. Clean up and destroy infected foliage in the fall. Cut back foliage that's showing signs to slow the spread. Disinfect your hands and pruners between plants. Avoid overhead watering and make sure plants have good air circulation.

PHOTOS: © Jerry Pavia ('My Pet'); © Image Botanica ('Siloam Double Classic'); © Donna & Tom Krischan ('Malaysian Monarch'); © Susan Bergeron (daylily rust)

GREAT DESIGN IDEAS

Botanical Names

Barberry *Berberis* hybrid
Blue oat grass *Helictotrichon sempervirens*
Daffodil *Narcissus* hybrid
Tulip *Tulipa* spp.

Designing with daylilies is easy! Just plop them in anywhere. Well, maybe there's a little more to it than that, but daylilies *are* pretty versatile. Cheery reds or sweet pinks are right at home in a casual, cottage-style garden, where the flowers can rise above shorter plants. And there's nothing more elegant than a clump of pale yellow or creamy white daylilies in a formal garden. If you prefer a zany look, try combining several of the ruffled, multi-colored ones!

Nothing says "summer" like a massed planting of mixed daylilies. It's a great way to showcase them, and it makes care easier, too, because they can all enjoy the same conditions. And many daylilies bloom in midsummer when other perennials are often a little droopy. This planting will distract your eye from areas of the garden that don't look so good. Choose daylilies with different bloom times to keep this display going on and on.

As you can see in photo 5, daylilies' big, bright flowers make them natural focal points. Here, yellow 'Mary Todd' is paired with burgundy barberries and blue oat grass. Against the backdrop of the finer-foliaged plants, the daylily really stands out. Use the bold blooms to draw attention to other garden features — plant daylilies near a garden sculpture or special bench to draw your eye straight to it. Once established, daylilies are pretty heat-tolerant, so they don't mind the reflected heat at the edge of this sidewalk. But give them a little extra water in a hot spot like this. (Read "How to grow great daylilies," at right, for more care tips.)

You can make any garden look pulled together by repeating a plant in several places. Red 'Chicago Apache', in photo 6, adds sparkle all around the edges of this pond, and it blends in well with other perennials, too. Tuck a few spring bulbs in among a planting like this — the daylily foliage is great for hiding fading daffodil and tulip leaves.

Once you get started with daylilies, it's hard to stop. Fortunately, there are so many choices, and they work so well just about anywhere, you really don't have to stop! Just keep on trying new ones — you can't go wrong with these easy plants. □

— *Stephanie Polsley Bruner*

(5) Plant daylilies with their arching leaves near ornamental grass foliage for a subtle contrast in texture and color.

(6) Repeating clumps of one kind of plant, like these red daylilies, makes any garden look unified and well-designed.

HOW TO GROW GREAT DAYLILIES

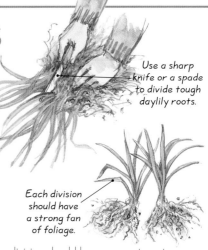

Use a sharp knife or a spade to divide tough daylily roots.

Each division should have a strong fan of foliage.

Daylilies are easy to grow. For the healthiest plants and showiest flowers, keep the following tips in mind.

CHOOSE THE RIGHT SPOT Full sun is best, although a little afternoon shade in the South keeps flowers from fading, especially dark colors. Most daylilies tolerate quite a bit of shade, but they won't flower as well. They may rot in soil that stays wet, so choose a well-drained location.

KEEP 'EM WATERED Once daylilies are established, they're pretty drought-tolerant. However, they'll bloom better and be healthier with plenty of water — about 1 in. per week. A layer of mulch keeps the soil moist and cuts down on weeding.

DON'T FUSS ABOUT FERTILIZER Fertilizing isn't very important for daylilies. They enjoy a sprinkling of all-purpose fertilizer in spring, when you feed all your perennials, and topdressing with compost adds nutrients to the soil. But don't overfertilize, or you'll get lush foliage and few flowers.

DIVIDE AND MULTIPLY You can divide daylilies any time except in the heat of summer, but the best time is late summer or early fall. (Divide rebloomers in spring.) Most cultivars need to be divided every 5 to 7 years.

Dig the entire clump and tip it on its side, as you can see in the top illustration. Use a spade or knife to cut the clump into four to six divisions. Each division should have one or two strong foliage fans, like the ones above. Replant the divisions at the same depth as they were originally growing, and trim off any damaged foliage. Keep the new transplants well-watered through the rest of the growing season.

ILLUSTRATIONS: Mavis Augustine Torke; GARDEN DESIGN: Diane Taylor (5)

Overwintering Geraniums

WEB extra

We'll show you step-by-step instructions in our online **video**.

Annual geraniums (*Pelargonium* hybrids) are tough little plants. One year, in the fall, a coworker gave me some that he dug before they froze. I stuffed them in a trash bag and forgot about them. In late February, I found them and scolded myself for being so cruel. Then I potted up the leafless plants. Lo and behold, most of them grew.

Now, geraniums are resilient, and I was lucky, but I don't recommend treating them quite so roughly! However, there's an easy process for keeping geraniums over the winter that doesn't need much storage space. And you'll save money in spring, when you don't have to buy new plants. You've heard of hanging geraniums up for the winter, but I think this method is even more successful. It's amazing what these leafless little stems can do. □

— *Marcia Leeper*

Out of the ground

Dig your geraniums before a hard freeze and shake the soil from the roots. You don't need to wash the roots or remove every little bit of soil. Set the plants in a shady spot and let them dry for a few days. Most of the leaves will dry up and fall off, as the one in the inset has. It's not critical to remove all the leaves, but the plants will overwinter better without them, as leaves can harbor mold.

Pick off dried and moldy leaves.

Into the box

Store the stems in a box, and close the top. Traditionally, you store them upside down. No one is quite sure why, but one theory is that it forces the moisture downward into the stems. Whatever the reason, keeping geraniums upside down improves the survival rate, in my experience. Keep them in a cool, dry location, at about 50 to 60 degrees F. Check for mold every few weeks, and clean any fallen leaves out of the box. The stems should stay firm. If you find shriveled, dried-out stems, throw them away. Soak the plants in water for a few minutes if you notice that a lot of them are shriveling. And if you find stems with black, mildewed tips, cut off the mildewed areas and dispose of them.

3 EASY-CARE GROWING TIPS

Three crucial things will keep your geraniums happy: Sun, dry soil and plenty of fertilizer.

STAY ON THE SUNNY SIDE Geraniums can tolerate some late afternoon shade, but they really need to have at least six hours of full sun. Otherwise, they won't bloom as well, and they'll be pale and spindly.

KEEP THE SOIL DRY Many people make the mistake of keeping geraniums too wet. They actually prefer to be on the dry side, so don't include water-holding crystals in the potting mix, and don't put the pot in a saucer. Check the soil before you water, and only water when the top inch of soil is dry.

FEED THEM WELL These heavy bloomers are also heavy feeders. Most annuals are happy with fertilizer once every few weeks, but geraniums need to be fed more often. To begin with, mix some balanced (10-10-10) time-release pelleted fertilizer in the soil at the bottom of the container, so the roots will have to stretch to reach it. Every time you water during the summer, use a half-strength 10-10-10 liquid fertilizer. This sounds like a lot of feeding, but your geraniums will love you for it. Be careful to water at the base of the plant — those fuzzy leaves will hold the fertilizer and water mixture, and it will cause white spots and scorched areas.

Cut stems back to healthy green growth.

All potted up

Leave your geraniums in the box until 6 to 8 weeks before the last frost date. Then it's time to pot them up. I like to use 5- or 6-in. terra-cotta pots, because they allow the soil to dry evenly. (You can use plastic pots, but don't let the soil stay too wet.) Fill the pots with damp, soil-free potting mix. Snip off any extra-long, straggling roots, and cut the stem back to healthy green growth, as you see in the inset above. I cut the one in the photo back to about 4 in. long. Tuck the plant into the potting mix deep enough that two leaf nodes are below the soil line — that's where new roots will emerge.

Ready to plant

After you pot up the geraniums, you'll start to see growth in 7 to 14 days. The real key to making this work is to water cautiously, only when the soil dries out about an inch down. In 4 to 6 weeks, the plants should look like the one in the inset at left. At this point, they're ready to transplant outside, or plant several into a bigger container like the one above.

Now your geraniums are ready for their big summer debut. But how do you keep them looking this gorgeous all summer long? Read "3 easy-care growing tips" above for a few hints on watering and fertilizing. Your geraniums will stop traffic this summer!

4 weeks after planting

Scott Kunst
on growing spectacular glads

PHOTO: Courtesy Scott Kunst

Show off your glads! For years gladiolus have been relegated to straight lines in cutting gardens or vegetable beds. But Scott Kunst showed me some creative tips on how to work these stately spires into your garden, and grow them straight and tall. Scott's the owner of Old House Gardens, a mail-order company in Ann Arbor, Michigan, that specializes in heirloom bulbs. Let me share his tips with you.

GLAD BASICS When buying glad corms, skip flat ones in favor of thick ones, even if they're smaller in diameter. You'll get the best flowers from thick corms.

In spring, about the same time you'd set out tomato seedlings, it's time to plant. Choose a spot in full sun with well-drained soil. And just because you bought a bag of 25 corms doesn't mean you have to plant them all on the same day. Stagger plantings every 2 weeks until late June or early July and you'll have flowers all summer.

Space the corms 4 to 6 inches apart. Small or dwarf cultivars, such as 'Atom', can be set a bit closer. I'll show you the secret to keeping your flowers standing up in the illustration below left. It's all in how you plant! You can plant corms as shallow as 2 inches. They'll bloom faster than ones planted deeper but you'll probably need to support the flower stalks.

After you backfill the planting hole with a couple inches of soil, water thoroughly to settle the corms in. Unless the weather turns very dry, don't water again until you see some growth, or the corm may rot. Once the foliage is up and growing, keep the soil moist. Mulch, such as compost or wood chips, is a big help.

In USDA zone 8 or warmer, you'll be able to leave the corms in the ground year round. Applying a thick layer of mulch or planting against a warm wall will usually bring the corms through zones 6 and 7 winters. Further north, you'll need to dig and store the corms after a frost — or replace them each year as you would annuals.

How to plant topple-proof gladiolus

3) MOUND THE SOIL UP AROUND THE STEM after the hole is filled. Another 2 to 4 in. will help keep the flowers standing straight.

2) BACKFILL THE HOLE with more soil every week as the stem grows, never completely covering the tops of the leaves.

1) SET CORMS 6 TO 8 IN. DEEP and cover them with 2 or 3 in. of soil.

(1) Frustrated with glads' short bloom time? Set pots in bloom into your perennial bed as they flower. When one finishes, slip in another pot that's ready to bloom (inset).

DESIGNING WITH GLADS Want to add some drama and color to your foundation planting? Set a few groupings of glads between shrubs like Japanese spirea or a low-growing deutzia. The tall spires will really stand out planted in front of evergreens or large-leafed hydrangeas for bright spots of summer color.

Glads are great accent plants in a perennial border. Tuck a few among Shasta daisies or tall sedum for interesting flower and foliage shape contrasts.

Shorter cultivars are especially good in mixed containers. You can enjoy their flowers for a couple of weeks and then leave the swordlike foliage to accent the arrangement.

In the photo above, the glads are in a 3-gallon pot so you can swap them in and out of your border. Starting in early spring, plant up a pot of glads every two weeks. Set the first pot in the border as it starts to flower. The one in the inset photo is waiting in the wings, ready to

be put in when the one in the garden is finished blooming. Your neighbors will wonder where you bought the ever-blooming glads!

To grow glads in pots, you'll need several 3- or 5-gallon plastic nursery pots. Dump some general-purpose potting mix in the bottom so the corms will be 6 to 8 inches below the lip of the pot. Set the corms an inch apart, cover them with a couple inches of soil and water them in. Just like you did with the corms in the ground, as they grow, gradually add more soil until the pot is full. Keep the soil moist and in bright sun.

See how easy glads are to grow? The hardest part may be choosing which cultivars to plant. In the box to the right is a short list of Scott's favorites to help get you started. Pick up a few corms, or check out Old House Gardens for some choice cultivars to enjoy next summer. You'll be "glad" you did! □

— *Jim Childs*

SCOTT'S FAVORITE GLADS

There are hundreds, if not thousands, of glad cultivars. And most all of them are beautiful. But we pinned Scott down to see which ones he likes best.

'Atom' — Each small red floret along a 3-ft.-tall stem has a silver-white edge

'Boone' — Small soft-apricot florets on 3-ft. spikes

'Friendship' — Soft pink-and-white flowers on sturdy, 4-ft.-tall flower stems

'Mexicana' — Ruffled yellow flowers with a crimson throat on 4-ft.-tall stems

'White Friendship' — Crisp white flowers on 4-ft.-tall stems

Old House Gardens
www.oldhousegardens.com
734-995-1486. Catalog $2

Orange Globe Mallow

4 ft.

3 ft.

2 ft.

1 ft.

0

Sphaeralcea munroana

Size 2 to 4 ft. tall and wide

Habit Upright to slightly sprawling

Bloom Early summer; sporadic rebloom throughout summer; deadhead to prevent reseeding if necessary

Soil Well-drained

Light Full sun

Pests None serious

Hardiness Cold: USDA zones 5 to 9
Heat: AHS zones 9 to 1

Soft, sherbet-orange flowers and fuzzy silver-gray leaves. Sounds like a cool combination on a hot day. And orange globe mallow stands up to the heat, too.

HIGH AND DRY Native to the Mountain West, orange globe mallow prefers not-too-humid climates and well-drained, nutrient-poor soil. But it blooms happily elsewhere, too, although it gets a little leggier in rich, moist soil. If you live in the Midwest or the eastern United States, sandy soil is best. Try planting it in a rock garden or along the top of a retaining wall. It'll appreciate the good drainage. In arid climates (less than 20 inches of rain a year), orange globe mallow will tolerate clay, too.

In my Iowa garden, this dry-soil lover gets a bit lanky. I plant several together so they prop each other up and look a little more full. In the illustration below, you'll see a planting that combines orange globe mallow with some other dry-soil plants.

EASY TO GROW As long as this plant's in well-drained soil, it's pretty carefree. Most pests, including rabbits and deer, leave it alone.

If you use a sprinkler in summer, put this plant where it won't get extra water. It doesn't appreciate extra fertilizer either.

The pretty ½- to 1-inch-diameter blooms show up in a big flush in early summer, then the plant will rebloom on and off until fall. Orange globe mallow dies to the ground in winter. In spring, just as new foliage starts to emerge, cut the old stems back to just an inch or two high.

If your orange globe mallow is happy, it may self-seed a little bit, but not enough to be a problem.

Strangely enough, this plant can have either a tap root or a mat of smaller roots, and it varies from plant to plant. The ones that form taproots don't like to be moved, but if yours has a clump of roots, it'll take being divided and transplanted better. (Unfortunately, it's hard to tell until you're already digging.) I *have* moved a couple with taproots, digging deep to get as much of the bright-orange root as I could. My plants struggled after being transplanted and in the future, I'd probably just get new ones.

If there's a hot spot in your garden, try planting this cool customer there. It'll take the heat. □

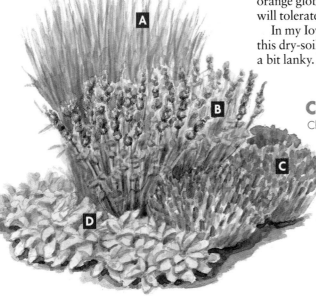

Cool combo for a hot spot

Looks good all summer? Check. Doesn't need a lot of care? Check. Cool, silver-gray foliage and plenty of flowers? Check. 'Heavy Metal' switchgrass, with its blue foliage and midsummer cloudy plumes, is a backdrop for orange globe mallow's cheery little blooms. 'Hidcote Superior' lavender likes the same dry conditions and a sweep of silvery lamb's ears enhances the gray foliage of the orange globe mallow and the lavender.

A Switchgrass *Panicum virgatum* 'Heavy Metal'
B Orange globe mallow *Sphaeralcea munroana*
C Lavender *Lavandula angustifolia* 'Hidcote Superior'
D Lamb's ears *Stachys byzantina* 'Big Ears'

Mail-order sources

High Country Gardens
www.highcountrygardens.com
800-925-9387. *Catalog free*

Big Dipper Farm
www.bigdipperfarm.com
360-886-8133. *Online catalog only*

Luna Pink Swirl
Hibiscus

Hibiscus moscheutos
Luna™ Pink Swirl

Size	2 to 3 ft. tall by 2 to 3 ft. wide
Bloom	Midsummer to frost
Soil	Well-drained
Light	Full sun to part shade
Pests	None serious
Hardiness	Cold: USDA zones 5 to 9
	Heat: AHS zones 9 to 1

You'd expect to see big, 8-inch flowers like these in a tropical oasis or a greenhouse. But coming back year after year in gardens even when winter temperatures stay below freezing — now that's something!

We received Luna Pink Swirl hibiscus when it was a new introduction. We liked it then and still like it today. Why? Those beautiful flowers, to begin with. And it's easy to grow!

Just take a look at the one in our test garden, at right. Grown with pentas and nicotiana up front and agastache and ninebark behind, it looked fantastic.

Pink Swirl is just one of the Luna series, which also comes in Red, White or Blush. All have the same cultural needs and grow about the same size. Individual flowers only last a couple of days but new ones keep coming from midsummer until frost.

GROW GLAMOROUS HIBISCUS You can find hibiscus plants at garden centers or from mail-order nurseries. But you probably wouldn't guess that Pink Swirl is easy to start from seed, too. Sow seed indoors 6 to 8 weeks before the last frost for blooms the same year.

Don't worry about staking once they're grown. These sturdy stems keep the flowers standing tall.

In fall, after a hard frost, put down a 4- to 6-inch layer of organic mulch. (To be honest,

ours doesn't always get mulched and still survives in our zone 5 winters.)

When spring arrives, pull the mulch away and cut stems back to within a couple inches of the ground. Pink Swirl may be slow to emerge, so be patient.

Plenty of deer visit our gardens, but they seem to leave Pink Swirl off the menu. And it doesn't have any serious disease problems, either.

LOOKING GOOD! This versatile hibiscus fits in perennial borders, cottage gardens, small gardens...you name it. And it's been a hit for us in a glazed container with elephant ears and other tender perennials. Try the hot-colored tropical design below and you'll feel like you're on vacation in your own yard! □

Tropical paradise Take a trip to an island paradise with this planting — even if it's only in your imagination. Big, colorful plants say "tropical," so hibiscus fits right in. Large, dark canna leaves make a great backdrop and are echoed at the front of the border by the dahlia leaves. Be sure to save both the canna and dahlia tubers indoors over the winter. Some bright spikes of yellow celosia add a spark to the hot-pink dahlia flowers at the front of the border.

A Hibiscus *Hibiscus moscheutos* Luna™ Pink Swirl
B Canna *Canna* Tropicanna® Black
C Celosia *Celosia plumosa* 'Fresh Look Yellow'
D Dahlia *Dahlia* 'Fascination'

Mail-order sources

W. Atlee Burpee & Co.
www.burpee.com
800-888-1447. *Catalog free*

Garden Crossings
www.gardencrossings.com
Online catalog only

Jupiter's Beard

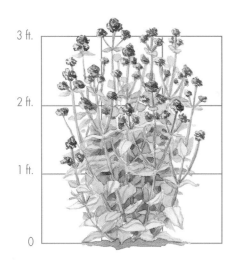

3 ft.

2 ft.

1 ft.

0

Centranthus ruber

Size	18 to 36 in. tall, 24 to 30 in. wide
Type	Perennial
Bloom	White, pink, or rose-red blooms from mid- to late spring until frost
Soil	Well-drained
Light	Full sun
Pests	None serious
Hardiness	Cold: USDA zones 5 to 8 Heat: AHS zones 8 to 1

If there's anything better than a tough plant that can take heat and drought, it's a tough plant that blooms all summer!

Jupiter's beard is 1½ to 3 feet tall and 2 to 2½ feet wide, with white, medium-pink or bright rose-red flowers. Gray-green foliage stays neat all summer, as insects, rabbits, deer and diseases usually pass this plant by.

The best thing about Jupiter's beard? It starts to bloom in mid- to late spring and keeps on going until frost, especially if you deadhead it. Although it blooms heavily at first, and again in late summer, there are always a few blossoms.

A traditional cottage garden plant, Jupiter's beard mixes happily with favorites like daisies and phlox. But it's also drought-tolerant

enough for dry landscapes. Butterflies and hummingbirds love the blooms too.

Jupiter's beard is great for a beginning gardener, or where you need a "quick" plant. I once purchased some tiny ones at the grocery store and they bloomed the first season.

CARE TIPS Like most tough plants, Jupiter's beard isn't picky about growing conditions. It likes full sun and well-drained, slightly alkaline soil. (Mine grows happily along the top of my limestone retaining wall.) Give it a little extra water the first season, but it's pretty drought-tolerant once established. It'll tolerate clay soil and some shade, but may get tall and lanky.

Your Jupiter's beard may flop over by midsummer. It's so full that it still looks great, but

be sure it's not smothering smaller nearby plants. You can stake it early in the season, cut fallen stems back or just leave a little extra room around the nearest neighbors.

As the blooms fade, Jupiter's beard sets fuzzy white seed heads. It will reseed freely too, although the seedlings are easy to pull. Regular deadheading will keep reseeding under control.

If you want to transplant a few of the seedlings, do it while they're small. Jupiter's beard develops big, heavy taproots that look like gnarled carrots. So it's hard to divide or transplant once it's established.

Choose a spot (any spot!) where you'd like flowers all summer. Plant some Jupiter's beard, stand back and let it amaze you. □

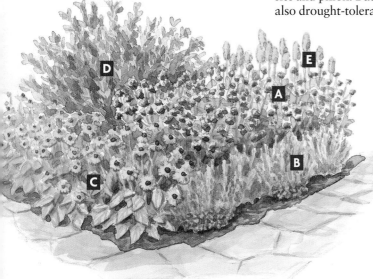

All summer long
Most gardeners want nothing more than a planting that looks great all summer. Anchor it with a long-blooming perennial like Jupiter's beard, add a few plants for spring, midsummer and fall bloom, and you're guaranteed success!

A Jupiter's beard *Centranthus ruber*
B Salvia *Salvia xsylvestris 'Mainacht' (May Night)*
C Black-eyed Susan *Rudbeckia fulgida sullivantii 'Goldsturm'*
D Caryopteris *Caryopteris xclandonensis 'Longwood Blue'*
E Torch lily *Kniphofia 'Primrose Beauty'*

Mail-order sources

Bluestone Perennials
www.bluestoneperennials.com
800-852-5243. *Catalog free*

High Country Gardens
www.highcountrygardens.com
800-925-9387. *Catalog free*

(1) 'Pixie' has flowers that last a long time in the garden and in a vase.

The secret to growing
Pinks

PINKS
Dianthus spp.

*3 to 24 in. tall by
18 to 24 in. wide*
*White, pink, lavender
and red flowers,
spring to summer*
Full sun to part shade
Well-drained soil
*Occasionally suffers
crown or root rot*
*Cold-hardy in
USDA zones 3 to 9*
*Heat-tolerant in
AHS zones 9 to 1*

Undemanding plants always make it to the top of my garden shopping list. I penciled pinks in a long time ago because they're easy to grow, have pretty flowers and many are fragrant.

Pinks are cousins of florists' carnations and the wildflower sweet William. Their flowers are like mini carnations and often have that spicy clovelike scent. They're relatively small but are jam-packed with blooms when they're at their peak. Check out the photo at left to see what I mean.

PINKS AREN'T JUST PINK You'll find pinks come in a variety of reds, lavenders, white and of course, pink. Add to that all the different patterns and fringed petals, and you'll see why I have so many of these beauties in my own garden.

Most pinks are relatively low-growing but they differ in habit. 'Tiny Rubies', for example, forms a mound with flowers that seem to float above the leaves. Others, like 'Zing Rose', grow in a spreading mat.

A PINK FOR ANY GARDEN STYLE A mixed border is an excellent place for a few showy pinks. Just make sure they're tucked in with other plants that like the same growing conditions. 'Pixie', in the photo at left, shares the garden with 'Matrona' sedum behind it and a couple of small blue fescues in front. None of these plants need a lot of watering. To top it off, the bright-pink patterned flowers bridge the gap between early-spring daffodils and the emerging late-summer-blooming sedum.

It's no surprise to find pinks in cottage gardens. The looser habit of taller varieties fits right in with this casual style, and they last a long time in a vase, too. Try 'Dad's Favorite' and 'Spring Beauty'. You'll enjoy their spicy fragrance. Add a few more flowers, such as daisies, snapdragons and larkspur, for a charming bouquet.

Not every plant is as versatile as pinks: They work just as well in formal gardens. Small clusters of the brightly colored annual bedding types brighten up the edges of a formal path. These little dynamos will bloom all season, putting on quite a show. Plus, their tidy clumping habit fits in with the straight lines and square corners so prominent in formal designs.

Because pinks love well-drained soil, they're perfect candidates for rock gardens. Mound-forming types even grow happily in hypertufa containers. Mat-forming varieties cascade over rocks or down the front of a stone wall.

GOOD-LOOKING FOLIAGE With all this talk about flowers, it's easy to forget the grasslike foliage. Few pests bother pinks, and the foliage holds up well all summer. Their slender leaves contrast nicely with broad-leafed plants, such as coral bells. Or try the blue-gray leaves of 'Feuerhexe' ('Firewitch') next to the shades of burgundy and green on 'Chocolate Chip' bugleweed foliage.

Now you can see why I keep a look out for pinks whenever I go plant shopping. A plant with pretty flowers *and* great-looking foliage can be used almost anywhere in the garden. On the next page I've pulled together a list of varieties that are easy to find, along with some information to help you decide which pink is best for you.

Botanical Names

Blue fescue *Festuca glauca*
Bugleweed *Ajuga reptans*
Carnation *Dianthus caryophyllus*
Coral bells *Heuchera hybrid*
Daffodil *Narcissus spp.*
Daisy *Leucanthemum xsuperbum*
Larkspur *Consolida ajacis*
Sedum *Sedum hybrid*
Snapdragon *Antirrhinum majus*
Sweet William *Dianthus barbatus*

Find out which pinks work best in your garden. ▶

PICK A PINK FOR YOU

Pinks have been popular for hundreds of years. While there are a few varieties still around from the 18th century, like 'Bat's Double Red' and 'Inchmery', most are gone. In fact, it's not uncommon for even modern varieties to be popular for a few seasons and then disappear from catalogs and garden centers.

One of the reasons for all this change is that pinks hybridize so easily. You may even find evidence of this in your garden if you grow several different pinks. It can be exciting to see seedlings popping up, in new colors, sizes and fragrances. Not all of them will be better than their parents, so don't be afraid to pull out less-than-stellar plants. On the following pages I'll show you some tips for growing pinks so you can keep your favorite varieties healthy and happy for years to come.

ROCK GARDEN PINKS
These diminutive gems are rock garden stars because they like the sharp drainage. But they're versatile enough to grow along the edge of a perennial border, too.

'Tiny Rubies' Cheddar pink; *Dianthus gratianopolitanus* (above); 6 to 8 in. tall by 6 to 10 in. wide; double pink flowers; cold-hardy in USDA zones 3 to 8; heat-tolerant in AHS zones 9 to 1

'Bath's Pink' Cheddar pink; *Dianthus gratianopolitanus*; 8 in. tall by 24 in. wide; single pink flowers; cold-hardy in USDA zones 3 to 8; heat-tolerant in AHS zones 9 to 1

'Pink Feather' *Dianthus* hybrid; 9 in. tall by 9 in. wide; single pink feathery flowers; cold-hardy in USDA zones 4 to 9; heat-tolerant in AHS zones 9 to 1

'Spotty' Cheddar pink; *Dianthus gratianopolitanus*; 4 to 6 in. tall by 6 in. wide; single rose pink flowers spotted with light pink; cold-hardy in USDA zones 3 to 8; heat-tolerant in AHS zones 9 to 1

CUT FLOWERS
Long-lasting and fragrant, these taller pinks make a nice bouquet. Add to the life of your bouqet by removing all foliage below the water line so it won't rot.

'Velvet and Lace' *Dianthus* hybrid (above); 12 in. tall by 6 to 10 in. wide; double burgundy flowers with white edge; cold-hardy in USDA zones 3 to10; heat-tolerant in AHS zones 9 to 1

'Bat's Double Red' *Dianthus* hybrid; 15 in. tall by 15 in. wide; double red flowers; cold-hardy in USDA zones 5 to 8; heat-tolerant in AHS zones 9 to 1

'Prairie Pink' *Dianthus* hybrid; 18 in. tall by 14 in. wide; double bright-pink flowers; cold-hardy in USDA zones 3 to 8; heat-tolerant in AHS zones 9 to 1

'Sonata' cottage pink; *Dianthus plumarius*; 12 to 15 in. tall by 12 in. wide; single white flowers with magenta eye; cold-hardy in USDA zones 5 to 9; heat-tolerant in AHS zones 9 to 1

FEATHERY PETALS
Some pinks look like their petals have been trimmed with pinking shears. The delicate and lacy flowers in the photo above are the most serrated of any of the pinks.

'Rainbow Loveliness' Allwood pink; *Dianthus xallwoodii* (above);15 in. tall by 10 in. wide; single flowers in a variety of pastel colors; cold-hardy in USDA zones 3 to 9; heat-tolerant in AHS zones 9 to 1

'Bewitched' *Dianthus* hybrid; 8 in. tall by 14 in. wide; single pale pink flowers with a ring of magenta; cold-hardy in USDA zones 4 to 8; heat-tolerant in AHS zones 9 to 1

'Crimsonia' fringed pink; *Dianthus superbus*; 20 in. tall by 14 in. wide; single crimson flowers; cold-hardy in USDA zones 3 to 8; heat-tolerant in AHS zones 9 to 1

'Arctic Fire' maiden pink; *Dianthus deltoides*; 8 in. tall by 12 to 15 in. wide; single white flowers with fuchsia ring around pink eye; cold-hardy in USDA zones 3 to 9; heat-tolerant in AHS zones 9 to 1

SO MANY CHOICES There are dozens of different pink species and hybrids available, and while it's wonderful to have all those choices, it can be a little overwhelming. Generally, their care is the same but there are some differences. Do you have part shade? Look for maiden pinks and their hybrids in the lists below. Fringed pinks, including many of the Allwood varieties, tolerate moisture better that some of the others so you can grow them easily in a mixed bed. Heat-tolerant cottage pinks are best for southern zones. And cheddar pinks are a good choice for rock or alpine gardens. With those things in mind, check out these lists of readily available pinks then find out how to grow them on the following pages. You're sure to find one (or more) varieties to brighten up your garden.

Mail-order sources

Bluestone Perennials

www.bluestoneperennials.com
800-852-5243. *Catalog free*

Joy Creek Nursery

www.joycreek.com
503-543-7474. *Catalog $3*

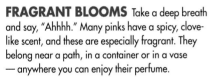

FRAGRANT BLOOMS Take a deep breath and say, "Ahhhh." Many pinks have a spicy, clove-like scent, and these are especially fragrant. They belong near a path, in a container or in a vase — anywhere you can enjoy their perfume.

'First Love' *Dianthus* hybrid (above); 15 in. tall by 18 in. wide; single flowers that start white and age to pink; cold-hardy in USDA zones 3 to 8; heat-tolerant in AHS zones 9 to 1

'Inchmery' *Dianthus* hybrid; 12 in. tall by 12 in. wide; semi-double pink flowers; cold-hardy in USDA zones 5 to 9; heat-tolerant in AHS zones 9 to 1

'Itsaul White' *Dianthus* hybrid; 12 in. tall by 12 in. wide; double white flowers; cold-hardy in USDA zones 3 to 8; heat-tolerant in AHS zones 9 to 1

'Mrs. Sinkins' cottage pink; *Dianthus plumarius*; 8 to 10 in. tall by 10 in. wide; double white flowers; cold-hardy in USDA zones 6 to 9; heat-tolerant in AHS zones 9 to 1

ENCORE PERFORMANCE Not every pink reblooms, but these varieties will give you a second show. Deadheading will help move the blooming cycle along.

'Feuerhexe' ('Firewitch') Cheddar pink; *Dianthus gratianopolitanus* (above); 10 to 12 in. tall by 12 in. wide; single pink flowers; cold-hardy in USDA zones 3 to 9; heat-tolerant in AHS zones 9 to 1

'Helen' Allwood pink; *Dianthus xallwoodii*; 12 to 14 in. tall by 6 to 8 in. wide; double salmon pink flowers; cold-hardy in USDA zones 3 to 8; heat-tolerant in AHS zones 9 to 1

'Confetti Cherry Red' maiden pink; *Dianthus deltoides*; 6 in. tall by 12 to 15 in. wide; single apple-red flowers; cold-hardy in USDA zones 3 to 9; heat-tolerant in AHS zones 9 to 1

'Rose de Mai' *Dianthus* hybrid; 10 to 12 in. tall by 24 in. wide; double pink flowers; cold-hardy in USDA zones 3 to 9; heat-tolerant in AHS zones 12 to 1

ANNUAL PINKS?

Have you noticed how your "annual" bedding-plant pinks from the garden center sometimes come back year after year? These pinks are actually hybrids of Indian pinks (*Dianthus chinensis*), a tender perennial that is reliably hardy to USDA zone 7. However, they can survive mild winters in colder zones or if they're planted in a protected place with a good layer of mulch. That's why you might get a bargain if you buy 'Supra Purple' above or its relatives in the annual aisle at the garden center!

PHOTO: John Holtorf ('Feuerhexe'); © Image Botanica ('Tiny Rubies')

GROWING
GREAT PINKS!

Botanical Names

Cheddar pink *Dianthus gratianopolitanus*
Mexican giant hyssop *Agastache mexicana*
Sedum *Sedum* hybrid
Wild strawberry *Fragaria vesca*

PHOTOS: © Donna and Tom Krischan; (2) John Holtorf (3)

Pinks aren't fussy. Planted in the right place, they'll bloom happily for many years. I've found that 5 to 6 hours of morning sun works best for my pinks. Flowers seem to last longer and those with blue-gray foliage keep their color better.

GOOD DRAINAGE IS KEY Though pinks have a reputation for being short-lived, you can get them to live longer with good soil drainage. They won't survive with a soggy crown. In fact, if you've ever had pinks with an ever-increasing center of brown, you're overwatering. Sometimes the plants can recover, but they'll be weaker. If you struggle with clay soil, try this recipe when you plant: Mix ⅓ compost and ⅓ poultry grit with ⅓ of the original soil you've removed from the hole. The coarse texture helps water drain quickly, and the nutrients from the compost nourish the plant.

Did you know that a simple rock or brick can help your pinks survive winter? The rock nestled in next to the pinks in photo 2 below radiates warmth all year, helping keep the crown and roots dry. Or try planting a brick at the same time you plant your pinks in spring. It's easy, just spread the roots over

(3) Deadhead reblooming types like 'Feuerhexe' to encourage more flowers to form. In between blooms, you can enjoy the blue-gray foliage.

the top of the brick and refill the hole with soil. The warmth the brick generates will help plants survive cold winter temperatures.

CONTAINER PINKS Even easier than amending poor soil is growing pinks in containers, as in photo 3. Start by choosing companion plants that don't need a lot of water. In this container, we have Acapulco™ Salmon Mexican giant hyssop, 'Purple Emperor' sedum and wild strawberry growing happily with 'Feuerhexe' cheddar pink. Be sure to choose a container with a hole in the bottom so water can drain. And don't bother with a saucer beneath it. Now go ahead and fill the container most of the way with a soilless potting mix. (Skip the water crystals so the soil doesn't stay too wet.) Then add all the other plants, except the pink. Commercial potting mixes generally drain well, but for added insurance, I like to throw a couple handfuls (about an inch) of gravel or poultry grit in the bottom of the hole just for the pink. Fill in any gaps with more soil, give it a good drink and watch it grow.

The illustration at right has even more tips for growing beautiful pinks in your garden so you can keep your favorites going for years to come. □

— *Sherri Ribbey*

(2) Stones tucked in the garden keep pinks like 'Diamond Pink' (in the foreground) happy.

GROW LONG-LASTING PINKS

MULCH Since pinks can rot in too much moisture, use rock mulch instead of bark. A 2-in. layer of medium poultry grit or pea gravel will keep the foliage and crown from coming into contact with damp soil but still help conserve moisture when the weather gets too dry.

PLANTING Spring is the best time to plant your pinks. Make sure the crown is at soil level so moisture doesn't pool and cause rot.

SOIL Work some compost and poultry grit into the soil when you plant. The compost will nourish the plant. An additional inch of grit at the bottom of the hole will help with drainage.

CUTTING BACK When each flush of flowers is done, the easiest way to deadhead pinks is to grab a bunch with one hand and cut the stems back by about half with your scissors. This will prevent unwanted seedlings and, for the reblooming varieties, produce another flush more quickly.

You may also need to cut pinks back in spring if they come through winter looking rough. Cut the foliage back by up to two-thirds and the plant will still come back.

Crown

Poultry grit

More pinks
For more of your favorite variety, you could divide them but they're more susceptible to disease when the crown is disturbed. Instead, take cuttings in late summer. Water the plant the night before. It'll root easier this way. Cut a non-flowering side shoot 4 to 5 in. long, place it in growing medium and keep it watered. You should have roots in 4 to 6 weeks. For more details on how to take cuttings, check out Make More Plants...It's Easy! on p. 266.

Day Breaker Rose

Rosa Day Breaker™ ('FRYcentury')

Size	5 to 6 ft. tall by 4 to 5 ft. wide
Bloom	Spring to autumn
Type	Shrub
Soil	Well-drained
Light	Full sun
Pests	Occasional blackspot

Hardiness

Cold: USDA zones 5 to 9
Heat: AHS zones 9 to 1

I used to be afraid of growing roses — they seemed too demanding. Then someone gave me Day Breaker™ and I've been hooked ever since. This easy-care beauty gives me dozens of flowers all summer long, and its light scent is a pleasure to have around.

Day Breaker shows the best of its floribunda and hybrid tea parents. Like floribundas, it's hardy with long-lasting clusters of flowers. It also has the hybrid tea fragrance and blossom. Sometimes Day Breaker even has single flower stems like hybrid teas do, but you never know when that will happen.

PRUNING IS A CINCH You may have heard that pruning roses is complicated. But it really isn't with this one. The only pruning I do is to cut off any dead canes at the base of the plant in late winter before new growth starts. If a tip is brown, cut it back at a 45-degree angle to healthy tissue, which is dark green outside and light green inside.

KEEP THOSE FLOWERS COMING To get as many flowers as possible from my Day Breaker, I do two things: Deadhead and fertilize. Roses bloom in cycles, so deadheading makes them look better, keeps them from spending energy forming hips and helps the plants start working toward the next cycle of bloom. Once all the flowers in a bloom cycle are done, cut the stems back by about half to encourage more growth.

Fertilizing keeps your plant well-nourished so it flowers a lot. I always start with a dose of fish fertilizer like Neptune's Harvest in spring when new growth appears. Sometimes, other than an annual dose of compost, that's all this rose gets, and it still looks good. But to be on the safe side, apply a balanced formula fertilizer whenever your rose takes a rest between blooms. Stop fertilizing about six weeks before the last frost date in your area so the rose can start shutting down for winter.

FUNGUS FEARS Day Breaker has great resistance to black spot, but as I found out, it's not immune. After several years with no real problems, mine came down with a bad case. The lower portion of this 5-foot shrub was completely defoliated. So in mid-July I cut the canes to within 12 inches of the ground. In a couple of weeks, it had several new canes and even bloomed in the fall.

Preventing black spot will save you some grief. Apply this easy recipe every five to seven days when the weather gets humid. Mix 1 tablespoon of baking soda and a squirt of a mild dish soap like Ivory® to 1 gallon of water and spray evenly over the foliage. Apply the spray in the evening to keep foliage from burning.

Thanks to Day Breaker, I know how easy a rose can be and I'm looking forward to more beautiful blooms next summer. □

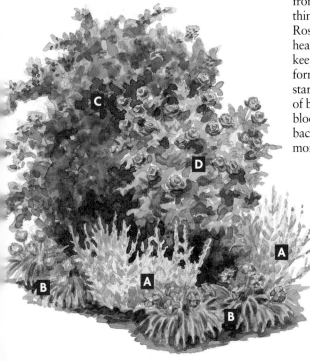

Winning combos Day Breaker doesn't need to be in a special rose bed to look good. This hardy, disease-resistant shrub is a great choice to grow alongside other plants, such as lilies, daisies and phlox. Here its bushy, upright habit and glossy green leaves help show off the wispy flowers of 'Little Spire' Russian sage. And speaking of foliage, the deep burgundy leaves of 'Diabolo' ninebark make Day Breaker's yellow, apricot and pink flowers glow. The rose-pink of the reblooming daylily repeats that warm tone and ties the color scheme together.

A Dwarf Russian sage *Perovskia atriplicifolia* 'Little Spire'
B Daylily *Hemerocallis* 'Rosy Returns'
C Ninebark *Physocarpus opulifolius* 'Diabolo'
D Rose *Rosa* Day Breaker

Mail-order sources

Northland Rosarium
www.northlandrosarium.com
509-448-4968. *Catalog free*

Witherspoon Rose Culture
www.witherspoonrose.com
800-643-0315. *Catalog free*

David &

on the perfect way to plant a tree peony

Kasha Furman

PHOTOS: Dean Batchelder (portrait); Susan Kahn (photo 1)

IN THE KNOW

FAVORITE FERTILIZER The Furmans recommend Neptune's Harvest fertilizer every two or three weeks during the growing season. Stop in late summer.

CONTAINER TIPS Chinese tree peonies grow great in containers. Plant one in a large container with well-drained potting mix. Make sure to move the plant to an area where temperatures stay around 35 degrees F over the winter.

Cricket Hill Garden
www.treepeony.com
877-723-6642. Catalog free

I bet I'm not the only one who's ever pulled over for a closer look at a Chinese tree peony in full bloom. There's a stunning one in my neighborhood. After I learned what it was, I gave Kasha and David Furman a call. They own Cricket Hill Garden, a nursery specializing in Chinese tree peonies, in Thomaston, Connecticut. I wanted to learn the secret to growing these traffic-stoppers in my own yard. They told me it's all in how you plant them. You won't believe how simple it is!

START WITH THE SITE Dappled shade, or just 5 hours of morning sun, is perfect to protect colorful blooms from fading. But if you only have a spot with full sun, don't fret — the blooms may just fade faster. And David and Kasha have a solution to full sun situations. They place large ornamental Oriental-inspired umbrellas over the flowers to protect them from harsh rays and even heavy rains.

Chinese tree peonies can grow up to 4 feet tall and wide in just 10 years. With more age, most grow even bigger. And keep in mind that they're extremely long-lived; many live more than 100 years. If a young plant looks small and lonely, go ahead and surround it with annuals or perennials that you can move out later.

PLANT FOR SUCCESS You can transplant a tree peony growing in a container any time you can dig. Just plant the root ball at the same level it was growing at in the pot. But bare-root tree peonies, the way most are sold by mail, transplant best in autumn. Get them into the ground six weeks before the soil freezes in your area. Like planting daffodils in fall, this gives the shrub time to send out a few new roots before winter, and more in early spring before the leaves grow. That helps them take hold quicker than tree peonies planted in spring.

DIG A GENEROUS HOLE IN THE RIGHT SOIL A well-drained sandy loam with a pH around 7 grows beautiful flowers. If you have clay, mix coarse sand and lots of compost into the hole. Or plant on a slope so water won't collect around the roots and drown the plant. Wet soil is the most common reason Chinese tree peonies don't survive.

For a bare-root peony you'll want to dig a hole at least 2 feet deep and wide, like the one in the illustration at right. If the soil is poorly drained, this is your chance to adjust or replace it with sandy loam. Make the hole wider and deeper if you have to swap soil so you don't create a spot where water puddles and the new plant drowns.

Once you refill the hole halfway, build a mound in the center, set the plant in and adjust the depth. Add enough soil over the roots to hold the plant in place. Fill the hole with water and let it drain away before you add the rest of the soil. Then water again. For this second watering, mix in some fish and seaweed liquid fertilizer.

That's the basics, but check out "Planting pointers" below, where you'll find a few more helpful tips. The only variation to this technique is if your tree peony is grafted. I'll show you the slight difference in "Is it grafted?" at right below.

PREP FOR WINTER Chinese tree peonies are cold-hardy in USDA zones 4 to 8. In zones 4 to 7, spread 6 to 12 inches of leaves or straw over the crown for winter protection. But wait until the ground freezes — your objective is to keep the soil frozen so the roots won't be damaged by repeated freezing and thawing. In following years, only tree peonies in zone 4 will need a deep winter mulch.

Start to remove the mulch six weeks before your peonies are expected to bloom, or about the time the first crocuses open. Keep an old blanket or some mulch handy to toss back over the plant to protect the buds if a cold snap is predicted.

OLD PEONY PERK UP Have a tree peony that's just not performing? Dig a trench 6 inches deep and wide around the dripline and fill it with well-rotted compost. Your plant will take off as if it has been transplanted into rich soil without the shock of actually moving it.

See, I told you growing these shrubs wasn't hard. Regardless of the size or style of your garden, your Chinese tree peony is sure to become a traffic-stopping beauty. □

—*Jim Childs*

(1) After your tree peony is fully established, it'll flower for up to three weeks each spring with 7- to 12-in.-diameter blooms. You'll find colors ranging from white to deep red.

Planting pointers

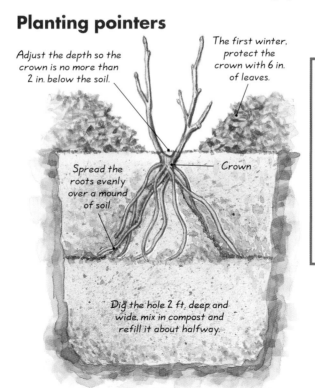

Adjust the depth so the crown is no more than 2 in. below the soil.

The first winter, protect the crown with 6 in. of leaves.

Spread the roots evenly over a mound of soil.

Crown

Dig the hole 2 ft. deep and wide, mix in compost and refill it about halfway.

IS IT GRAFTED? If your tree peony is grafted, the point where the root and stem join needs to be set 4 to 6 in. deep. That way the plant above the graft will eventually develop its own roots, ensuring stronger growth and a long life.

Graft

6 plants for the patient gardener

Worth the Wait

I t's hard to hurry perfection — in the garden or anywhere else, for that matter. And these days, when everyone seems to be short on time, it's good to slow down and enjoy some plants that may move at a slower pace, but are sure to please.

From gorgeous variegation to impressive plant size or spectacular bloom, here are six of my favorite "less-than-speedy" plants. I'll tell you what makes each one worth the wait, when you can expect it to look its best, and tips on how to hurry it along! □

— *Deborah Gruca*

Martagon lily *Lilium martagon*

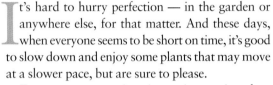

Good things come to those who wait. It often takes more than five years for martagon lily to start blooming in your garden. But you won't mind the time once you see a mature clump of dozens of plants with up to 50 of the 2-in., downward-facing flowers on each stem! Martagon hybrids bloom in white, pink, yellow, mauve, lavender, purple and red. 'Claude Shride' in the photo has stunning copper-red flowers.

With a strong scent, the large mass of flowers makes an impact in any sun to part-shade garden. The sturdy stems hold whorls of deep green leaves and don't require any staking to keep them standing tall. Mark the spot where you plant the bulbs so you don't accidentally dig them up — sometimes the plants don't emerge for a couple of years after planting!

BLOOM Small blooms in summer **SIZE** 5 to 6 ft. tall, 1 ft. wide **SOIL** Moist **LIGHT** Sun to part shade **COLD-HARDY** USDA zones 3 to 8 **HEAT-TOLERANT** AHS zones 8 to 1

HURRY IT ALONG Buy the biggest plants or bulbs you can find, but more importantly, once you plant them, don't disturb or move them.

Clivia *Clivia miniata*

Clivia is not a plant for the impatient gardener. The large, eye-catching flowers look great in the garden or, for gardeners in areas colder than zone 9, in a container. A mature plant can send up as many as 15 to 20 fabulous blooms on a half dozen sturdy stalks. But a young plant may take five or more years to bloom. Fortunately, its strappy foliage is attractive on its own. If you're not willing to wait that long, you might want to start with a larger plant that's already setting buds.

Indoors, clivia does well in a bright north window. Clivia flowers best when its roots are a tad overcrowded, so keep the plant in the same pot as long as possible.

BLOOM Orange, red or yellow blooms in winter to spring **SIZE** 18 to 24 in. tall, 24 in. wide **SOIL** Humusy, well-drained **LIGHT** Shade to part shade **COLD-HARDY** USDA zones 9 to 11 **HEAT-TOLERANT** AHS zones 11 to 1

HURRY IT ALONG Let the plant get potbound and stop watering it in winter to encourage flowering.

Variegated horseradish
Armoracia rusticana 'Variegata'

Here's a variegated plant that stops people in their tracks. The 18-in.-long, wavy, crepe-paper-like leaves develop striking patterns of cream splashed on dark green — but not right away. It may take two or three years for it to become completely variegated, and then only if it's left undisturbed. If you move it, you'll have to start your wait all over again.

Like other horseradishes, the root of this plant is edible. Unlike them, it does not spread aggressively, but instead, forms polite clumps gradually growing to 3 ft. across. Once the variegation does get going, the splotches and speckles are most pronounced in early spring.

BLOOM Insignificant white flowers in early summer **SIZE** 3 ft. tall, 3 ft. wide **SOIL** Well-drained **LIGHT** Full sun to part shade **COLD-HARDY** USDA zones 3 to 10 **HEAT-TOLERANT** AHS zones 10 to 1

HURRY IT ALONG Give it even moisture, especially in hot summer areas.

MORE WORTH-THE-WAIT PLANTS

False indigo *Baptisia australis*

Even after the spikes of blue spring flowers fade, this plant has several great features going for it. The first thing you notice is the attractive upright form that almost never requires staking. Blue-green foliage makes a beautiful background for shorter plants and camouflage for fading spring bulb foliage. And finally, after blooming is done, false indigo forms fascinating, fat green seedpods that dry to brown or black and rattle in the wind.

You can grow this perennial from seed, but even in full sun and average soil, a plant takes several years to form a good-sized clump. So buy a large plant and set the crown an inch higher than the surrounding soil for good drainage. And once it's established, don't divide or move it, or you'll end up waiting a little longer for that impressive mass of beautiful blue blooms.

BLOOM Blue flowers in spring   **SIZE** 4 to 5 ft. tall, 3 to 4 ft. wide
SOIL Moist, well-drained   **LIGHT** Sun to part shade
COLD-HARDY USDA zones 3 to 9   **HEAT-TOLERANT** AHS zones 9 to 1

HURRY IT ALONG Buy the largest plant you can afford.

Hosta *Hosta* 'Sum and Substance'

With its enormous, puckered gold leaves, 'Sum and Substance' really demands the spotlight in a garden. But eye-catching as it may be, fast-growing it is not. It takes time to grow the roots needed to produce those huge leaves. Fortunately, 'Sum and Substance' looks stunning even when it's small.

An early spring application of a balanced slow-release fertilizer and then one more feeding of water-soluble food in midsummer will keep your clump in top shape. For the brightest gold leaf color, plant this hosta in plenty of sun. But if you garden where summers are hot, some afternoon shade will prevent the leaves from scorching.

BLOOM Purple summer flowers   **SIZE** 30 in. tall, 5 ft. wide
SOIL Moist, well-drained   **LIGHT** Sun to part shade
COLD-HARDY USDA zones 3 to 8   **HEAT-TOLERANT** AHS zones 8 to 1

HURRY IT ALONG Give it lots of space away from trees with competitive roots, and don't divide or move it.

GARDEN DESIGN: Linda Ernst (hosta); PHOTO: © Ed de Grey (giant Himalayan lily inset)

Giant Himalayan lily
Cardiocrinum giganteum

Can you picture dozens of these 12-in. trumpet-shaped white or pink blooms on towering stems in your garden? The showy flowers are very fragrant and are followed by decorative pale brown seed capsules. Because the seeds need a specific cold-then-warm cycle, they rarely germinate in the garden. But big stems, leaves and flowers like these don't happen overnight. Giant Himalayan lily bulbs grow for several years before they reach blooming size, producing small bulb offsets in the soil all the while. Then, once the plant finally blooms, it fades and dies. And the waiting starts again as the remaining bulb offsets take several years to produce their own flowers.

Though the enormous flowers are worth waiting for, you can shorten the time between bloom periods. Simply plant new bulbs just below the soil's surface each autumn for three to five years in a row. Then, once they start blooming, you can enjoy the flower show every year!

BLOOM Large flowers early to midsummer **SIZE** 5 to 12 ft. tall, 18 to 24 in. wide **SOIL** Humus-rich, moist **LIGHT** Part shade **COLD-HARDY** USDA zones 7 to 9 **HEAT-TOLERANT** AHS zones 9 to 1

HURRY IT ALONG Don't bother with seeds; plant the biggest bulbs you can find.

ONE-BLOOM WONDERS

It may seem odd that giant Himalayan lily blooms only once after many years and then dies. But it's not the only plant with this strange life cycle:

HEN AND CHICKS (*Sempervivum* spp.) This plant will grow for years before flowering. Suddenly, out of the blue the mother plant sends up the bizarre-looking flower stalk you see at right. Afterward it dies, leaving the "chicks" to carry on.

BROMELIAD (*Bromelia* spp.) It can take a member of this family months to years to bloom just one time. Afterward, it makes lots of "pups," then slowly dies over a period of a year or two.

CENTURY PLANT (*Agave americana*) You may wait up to 100 years to see this plant bloom! Be warned — it grows and spreads quickly in zones 9 and 10, and is a chore to remove from your garden.

Hen and chicks

Seasonal Companions

Want a show-stopping garden week after week? A garden with something blooming in every corner, whether it's midspring or late summer? You can have it! With just a little planning and some creative plant placement, you can clear the path for blooms all season long. Below are a few surefire tips. Then check out the plans at right to see how to put these ideas to work in your garden.

CHOOSE THE RIGHT COMBOS

Often, you can create a scene of continuous blooms by changing the focus throughout the season. To enjoy color week after week, choose plants that differ in bloom times: Where the peonies leave off, the roses pick up. Just be sure to keep up with your deadheading. Spent flowers might detract from new blooms. Plus, deadheading helps some plants bloom longer.

If you've planted a new garden, you might have to wait several seasons for your plants to grow up to size. You can fill the empty spaces with colorful annuals. Fast-growing perennials work, too, especially ones that move easily, such as iris or tickseed.

FILL IN WITH CONTAINERS

To fill in where there's a gap between flowering plants, use a pot filled with colorful annuals or tender perennials that you've overwintered, such as a tropical hibiscus or cannas. Some plants die back, foliage and all, when they're done blooming — Oriental poppies and bleeding heart, for example. If that's the case, place the pot directly over it. Just be sure to lift the pot off the ground by an inch so you don't smother the dormant plants underneath. Broken pieces of terra-cotta or small stones work well. Or if you want more height, use bricks.

LAYERS OF BULBS

Get layers of blooms above ground by layering bulbs underground. The illustration at right shows you how you can pack several different bulbs in a small space because they go in at different depths. In general, the larger the bulb, the deeper you plant it. Don't be afraid to mix your bulbs in with annuals and perennials. You can get a lot of blooms in a small space this way!

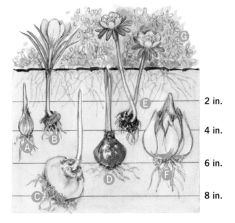

2 in.

4 in.

6 in.

8 in.

This cross section shows a combination of bulbs and a perennial that is colorful from early spring through summer. In this combo, the smaller the bulb, the earlier it blooms. **A)** Allium *(Allium caeruleum)*, **B)** Crocus *(Crocus flavus)*, **C)** Fritillaria *(Fritillaria imperialis)*, **D)** Hyacinth *(Hyacinthus orientalis)*, **E)** Winter aconite *(Eranthis hyemalis)*, **F)** Lily *(Lilium concolor)*, and **G)** Lemon thyme *(Thymus citriodorus)*.

THREE SEASONS OF COLOR

One beautiful spring combination is bright-yellow 'Dutch Master' daffodils in a deep-blue sea of grape hyacinth. But after their spring show, what happens to that garden space? Here's a solution for a sunny, well-drained garden: As the bulbs die back, cut flower stems to the ground. Leave the foliage until it turns brown so the plants can store energy for next year. Red and white columbine and peach and white bearded iris take the stage in late spring and early summer. If the columbine foliage becomes damaged with leaf miner trails, just cut it back to the ground. The sedum foliage will fill in the gap while the columbine grows new, healthy leaves. Later in summer, globe thistle shows up with rounds of blue blooms that will last well into autumn, when the sedum is flowering. You might even get another display from the iris.

A WATER-WISE GARDEN

Here's a suggestion for a drought-tolerant garden. Baby's breath blooms in early summer, reaching almost 3 ft. tall. At the same time, you'll have a carpet of white candytuft about 1 ft. tall, and globes of silvery purple star of Persia. In summer, Russian sage takes center stage with two months of soft-blue blooms. For a contrast of shape and color, you'll also have the vibrant-yellow black-eyed Susan blooms and the bright-green candytuft foliage. As the plants become established, they'll need a few extra helpings of water. Then they'll be set for your dry, sunny space. Keep in mind that even though this is a dry garden, you'll still want to give your plants a drink if they start to wilt. And to fill in, add a spot of pink with a pot of moss rose.

SPRING Once daffodils are done blooming, cut back only the flower stems. Leave the foliage so the plant can store energy for next year's blooms. Cut it back to the ground when it turns brown.

SUMMER A remontant, or reblooming, iris will bloom with other irises in early summer, and then reward you again with another show in late summer or fall.

AUTUMN If you find your sedum gets too tall, you can pinch back the stems in early summer.

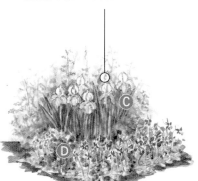

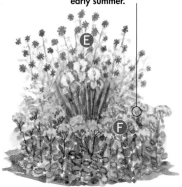

PLANT LIST

Code	Plant Name	Cold/Heat Zones	Height/Width
Late spring peak			
A	**Daffodil** (*Narcissus* 'Dutch Master')	3 to 8/8 to 1	14 in./12 in.
B	**Grape hyacinth** (*Muscari armeniacum*)	4 to 8/8 to 1	8 in./3 in.
Early summer peak			
C	**Iris** (*Iris* 'Champagne Elegance')	3 to 9/9 to 1	30 in./18 in.
D	**Columbine** (*Aquilegia* 'Crimson Star')	3 to 8/8 to 1	24 in./12 in.
Late summer and autumn peak			
E	**Globe thistle** (*Echinops bannaticus* 'Taplow Blue')	3 to 9/12 to 1	36 in./18 in.
F	**Sedum** (*Sedum telephium* 'Matrona')	3 to 8/8 to 1	30 in./18 in.

EARLY Baby's breath is a cloud of flowers when it blooms. But after it's finished, cut back the flower stems to the ground.

MIDSUMMER AND BEYOND Deadhead black-eyed Susan blooms as they fade to keep plants blooming longer.

PLANT LIST

Code	Plant Name	Cold/Heat Zones	Height/Width
Early summer peak			
A	**Baby's breath** (*Gypsophila paniculata* 'Perfekta')	5 to 8/8 to 1	18 in./18 in.
B	**Candytuft** (*Iberis sempervirens*)	5 to 9/9 to 1	12 in./16 in.
C	**Star of Persia** (*Allium cristophii*)	4 to 9/9 to 1	36 in./36 in.
Late summer peak			
D	**Russian sage** (*Perovskia atriplicifolia* 'Filigran')	3 to 7/7 to 1	24 in./18 in.
E	**Black-eyed Susan** (*Rudbeckia hirta* 'Irish Eyes')	4 to 9/9 to 4	30 in./30 in.
F	**Moss rose** (*Portulaca grandiflora* 'Giant Pink Radiance') (in container)	Annual/12 to 1	6 in./6 in.

did you know...

Virginia creeper
Parthenocissus quinquefolia
50 ft. tall; vigorous vine with black or dark blue late-summer berries; full sun to part shade; cold-hardy in USDA zones 4 to 9; heat-tolerant in AHS zones 9 to 1

American bittersweet
Celastrus scandens
(not the invasive Oriental bittersweet *C. orbiculatus*)
30 ft. tall; red-seeded, orange fall fruit; full sun to light shade; cold-hardy in USDA zones 3 to 8; heat-tolerant in AHS zones 8 to 1

Grape *Vitis* spp.
25 ft. tall; fruit in late summer to autumn; most fruit in full sun; cold-hardy in USDA zones 5 to 9 (varies with species); heat-tolerant in AHS zones 9 to 5

Vines birds love
Charlene Ray, Minnesota

Q *We built a large arbor last fall. What vines should we plant on it to attract some birds?*

A Birds in your garden are not only fun to watch, they also help keep bad bugs from taking over.

Lots of vines offer quick cover, food and nesting sites for birds — I've shown three at left that do all these things. When choosing vines for your arbor, consider the height of the plant and if it'll grow in your zone. And try to choose one that has multiple seasons of interest, such as berries and fall color, so it'll look good for much of the year.

Blasted daffodils!
Jim McKenna, Colorado

Q *I have a batch of double daffodils whose buds just dried up on the stems this year. Why?*

A Your daffodil buds are *blasting* — forming and then simply drying up. Late-blooming, double

cultivars are especially susceptible to this. Unseasonably warm spring days alternating with freezing temperatures keep the buds from opening. There's not much you can do to correct the problem — some years you may get great late daffodils, others not.

Unfortunately, almost all double-flowered daffodils bloom late in spring. But if you want to grow doubles, 'Sir Winston Churchill' and 'Tahiti' are blast-resistant cultivars worth trying. If you still have trouble with buds drying up, it's probably best to stick to only early blooming single daffodils.

You *can* take them with you...
Sylvia Mabry, Tennessee

Q *I plan to move this fall and would like to take some of my daylilies, roses and a small hydrangea. How long can these bare-root plants be kept out of the ground?*

A Following a few easy steps, you can store these plants for several months.

Plants with fleshy or woody roots, such as the ones you mention, store well bare root.

Dig the plants as late in fall as possible, preferably after a hard freeze but before the ground freezes. Wait to lift them until after the

leaves drop. Cut the daylilies back to the ground after the tops have died back.

Carefully dig up the root ball and wash off as much soil as you can with a garden hose. If you want to divide the clump, wait until just before replanting it in spring. Cutting the clump apart in fall will open the plants up to infection from bacteria and fungus. Wrap the roots in moist (but not wet) shredded paper or sphagnum moss. Keep them in sealed plastic bags in a refrigerator or other dark place that stays 34 to 40 degrees. Your plants can be kept like this right through to spring.

Tag-team annuals
Rachel Miller, Kentucky

Summer heat often makes petunias look pretty rough. To keep her containers looking good, Rachel pulls out the faded petunias and substitutes verbena, another colorful annual that she starts from seed.

The trick is to have the verbena plants ready to transplant at just the right time. So Rachel postpones starting the verbena seed until May.

She says if you start the seed earlier, you'll get leggy, root-bound plants instead of full, healthy ones.

Use fencing with at least 4-in. openings to make harvesting easier.

Wire cage to two 4-ft. lengths of ½-in. rebar.

More tomatoes, please
Agatha Baker, California

Q *The tomatoes that I grew last year looked healthy but had fruit for just a few weeks and then stopped. What happened?*

A It sounds as if you grew a determinate type of tomato.

Tomato varieties develop into one of two basic forms: determinate and indeterminate. Determinate plants have a bushy habit and usually don't grow taller than about four feet. The branches end with flower clusters, which turn into the fruit. Once the tomatoes form, the plant stops growing taller. Since they don't get very tall, these plants may not need staking, but all of the fruit will ripen during a short time in the summer. 'Celebrity' and 'Taxi' are two popular determinate varieties.

You may want to grow indeterminate tomatoes. They have a vining habit that keeps growing (up to 10 feet or more) and making fruit all season long. You'll find that most of the tomato plants garden centers carry are this type. 'Brandywine' and 'Sun Gold' are a couple of popular ones.

Because they get so big, indeterminate plants require staking for support. You can see an easy-to-make cage for your tomatoes above. Form stiff wire fencing into a tube 30 to 36 inches in diameter and 3 to 4 feet tall.

Place the cage over the young plant before it reaches about 2 feet high. This cage will contain the vines and keep the fruit up out of the mud. It'll make harvesting the fruit a snap so you can enjoy all the tomatoes you'll get from summer until frost.

product pick

The Plant Finder

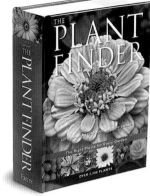

You don't have to be a botanist to identify all the plants in the neighborhood — just get *The Plant Finder*, edited by Tony Rodd and Geoff Bryant. This pint-sized reference book is hefty but only 6 by 8 inches, so it's easy to handle. There are 10 color-coded plant categories so you can flip to the right section without a hassle. Charts at the beginning of each section help you find the plants you want quickly by size, light requirements, fragrance and other characteristics.

Bottom line: Easy to hold and full of information. This is a handy little book to have around.
Source: Local or online bookstores or www.GardenGateStore.com
Price: $49.95; hardcover; 992 pages

in the news

What's the best lamb's ear?
For six years, researchers at the Chicago Botanic Garden have been growing lamb's ear (*Stachys byzantina*) and the results are in. Several popular cultivars scored highly. 'Big Ears', 'Cotton Boll' and 'Silver Carpet' were solid performers as was the straight species. Good drainage appears to be the key to keeping these fuzzy leafed plants coming back year after year. This study also looked at betony, another member of the *Stachys* family. Taller and with plain green leaves, *S. monieri* 'Hummelo' came out on top because of a long bloom time and hardy constitution. For a complete report, go to www.chicagobotanic.org/downloads/planteval_notes/no27_stachys.pdf or send $3 to Plant Evaluation Notes, c/o Richard Hawke, Chicago Botanic Gardens, 1000 Lake Cook Road, Glencoe, IL 60022.

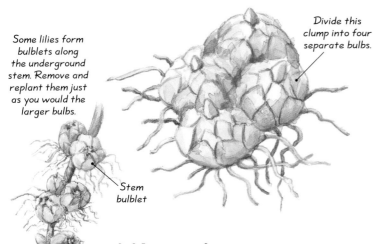

Some lilies form bulblets along the underground stem. Remove and replant them just as you would the larger bulbs.

Divide this clump into four separate bulbs.

Stem bulblet

Divide to revive
Marcia Hansen, Iowa

Q *I have about 50 lilies. I fertilize them regularly, but this year they have really small blooms. What's wrong with them?*

A Your plants are trying to tell you it's time to divide them. Lilies (*Lilium* spp.) multiply quickly and need to be divided every two to three years. You'll know it's time to divide when your plant's not blooming like it used to and you see smaller lily plants crowding the original space.

The best time to divide lilies is in the fall, after the foliage has died back. Carefully dig up the entire clump. You'll find bulblets or clumps of bulbs like the illustrations above. Separate the individual bulbs and replant them, along with the original bulb, 3 to 4 inches deep and 6 to 8 inches apart. Water the area well before the ground freezes and you should see plenty of healthy new lilies in the spring.

Forced bulbs worth saving?
Linda Firman, Colorado

Q *What can I do with my potted tulip bulbs after I've forced them to bloom?*

A Unless you have a lot of patience, throw them in the compost pile. This goes for hyacinths and daffodils, too. If you're willing to wait a few years for blooms, you can plant the bulbs in the garden.

After your flowers fade, cut off the stems. Place the pots in direct sunlight and continue to water and fertilize. This will keep the foliage growing and restoring energy to the bulb. Don't cut off the foliage until it has completely withered and turned brown. Store the bulbs (in the pots) in a cool, dry spot in your home, and stop watering. In early fall, take them out of the pots and plant them in the garden, treating them as you would your other spring flowering bulbs.

Which bulbs like soggy soil?
Melinda Martin, Michigan

Q *The soil in much of my garden is damp or wet most of the time. Is there any way I can grow spring bulbs?*

A While most spring-blooming bulbs like very well-drained soil, here are three that thrive in damp conditions:

Spring snowflake
Leucojum vernum
8 to 12 in. tall
White bell-shaped flowers with green tips in early spring
Sun to part shade
Cold-hardy in USDA zones 4 to 8
Heat-tolerant in AHS zones 9 to 3

Quamash
Camassia quamash
8 to 32 in. tall
Cup-shaped blue flowers in late spring
Sun to part shade
Cold-hardy in USDA zones 4 to 11
Heat-tolerant in AHS zones 12 to 1

Checkered lily
Fritillaria meleagris
12 in. tall
Bell-shaped purple, pink or white flowers in spring
Sun to part shade
Cold-hardy in USDA zones 4 to 9
Heat-tolerant in AHS zones 8 to 2

in the news

Daffodils help Alzheimer's patients
Daffodils may soon be helping in the fight against Alzheimer's disease. Galanthamine, an alkaloid extracted from snowdrops, has been helpful in relieving memory loss but is very expensive. Recently, scientists found that daffodils (a snowdrop relative) grown in the Black Mountains of Wales contain a higher level of this valuable substance than other daffodils or even snowdrops. Scientists hope that once full-scale production gets going, the drug will become more affordable.

Check gladiola corms for pale yellow spots that turn sunken and brown.

Well-behaved bamboo

Beth Laverdiere, Ohio

Q *I'm interested in planting a non-invasive bamboo that would be hardy in USDA zone 5. Is there such a thing?*

A Well, believe it or not, there is! The difference between invasive and non-invasive bamboo is the root structure. Most bamboos have running roots, which allow the plants to spread far and wide. In the illustrations below, you can see how this differs from the more well-behaved bamboos with clumping roots.

In general, clumping bamboos aren't cold-hardy past USDA zone 7, but umbrella bamboo (*Fargesia murieliae)* and blue fountain bamboo (*Fargesia nitida*) are cold-hardy to USDA zone 5 (heat-tolerant to AHS zone 4) and both grow best when planted in part shade.

Spot treatment for glads?

Pam Keltz, Minnesota

Q *My gladiola bulbs have round brown spots on them. What is this and what should I do about it?*

A It sounds as if you're describing gladiola scab, which is caused by the bacteria *Pseudomonas marginata*. Scab infection first appears on the bulbs or corms as pale yellow spots that eventually turn brown and sunken. The bacteria spread by splashing water or insect feeding.

Throw infected corms away, not on your compost pile. And before you store glad corms next fall, inspect them and get rid of any infected ones. Dry the remaining corms in a well-ventilated area out of direct sunlight for 2 to 3 weeks. Keep the temperature around 60 to 70 degrees F. Once they're dry, store them in paper bags at 35 to 40 degrees F.

In spring, when you replant your glads, don't overwater them, as scab spreads more easily in wet soils.

product pick

The Complete Flower Gardener

If you dream of flower-filled borders and containers, this new book by Karan Davis Cutler and Barbara W. Ellis can help make your dreams a reality.

The first few chapters tell you everything you need to know to get your flower bed going, starting with site analysis and finishing up with maintaining that garden full of blossoms. There are lots of organic solutions to your garden problems, including a very educational section on environmentally friendly chemical controls like pyrethrum. The plant profile chapter is generous, covering 175 plants, with enough information to help you decide what to put where. With its easy-to-read style, this big book is a great garden resource.

Bottom line: Easy to read, plenty of design advice and lots of organic gardening tips.
Source: Local or online bookstores or www.GardenGateStore.com
Price: $34.95; hardcover; 488 pages

Watch them spread: Runners vs. clumpers

New growth forms in clumps.

New shoots form on running roots.

Two well-behaved clumping bamboos

Umbrella bamboo grows to 15 ft. in a weeping form.

Blue fountain bamboo's foliage arches a bit and grows to 12 ft.

Floribunda: Clusters contain blooms at different stages, from bud to fully open.

Hybrid tea: Single blooms on long stems make great cut flowers.

Grandiflora: All the blooms in each cluster are at the same stage.

A mound of soil helps support the new plant and encourages roots to grow out into the soil.

A rose isn't just a rose
Cheryl Geisinger, Washington

Q *What's the difference between a hybrid tea, floribunda and grandiflora rose?*

A Hybrid teas are known for their large, showy blooms in spring through fall. Because they have long stems, usually with one fragrant bloom on each, they make good cut flowers. Most hybrid teas grow 3 to 6 feet tall and are generally cold-hardy in USDA zones 5 to 9. Disease resistance varies across this very large group.

Floribundas bloom all summer with smaller flowers than those of hybrid teas. But instead of one bloom per stem, they grow in clusters of three to 15. They tend to be more disease-resistant and cold-hardy (zones 4 to 9) than hybrid teas. Most floribundas reach 3 to 5 feet tall and look great if you plant them in masses.

Grandifloras are a cross between hybrid teas and floribundas. They bloom with larger flowers like those of hybrid teas but in clusters like floribundas. The fragrant clusters bloom repeatedly all season long. Generally speaking, grandifloras are taller than either parent — up to 6 feet — so these roses are good for larger gardens or for the back of the border. Hardy in zones 4 to 9, they are more disease-resistant than hybrid teas.

Do the math
Cindy Brandt, Georgia

Q *Can I plant last year's leftover vegetable seeds?*

A Yes, but before you do, check their germination rate.

To do this, roll 10 seeds inside a damp paper towel. Seal them in a plastic bag and mark it with the date and type of seed.

After the normal germination time for that plant (found on the seed packet) has passed, open the bag and count the number of seeds that have sprouted. Multiply that number by 10 to calculate the percentage of seed that has germinated. If germination is 70 percent or more, plant the seed normally; 40 to 69 percent, plant the seed more thickly; below 40 percent, discard and buy new seed.

Help for root-bound plants
Rose Loveall, Pennsylvania

For gardeners, finding a good plant sale is like finding a gold mine. But some of those late-summer sale plants are root-bound after sitting around all season in a pot. From some master gardener friends, Rose learned a valuable technique that ensures any bargain perennials she buys will be a success. It's called "butterflying." Just take a soil knife or spade and slice the root mass one-third to one-half up from the bottom of the root ball.

The illustration above shows you how to spread the two "wings" over a mound of soil in the bottom of the planting hole. Make sure that the ends of the wings touch the bottom. Then backfill the hole with soil and water well.

Butterflying encourages roots to grow out into the surrounding soil, rather than growing in a circle, girdling the plant. The mounded soil in the center of the root mass keeps the roots from winding back together.

Bug-busting plants
Janie Jackson, Mississippi

Q *Are there plants that mosquitoes and other insect pests don't like?*

A If you're looking for a plant that repels mosquitoes while grow-ing in the ground or in a pot, the answer is "no."

Studies show the cit-ronella plant, supposedly bred to repel mosquitoes, doesn't affect the bugs at all. But there are some plants — lemon thyme, verbena and fennel to name three — that release repel-lent oils when their leaves are crushed and rubbed on the skin. Test a small amount on your skin first to see if you are allergic.

Never-blooming wisteria
Janet Tolbert, Maryland

Q *I have a 5-year-old wisteria that's never bloomed, but it's very healthy otherwise. Why hasn't it bloomed?*

A Many wisterias don't flower much for the first six or seven years because they have to reach their full height first. At that point, the blooms are dependent upon four factors: Light, fertilizer, pruning and weather.

Wisterias grow and bloom best when planted in full sun. If yours gets at least 6 hours a day, try feed-ing it with a fertil-izer high in phosphorus. Too little of this essential element, and you'll get a lot of leaves, but very few flowers.

Proper pruning, best done twice a year, is also important for blooming. First, in July or August, cut the long new side shoots back to about half of their length, as in (A) below. This lets more light reach the wood and helps flower buds to form. Then in January or February, cut those side shoots back farther, leaving only three to four buds on each stem (B) to encourage heavier flowering.

Even after proper pruning, a dry fall or cold spring could also prevent buds from forming or opening. You can't do anything about late spring freezes, which kill the emerging buds. But water your plant if you have a dry autumn so it's able to set flower buds. The gor-geous blooms in spring are well worth the effort!

in the news

Regional daylily picks
With the hundreds of daylily varieties for sale, it's hard to know which one to choose. Tap into the experience of gardeners in your region who've grown them for years with the American Hemerocallis Society's popularity poll. Each year the AHS polls members across the United States and Canada to see which daylilies did the best for them. It lists the top performers on its Web site. To see the top daylilies for any region and the top 20 in the nation, go to www.daylilies.org and click on "Popularity Polls."

Competitive ground covers
Wouldn't you rather see lamb's ear in your garden instead of dandelions? Ground covers make beau-tiful weed control, and Cornell University's Allstar Groundcover Web site tells you which plants are competitive enough to keep weeds at bay. Visit www.entomology.cornell.edu/Extension/Woodys/CUGroundCoverSite/GroundcoverMain.html and click on the link "Data on Competitiveness" to find out which plants can help you in your quest for a weed-free garden.

Good scents = fewer pests?
New flowers are often bred to be big and colorful but not fragrant. Fortunately, a scientist at Purdue University is looking into how volatile com-pounds, the enzymes that produce scent, work on a genetic level. Volatile compounds combine to create scents that attract pollinators and repel pests. There are even examples of infected plants releasing the compound to "warn" other plants. Scientists hope that by understanding volatile compounds better, they'll be able to manipulate the genes to enhance benefits like repelling pests. The big plus for us will be great-smelling flowers that are also pest-free!

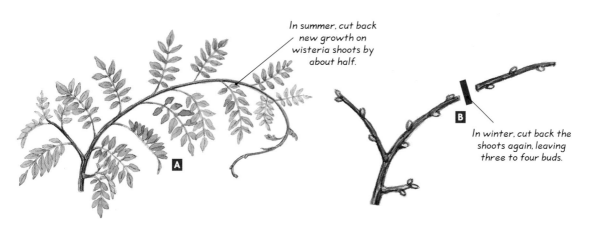

In summer, cut back new growth on wisteria shoots by about half.

A

B

In winter, cut back the shoots again, leaving three to four buds.

What is this stuff?

Tammy VanGrowski, Illinois

Q *The soil in some of my house plants has a flaky white substance on it. What can I do about it?*

A It sounds like you're describing mineral buildup in the soil caused by the way you water and fertilize.

If you use water that's very hard or has been treated in a softener using sodium, the minerals and sodium can build up in the soil. The problem is worse if you let the pot sit in the saucer holding the drained water. And salts from water-soluble synthetic fertilizers can also add to the trouble.

A light buildup won't harm plants. Just scrape off the white residue, set the pot in the sink and flush it with distilled or unsoftened water to leach the minerals out of the soil. Do this once a month to avoid a heavy buildup.

If you *do* have a heavy buildup on the soil, with a crust around the drainage hole or on the outside of the pot, start fresh and repot the plant in a new container. Use a well-drained potting mix and water deeply when the top inch of the mix is dry. (Light, frequent watering makes the minerals build up faster.) Empty the saucer or raise the container on a layer of gravel so the drained water isn't taken back up into the pot.

Reviving lady's mantle

Ruth Brown, Michigan

Q *My lady's mantle looks very bad by midsummer. Is there anything I can do to improve it?*

A You have a couple of options.

Lady's mantle (*Alchemilla mollis*) will grow in full shade to full sun. But by midsummer, its flowers and foliage often look scorched when it's growing in more light.

If you have just a few plants, grab the green foliage in the center of the clump with one hand. With the other, use a pair of scissors to cut away the brown foliage and flowers around the edge, as you see in the illustration at right.

To do a lot of plants at once, use hedge shears to cut back the entire plant by about two thirds. Either way you do it, the plant will put out new growth and soon look great again.

Why evergreen hellebores aren't...

Sherri Lochmann, Colorado

Q *Help! I thought my hellebores were supposed to be evergreen, but the leaves on mine turn brown in winter. What's the deal?*

A The brown hellebore leaves, like those in the photo, are caused by cold, dry weather. Though they often come through a mild winter unscathed, you're likely to see some leaf dieback in colder zones. A severe winter in any zone, especially if there isn't much snow cover, can also take a toll on them. On the other hand, a blanket of snow gives plants moisture and protection from drying sun and winter wind. When the snow melts, leaves will come through fresh and green.

In spring, remove any winter-burned leaves and debris. Your flowers will look their best and you'll protect your plants from rot and diseases.

Refresh your lady's mantle in midsummer by cutting away anything that looks dead or brown.

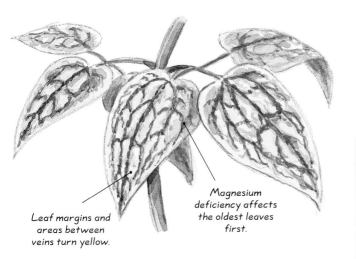

Leaf margins and areas between veins turn yellow.

Magnesium deficiency affects the oldest leaves first.

Yellow clematis leaves
Nancy Williams, California

Q*The leaves of my 'Ernest Markham' clematis are turning yellow. Can you help?*

A Yellow leaves on your clematis *can* be caused by too much moisture. But if your clematis is in well-drained soil, they're likely a symptom of magnesium deficiency. One cause is using too much fertilizer high in potassium. The illustration above shows how the areas between the leaf veins and around the edges turn yellow in early summer. Without enough chlorophyll, the plant becomes stunted and weak and may even die.

Mix ¼ cup Epsom salts (magnesium sulphate) into a gallon of water and spray the leaves in summer. You may need to treat it several times before you see improvement. Or sprinkle the dry Epsom salts right on the soil (¼ to ½ cup per 10 square feet) around the plant. This can be done once, at any time of the year.

Foamy stems
Beverly Eaton, Idaho

Q*There's a watery white foam on some of my plants. What causes this and how do I get rid of it?*

A What you're seeing is the frothy foam produced by the nymphs of spittle bugs, sometimes called frog-hoppers. The ¹⁄₁₆-inch-long nymphs feed on the sap of many plants, including pines, holly, salvias, goldenrod and chrysanthemums. They excrete a clear liquid that they mix with sap and air to create foam that protects them from drying out and hides them from their predators.

Spittlebugs don't cause much damage. Handpick or knock them and the foam off the plant with a stiff spray of water. Then, in fall, send any foliage that had the foam out with the trash to keep the eggs from overwintering in your garden.

product pick

Plant Solutions

Do you need a perennial for a dry, sunny border? Or do you have a shady spot in need of a shrub? Look through *Plant Solutions* for the answers. We found the color-coded bars at the top of the pages made it easy to flip through this book to find plants for specific situations. "Perennials for full sun" or "Small trees for sheltered sites" are examples of the numerous categories. Each plant profile has a photograph, growing specifications and a brief description.

Bottom line: If you're stumped about what plant to put where, this book is a great guide.
Source: Local or online book stores or www.GardenGateStore.com
Price: $39.95

in the news

Online perennial library
Trying to figure out which perennial would work in that sun-filled bed? Or maybe you have an empty space in the shade garden. Check out this helpful online library at www.perennialresource. com to find a variety that fits your needs. The site is maintained by wholesale plant distributor Walters Gardens. Plants are listed alphabetically and each includes a photo so you can see the color of the flower or foliage. Click on the photo of one you like and you'll get a more complete description of the plant, along with growing information and design suggestions. Then add it to your shopping list. You can't buy plants through this site, but you can take the printed list with you when you go shopping. That way you'll have the name, photo, size and hardiness at your fingertips.

Choose a pot that's about a third as wide as your African violet's leaf span.

Better-blooming African violets
Carol Baltz, Florida

Q *Why isn't my African violet plant blooming?*

A If it's not blooming, there's usually a problem with one of the following:

Light — African violets need at least 10 hours of bright, filtered light per day, but must have 8 hours of darkness to bloom.

Fertilizer — Be sure to feed your plants weekly with a good-quality African violet fertilizer (7-7-7).

Medium — Your potting mix should be a light, soilless mix. You won't see many flowers if the mix is too heavy.

Pot size — African violets like to be crowded. Make sure your pot is no more than 4 inches deep and the width is only a third the size of the leaf span.

How and when to move alliums
Warren Gould, New York

Q *I'd like to move some established alliums. How do I do this? Do I need to replant them right away?*

A Alliums can be transplanted right after they finish flowering, but you can also dig and store them over the summer for fall planting.

Though the foliage doesn't last long, you can locate the bulbs in your bed beneath the long-lasting flowers. Dig into the soil several inches out from the stem so you don't accidentally spear the bulbs. Carefully lift, separate and replant them in their new home so the base of the bulb sits at a depth three times the bulb's height. Add a little 7-10-5 bulb food into the soil, backfill and water.

If you can't replant the bulbs right away, store the ones free of mold or soft spots in mesh bags in a dark, dry area. Keep them around 68 degrees F. (except *A. giganteum*, which should be stored between 73 and 77 degrees.) Then in fall, plant them as usual. Top with a little light mulch to help keep the soil moist until the roots get established.

It's time to transplant
Jean Coffey, Illinois

Q *How and when is the best time to move a rose of Sharon?*

A The best time to move your rose of Sharon (*Hibiscus syriacus*) is right after it's dropped its leaves in the fall or in early spring before new leaves emerge. Moving a deciduous tree or shrub while it's dormant is easier on the plant. Plus, it'll weigh less without the leaves.

If your plant is big, prune the tallest of the branches to 5 or 6 feet to make moving easier. That way there's less foliage to support while the roots gets re-established, as well.

To lift the root ball, dig a foot out from the trunk, getting as much of the main roots as possible. Use a sharp spade and keep loppers or a small saw handy to cut through roots. Dig the new hole at least twice as wide as the root ball and about the same depth.

Water the plant in well to get rid of any air pockets in the soil. When the weather warms up in spring, the roots will be established and ready to go.

Transplant TLC
Larry Sohren, Colorado

Have you ever tried transplanting a perennial only to have it wither in the sun? Larry found a little TLC goes a long way to getting his transplants to survive. He puts some of those narrow green bamboo stakes in the ground, just outside the planting area. Then he attaches 50 percent shade cloth, found at the local hardware store, to the stakes with some heavy duty clothespins. The shade cloth keeps the harsh sun from drying out the new plants. Three to five days is usually enough time for plants to get settled in.

It takes about four weeks for CowPots to decompose in the soil.

product pick

CowPots™

These may look like your typical peat pots, but they're not. They're made of dried cow manure! Put away your clothes pins, though, because CowPots are odorless. Great for starting seeds or cuttings, these organic pots strike a good balance between holding up well for starting seeds and decomposing quickly in the soil. When we did some spring planting in CowPots, we found that soaking the soil and pots before planting the seeds kept the soil moisture high while the seeds got started.

Bottom line: Your transplants will really take off in these environmentally friendly pots. CowPots decompose quickly and add nutrients at the same time, and they don't restrict root growth.
Source: Gardener's Supply Company at 888-833-1412 or www.gardeners.com
Price: $11.95 for a pack of 15 3½-inch diameter pots

in the news

A piece of pine history

A few years ago, we told you about the discovery of the once-thought-extinct Wollemi™ pine (*Wollemia nobilis*), in a remote canyon of Australia's Wollemi National Park. Now you can buy one of these beauties and contribute to its conservation, too. This versatile tree is cold-hardy from USDA zone 7 to 11 and does well in sun or shade. You can even grow one indoors. Get your own 10-inch-tall Wollemi pine at select independent garden centers or visit National Geographic at www.nationalgeographic.com/Wollemipine. The cost is $99.95, which includes a care manual.

Top elm varieties

Dutch elm disease has decimated the American elm (*Ulmus americana*) in our urban landscapes, but thanks to the efforts of The United States National Arboretum, this beautiful tree may make a comeback. A recent study by the arboretum compared the disease tolerance of 19 elm clones and cultivars. No tree is completely immune, but several show very good resistance to Dutch elm disease. One of the best in the study was 'Jefferson', a new clone that should be available in about four years. 'Valley Forge', 'Princeton', 'Delaware' and 'New Harmony' are available now and also have excellent tolerance.

Find the right tree

When you plant a tree, make sure you get the right one with the online tree selector at http://orb.at.ufl.edu/TREES/index.html. Created by the University of Florida, Rutgers University and the USDA Forestry Service, this Web site profiles trees cold-hardy in USDA zones 2 to 7. And additional information for gardeners in zones 8 to 11 is just a click away. You can find trees in the index listed by common or botanical name, along with a photo and growing information. Or click on "Tree Identification" to select characteristics, such as bloom time, zone and leaf pattern for a list of trees fitting that description.

Minnesota's most wanted

When you're faced with all the annuals and perennials at the garden center, it's hard to know what to choose. Gardeners in the upper Midwest need plants that take off quickly and tolerate the cooler temperatures. Check out the University of Minnesota's Tough and Terrific™ Web site at www.florifacts.umn.edu and click on "Annual and Perennial Trials" to help you decide. University researchers evaluate plants for cold hardiness, disease resistance, size and flowering at three locations around Minnesota. For a quick guide, click on the "Top 10 performing annuals and perennials." If you'd like more information, go to the "Final Flower Report" and for the complete listing.

A tiger swallowtail sips
nectar from flowering
crabapple blossoms.

top picks

our favorite perennials, butterflies and more!

EVERYONE HAS AN OPINION

and we're taking the opportunity to share ours...We'll let you know what we think are the best new plants, and introduce you to some not-often-grown annuals and even our favorite pink perennials. Plus, we'll show you how to identify 7 butterflies you're likely to find in your garden and how to attract them, even in spring. Finally, enough about us — what are *your* favorites? We'll share the results of our readers' poll on best-loved annuals.

new plants

Ordering new plants is a lot like reading a good book. There's excitement: Hey, it's new! There's mystery: Will it perform well and look good in my garden? There's adventure: Sometimes despite our best efforts, pests or disease sneak in on good plants. And as the season progresses, you hope for a happy ending. But since gardening has enough adventure without the unknowns of a new plant, I'm going to provide you with a sneak peek at some of the latest varieties to get you off to a good start.

We had a hot, dry summer in our test garden last year, and watering became quite a chore. Thankfully, some much-needed rain arrived in fall to refresh our wilting spirits and withering plants. Every season has its challenges, and plants that can stand up to difficult weather and pests are a must.

This year's crop of new plants has a lot to offer: Interesting foliage, drop-dead gorgeous flowers and improvements on old standbys. And be sure to check out our online video to see more of our favorites. I think you'll find they'll all put in a solid performance, and I wouldn't be surprised if some of them are on the best-seller list next year. □

— *Sherri Ribbey*

Check out more new plants in our online **video**.

'Berry Basket' zinnia
Zinnia hybrid

You'll see zinnias in a whole new light with 'Berry Basket', the mix in the large photo, or 'Décor', in the small photo. The colors are fantastic. Full, luscious flowers bloom in a range of sizes but most are around 4 inches.

Our zinnias looked great last summer. They branched well, and since we cut some flowers for bouquets, the side branches bloomed more quickly. Like most zinnias, ours had some trouble with powdery mildew. To keep this fungus at bay, avoid overhead watering and make sure your zinnias have good air circulation.

Type	Annual
Size	3 to 3½ ft. tall, 10 in. wide
Bloom	Summer
Soil	Moist, well-drained
Light	Full sun
Hardiness	
	Cold: Annual
	Heat: AHS zones 12 to 1
Introducer and Source	
	Renee's Garden Seeds
	888-880-7228
	www.reneesgarden.com
What's new?	
	Bright new color mixes

'Gage's Shadow' perilla
Solenostemon xperilla

A vigorous plant with great foliage can't be beat. The colors are subtle enough to make a nice background for colorful annuals. But it makes a nice centerpiece, too. Ours quickly filled a purple-glazed container. Surrounded by the pink impatiens in the photo above, it looked wonderful. Pinch plants at the leaf joint to keep them more compact, if needed. 'Gage's Shadow' won't reseed everywhere, like some perillas do.

It's named in honor of the breeder's son, Gage, who has cerebral palsy. A portion of the cost for each plant is donated to United Cerebral Palsy.

Type	Annual
Size	18 to 24 in. tall, 3 ft. wide
Bloom	N/A
Soil	Moist, well-drained
Light	Part shade to shade
Hardiness	Cold: Annual
	Heat: AHS zones 12 to 1
Introducer	Proven Selections
Source	Local garden centers

What's new?
Beautiful new foliage color combo on a vigorous plant

'Candy Mountain' foxglove
Digitalis purpurea

Beautiful foxglove is now even better. 'Candy Mountain' lifts its flowers to the sky instead of producing the usual downward-facing bells. These dainty blossoms go all the way around the stem for a fuller spike. And there's no need to stake these sturdy stems.

A biennial, foxglove forms a rosette of foliage the first year and flowers the next. Removing spent flower stalks encourages a second, though smaller, round of blooms.

You can start seed indoors in early spring. Direct sow your foxglove by early summer at the latest so the plants have time to get established.

Type	Biennial
Size	36 to 56 in. tall, 18 to 24 in. wide
Bloom	Summer
Soil	Well-drained
Light	Sun to part shade
Hardiness	Cold: USDA zones 4 to 8
	Heat: AHS zones 8 to 1
Introducer and Source	Thompson and Morgan
	800-274-7333
	www.thompson-morgan.com

What's new?
Upward-facing flowers all around the stem

PHOTO: © Thompson & Morgan (Group) Ltd. (foxglove)

'Jethro Tull' tickseed
Coreopsis hybrid

Liven up your perennial border with this new twist on an old favorite. 'Jethro Tull' tickseed has fluted sunshine-yellow petaled flowers that keep coming from summer to frost. The first flush of blooms is the biggest — the plants are just covered. Cut a few flowers to add to a wildflower bouquet. Later, remove spent stems below the foliage for a fresh supply of blooms in a few weeks. In the meantime, enjoy the deeply lobed green leaves and full, mounding habit as a ground cover.

To keep your coreopsis coming back, make sure it has well-drained soil. It doesn't like "wet feet."

Type Perennial
Size 12 to 15 in. tall, 18 in. wide
Bloom Summer
Soil Well-drained
Light Full sun
Hardiness
  Cold: USDA zones 5 to 9
  Heat: AHS zones 9 to 1
Introducer
  ItSaul Plants
Source Garden Crossings
  www.gardencrossings.com
What's new?
  Bright, sunny yellow fluted petals

'Piglet' fountain grass
Pennisetum alopecuroides

Here's an ornamental grass that fits in anywhere. 'Piglet' fountain grass grows only 6 to 8 inches tall and 18 inches in flower. Fluffy tan flowers start showing up in late summer and last through late fall. Whether your garden is large or small, you can edge a sunny border or tuck 'Piglet' into that last open space in the garden.

During the growing season, make sure 'Piglet' gets regular watering to keep the foliage looking good and ensure plenty of flowers. You may notice a few seedlings in spring, but they're easy to pull if you don't want more.

Type Perennial
Size 18 in. tall in flower, 24 in. wide
Bloom Fall
Soil Moist, well-drained
Light Full sun to light shade
Hardiness
  Cold: USDA zones 5 to 9
  Heat: AHS zones 9 to 1
Introducer
  Intrinsic Perennial Gardens
Source Klehm's Song Sparrow Farm and Nursery
  800-553-3715
  www.songsparrow.com
What's new?
  A small fountain grass for any space

'Ruby' Volcano® phlox
Phlox paniculata

How would you like a phlox that's resistant to powdery mildew, flowers summer to fall on sturdy stems and has a heavenly fragrance? You'll get it all with 'Ruby', the latest color in the Volcano phlox series. Try these vibrant pink flowers with other summer-bloomers like strawflower, salvia and cosmos.

In spring, apply some slow-release fertilizer such as Vigoro®. Then after the first flush of flowers, cut the plant back by a third to encourage more stems.

Divide plants in spring every three to five years. Just dig the clump, pull it apart and replant.

Type	Perennial
Size	16 to 24 in. tall, 24 in. wide
Bloom	Early summer to fall
Soil	Well-drained, fertile
Light	Full sun
Hardiness	Cold: USDA zones 4 to 9
	Heat: AHS zones 9 to 1
Introducer	Anthony Tesselaar Plants
Source	Local garden centers

What's new?
New color in this series of long-blooming, compact plants

'Edge of Night' calla lily
Zantedeschia hybrid

Simple and elegant, yet bold, 'Edge of Night' is fantastic in the border or containers. Deep-purple to black 3-inch flowers on dark stems are set off by speckled leaves with purple-black edges. They make wonderful cut flowers, often lasting up to two weeks in a vase.

Where 'Edge of Night' isn't hardy, dig and store the tubers like you would cannas. It's even easier when you grow them in containers. Bring the whole pot inside. If a light frost hasn't killed the foliage, go ahead and cut it off. Store it in a cool, dry place through winter and water lightly about once a month.

Type	Perennial tuber
Size	36 in. tall, 20 in. wide
Bloom	Summer
Soil	Rich, moist
Light	Sun to part shade
Hardiness	Cold: USDA zones 7 to 10
	Heat: AHS zones 12 to 1
Introducer	Terra Nova Nurseries, Inc.
Source	Plant Delights Nursery, Inc.
	919-772-4794
	www.plantdelights.com

What's new?
Dramatic dark-purple flowers with a backdrop of purple-edged leaves

PHOTO: Courtesy of Skagit Gardens (lickseed); courtesy of Intrinsic Perennial Gardens (fountain grass); courtesy of Anthony Tesselaar Plants USA, Inc. (phlox); courtesy of Terra Nova Nurseries, Inc. (calla lily)

Strike It Rich™ rose
Rosa 'WEKbepmey'

Strike It Rich is the perfect name for this rose. Every year you get a wealth of long-lasting, 5-inch golden-yellow flowers all season. The sweet and spicy fragrance is wonderful. When temperatures dip, there's a pink blush on the petals.

The glossy green foliage stayed clean with only a touch of black spot at the end of our hot, humid summer.

Like most roses, the height depends on where you live and how you prune. For mild climates, Strike It Rich reaches at least 6 feet. In colder areas, plan on 4 to 5 feet. By the way, you can still grow this rose in zone 4 with winter protection.

Type Grandiflora rose
Size 4 to 6 ft. tall, 2 ft. wide
Bloom Late spring to fall
Soil Well-drained
Light Full sun
Hardiness
  Cold: USDA zones 5 to 9
  Heat: AHS zones 9 to 1
Introducer Weeks Roses
Source Jackson & Perkins
  877-322-2300
  www.jacksonandperkins.com
What's new?
  Vigorous rose with big, fragrant flowers

'Purple Butterfly on the Wind' tree peony
Paeonia rockii

How would you like to have 8-inch flowers like this for two to three weeks at a time every spring? You can, with 'Purple Butterfly on the Wind'. We planted this tree peony in fall and it flowered beautifully the following spring. To help the flowers stay bright, keep them out of intense afternoon sun. And to make sure your tree peonies really take off, plant them in fall rather than spring. They'll need six weeks before the ground freezes to form roots and get established. Make sure they have good drainage too; soggy soil causes rot.

Type Shrub
Size 5 ft. tall, 4 ft. wide in 10 years
Bloom Spring
Soil Well-drained
Light Full sun
Hardiness
  Cold: USDA 4 to 9
  Heat: AHS 9 to 1
Introducer and Source
  Cricket Hill Garden
  877-723-6642
  www.treepeony.com
What's new?
  Big, red-purple flowers

Frosty Pearl™ euonymus
Euonymus fortunei **'Duncanata Variegated Vegeta'**

Got shade? Get Frosty Pearl. It does more than tolerate low-light conditions — it looks its best there. The creamy white edges are even whiter in shade. Hardier than other variegated euonymus, the foliage is evergreen so you can enjoy it even in winter.

Pearl-sized frosted pink berries, in the small photo, start showing up in fall. By winter, they age to red and open to reveal bright orange seeds.

Frosty Pearl naturally forms a low-growing mound as you see in the illustration. You can also train the long stems up a trellis or a tree.

Type Shrub
Size 50 to 60 in. tall, 24 in. wide
Bloom Summer
Soil Well-drained
Light Part shade to shade
Hardiness
Cold: USDA zones 4 to 8
Heat: AHS zones 9 to 3
Introducer Zelenka Nursery
Source Local garden centers
What's new?
A hardier variegated euonymus

My Monet™ weigela
Weigela florida **'Verweig'**

This shrub is as pretty as a bouquet of flowers. Green leaves with creamy white edges change to pink with plenty of sun. In spring, when the pink flowers open, it's even prettier.

At only 12 inches tall, it has a neat mounded habit, and it stays that way without a lot of pruning. Like most weigelas, this colorful variety doesn't have any serious pest or disease problems.

My Monet is perfect for lining a path or border. It even does well in containers. Weigela flowers are hummingbird magnets, so make sure to plant a few near your deck so you can catch a glimpse of some hungry hummers.

Type Shrub
Size 12 to 18 in. tall, 18 in. wide
Bloom Spring
Soil Moist, well-drained
Light Full sun to part shade
Hardiness
Cold: USDA zones 4 to 9
Heat: AHS zones 9 to 1
Introducer Proven Winners® ColorChoice®
Source Wayside Gardens 800-213-0379 www.waysidegardens.com
What's new?
Pastel variegation and nice tight habit

PHOTO: Courtesy of Zelenka Nursery (euonymus); courtesy of Spring Meadow (weigela)

Long-Blooming Perennials

WEB extra

At-a-glance **pruning guide** for 59 perennials.

With the hectic pace of life these days, most of us don't get to spend as much time gardening as we'd like to. That's why I love perennials. You only plant them once, they're easy to take care of and there are so many to choose from.

We also dream of gardens filled with a profusion of blooms from early spring right up until frost. But most perennials bloom for only a short time. Or do they? Why not try some long-blooming perennials?

When you hear the words "long-blooming perennials," what comes to mind? Because most perennials only bloom for a few weeks, you may not have high hopes. What if I could show you 10 plants that bloom for 8, 10 or even up to 12 weeks? Pretty amazing for a perennial!

And just to make those dreams a little sweeter, you'll find plants in many different sizes, shapes, colors and bloom times. There are perennials in new and exciting colors, and some that will thrive in shade gardens. And finally, while a few tried-and-true plants made the list, I've also included a couple of lesser-known perennials, such as masterwort and corydalis, that every gardener should try.

Some of the plants are specific cultivars, while others represent an entire species. That's because in some cases, a particular cultivar really stands out above the rest, while in a few cases, all the relatives are long-blooming.

Deadheading, or cutting back spent blooms, keeps many perennials blooming longer or gets them to rebloom. With each of these plants, I've given you some tips about that. But for more information about keeping your other perennials blooming longer with pruning, check out our Web extra.

Give a few of these long-blooming perennials a try, and your dreams for a profusion of blooms from spring through fall just might come true. □

— *Penny Verran*

'Homestead Purple' rose verbena
Verbena hybrid

'Homestead Purple' is a tumbling, spreading verbena that forms a lush carpet nearly 3 feet wide. Its flowers turn rosy magenta in part sun and a vibrant, rich purple in full sun. And I guarantee that you won't be disappointed in its fantastic color display, which lasts from midspring right up until the first frost.

Although it's extremely heat-, humidity- and drought-tolerant, 'Homestead Purple' also thrives in cool summer regions. This tough little verbena is extremely cold-hardy and has been known to grow well even in zone 4 with a little bit of winter protection.

Size	6 to 18 in. tall, 24 to 36 in. wide
Blooms	Midspring to midfall with regular deadheading
Soil	Well-drained to dry
Light	Full sun to part sun
Hardiness	
	Cold: USDA 5 to 10
	Heat: AHS 12 to 1

Mail-order source
Classy Ground Covers
www.classyground
covers.com

Royal Candles speedwell
Veronica spicata 'Glory'

Royal Candles will provide you with a spectacular display of its violet-blue blooms for 6 to 7 weeks or more, usually beginning in late spring.

It also happens to be relatively carefree. Just plant in well-drained soil in full sun and watch it take off. This plant will tolerate some shade, but you won't get quite as many flowers and it may need to be staked.

Some veronicas' bottom foliage dies out late in the season, but not this one. So don't be afraid to give this plant the royal treatment and plant it in the front of your garden.

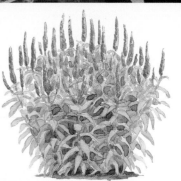

Size	15 to 18 in. tall and wide
Blooms	Late spring to early fall; will rebloom with deadheading
Soil	Well-drained
Light	Full sun to part shade
Hardiness	
	Cold: USDA 3 to 8
	Heat: AHS 8 to 1

Mail-order source
Bluestone Perennials
800-852-5243
www.bluestone
perennials.com
Catalog free

Torch lily
Kniphofia hybrids

With its big clumps of sword-shaped leaves and unique multi-colored flower spires, torch lily creates a showstopping focal point. Easy to see how it got its name. It's great as a single specimen, or in groups of three or four. And it'll bloom for 10 to 12 weeks throughout the summer.

Torch lily is a sun-lover that likes it hot and dry and can tolerate drought conditions. One thing it won't tolerate is wet feet. In zones 5 and 6, tie the foliage up over the crown of your plant in the fall to keep water from freezing there.

Size 18 to 60 in. tall, 18 to 36 in. wide

Blooms Early to late summer with regular deadheading

Soil Well-drained

Light Full sun

Hardiness
Cold: USDA zones 5 to 9
Heat: AHS zones 9 to 4

Mail-order source
Plant Delights Nursery, Inc.
919-772-4794
www.plantdelights.com
Catalog free

Blanket flower
Gaillardia xgrandiflora

This perennial's heat and drought tolerance and extremely long bloom time make it perfect for first-time gardeners *and* seasoned veterans alike.

Blanket flower's flame-red flowers tipped with yellow will ignite a fire in any garden from early summer until the first frost. And there are lots of new color variations on the market these days.

Deadheading helps extend the bloom time, but I leave the spent flower heads intact at the end of the season for winter interest.

Blanket flower has a reputation for being short-lived, but I've had the same plants in my garden for 8 years.

Size 24 to 36 in. tall, 24 in. wide

Blooms Early summer to midfall with regular deadheading

Soil Well-drained to poor

Light Full sun

Hardiness
Cold: USDA zones 3 to 10
Heat: AHS zones 8 to 1

Mail-order source
High Country Gardens
800-925-9387
www.highcountry
gardens.com
Catalog free

'Romantic Returns' daylily
Hemerocallis hybrid

'Romantic Returns' is certainly a fitting name for this rose-pink daylily. And unlike most reblooming daylilies, its flowers don't appear in recurring waves. Instead, it blooms nonstop from early summer until frost.

Like most daylilies, 'Romantic Returns' grows best when planted in full sun. And while it's not fussy about soil type, it does prefer a spot with good drainage. Not much gets this tough little performer down, including heat, humidity, drought or cold.

Size 21 to 26 in. tall, 23 to 30 in. wide

Blooms Early summer to midfall; pull out spent stalks to keep it going

Soil Well-drained

Light Full sun

Hardiness
Cold: USDA zones 5 to 9
Heat: AHS zones 9 to 1

Mail-order source
Wayside Gardens
800-213-0379
www.waysidegardens.com
Catalog free

'Snowflake' catmint
Nepeta racemosa

Catmint has been a garden staple for many years, but 'Snowflake', as its name implies, offers a white alternative to the more common blue varieties. It's covered with tiny white blossoms all season with a fragrance just as enticing as that of other catmints.

In zones 3 to 6, the best spot for this catmint is a sunny one with well-drained soil. In zones 7 to 9 it needs afternoon shade.

Try planting 'Snow-flake' around your roses. It's a winning fragrance combination, and a great way to cover up the "knees" of your roses.

Size 12 to 15 in. tall, 12 to 18 in. wide

Blooms Late spring to early fall with regular deadheading

Soil Well-drained

Light Full sun to part shade

Hardiness
Cold: USDA zones 3 to 9
Heat: AHS zones 12 to 2

Mail-order source
Digging Dog Nursery
707-937-1130
www.diggingdog.com
Catalog $4

PHOTO: © Image Botanica (daylily); © Neil Soderstrum (torch lily); © Donna and Tom Krischan (blanket flower)

'Rubra' masterwort
Astrantia major

Masterwort's starry little flower gems shine brightly from midspring into the fall. Because of its long bloom time and tolerance for shade, you'll probably see more and more of it.

These red-pink flowers are nothing less than spectacular. But 'Rubra' does prefer areas with cool summer night temperatures.

As delightful as the dried flower heads look, you should cut the stems down as soon as the flowers have faded. Masterwort will self-seed, but the flower colors don't stay true.

Size	6 to 18 in. tall, 12 in. wide
Blooms	Midspring to early fall with regular deadheading
Soil	Moist, well-drained
Light	Part shade to full sun
Hardiness	Cold: USDA zones 4 to 7 Heat: AHS zones 7 to 1

Mail-order source
Crownsville Nursery
540-631-9411
www.crownsvillenursery.com
Catalog free

'Pink Chablis' spotted deadnettle
Lamium maculatum

Spotted deadnettle is well-known for its showy variegated foliage and the highlights it brings to any shady garden. You might never have considered it as a long-blooming perennial, but 'Pink Chablis' may just change the way you think. It's covered with light-pink blooms from late spring right up until the first hard freeze.

And there's another bonus. While most varieties of spotted deadnettle prefer cooler conditions, 'Pink Chablis' can stand the heat. It will grow just as well whether you plant it in the sun or shade. How's that for versatility in the garden?

Size	8 to 12 in. tall, 12 to 18 in. wide
Blooms	Late spring to midfall; no deadheading necessary
Soil	Moist, well-drained
Light	Sun or shade
Hardiness	Cold: USDA zones 4 to 8 Heat: AHS zones 8 to 1

Mail-order source
Garden Crossings
www.gardencrossings.com

Corydalis
Corydalis lutea

When you think of shade plants, this one doesn't usually jump to mind. But give corydalis a try. Its foliage resembles bleeding heart, but its flowers provide a splash of vibrant yellow color from midspring until frost. This plant has been known to bloom for as long as 12 weeks.

Corydalis requires very little care. It prefers to be planted in part shade, but will also grow in full sun with plenty of water.

This is a plant that will self seed. You can leave the seedlings alone or they can easily be removed and either discarded or moved to another location.

Size	9 to 15 in. tall, 12 to 15 in. wide
Blooms	Midspring to midfall; no deadheading necessary
Soil	Moist, well-drained, alkaline
Light	Part shade to full sun
Hardiness	
	Cold: USDA zones 5 to 7
	Heat: AHS zones 8 to 3

Mail-order source
Busse Gardens
www.bussegardens.com
800-544-3192
Catalog $3

Cardinal flower
Lobelia cardinalis

Here's a plant that's more often thought of as a wildflower than a perennial garden staple, but its adaptability to a wide range of conditions makes it a great addition.

Cardinal flower grows very well in moist areas so it's perfect around ponds. It also does well in normal garden conditions, and with plenty of water, it will grow in full sun.

The brilliant red blooms appear a little later in the season, so cardinal flower's sure to give your garden the pick-me-up it needs in the waning days of summer.

Size	24 to 48 in. tall, 12 to 24 in. wide
Blooms	Midsummer to midfall
Soil	Wet to well-drained
Light	Part shade to full sun
Hardiness	
	Cold: USDA zones 3 to 9
	Heat: AHS zones 8 to 1

Mail-order source
Big Dipper Farm
www.bigdipperfarm.com

PHOTO: © Jessie Harris (cardinal flower)

Beautiful Butterflies

One of the best things about gardening is getting to enjoy nature up close: The surprise of a snake sunning itself in your perennial bed. The whirring when a hummingbird buzzes by. The tickle when a butterfly lands on your head. This is the stuff that gets me out in the garden every chance I get.

If you've ever wondered what you were looking at as you enjoyed a butterfly, this guide will help you identify seven common ones that you might see. For each butterfly, I've listed some host plants for egg laying and food for the caterpillars as well as nectar plants to feed the adults. These all live in North America, but some are pretty widespread, while other are found in smaller areas. Range maps will help you know where you're likely to see them.

As with so many beautiful things, there's more to these pretty butterflies than meets the eye. So I've shared some cool facts about each one to help you get to know them just a little better. □

— *Deborah Gruca*

Viceroy, monarch or queen?

Viceroy   Monarch   Queen

Stripe

Though they look similar, there's a quick way to tell the viceroy from the monarch or queen: It has a prominent stripe across its lower wing.

Viceroy
Limenitis archippus

You'll have to look closely to tell this butterfly from the similar-looking monarch and queen butterflies. The viceroy is smaller than the other two, and normally rests with its wings half open instead of closed. But it resembles the bad-tasting monarch enough that it's pretty safe from becoming somebody's supper.

Look for the viceroy near willows, aspens and other moisture-loving plants in meadows or damp areas. The caterpillar hatches from a single light green egg laid at the leaf tips of these plants. Predators usually leave the caterpillar and chrysalis alone — they look just like bird droppings.

Where you'll find it

Wingspan 3 in.

Nectar plants
Coneflower *Echinacea* spp.
Milkweed *Asclepias* spp.
Zinnia *Zinnia elegans*

Host plants
Apple *Malus* spp.
Poplar *Populus* spp.

Zebra longwing
Heliconius charitonius

Long black wings with vivid yellow stripes give the zebra longwing an exotic look. It tends to stay in the southern part of the United States, venturing a little farther north at times.

Unusual-shaped wings seem to confuse potential predators (which direction will it fly?), making this butterfly hard to catch. If you spot one in the garden, listen closely — a zebra longwing makes a creaking sound when it's startled.

Clusters of head-of-a-pin-sized yellow eggs on leaves and tendrils resemble tiny ears of corn. The hatched caterpillar has black spines on its body that look lethal, but are actually soft and harmless.

Wingspan 3¼ in.
Nectar plants
   Butterfly bush
      Buddleja spp.
   Lantana *Lantana camara*
   Starflower *Pentas lanceolata*

Host plants
   Passion vine *Passiflora* spp.

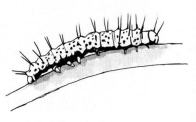

Common buckeye
Junonia coenia

From a single, fat green egg hatches the black spiny caterpillar of the common buckeye. With feet like tiny suction cups, it clings to stems upside down to feed. But when frightened, it drops off to escape danger.

Three pairs of eyelike spots on its wings make this butterfly easy to find and identify. Used to scare away potential predators, the spots, called *ocelli*, give it protection as it feeds and even as it sits on the bare ground basking in the sun. (Males especially can spend hours there, waiting for that perfect female.) When cold weather hits, the butterfly migrates in large flocks to the southern parts of its range.

Wingspan 2¼ in.
Nectar plants
   Cosmos *Cosmos bipinnatus*
   Sedum *Sedum* spp.
   Lantana *Lantana camara*

Host plants
   Snapdragon
      Antirrhinum majus
   Plantain *Plantago major*

PHOTOS: © Joseph G. Strauch, Jr. (viceroy); © Catriona Tudor Erler (zebra longwing);
© David C. McClure (common buckeye) ILLUSTRATIONS: David Kallemyn

Cabbage white
Pieris rapae

As its name implies, the caterpillar of this diminutive butterfly actually enjoys eating its vegetables. The tiny, singly laid eggs can be found on many edibles, including cabbage and radishes, and even Brussels sprouts. In large numbers, caterpillars can do quite a bit of damage.

Common throughout North America, cabbage whites are among the first butterflies to appear in spring, and can be seen as late as November in some areas.

The wings are white on top with pale yellow-green undersides. Unlike many other butterflies, you can easily tell the boys from the girls: Males have a single black dot in the middle of the top wing; females have two.

Where you'll find it

Wingspan 1½ in.

Nectar plants
Verbena *Verbena* hybrids
Cosmos *Cosmos bipinnatus*

Host plants
Nasturtium *Tropaeolum majus*
Cabbage *Brassica oleracea*
Spider flower
 Cleome hassleriana

Pearl crescent
Phyciodes tharos

Some gardeners also call this a pearly crescent-spot. This small common butterfly can be found throughout a large area of North America. You'll notice it in gardens, woods and meadows starting in late summer as the asters start to bloom. Males tend to have larger areas of orange on their wings, while the females (like the one in the photo above) have more black.

Though the females lay large clusters of green eggs on the leaves of asters, the small, spiny brown and yellow caterpillars do little damage to the plants. Later they spin brown chrysalises that look just like dead leaves dangling from a stem.

Wingspan 1¼ in.

Nectar plants
Marigold *Tagetes* spp.
Starflower *Pentas lanceolata*
Verbena *Verbena* hybrids

Host plants
Aster *Aster* spp.

Red-spotted purple
Limenitis arthemis astyanax

The red spots of this butterfly's common name can be seen on the undersides of its large iridescent blue wings. It looks a bit like a spicebush swallowtail, which lives in the same areas. Because it also resembles the nasty tasting pipevine swallowtail, few predators bother it. A tip to tell it apart from the swallowtails? The red-spotted purple has no tail!

This butterfly has a taste for the flowers of several plants, but you're just as likely to see it dining on rotting fruit, dung or decayed matter when it can find them.

Females lay single miniature golfball-like eggs on the tips of the leaves of several kinds of trees.

Wingspan 3¼ in.

Nectar plants
Lantana *Lantana camara*
Zinnia *Zinnia elegans*
Butterfly bush
Buddleja spp.

Host plants
Willow *Salix* spp.
Apple *Malus* spp.
Poplar *Populus* spp.

Zebra swallowtail
Eurytides marcellus

Talk about fun to watch! This bold black and white beauty is one of the largest butterflies found in North America and has the longest tail. The top surface of the wings has scarlet and blue dots while the lower surface sports a striking red stripe. Several generations hatch during the season with earlier ones quite a bit smaller and duller in color than those later in the year.

Females lay single green eggs on the leaves of pawpaws, the only host plant for the zebra swallowtail. The caterpillar's strong smell helps keep predators away. Later, it creates a compact green or brown chrysalis that looks like it'd be a tight fit for such a large butterfly.

Wingspan 4½ to 6 in.

Nectar plants
Lilac *Syringa* spp.
Sweet William
Dianthus barbatus
Cosmos *Cosmos bipinnatus*

Host plants
Pawpaw *Asimina triloba*

PHOTOS: © Jay Gilliam (cabbage white, pearl crescent, red-spotted purple); © David C. McClure (zebra swallowtail)

Kathleen Ziemer
on attracting spring butterflies

PHOTO: © Jay Gilliam (1,2); LOCATION: Fertile Crescent Nursery (3)

IN THE KNOW

WANT MORE SPRING BUTTERFLIES?
Kathleen's best tip for getting more spring butterflies next year is to grow host plants. That's where adult butterflies lay eggs and their hungry caterpillars feed before changing into adults. For example, mourning cloak butterflies have a fondness for willow and elm leaves. Want to see a list of host plants and the caterpillars they attract? Check out our Web extra.

WEB extra

Our *list* of host plants matched with the caterpillars that find them tasty.

When you picture a butterfly, you probably see it gathering nectar from a flower. But I bet you picture summer flowers like zinnias or butterfly bush rather than the flowering crabapple in photo 3 to the right. The truth is butterflies aren't just summer visitors. There are plenty that like spring flowers. I spoke with Kathleen Ziemer, from Butterfliz of Iowa, about ways to attract these early visitors. Here's what she shared with me.

GROW FOOD Spring butterflies need plenty of it for energy. Many drink nectar from flowers. Lilacs, grape hyacinths and even weeds like dandelions and clover, in photo 1, are among their favorites. In the list to the right, you'll find some more well-known spring flowers to feed early visitors.

But not all of the nutrients butterflies need come from nectar. Mourning cloaks, for example, can appear in gardens before flowers bloom, feasting on sap as it drips from cuts or wounds on trees and shrubs. If that's not on the menu in your garden, put out some overripe, or even rotting, fruit. Instead of throwing out those wrinkled grapes or that brown banana, slice them and lay them on a sunny rock or directly on the ground for butterflies to enjoy.

ADD WATER Ever been strolling in your garden or the woods and spotted a flock of butterflies around a mud puddle? It's called a "puddle club," where butterflies drink water that contains minerals and other nutrients they need.

You can organize your own club. Set a plastic or clay saucer on the ground and fill it with sand or gravel, like the material in photo 2. Keep it wet with water, stale soda or beer — they all help provide salts and nutrients adult butterflies need.

(1) Sulphurs are some of the earliest spring butterflies. Even early blooming weeds, like this red clover, are popular nectar sources.

(2) Gravel areas and mud puddles provide minerals and nutrients that this red-spotted purple and other butterflies can't get from nectar.

(3) Flowering crabapple blossoms are a good source of nectar for spring butterflies like this yellow swallowtail.

A SPRING FEAST

Butterflies love nectar. Here is a list of spring-blooming flowers and the early arrivals they attract.

Chives *Allium schoenoprasum*
Swallowtails, hairstreaks, commas, admirals, fritillaries

Clover *Trifolium repens* and *T. pratense*
Whites, sulphurs, blues, hairstreaks, crescents, buckeyes

Dame's rocket *Hesperis matronalis*
Red-spotted purples, swallowtails

Dandelion *Taraxacum officinale*
Red admirals, commas, sulphurs, common blues

Grape hyacinth *Muscari* spp.
Skippers, whites, sulphurs, alfalfas

Lilac *Syringa* spp.
Swallowtails, spring azures, tortoiseshells

Moss phlox *Phlox subulata*
Swallowtails, pearl crescents, skippers, painted ladies

Peony *Paeonia* spp.
Swallowtails, skippers, satyrs

Privet *Ligustrum* spp.
Red admirals, commas, azures, duskywings, swallowtails

Spicebush *Lindera benzoin*
Spring azures, swallowtails

Virginia bluebell *Mertensia virginica*
Skippers, sulphurs

KEEP THEM SAFE AND WARM

To get the most spring butterflies, you need more than food and water. Shelter is also very important. Have you ever wondered where butterflies go when it rains? If they can't go inside a structure, they attach themselves to the undersides of leaves. So make sure you have a few plants with large foliage, such as redbuds, so butterflies can duck under when it starts to pour.

It's fun to watch butterflies gliding on the breeze, but a strong wind can damage their fragile wings. Plus wind makes it hard for butterflies to get around. Grow nectar plants or set food in areas along fences or where prevailing winds are blocked by trees and shrubs, and butterflies are much more likely to stick around.

All butterflies, but especially those that you see in cool spring temperatures, require a spot where they can bask in the warm sun. Since butterflies are cold-blooded, they need warmth before they can fly. And after a cold spring night, they like to warm up thoroughly before taking off. Rocks or chunks of concrete set in sunny spots are perfect places. They absorb heat quickly and hold it well into the evening.

At right, you'll find a list of nectar plants that spring butterflies like. I'm sure you already have one or two of them growing in your garden — I know I have plenty of dandelions! Add a few cultivated flowers, and you'll have more spring butterflies to enjoy. □
— *Jim Childs*

Pink Perennials

Pink has a lot going for it. It can be soft and sweet, but it can also be playful or kitschy, like a pink flamingo. Using shades of pink — whether it's fuchsia, coral, salmon or dusty rose — and combining them with other colors, you can really set a mood in your garden.

And remember that there are no laws about what colors you can use with pink. If you like it, plant it! Who knows, you might even start the next color trend.

Let me introduce you to seven of my favorite pink perennials. I've picked lots of different shades and arranged them on these pages by approximate bloom time. (Things like weather and microclimate can affect when a plant blooms.)

I'll give you the lowdown on each plant's size and care needs so you'll know if it'll work in your situation. You'll also see suggested planting partners that like the same conditions and make that shade of pink really pop.

And to give you some ideas for designing with these and other pink plants, on p. 106 I'll include three pretty combos using pink flowers. Maybe one of them will be just perfect for that empty space in your perennial border!

'Pink Snowflakes' primrose
Primula sieboldii

The ruffled olive-green leaves of this dainty primrose emerge in early spring, followed shortly by clusters of frilly pink flowers. Held over the foliage on stiff stems, the blooms of 'Pink Snowflakes' are well-named. A white eye zone and unusually fringed petals give the flowers a delicate look.

Use primrose for an early splash of color in a container or at the front of a bed. The foliage disappears after the flowering is finished, so place this plant next to later-season companions that will fill in the space. But plant plenty — with its long stems, it also makes a pretty cut flower.

Size 12 in. tall, 18 in. wide
Bloom Early spring
Soil Moist, acid, well-drained
Light Part shade to shade
Hardiness
　　Cold: USDA 5 to 8
　　Heat: AHS 8 to 1
Good neighbors
　　Silver-leafed brunneras or lungworts shine even in the shade.
Mail-order source
　　Big Dipper Farm
　　www.bigdipperfarm.com
　　360-886-8133
　　Online catalog only

Bloody cranesbill
Geranium sanguineum striatum

Looking for a pink-flowering ground cover? Look no farther than this compact, clump-forming geranium. Five-petaled soft-pink flowers are self-cleaning and cover the plant all summer. The heaviest flush of bloom comes early in the season.

Clumps of deeply cut dark-green leaves tend to sprawl out a bit, so don't be afraid to snip them back to keep them in bounds. And if the plant starts to flag in the heat of late summer, cut it back to the new growth at the crown.

This geranium prefers full sun and a moist spot, but will tolerate a little drought. You'll get the most flowers and the best fall leaf color in more light.

Size   6 to 9 in. tall, 18 in. wide

Bloom   Early summer

Soil   Moist, well-drained

Light   Sun to part shade

Hardiness
Cold: USDA 3 to 8
Heat: AHS 8 to 1

Good neighbors
Deep-blue lobelias and torenias perk up soft pinks.

'First Love' cheddar pink
Dianthus hybrid

'First Love' is one of the more fragrant hybrids in the dianthus family. The plant is covered from spring to frost with flowers in a mix of colors. Each flower opens white, then gradually turns to pink and finally a deep rose.

You may have heard that dianthus can be short-lived, but give it good drainage and you'll get it to last longer in your garden. A dianthus that turns brown in the center is getting too much moisture. Amend the soil with 2 inches of compost and an inch of poultry grit before you plant. Once flowering is finished, cut the stems back to the foliage to rejuvenate the plant.

Size   15 to 18 in. tall, 18 in. wide

Bloom   Early to midsummer

Soil   Well-drained

Light   Full sun to part shade

Hardiness
Cold: USDA 3 to 8
Heat: AHS 8 to 1

Good neighbors
Purple calibrachoas or 'Wave' petunias make a cool background even in full sun.

Mail-order source
Bluestone Perennials
www.bluestoneperennials.com
800-852-5243 *Catalog free*

'Morris Berd' smooth phlox
Phlox glaberrima

If you don't currently grow phlox because you're concerned about powdery mildew, give 'Morris Berd' a try. It's particularly resistant to that fungus *and* root rot. In fact, this phlox is more tolerant of moisture, heat and humidity than other phloxes, and will happily thrive in moist areas, even at the edge of ponds.

In early summer, large clusters of rose-pink flowers open atop stalks that don't need staking. The lightly fragrant blooms attract butterflies. Deadhead spent blooms to prolong flowering through the summer or leave them and the plant will self-seed to give you even more of a good thing.

Size 24 in. tall, 18 in. wide
Bloom Early summer
Soil Medium wet to moist, well-drained
Light Sun to part shade
Hardiness
　　Cold: USDA 3 to 8
　　Heat: AHS 8 to 1
Good neighbors
　　Fuzzy lamb's ear leaves contrast with, as well as complement, phlox.
Mail-order source
　　Forestfarm
　　541-846-7269
　　www.forestfarm.com
　　Catalog $5

Gas plant
Dictamnus albus purpureus

With their long, thin stamens, the flowers of this early summer bloomer look a little like pink shooting stars.

Gas plant is a long-lived perennial with a woody base and sturdy stems. It has a long taproot that makes the plant quite drought-tolerant once it's established, but also makes it hard to transplant.

The common name comes from volatile oils in the leaves and stems that on hot evenings can ignite when touched with a lighted match. These oils can cause a rash for some people. And eating any part of the plant will give you a nasty stomachache.

Size 24 to 36 in. tall and wide
Bloom Early summer
Soil Moist, well-drained
Light Full sun
Hardiness
　　Cold: USDA 3 to 8
　　Heat: AHS 8 to 1
Good neighbors
　　Yews or boxwoods show off gas plant's flowers and seedheads.

Joe-Pye weed
Eupatorium maculatum 'Atropurpureum'

If you think pink flowers are shy or demure, think again. This towering 7-footer, with its large blooming domes, makes quite an impact in any bed. Its size makes it a perfect back-of-the-border plant. Like the plant, but want a shorter version? Cut the stems back by half in June.

Deep green leaves form in whorls around the stem and look attractive until the flowers open in late summer. Then, the nectar-rich blooms attract clouds of butterflies and bees. After the flowers fade, the fuzzy brown seedheads provide interest right through winter. In early spring, cut the plant back to 4 inches tall.

Size   5 to 7 ft. tall, 2 to 4 ft. wide

Bloom   Late summer

Soil   Alkaline, moist

Light   Full sun

Hardiness
Cold: USDA 3 to 9
Heat: AHS 9 to 1

Good neighbors
Gold 'Butterpat' helenium and false aster appreciate the same even moisture.

Turtlehead
Chelone lyonii

Just one look is all it takes to see the reason for this plant's common name. But unusual flowers aren't its only feature.

Shiny, dark green leaves offer a lovely background for the clusters of showy flowers. And while the plant attracts butterflies, deer tend to pass it by.

Turtlehead happily grows in moist, part-shade gardens where other plants might struggle. (In deep shade, you may want to support the stems with stakes or pinch back the growing tips a bit in early spring to keep the plant more compact.) Full-sun settings are OK with turtlehead, if you give it plenty of moisture. A 2-inch layer of composted leaf mulch helps, too.

Size   2 to 3 ft. tall, 1 to 2 ft. wide

Bloom   Early to midfall

Soil   Moist, rich

Light   Sun to part shade

Hardiness
Cold: USDA 4 to 9
Heat: AHS 9 to 3

Good neighbors
Gold or chartreuse hostas brighten a shady border.

designing with pink

Like other colors, pink can be either cool or warm, depending on whether it leans more toward blue or orange. Fortunately, different shades of pink play together nicely, so you don't have to worry about them clashing when you combine them in the same bed. Notice how each plant in "Purely pink" at right gets along with its pink neighbors.

Pinks also stand out against deep greens and blues and really shine when combined with frosty or silvery shades.

Each color combination sets its own mood, and the sky's the limit! To get you started, I've put some plants of different colors together here to show you a few of the effects you can get. □
— *Deborah Gruca*

Monkshood

Turtlehead

Sedge

Persian shield

Soothing shades Combine other pastels or soft colors with pinks to add a little snap to the scene, without losing pink's calm composure. The subtle colors of the blue and white monkshood flowers complement the pink turtlehead in late summer to fall. Persian shield provides deep pink and purple that both echo and accent the pink flowers.

Remember to use foliage, too, to add interest to your garden. Grassy sedge and dramatic shimmery Persian shield add great contrast to give this bed even more life.

Monkshood *Aconitum xcammarum* 'Bicolor'
  4 ft. tall, 1 ft. wide
  Cold-hardy in USDA zones 3 to 7
  Heat-tolerant in AHS zones 7 to 1

Turtlehead *Chelone lyonii*
  2 to 3 ft. tall, 1 to 2 ft. wide
  Cold-hardy in USDA zones 4 to 9
  Heat-tolerant in AHS zones 9 to 3

Sedge *Carex* 'Ice Dance'
  9 to 12 in. tall, 1 to 2 ft. wide
  Cold-hardy in USDA zones 5 to 9
  Heat-tolerant in AHS zones 9 to 1

Persian shield *Strobilanthes dyeriana*
  1 to 3 ft. tall and wide
  Treat as an annual

Purely pink Like little girls, bubble gum and cotton candy, multiple shades of pink together play up the sweeter, softer side of the color. Looking at this planting, you can't help but feel calm and relaxed. And calm is good, but sometimes single-color beds can look, well…a bit boring. A tip for banning the blahs? Vary the sizes and shapes of the plants you put together to give the pink more punch. The different shapes of the early summer-blooming Martagon lily, gas plant and cranesbill offer loads of interest.

Martagon lily *Lilium martagon* 'Pink Taurade'
4 to 5 ft. tall, 1 ft. wide
Cold-hardy in USDA zones 3 to 7
Heat-tolerant in AHS zones 7 to 1

Gas plant *Dictamnus albus purpureus*
24 to 36 in. tall and wide
Cold-hardy in USDA zones 3 to 8
Heat-tolerant in AHS zones 8 to 1

Bloody cranesbill *Geranium sanguineum striatum*
6 to 9 in. tall, 18 in. wide
Cold-hardy in USDA zones 3 to 8
Heat-tolerant in AHS zones 8 to 1

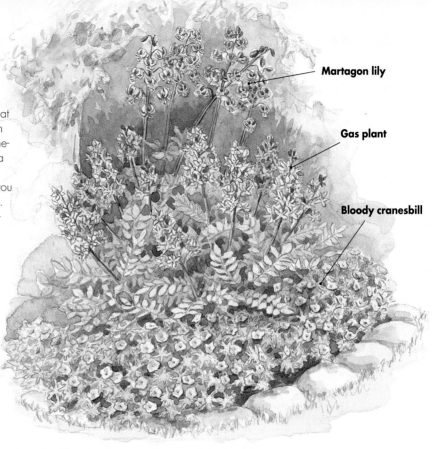

Martagon lily

Gas plant

Bloody cranesbill

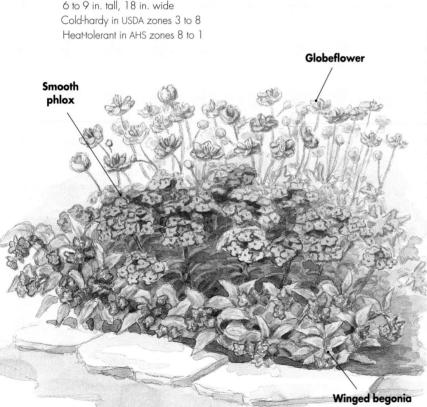

Globeflower

Smooth phlox

Winged begonia

High-energy hues If you're not tickled pink with the natural softness of the color, introduce it to some crazy companions. You might not usually think of putting orange and pink together on purpose. But check out how the hot orange summer blooms of these begonias and globeflowers jazz up the proper pink of the phlox. Feel free to try out what might seem like odd color combinations in your garden. You might be surprised with what happens. And you can always change it later, if you decide you don't like it.

Globeflower *Trollius xcultorum*
36 in. tall, 18 in. wide
Cold-hardy in USDA zones 3 to 7
Heat-tolerant in AHS zones 7 to 1

Smooth phlox *Phlox glaberrima* 'Morris Berd'
24 in. tall, 18 in. wide
Cold-hardy in USDA zones 3 to 8
Heat-tolerant in AHS zones 8 to 1

Winged begonia *Begonia* 'Orange Rubra'
14 in. tall, 15 in. wide
Treat as an annual

Readers'
Favorite
Annuals

What's *your* favorite annual? We asked our readers to share their favorites, and here they are! Long bloom time, bright colors, easy to grow...that's what you said about these plants, and we couldn't agree more. One or two of these plants are actually tender perennials, but most people grow them as annuals.

In case you're wondering why a couple of old stand-bys, like geraniums, aren't on the list, it's because we narrowed down your answers to annuals that you told us you usually plant in the ground, not in containers.

One of the best things about annuals is that you can find lots of cultivars at local garden centers. Check out the "Try these" boxes at the bottom of each description for a few specific cultivars to look for.

In "Six-pack to impact" on p. 264, we'll show you how to care for annuals to get great flowers all summer. You can start any of these from seed indoors, but in our list, I'll let you know if you can direct sow the seeds outdoors or if you're better off buying plants at the garden center. However you get started, you're off to a showy summer! □

— *Stephanie Polsley Bruner*

Marigold
Tagetes spp.

Even if you don't like the smell of marigolds (although I do!), you have to love the nonstop color. Plants can be 6 or 8 inches tall (like 'Janie Flame' shown here) to 3 feet tall, and flowers can be 1 to 3 inches across.

As long as they're warm enough, marigolds don't need a lot of care. They like full sun, and while they tolerate drought, they'll flower better with plenty of moisture. If marigolds are drought-stressed, you may find spider mites on them — the leaves turn bronze-green and there's webbing on the undersides. Just hose off the plants, then keep them well-watered for the rest of the season.

Size 6 to 36 in. tall, 8 to 16 in. wide

Blooms Yellow, orange, red, bicolors; single or double

Getting started Seeds or plants

Light Full sun

Pests Occasional spider mites

Try these
Huge, clear-yellow flowers: 'Inca Yellow Hybrid'

White flowers and no odor: 'French Vanilla'

Petunia
Petunia hybrid

Readers love petunias for their bright colors and spreading habit. They can have single or double flowers, and they come in a range of colors. Small, mounding ones are great in containers, while spreaders like this Wave® Purple, shown here with annual salvia, spill over retaining walls or cover a lot of ground. New cultivars have flowers that stand up to rain and wind better than the old-timers did.

To keep petunias blooming their best, give them plenty of water. You may need to pinch them back a bit if they get straggly, but many of the newer hybrids don't even need that much care.

Size	6 to 18 in. tall by 1 to 5 ft. wide
Blooms	White, pink, red, purple, blue; may have striped petals or contrasting veins; large or small flowers; double or single forms
Getting started	Plants
Light	Full sun
Pests	Occasional aphids or slugs

Try these

Pink with a white eye:
Easy Wave® Rosy Dawn
Bright colors with white stripes:
'Razzle Dazzle' hybrid mix

Zinnia
Zinnia hybrid

Most of us planted a pack of zinnia seeds as kids. And we never outgrew these sizzling bright colors. 'State Fair Mix', planted with statice in the photo above, is a classic.

Some zinnias have rounded, ball-shaped blooms (dahlia-flowered), while others have spiky petals (cactus-flowered). Upright zinnias can be 3 to 4 feet tall with blooms 4 or 5 inches across, while spreading, ground cover types, like the 'Profusion' series, grow only a foot tall.

You're not the only one in the garden who likes zinnias. Butterflies love 'em! They're also a great cut flower — the more you pick, the better the plants branch.

Size	10 to 48 in. tall by 6 to 18 in. wide
Blooms	Any color but blue; may be spotted or streaked; double or single
Getting started	Seeds or plants
Light	Full sun
Pests	Powdery mildew in mid- to late summer

Try these

Unusual flower shape:
'Red Spider'
Eye-catching red-and-yellow blooms: 'Old Mexico'

Snapdragon
Antirrhinum hybrid

Greet the spring with these cool-season beauties. In USDA zone 7 and warmer, snapdragons are often planted in fall so they'll bloom in the spring, then they're removed to make way for summer annuals. But in colder gardens, you can plant them either in early spring for cool-weather color or in late summer to enjoy fall blooms.

I like the short ones best, like 'Chimes Yellow' above, because they stand up without staking. But you can stake the taller ones, and they make beautiful cut flowers. Some new trailing snapdragons are available, and they're a bit more heat-tolerant than other snaps.

Size 6 to 36 in. tall by 8 to 12 in. wide

Blooms Yellow, peach, orange, burgundy, red, pink, white, bicolor; most are single, a few are double

Getting started Plants

Light Full sun to part shade

Pests Rust may be a problem in hot weather

Try these

Trailing: Lampion Mix
Dark-red flowers: 'Black Prince'
Tall, white spikes: 'Royal Bride'

Spider flower
Cleome hassleriana

It may be called spider flower, but I think these blooms look like fireworks. Either way, the plants attract hummingbirds and butterflies to your garden. The only drawback? To most people, they smell like a skunk, but it's only noticeable if you're very close or handling the foliage.

Spider flower's stems can look ratty at the base, so plant something shorter in front, like the red celosia with the 'Sparkler White' spider flower in the photo.

Reseeding can be a bit of a problem, but the little seedlings are easy to pull. Or snip off the seed pods as they form along the stem to keep the plant from reseeding.

Size 18 to 48 in. tall by 12 to 36 in. wide

Blooms White, pink, purple; bicolor

Getting started Seeds or plants

Light Full sun

Pests None serious

Try these

Short, 18-in. plants:
'White Spider'
Pink-and-white flowers:
'Sparkler Blush'

Nicotiana
Nicotiana hybrid

They're sometimes called flowering tobacco, but there's nothing smoky about these flowers. This is an old cottage garden favorite, but new, shorter hybrids with showier flowers, like 'Apple Blossom' in the photo, work in any garden. Nicotiana can be very fragrant, but some new cultivars have been bred for looks, not fragrance. If you want the sweet scent, check the tags to be sure you're getting one that smells good. Hummingbirds flock to nicotiana flowers, too.

In areas with cool summers, nicotiana likes full sun, but in USDA zone 6 and warmer, it does better with afternoon shade.

Size	12 to 36 in. tall by 12 to 24 in. wide
Blooms	White, yellow, pink, red, purple, green
Getting started	Seeds or plants
Light	Full sun
Pests	Occasional aphids

Try these

Sweet scent and dark-purple flowers: 'Perfume Deep Purple'
Pink petals with lime-green backs: 'Tinkerbell'

Impatiens
Impatiens walleriana

These may be the most popular annuals in the world — and also with our readers!

Plant them among hostas for summer color, or grow them in containers on the patio. You'll find mixes, like the 'Super Elfin' mix in the photo, or single colors. Some are double, looking almost like miniature roses. They aren't fragrant, but they're so pretty that it doesn't really matter much.

Impatiens are slow to get started in cool spring weather, so plant them a little later than most annuals. I keep a couple of old sheets handy to cover mine in case of a light frost in early fall as they're very sensitive to cold.

Size	6 to 18 in. tall and wide
Blooms	White, pink, purple, red, orange; bicolors; picotee edges; singles and doubles
Getting started	Plants
Light	Part shade
Pests	Occasional slugs

Try these

Double flowers: Fiesta™ series
Light-pink flowers with dark-pink edge: Dazzler® Rose Swirl

Cosmos
Cosmos **spp.**

Nothing looks as airy as a planting of cosmos. And boy, can they bloom!

In fact, they may bloom so heavily that the plants start to fade. If that happens, just sow some more seed in midsummer to keep the show going.

Sulfur cosmos has yellow, orange or red flowers in 1- to 2-foot-tall plants, like 'Polidor' in the main photo. Tall cosmos comes in shades of white, pink and burgundy, and the plants are usually 3 to 4 feet tall. (That's 'Seashell' in the small inset photo.) Both types are often sold as color mixes.

Plant cosmos in clumps for a really dramatic look. Those wiry stems make great cut flowers.

Size 1 to 4 ft. tall by 1 to 2 ft. wide

Blooms White, pink, burgundy, orange, red, yellow; picotee edges; rolled petals

Getting started Seeds or plants

Light Full sun

Pests None serious

Try these
Double flowers, color mix:
'Double Click' tall cosmos
Bright orange-red flowers:
'Dwarf Ladybird Scarlet' sulfur cosmos

Globe amaranth
Gomphrena **spp.**

I love unusual flowers, and these balls of color are certainly unique.

'Strawberry Fields', above, is a little taller than most globe amaranth, at 18 to 24 inches. Other hybrids, like 'Bicolor Rose', tend to be a bit smaller. But other than that, all globe amaranths have the same papery, long-lasting blossoms.

And speaking of papery blossoms, those aren't petals, they're bracts. (The true flowers are tiny and yellow — you might not even notice them.) Globe amaranth dries well, like most papery flowers. Cut the blooms when they've just opened, and hang them in a dry, shady place.

Size 6 to 24 in. tall by 6 to 12 in. wide

Blooms White, pink, purple, lavender, red

Getting started Seeds or plants

Light Full sun

Pests None serious

Try these
Pale lavender flowers, darker at the tips: 'Lavender Queen'
6-in.-tall plants: 'Gnome Purple'

Lantana
Lantana camara

Great for hot summers, lantana not only stands up to heat, but thrives in it. This is the plant you'll want in your garden in August when everything else is drooping. (And it'll be surrounded by butterflies, too.)

See how 'Confetti' lantana in the photo has two colors in the same flower cluster? That's common with lantanas — often the blooms are one color in bud, then they change to another as they age.

This is a tender perennial. (You can keep it over the winter in a container.) Where lantana is hardy, it's a woody shrub, but if you're growing it as an annual in a cooler area, it won't get quite so big.

Size 1 to 6 ft. tall by 2 to 8 ft. wide

Blooms White, yellow, pink, orange, red; many have multiple colors in a single flower

Getting started Plants

Light Full sun

Pests None serious

Try these
Solid-yellow flowers: 'Sonshine'
Bright-red flowers, hardier than most: 'Miss Huff'
Pastel pinks and yellows: 'Tropical Fruit'

Tall verbena
Verbena bonariensis

Looking for an airy "filler" plant? Look no further! This verbena is cold-hardy to USDA zone 7, but elsewhere, it reseeds happily. You can pinch off or cut back the flowers as they fade, before the plant sets seed. Or just pull the unwanted seedlings in spring.

My favorite thing about this verbena is that when it comes up in my flower bed next spring, it never comes up quite where it was before. It often creates beautiful combinations that I wouldn't have considered. I like it at the back of the flower border, where it weaves up through other plants. (And they'll help cover the bare verbena stems.)

Size 3 to 5 ft. tall by 1 to 2 ft. wide

Blooms Lavender

Getting started Seeds or plants

Light Full sun

Pests None serious

Try these
Shorter verbena hybrid: 'Homestead Purple'
Spike-shaped flowers: Blue vervain (*Verbena hastata*)

Annuals
You Should Meet

Are you one of those folks who reads photo-filled seed catalogs until they're dog-eared? And all the while, you're dreaming about the annuals you want to grow in your garden next spring? You skip over the common stuff like marigolds and petunias to read about annuals you've never grown but always wondered about. Funny names like painted tongue or farewell-to-spring always draw my attention. For years I fell back on the standards I found at the garden center. But like many gardeners, I like to try something new every now and again.

The annuals I'll talk about here have all been around for years. In fact, your mother or grandmother may have been familiar with them. Sadly, in recent decades, they've been overshadowed by plants greenhouses found easier to grow. Things like four o'clocks and monkey flowers were shoved aside in favor of annuals that bloomed in their little packs. Gardeners wanted instant color, no time to wait for seeds to grow. And some of these flowers were forgotten in the boom of new "low-maintenance" perennials that have been introduced over the past several years.

But what could be easier than scratching up the soil and sprinkling a packet of seeds or tucking in a few seedlings? With many of these annuals you get to enjoy flowers all summer. And some of them even reseed so you really don't have to do anything next year. At the most, for some, you may need to repeat the seeding process or do a bit of thinning. Plus, all annuals give you the option to simply choose a completely new flower to try next year. Now I ask you, is that harder than digging up those heavy clumps of perennials to divide? Or having to haul in mulch to protect the tender crowns over winter only to pick it up and haul it away again in spring? I don't think so.

Have you ever noticed the terms "hardy" or "half-hardy" annual when you browsed those catalogs? Check out "Annual terms" at left to find out what those terms mean and how they can help you figure out when to start your seeds.

There are more annual flowers available than you can shake a hoe at. Let me share details on 10 favorites I've rediscovered. □

— *Jim Childs*

Annual terms

HARDY ANNUALS can survive a light frost and are often sown directly in the garden when it's still quite cold. Fall is the time to plant them in Southern gardens. In USDA zones 6 and colder, plant when forsythia blooms.

HALF-HARDY ANNUALS will grow in cool weather but won't tolerate any frost. Start them indoors to be moved out when the flowering crabapples finish blooming. Or sow seeds outdoors several weeks after that.

Peek-a-boo plant
Acmella oleracea

Looking for a conversation piece for your containers or border? Plant a few peek-a-boo plants. The flowers are small, so mass several plants together for the best effect. And be sure to grow enough so you can cut blooms for indoors.

Plant peek-a-boo plant where you can occasionally pluck a leaf and crush it. You'll get a peppery or minty scent. It's also called "toothache" plant as the leaves were an old remedy for that malady.

As you're browsing catalogs, you may also find this plant called *Spilanthes*, which is its old botanical name.

Size	12 to 18 in. tall, 12 to 24 in. wide
Type	Half-hardy annual
Bloom	Orange and yellow globes most of the summer
Soil	Humus-rich, moist, well-drained
Light	Full sun to part shade
Starting method	
	Start seed indoors to transplant out in summer. Can also root cuttings in fall.
Source	Thompson and Morgan www.thompson morgan.com 800-274-7333 *Catalog free*

Laurentia
Isotoma axillaris

If you live where summers are hot and humid, that's what laurentia, also called "blue stars," likes best. In USDA zones 8 or warmer, this plant can be treated as a perennial. But the rest of us have to enjoy it as an annual.

Laurentia's fine texture makes it an ideal companion as a border plant or in a hanging basket or container. Pair it with plants that have coarser flowers or leaves, such as licorice vine.

When you start to shop for this plant, you may find lots of confusion on the name. The preferred botanical name is *Isotoma*, but you may find it listed botanically as *Laurentia* or *Solonopsis*.

Size	10 to 12 in. tall, 10 to 12 in. wide
Type	Half-hardy annual
Bloom	Sky blue or lavender, all summer
Soil	Moist, well-drained to dry
Light	Full sun to part shade
Starting method	
	Start seed indoors 8 to 10 weeks before last frost. Can take cuttings to save over winter.
Source	Annie's Annuals www.anniesannuals.com 888-266-4370 *Catalog free*

PHOTO: © Marilynn McAra (laurentia)

Painted tongue
Salpiglossis sinuata

Not very tolerant of heat or drought, painted tongue does best in areas with cool summer temperatures. It'll tolerate 80 degrees for a few days, but not for weeks. And painted tongue performs best if you mulch the soil with a thick layer of an organic material, such as compost, to help keep the roots cool.

Keep tall varieties a bit shorter and better branched by pinching out the growing tip. Do it just once when the seedling is about 6 inches tall. Even so, you may need to stake tall cultivars to keep the stems upright. If you don't like to stake or pinch, grow a compact cultivar, such as 'Royale Mix'.

Size	12 to 36 in. tall, 12 in. wide
Type	Half-hardy annual
Bloom	Multiple colors, including pastels, all with contrasting veins
Soil	Fertile, moist, well-drained
Light	Full sun
Starting method	Start seeds indoors or direct sow in spring.
Source	Johnny's Selected Seeds www.johnnyseeds.com 877-564-6697 *Catalog free*

California poppy
Eschscholzia californica

In their native California, these vibrant flowers tend to be biennial or even perennial. But in most areas of North America, they make a great, easy-to-grow annual.

Blooming in the heat of summer, the flowers close on cloudy days, waiting for bright sun. Make several sowings, about two weeks apart, to keep the color coming.

You can let a few seedheads ripen so California poppies will reseed. However, if you plant one of the newer cultivars, the seedlings may revert. Instead of being the pale cream color or vivid pink that you purchased, they'll change back to the yellow-orange species over time.

Size	12 to 18 in. tall, 6 in. wide
Type	Hardy annual
Bloom	Vivid yellows, oranges and pinks as well as pastels
Soil	Well-drained
Light	Full sun
Starting method	Direct sow the seeds as soon as the soil can be worked in spring.
Source	Seeds of Change www.seedsofchange.com 888-762-7333 *Catalog free*

Red Malabar spinach
Basella rubra

Sometimes a foliage plant is just what your garden needs as a background or frame. Enter climbing spinach. It's not only pretty to look at, but edible, too. Harvest a few leaves to eat cooked — they do taste like spinach.

The succulent leaves can get quite heavy, so grow red Malabar spinach on a sturdy trellis or lattice. As the vine twines, pinch out the tips occasionally to encourage more branching. Some folks cut the flowers off, but leave a few and you'll get ornamental purple berries.

Red Malabar spinach is easy to share. Pinch off a 4- to 6-inch-long tip and root it in potting mix.

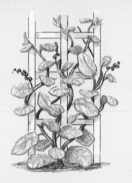

Size	12 ft. tall, 3 ft. wide
Type	Half-hardy annual
Bloom	Pink flowers in summer are not showy
Soil	Rich, well-drained with high nitrogen
Light	Part shade to full sun
Starting method	
	Start indoors or direct sow when daytime temps are near 70 degrees.
Source	Johnny's Selected Seeds www.johnnyseeds.com 877-564-6697 *Catalog free*

Farewell-to-spring
Clarkia hybrid

If you live where summers are cool, farewell-to-spring blooms in mid-summer. In areas with hot summers, you'll have to wait until the cooler days of fall for flowers. But this annual will tolerate light frost, blooming until a hard freeze knocks it out.

Farewell-to-spring, or godetia, as it's sometimes called, grows best when it is crowded by neighbors. So thin the seedlings to stand no more than 4 inches apart.

Stick a few twiggy branches among the seedlings to keep the stems standing tall. And don't fertilize farewell-to-spring; you'll get leggy plants and few flowers. It prefers a lean, well-drained soil.

Size	18 to 36 in. tall, 10 in. wide
Type	Hardy annual
Bloom	Shades of pink, cream and yellow, midsummer into fall
Soil	Lean, well-drained
Light	Full sun to part shade
Starting method	
	Resents transplanting, so direct sow in spring as soon as you can work the soil.
Source	Thompson and Morgan www.thompson morgan.com 800-274-7333 *Catalog free*

PHOTOS: © Marilynn McAra (farewell-to-spring, painted tongue)

Opium poppy
***Papaver somniferum
paeoniiflorum***

Just scatter a few seeds
in your garden and you'll
have flowers for years to
come. Each bloom lasts
only two or three days,
but the flower show will
continue for three or four
weeks in summer. After
the petals drop, you get
to enjoy the unique seed
pods for a few more
weeks. Pull all but a few,
leaving some to produce
seed so you get poppies
next year. In fact, you'll
need to do a bit of thin-
ning or the plants will be
much too close together.

You may need to stake
tall, double-flowered
cultivars. Or grow them
among tall plants that can
lend support. There are
single-flowered forms that
usually stand up better.

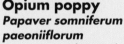

Size	2 to 4 ft. tall, 1 ft. wide
Type	Hardy annual
Bloom	Shades of pink and white in summer
Soil	Moist, well-drained and low in nitrogen
Light	Full sun
Starting method	Direct sow in late winter. Reseeds easily.
Source	Park Seed www.parkseed.com 800-213-0076 *Catalog free*

Monkey flower
***Mimulus* hybrid**

Monkey flower needs
water, and lots of it. The
wetter the soil, the more
sun it can take. It's perfect
at the edge of a water
garden or pond. Part
shade is best if the soil
tends to dry out.

It's great in mixed con-
tainers, but I think this
annual works best in a pot
of its own where you can
keep it constantly wet. A
self-watering style or any
pot with a saucer under it
will hold extra water.

Deadhead the spent
flowers occasionally to
keep monkey flower
blooming. Or, if it starts
to grow tall and floppy,
snip the upright stems
back to the low rosette
of leaves. In a few weeks
it'll cheerfully resume
flowering again.

Size	6 to 12 in. tall, 10 to 12 in. wide
Type	Half-hardy annual
Bloom	A rainbow of colors, often speckled, in late spring into summer
Soil	Wet
Light	Full sun to shade
Starting method	Sow the dust-fine seeds indoors about 8 weeks before the last frost date.
Source	Park Seed www.parkseed.com 800-213-0076 *Catalog free*

Four o'clock
Mirabilis jalapa

Sweetly scented flowers open in late afternoon, as the sun heads toward the horizon. By dawn the flower is tightly closed.

Four o'clocks, also called "marvel of Peru," need warmth, so there's no point rushing them to the garden. But once things warm up, they make a fast growth spurt and start to flower in late summer. If you want to get a quick start next year, dig the fleshy tubers and store them as you would dahlias. But they're so easy from seed I don't bother digging them.

Hummingbirds and night-flying moths are drawn to the seductively sweet fragrance. And the pale colors are great in moon gardens.

Size	24 to 36 in. tall, 24 in. wide
Type	Half-hardy annual
Bloom	Mixed colors, sometimes striped and streaked, in late summer
Soil	Tolerant of sand to clay
Light	Full sun to part shade
Starting method	Start 4 to 6 weeks before the last frost date or direct sow. Soak the seeds in warm water for a day before planting.
Source	The Fragrant Path www.fragrantpath seeds.com *Catalog $2*

California bluebell
Phacelia campanularia

Give California bluebell extremely well-drained to sandy soil. Anything else, even high humidity, and it tends to be sluggish or rot away. But it'll tolerate a light frost or two with no problem.

Try this low grower in a rock garden or between stepping stones laid on a sand and gravel base. In fact, California bluebell can take a bit of foot traffic. If you step on a plant occasionally, you might pick up a fresh, delicate sweet scent from the crushed leaves.

A long taproot makes California bluebell difficult to transplant. It's best to sow it directly where you want it. If it's happy, it may reseed.

Size	6 to 12 in. tall, 6 to 10 in. wide
Type	Hardy annual
Bloom	Blue flowers late spring into summer
Soil	Well drained to dry
Light	Full sun
Starting method	Direct sow in early spring or late fall.
Source	Stokes Seeds, Inc. www.stokeseeds.com 800-396-9238 *Catalog free*

PHOTO: © Mary Howell-Williams (four o'clock)

before &
after

transform *your* garden,
we show you how

WHO DOESN'T LOVE A
HAPPY ENDING? We all have
those problem spots in our yards —
the entryway without much pizzazz, a
daunting slope, a dated patio. Here's
how five gardeners took those kinds
of challenges and turned them into
dream gardens.

Car-stopping Curb Appeal

If your garden looked good for people driving by, people walking by and from your window, wouldn't that be great? Find out how you can grow a front yard garden that's so colorful it stops traffic.

Twenty years ago this home had just an average yard with a few shrubs dotting the foundation, as you can see in the small "before" photo. But now, what a difference!

GETTING TO THE ROOTS Linda Klein's Cleveland, Ohio, soil was all clay, making the good drainage most plants prefer only a dream. When you have poor soil of any kind, you have two choices: Use plants that are adapted to that situation or change the soil. She decided to change the soil by digging out the clay in an area about 30 feet long by 12 feet wide and 16 inches deep! Then she replaced it using her own special mix that you can see in "Super soil recipe" below. The loose, airy texture of this mixture has enough space and oxygen to help roots grow strong and healthy. Plus, it's chock-full of nutrients from the manure and leaf humus. With such good soil as a foundation, the plants are going to look fantastic.

You may not be able to see it, but all that good soil is piled about 12 inches high into a berm. Technically a berm is just a low hill with a garden on top and this one is a key ingredient to the success of this bed. The small rise gets the plants up at a slight angle so they can be seen — even from a distance.

EYE-POPPING COLOR That sweep of impatiens is the most eye-popping piece of this garden. Flowers of shocking pink, deep red and vibrant magenta run like a river of color, leading your eye up to the entrance. Bright colors are easy to see, and appreciate, from any distance. And because each color is grouped together, it has more punch than if the colors were mixed together in a random pattern.

Another thing that keeps this garden looking good isn't so obvious. Instead of being lined up by height, like a group photo, the plants here are staggered for a more natural look. You can see what I mean when you look at the impatiens. They're neat and even along the edge of the lawn. But follow the plants into the bed and you'll notice they weave in and out of the other plants. Now look at the purple floss flower to the right. It has pink geraniums on three sides, and as you look further along the bed the plant heights dip again. In fact, there's an up-and-down movement that ultimately leads to the tallest plants near the entrance. Another perk to staggering plant height is that you have a different view from different places throughout the garden and you can't always see everything at once.

One of the advantages of using so many annuals is that the show can change every year. If you get tired of impatiens, try some begonias or line the border with colorful snapdragons.

Now turn the page to walk up the driveway to the path and take a closer look at the other side of this garden.

(1) Intense color gets a lift from the berm beneath. Getting flowers up at an angle, like seats in a stadium, allows you to see more of these vibrant blooms.

Botanical Names

Begonia
Begonia hybrid
Floss flower
Ageratum corymbosum
Geranium
Pelargonium hybrid
Impatiens *Impatiens walleriana*
Snapdragon
Antirrhinum majus

SUPER SOIL RECIPE
1 40-lb. bag Michigan peat moss
3 10-in. pots sphagnum peat moss
3 quart-sized nursery pots dehydrated manure
1 10-in. pot of leaf humus
Mixed together, this recipe fills a small wheelbarrow and covers an area about 12 square ft. 2 in. thick.

PHOTOS: Dean Tanner; Courtesy of Linda Klein (before)

Turn the page to learn how to grow this garden.

Before

HOW TO GROW
A BOLD BED

The path that takes you to the front door is no less energetic than the view on the street side. Colorful impatiens reappear to escort you along the path and create a cohesive look to the garden as a whole. All the lush growth combined with the height of the plants could give this path an intimidating feel. But thanks to bright colors and familiar plants like sweet potato vine, geranium and astilbe, this walkway seems friendly, inviting you to walk up the path to the door. And did you notice the geranium in the container to your right? That's an easy way to get quick height if you lose a plant or just have an empty spot in the garden.

PRETTY PATH Would you believe this flagstone path is actually 4 feet wide? The original plan called for a path only 1 foot wide. It was later modified to 4 feet, which is a standard width that's comfortable for two people walking side by side. It's a good thing the path was widened because when this garden is at its peak from midsummer to fall, these healthy plants creep out so far there's only about a foot left.

SEASONS OF BEAUTY You might think that such exuberant growth would take days to care for. But what really keeps a garden like this in full swing is some planning along with the seasons. For example, a yearly application of compost keeps the soil healthy and the berm from leveling out. To avoid damaging new spring growth, wait until fall, when annuals are pulled and perennials cut back, to shovel on your yearly layer of compost.

Now that you know all about this garden, how would you like to try it on your own? Check out Linda's season-by-season tips to help get you on your way to a stunning color-filled garden. □

—*Sherri Ribbey*

Botanical Names

Astilbe
   Astilbe hybrid
Delphinium
   Delphinium hybrid
Geranium
   Pelargonium hybrid
Impatiens *Impatiens walleriana*
Monkshood
   Aconitum spp.
Phlox *Phlox* hybrid
Sweet potato vine
   Ipomoea batatas

SPRING

BOOST NUTRITION Plants this nice need good nutrition, so add bone meal to the hole when you plant. Bone meal is an excellent source of phosphorus, which aids root development. And water-loving plants like impatiens benefit from a dose of water crystals, too. Amounts for both additives vary depending on the size of the plant, so check labels first. Finish off by applying a slow-release fertilizer, such as Osmocote®, and you're set for the year.

Take cuttings of your monkshood in fall.

Treat phlox for powdery mildew early.

INSTANT FILLER

Take advantage of season-end clearance sales at nurseries to buy backup perennials. That way, if a plant in the garden dies, you have a more mature plant to replace it with. And you've saved some money, too! In the meantime, display it with other containers — at first glace I bet you didn't guess the garden above is really just a bunch of nursery pots crammed together on a driveway. In the late fall, cut your bargain perennials back and move them inside. The next spring, they'll be as good as new.

Huge impatiens take lots of water.

SUMMER

WATER LOTS For big impatiens like these, make sure they get plenty of water. The outside of this bed needs watering more often than the inside because it gets more sun.

TREAT PROBLEMS Take preventative steps to keep plants looking good. For example, this beautiful phlox by the entry is prone to powdery mildew. Treat it with a fungicide every 10 to 14 days before humid weather starts in midsummer or follow label directions.

FALL

TAKE CUTTINGS If you love delphiniums but can't get them to grow, try monkshood instead. To get more plants, you can wait until they stop blooming in fall and cut a piece off the top about 12 in. long, stick it in the ground and water well. Next spring, you'll have a bigger grouping. Just be sure to wear gloves while doing this since all parts of monkshood are poisonous.

Exuberant, Easy-care
Entry Garden

PHOTO: Denise Cosgrove (before)

Botanical Names

Arborvitae
  Thuja occidentalis
Barberry
  Berberis thunbergii atropurpurea
Coral bells
  Heuchera hybrid
Hakonechloa
  Hakonechloa macra 'Aureola'
Honeysuckle
  Lonicera nitida
Hosta
  Hosta spp.
Oakleaf hydrangea
  Hydrangea quercifolia
Redtwig dogwood
  Cornus sericea
Rhododendron
  Rhododendron hybrid
Spirea
  Spiraea japonica
Tulip
  Tulipa spp.
Witchhazel
  Hamamelis xintermedia

At first glance, this charming Victorian cottage may look old, but it isn't. When Denise Cosgrove bought this house 13 years ago, it had just been built and had the typical "builder's landscaping." In the Seattle area, that's usually an arborvitae and a few rhododendrons. Since Denise loves to garden, she got started right away by planting the tulips and annuals in the "Before" photo. But the original shrubs never really took off so she removed them and got a fresh start. The result? A beautiful garden that's also easy to care for.

STYLISH GARDEN, STYLISH HOME An entry planting works best if it matches the style of your home. This contemporary house has a touch of the historic and, in a way, so does the garden. The plants are modern varieties but the repeated bright colors and annuals laid out in a pattern echo the spirit of those Victorian "carpet beddings" of the past.

Like the steps that lead to the front door, this garden gets taller as it nears the house. Stair-stepping the plants smooths the transition from lawn to house and directs your attention to the door. A window box tops off the planting with more annuals. Though the plants are different from the those in the foundation bed, the windowbox has the same colors to tie it to the garden. For a similar plan from the same garden, check out our container recipe on p. 256.

Don't forget, the color of your house plays a role, too. This sage green is a great backdrop for the chartreuse and burgundy of the plants. It has enough green to complement the plants but enough gray to be neutral. Even the accent colors, like the white trim and the bright coral of the door, can be found in this planting.

PICK YOUR PLANTS Getting the right plants for your area is one of the keys to keeping a garden low maintenance. Plants adapted to the climate and soil can handle the inevitable stresses that occur each growing season and still look good.

Shrubs are a great investment, too. They're usually easy to care for and add structure and interest all year. Here,

reliable Magic Carpet spirea and 'Rose Glow' barberry provide eye-catching color from spring to fall. And 'Baggesen's Gold' honeysuckle keeps its bright gold leaves all year long.

Witchhazel, redtwig dogwood or oakleaf hydrangea also have multiple seasons of interest, and they're hardier than the plants in this garden.

FAVOR FOLIAGE Emphasize foliage over flowers for all season interest. Along with the colorful shrubs in this garden, there are perennials with beautiful leaves, such as hosta, coral bells and hakonechloa.

Now you know what it takes to get a beautiful and easy-care entry. Check out the next page for this garden plan and how to care for it.

Before

Turn the page to learn how to grow this garden.

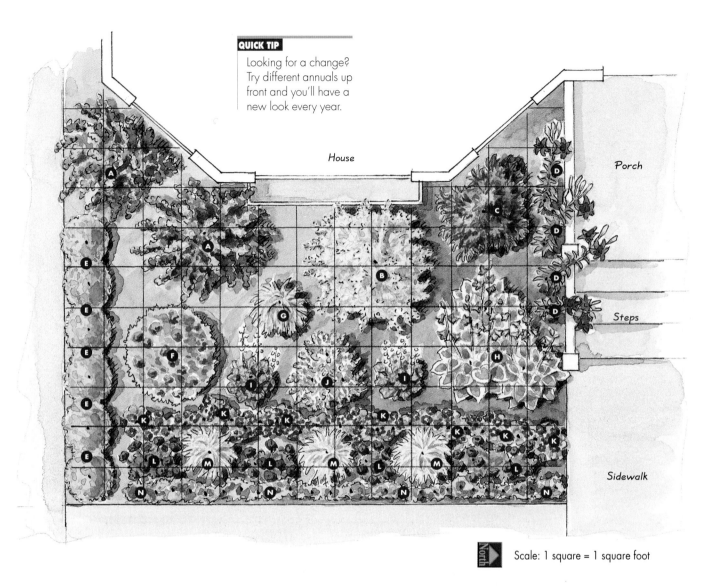

QUICK TIP

Looking for a change? Try different annuals up front and you'll have a new look every year.

House

Porch

Steps

Sidewalk

North   Scale: 1 square = 1 square foot

TIME-SAVING BEAUTY TIPS

We're all busy, but wouldn't it be nice to have time to relax and enjoy our gardens? Keeping garden chores to a minimum will help you do just that. But of course "low-maintenance" doesn't mean "*no* maintenance," so here are some tips for keeping this garden in great shape all season.

JUST THE BASICS You might think a garden this lush needs a lot of fertilizer. But all Denise does is shovel a couple inches of compost onto the beds every fall. Since this Washington garden

gets plenty of rain, there's no need for mulch. If you live where rain isn't as reliable, a 3- to 4-inch layer of organic mulch will keep soil moist. Look for pine bark in the garden center. Oils in the wood have been shown to have disease-suppressing qualities.

Keep an eye on plants the first year you have them. Regular, deep watering will help the new transplants develop a good root system so they can withstand dry spells more easily in the future. If you

garden where winters get below freezing, check out the alternate plant list that's just as colorful and easy to maintain.

CUTTING BACK Pruning can take a lot of time, but these shrubs are a cinch. Trim the honeysuckle in winter and the barberry in early spring to maintain their size and shape. Spirea stays compact, but if it does get too big, give it a quick haircut in early spring. You can cut this variety to within a few inches of the ground and it'll still reach its mature size and

COLORFUL ENTRY GARDEN

Code	Plant Name	No. to Plant	Type	Cold/Heat Zones	Height/Width
A	Barberry *Berberis thunbergii atropurpurea* 'Rose Glow'	2	Shrub	4-8/8-3	4-6 ft./4-7 ft.
B	Honeysuckle *Lonicera nitida* 'Baggesen's Gold'	1	Shrub	7-9/9-6	3-4 ft./3 ft.
C	Japanese maple *Acer palmatum* 'Shaina'	1	Tree	6-9/9-1	6-10 ft./6 ft
D	Lily *Lilium* 'Monte Negro'	4	Bulb	4-8/9-1	3-4 ft./1 ft.
E	Boxwood *Buxus* 'Green Ice'	6	Shrub	5-9/9-3	3 ft./3 ft.
F	Spirea *Spiraea japonica* 'Walbuma' (Magic Carpet)	1	Shrub	4-9/9-1	2 ft./2 ft.
G	Japanese forest grass *Hakonechloa macra* 'Aureola'	1	Perennial	6-9/9-1	10-12 in./18 in.
H	Hosta *Hosta* 'Patriot'	3	Perennial	4-8/8-1	15 in./36 in.
I	Coral bells *Heuchera* 'Plum Pudding'	2	Perennial	4-9/9-1	26 in./16 in.
J	Scotch heather *Calluna vulgaris* 'County Wicklow'	3	Perennial	4-6/7-1	10-12 in./18 in
K	Wax begonia *Begonia xsemperflorens* Harmony Scarlet	26	Annual	12/12-1	6-8 in./6-8 in.
L	Verbena *Verbena* Quartz Burgundy	8	Annual	9-12/12-1	10-12 in./8-12 in.
M	Japanese forest grass *Hakonechloa macra* 'All Gold'	3	Perennial	6-9/9-1	10-12 in./8-12 in.
N	Lobelia *Lobelia erinus* Riviera Marine Blue	26	Annual	12/12-1	5 in./5 in.

A PLAN FOR COLDER CLIMATES

Code	Plant Name	No. to Plant	Type	Cold/Heat Zones	Height/Width
A	Barberry *Berberis thunbergii atropurpurea* 'Rose Glow'	2	Shrub	4-8/8-3	4-6 ft./4-7 ft.
B	Arborvitae *Thuja occidentalis* 'Golden Globe'	1	Tree	2-8/7-1	2-4 ft./2-4 ft.
C	Smokebush *Cotinus coggygria* 'Royal Purple'	1	Tree	4-8/8-3	15 ft./10-12 ft.
D	Lily *Lilium* 'Caravan'	4	Bulb	3-8/8-1	4-5 ft./1 ft.
E	Boxwood *Buxus* 'Green Velvet'	6	Shrub	4-9/9-3	4 ft./3 ft.
F	Spirea *Spiraea japonica* 'Walbuma' (Magic Carpet)	1	Shrub	4-9/9-1	2 ft./2 ft.
G	Hosta *Hosta* 'Pineapple Upsidedown Cake'	1	Perennial	3-8/8-1	15 in./28 in.
H	Pigsqueak *Bergenia* 'Bressingham Ruby'	6*	Perennial	3-10/9-2	12-15 in./16 in.
I	Coral bells *Heuchera* 'Plum Pudding'	2	Perennial	4-9/9-1	26 in./16 in.
J	Speedwell *Veronica* 'Eveline'	3	Perennial	4-9/9-1	12-18 in./18 in.
K	Vinca *Catharanthus* Titan™ Rose	12*	Annual	12/12-1	14-16 in./10-12 in.
L	Dianthus *Dianthus* 'Supra Purple'	8	Annual	12/12-1	10-12 in./10 in.
M	Hosta *Hosta* 'Little Sunspot'	3	Perennial	3-8/8-1	6 in./16 in.
N	Ageratum *Ageratum* Neptune™ Blue	26	Annual	10-12/12-1	6-8 in./6-8 in.

*Number of plants has changed from the original plan.

flower the same year. If you're planting the smokebush in the alternative plan, cut it back to within a foot of the ground each spring to keep it a size that will better fit this space.

A garden that's mostly foliage cuts down on chores like deadheading. And many modern annuals are self-cleaning, so there's no need to remove the spent blossoms.

With plants this easy to care for, you'll have time to start a whole new garden bed! □

— *Sherri Ribbey*

QUICK CHANGE

Keep window boxes looking great all year by changing the plants out seasonally just like this gardener does. Plant bulbs in early spring, annuals for summer color and cold-tolerant plants like kale and pansies in fall. Don't stop when winter sets in. Try a variety of evergreens, some redtwig dogwood branches and pinecones.

Rise to the Challenge

Before

Starting from scratch can be intimidating. Add to that a big slope in your front yard and it's downright scary. Raquel Feroe's narrow 25-by-50-foot front yard started out full of weeds and scrubby trees. The construction of the house took care of all that, but it left behind a slope of bare soil.

KEEP SOIL IN PLACE There are lots of different ways to keep soil from washing away over time. Sometimes all you need are a few well-placed stones. Other times sophisticated retaining walls are best.

This solution is somewhere in the middle. In the "before" photo you can see that there are three levels here, with a small 20-foot-deep terrace in the middle that helps stabilize the incline. It also creates a resting place along the climb so it doesn't seem as steep.

Low-maintenance ground covers like those in the "after" photo are great soil savers, too. Since they mostly grow *out* instead of *up*, they form a dense cover that protects soil from pounding rains that cause erosion. Below ground, fibrous roots weave through the soil, holding it in place. Even better, plants like the thyme and sedum here root along the stem so they can cover a large area. You can help them along by pinning the new growth down to the soil with hairpins or small rocks.

Shredded bark mulch also provides soil protection and conserves moisture for plants. Large areas of bare soil may need an extra layer of burlap or jute netting to keep the soil in place until plants get going.

GOOD DESIGN MAKES A GOOD CLIMB Lumpy, bare soil isn't much of a front yard. It's amazing what a couple of years and some hardy ground covers can do. With color, texture and shape, this beautiful tapestry of low-growing plants is quite a view.

You don't need a lot of different colors for a pretty garden. In fact, limiting the number of colors helps create a unified and harmonious design. This garden works quite well with purple, white and shades of greens. Did you notice that the color of the slate stepping stones is similar to the house trim? What a great way to tie house and garden together!

Ground covers come in lots of different shapes and sizes. Play the different habits, sizes and leaf shapes off each other for an interesting composition. Take another look at that thyme. Those purple mounds are a nice contrast to the arching stems of the creeping Jenny to the right. Just below that is the white snow-in-summer that seems to march across the soil back toward the thyme. Up near the house and on the left you'll see clumps of flax and shasta daisies, taller plants that help cover the bare base of the deck. Across the yard on the right are more tall plants to help create a balance and define the border. Without it, that side would look dark and empty. In addition, these plants create a backdrop that softens the cluster of rocks.

WANDERING PATH It's a little hard to tell in the photo but the path that starts in the lower left winds across the middle and up to the front door at the top. A meandering path has a more natural feel than one that shoots straight ahead and it's not as steep, either. Because it winds this way and that, it encourages visitors to slow down to enjoy the different views along the way. The walk is so pleasant you won't even notice the climb.

Find out how to have a fantastic slope like this one on p. 132.

Botanical Names

Creeping Jenny
Lysimachia nummularia
Creeping thyme
Thymus serpyllum
Shasta daisy
Leucanthemum xsuperbum
Flax *Linum perenne*
Sedum *Sedum kamtschaticum*
Snow-in-summer
Cerastium tomentosum

PHOTOS: © Marilynn McAra (lead); Raquel Feroe (before)

Turn the page to get a slope as good-looking as this one.

5 HILLSIDE **HINTS**

_____

Botanical Names

Creeping Jenny
  Lysimachia nummularia
Creeping thyme
  Thymus serpyllum
Dianthus *Dianthus hybrid*
Sea thrift *Armeria maritima*
Sedum *Sedum kamtschaticum*
Snow-in-summer
  Cerastium tomentosum

Getting the right plants in the right place is a key ingredient to a good-looking slope. Annuals, containers and perennials that need extra care go at the top near the house — and the hose. The rest of the yard is planted with vigorous, low-maintenance ground covers.

Raquel used thyme, creeping Jenny, sedum and snow-in-summer, which all took off quickly without being invasive. The first three are easy to propagate from cuttings. In fact, you can even cut a piece, make a hole in the ground with a pencil and stick the cutting in. Give new transplants a little extra water until they root and you have another plant to take cuttings from. Snow-in-summer is best divided, but may also reseed. Once established, these plants are pretty drought-tolerant and they don't need any pruning or fertilizing to stay looking good.

Speaking of fertilizer, runoff from this and other chemicals, such as pesticides, is a serious concern for gardeners with a slope. To avoid contaminating water sources, stick with natural solutions like compost for plant nutrition and avoid pesticides as much as possible.

How a plant grows makes a difference in how you plant it on a slope. Low-growing and cascading plants or even vines can easily handle a landscape at an angle. You'll find some in the list "Great ground covers" below. But your average perennial needs a little extra help to keep from growing along the ground and then up. The tip at right shows you how to plant your perennials so they stay upright. Check out the rest of the tips and you'll see what else you can do to get a beautiful garden even on a slope. □

— *Sherri Ribbey*

GREAT GROUND COVERS

There are a lot of plants that are good at keeping your soil in place. Here are a few to get you started. You can find even more versatile ground covers online. Visit Allstar Groundcovers! at www.entomology.cornell.edu/Extension/Woodys/CUGroundCoverSite/GroundcoverMain.html.

Plant Name	Cold/Heat Zones	Comments
Barrenwort *Epimedium grandiflorum*	4-8/8-2	Shade; spring flowers in a variety of colors
Bugleweed *Ajuga reptans*	3-9/9-1	Sun to part shade; blue flowers in spring
Catmint *Nepeta* (Faassenii Group)	4-8/8-1	Sun; lavender flowers spring to fall
Creeping speedwell *Veronica peduncularis*	5-8/8-2	Sun; sky-blue flowers in late spring
Fragrant sumac *Rhus aromatica* 'Gro-Low'	3-9/9-5	Sun to part shade; red berries in fall
Ice plant *Delosperma cooperi*	5-11/12-1	Sun; fuchsia flowers all summer
Siberian cypress *Microbiota decussata*	2-7/7-1	Sun; evergreen foliage turns bronze in fall
Sweet autumn clematis *Clematis terniflora*	4-9/9-1	Sun to part shade; white flowers in fall
Sweet woodruff *Galium odoratum*	4-8/8-1	Shade; white flowers in spring

1 PLANT IN POCKETS When tucking small plants in between rocks, shake off soil from the root ball and tease the roots apart. Place the plant in the crevice and fill the remaining space with a mixture of peat and clay or top soil. The thick clay holds the plant in place while the crumbly texture of the peat keeps air and moisture around the roots.

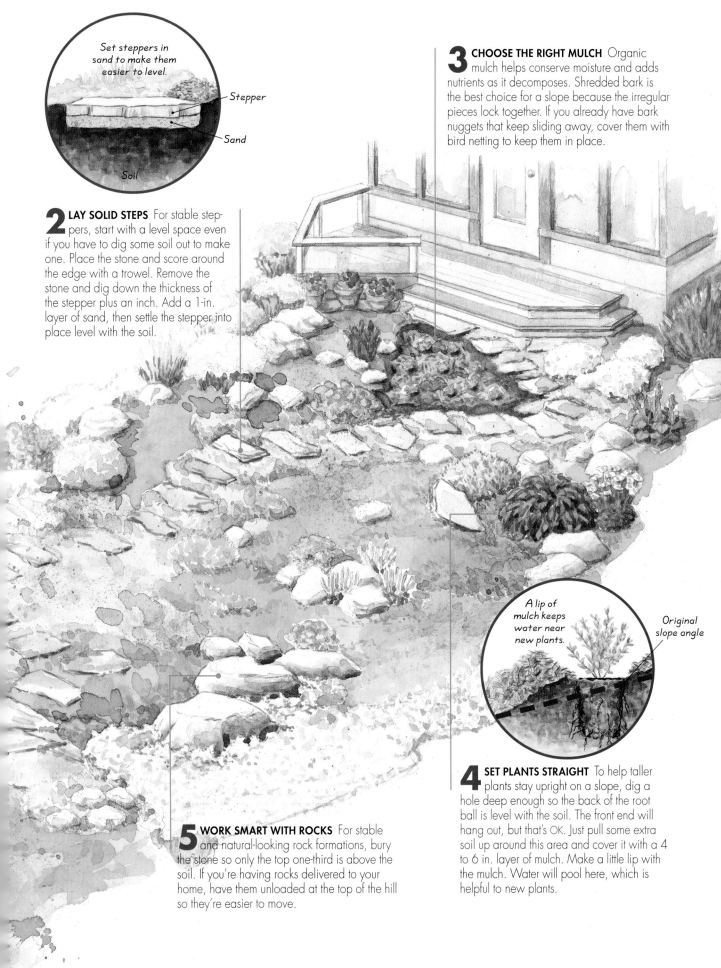

Set steppers in sand to make them easier to level.

Stepper

Sand

Soil

3 CHOOSE THE RIGHT MULCH Organic mulch helps conserve moisture and adds nutrients as it decomposes. Shredded bark is the best choice for a slope because the irregular pieces lock together. If you already have bark nuggets that keep sliding away, cover them with bird netting to keep them in place.

2 LAY SOLID STEPS For stable steppers, start with a level space even if you have to dig some soil out to make one. Place the stone and score around the edge with a trowel. Remove the stone and dig down the thickness of the stepper plus an inch. Add a 1-in. layer of sand, then settle the stepper into place level with the soil.

A lip of mulch keeps water near new plants.

Original slope angle

4 SET PLANTS STRAIGHT To help taller plants stay upright on a slope, dig a hole deep enough so the back of the root ball is level with the soil. The front end will hang out, but that's OK. Just pull some extra soil up around this area and cover it with a 4 to 6 in. layer of mulch. Make a little lip with the mulch. Water will pool here, which is helpful to new plants.

5 WORK SMART WITH ROCKS For stable and natural-looking rock formations, bury the stone so only the top one-third is above the soil. If you're having rocks delivered to your home, have them unloaded at the top of the hill so they're easier to move.

Make Your Side Yard Beautiful

Before

Every gardener I know has at least one spot in the garden he or she considers a problem. Often it's the side yard. Utilities, such as meters and air conditioners, usually get stuck in the side yard. If you look closely at Rosemary Kautzky's "before" photo below, you see an air conditioner unit tucked in the corner. And the house and fence create lots of hard angles in a small space.

Rosemary started with a few shrubs along the fence and foundation, but they didn't hide the air conditioner or cover the angles enough. So the beds got wider until there was only the grass path you see in the after photo. The curving design distracts your eye from all of the straight edges that were so prominent in the before photo. Some of the plantings are tall enough to break up and soften the strong horizontal lines of the fence and house. And dense plantings cover the blank fence and disguise the utilities.

Maybe your side yard isn't laid out like this. Perhaps it's on a steeper hillside with a large blank house wall and several window wells you want to hide. Or maybe you have to walk through a boring narrow area to get to the kitchen door. On the next pages, I'll show you three creative and inspiring ways to turn your side yard into a beautiful, useful garden.

(1) The vertical evergreens in the "before" photo are a good start. They'll eventually break the strong horizontal lines of the fence so it doesn't look so severe. In the "after" photo, more plants and a narrow path have turned this side yard into a beautiful garden.

PHOTOS: © Rosemary Kautzky

Turn the page and learn more tips to help you customize your own side yard.

CREATE A SIDE YARD **JUST FOR YOU**

To help you get started with your side yard, I've designed three that have situations you might encounter in your own garden.

All of the gardens share a similar location — between the house and a privacy fence. And these side yards take you from the front garden to the back. You may want a gate at one end, or you may like an open entrance — I'll leave that up to you.

In "On the wide side," the garden is the same size as the one on the last page. However, this side yard has been transformed into a spot for a relaxing meal or quiet conversation.

In "Skinny spaces" on the next page, the first garden has an incline, so the path has been divided with steps. Because the long wall has no windows, it seems to loom. Utilities and window wells also need to be disguised.

Below right is another narrow garden. This one is a spot where it would be nice to have some extra living space. But it's too narrow to plant trees and shrubs to disguise the wall.

Even if none of these designs is exactly like your garden, I bet you'll find ideas to help you turn your side yard into a beautiful place. □

— *Jim Childs*

ON THE WIDE SIDE

An outdoor dining room

What if your back door is really a side door that opens into your side yard? You can make this area work for you by turning it into a summer dining room. If it's right off the kitchen, it's a handy spot for grilling or entertaining. There's a lot of foot traffic in this area. Prevent tracking grass and mud into the house by installing a hard-surfaced path, like these bricks.

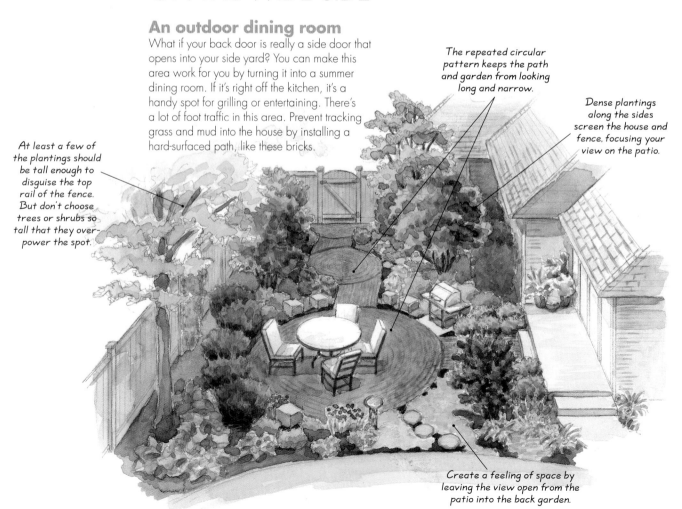

The repeated circular pattern keeps the path and garden from looking long and narrow.

Dense plantings along the sides screen the house and fence, focusing your view on the patio.

At least a few of the plantings should be tall enough to disguise the top rail of the fence. But don't choose trees or shrubs so tall that they overpower the spot.

Create a feeling of space by leaving the view open from the patio into the back garden.

SKINNY SPACES

Eye-level wall planters and taller decorative panels cover a blank wall. They also pull your eye away from the window wells and utility meters near the ground.

Choose narrow or columnar trees and shrubs so they won't comb your hair as you walk by.

If your path is 5 or 6 ft. away from the wall, you'll have plenty of planting space to cover up the side of the house.

Design clever disguises

Since there's not enough room to hide the air conditioner with shrubs, a lattice cover does the trick. Just make sure you can remove it easily for maintenance. And a dwarf tree also draws attention away from the AC unit. Placing a large shrub or a small tree in a narrow spot like this partially blocks the long view, making the garden appear shorter. Keep it no more than about two-thirds the height of the wall behind it. If it's taller, it'll overpower the small space. Soften the look of the fence with colorful vines growing on trellises.

I've added steps to this flagstone path so it's easier to travel the slope, especially in wet weather.

Make your side yard productive. Dwarf fruit trees can be pruned flat against a tall privacy fence.

Step into a hideaway

Right outside the door is a perfect spot to relax and unwind. An arbor with a comfortable bench tucked inside helps break up the long expanse of bare wall *and* gives you a place to sit. Across from the arbor is a low, gurgling fountain to help shut out unwanted noise.

If your fence is in full sun, a few espaliered fruit trees are a great choice to cover the bare boards. You'll have lovely spring blooms *and* edible fruit — what more could you want outside the kitchen door? Maybe a few herbs?

And finally, the main part of the brick path is a basket weave, rather than a running bond pattern. This helps shorten the look of a long path.

Let herbs and perennials billow over the edge of the path to disguise the straight line.

A diamond pattern in the bricks breaks up the long stretch of path, making it seem shorter.

An Inviting
Patio Update

If anyone knows about change, it's a gardener. Seasons change, plants grow, tools and hardscaping wear out. Even our gardens change over time. Susan Koelink knows this well. Her British Columbia patio garden has evolved over the years, as you can tell by the time line below, to meet the changing needs of her family. It started with a red brick patio filled with children's toys and furniture for family picnics. But once the children were grown, it was time to renovate.

The footprint of the garden hasn't changed but a smaller patio with a glass roof (on the left side of the large photo) replaced the hot sun room. And the stone that replaced the brick and rotten landscape timbers ties things together and adds a sense of age and permanence.

Is your patio ready for an update? Try these tips for a beautiful transformation.

FIT THE STYLE TO THE SITE Whether starting from scratch or renovating, take stock of what you have and fit your garden style to the situation. Here, a flower-filled cottage garden would be charming, but because there are several shade trees, it wasn't practical. No matter what your growing conditions are, use similar foliage, texture and plant habits to keep your garden unified.

COLOR COORDINATED Flower and foliage color are obvious concerns in garden design. But the color of the house and patio can have a big impact, too.

Isn't it amazing the difference color makes here? The updated soft yellow paint and bluestone help the patio fit in better with the pastel flower colors in the garden. The home's upper story, now deep violet, seems to recede, keeping the focus below on the patio and garden.

PATIOS WITH PURPOSE A large patio like this one, about 16½ feet square, is perfect for entertaining. With a big open space, it's easy to arrange tables and chairs to suit the occasion. And there's still room left over for folks to mingle.

For more intimate gatherings, like time with the grandkids or an early-morning cup of coffee, maybe you'd like a second, smaller patio. The cozy furniture arrangement here makes conversation easy. And heating elements under the glass roof make it possible to enjoy cool evenings outside.

Fitting your design to the space and coordinating colors make any outdoor living space look good. But plants play a role, too. Turn the page to find out how to design a garden around your patio.

Botanical Names

Japanese maple
Acer palmatum
Plum *Prunus* hybrid

Changing with the times

1982

PHOTOS: Courtesy of Susan Koelink (1982 and 1999)

1983
A large plum tree dies, letting in more sun.

1999
Earlier version of the garden under the Japanese maple.

2000
The kids are grown; time to renovate the garden.

Turn the page
for tips on
planting around
your patio.

CHOOSE YOUR **PLANT PALETTE**

To make your patio the perfect place to relax after a hard day at work, enjoy family time and entertain friends, start with the hardscaping. When that's done, surround the patio with plants to create a view you can't wait to come home to. Here are some tips to get you started.

IF IT SMELLS GOOD, GROW IT Just a whiff of a special aroma can take you back in time to a favorite person or moment. It can even help you relax. So surround yourself with some fragrant favorites. In this garden, 'Little Grapette' daylily and Abraham Darby rose perfume the patio from late spring through summer. Other fragrant plants you

might enjoy are lilies, peonies and phlox. Some, such as moonflower and jasmine, are most aromatic in the evening.

PLACE PLANTS WITH CARE Everyone is drawn to flowers — including insects. While butterflies are colorful and fun to watch, bees are another matter, especially if you're allergic. Be sure bee magnets like bluebeard and tall sedum are well away from the seating area. Thorns are another unpleasant surprise, so keep them away from places where they might snag skin or clothing.

A PATIO WITH A VIEW Summer isn't the only time you can enjoy your patio. Make sure you have

plants with a variety of bloom times so there's something to look at from spring right through fall. This garden has spring-blooming alliums with seed heads that last well into fall. Roses and geraniums bloom all summer into early fall when the anemones take over.

Flowers are beautiful to look at but they're not the only show in town. Look for annuals, perennials, trees and shrubs with variegated or interesting seasonal foliage, berries, unusual bark or colorful stems.

GOOD HABITS MAKE GOOD NEIGHBORS A plant's habit, or how it grows, is another important consideration when you're designing a patio planting. Those that grow tall and upright can help create a sense of privacy by screening off an area. On the other hand, loose low-growers and shorter plants growing near the patio preserve the view of the yard. Watch out for overly enthusiastic low-growing plants that creep out too far on the patio and create a walking hazard.

Sometimes a little privacy is what you need. The small patio garden in the photo at left has a lush border that sets it apart from the larger space without cutting it off entirely.

Change is inevitable, but it can be a good thing, too. In fact, with a patio like this to sit on, you might find yourself spending more time outdoors than in your living room easy chair. □

— *Sherri Ribbey*

Create privacy with plants This small patio, in the upper left of the plan, is a great place to relax. How do you turn a plain patio into a hideaway? Include tall plants like the magnolia to the right as a screen — but not too many or it's stifling. Also, the arching branches of the Japanese maple above create a sense of shelter. Up close to the patio, smaller plants like the daylilies and allium separate the area from the rest of the garden but still allow you to see out.

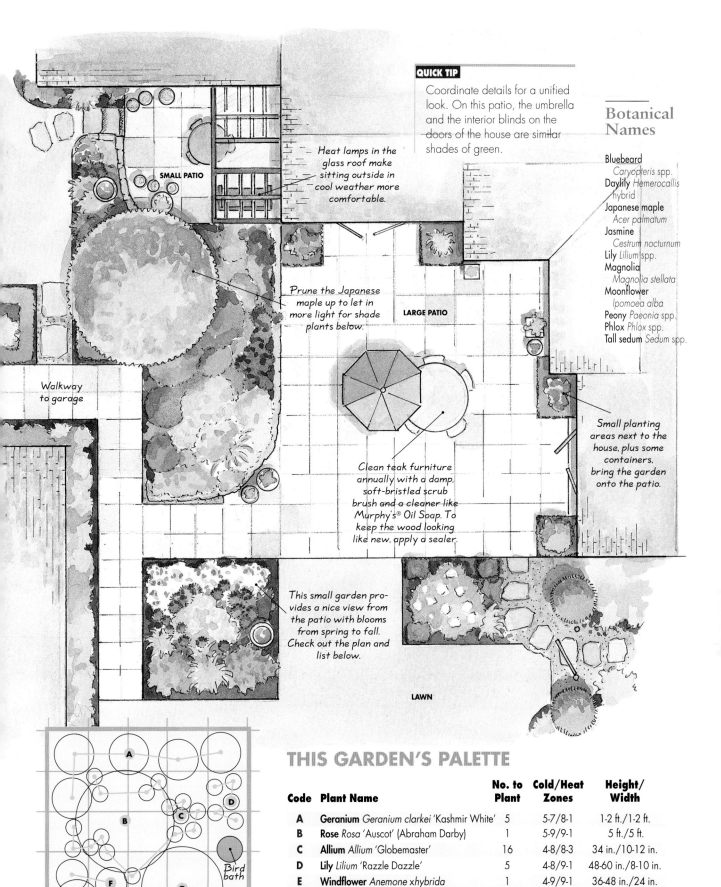

Coordinate details for a unified look. On this patio, the umbrella and the interior blinds on the doors of the house are similar shades of green.

SMALL PATIO

Heat lamps in the glass roof make sitting outside in cool weather more comfortable.

Botanical Names

Bluebeard
   Caryopteris spp.
Daylily *Hemerocallis* hybrid
Japanese maple
   Acer palmatum
Jasmine
   Cestrum nocturnum
Lily *Lilium* spp.
Magnolia
   Magnolia stellata
Moonflower
   Ipomoea alba
Peony *Paeonia* spp.
Phlox *Phlox* spp.
Tall sedum *Sedum* spp.

Prune the Japanese maple up to let in more light for shade plants below.

LARGE PATIO

Walkway to garage

Small planting areas next to the house, plus some containers, bring the garden onto the patio.

Clean teak furniture annually with a damp, soft-bristled scrub brush and a cleaner like Murphy's® Oil Soap. To keep the wood looking like new, apply a sealer.

This small garden provides a nice view from the patio with blooms from spring to fall. Check out the plan and list below.

LAWN

THIS GARDEN'S PALETTE

Code	Plant Name	No. to Plant	Cold/Heat Zones	Height/ Width
A	**Geranium** *Geranium clarkei* 'Kashmir White'	5	5-7/8-1	1-2 ft./1-2 ft.
B	**Rose** *Rosa* 'Auscot' (Abraham Darby)	1	5-9/9-1	5 ft./5 ft.
C	**Allium** *Allium* 'Globemaster'	16	4-8/8-3	34 in./10-12 in.
D	**Lily** *Lilium* 'Razzle Dazzle'	5	4-8/9-1	48-60 in./8-10 in.
E	**Windflower** *Anemone* xhybrida 'Honorine Jobert'	1	4-9/9-1	36-48 in./24 in.
F	**Daylily** *Hemerocallis* 'Little Grapette'	3	3-9/9-1	12 in./24-36 in.
G	**Snakeroot** *Actaea racemosa*	1	3-8/8-3	4-6 ft./2-4 ft.

Bird bath

North Scale: 1 square = 4 square feet

garden design

great *ideas* you can use!

SPECTACULAR RESULTS ON A DO-IT-YOURSELF BUDGET is what most of us dream of. We'll give you solid design ideas for creating beautiful gardens in the front, in the back and everything in between. Plus we'll show you how to attract birds, pass along other readers' tips and share ways to make gardening easier, no matter what your age.

Smart design saves you time.
Colorful Curb Appeal

Your front yard can be anything you want — a sweep of green or a kaleidoscope of color, like this one. Would you believe it's low-maintenance? The style of Ann Weckbaugh's Colorado garden resembles an English border, but these plants are both beautiful *and* tough. And the design follows through with an easy-to-maintain layout.

Front yard fences aren't uncommon, but they're often close to the street. This one leaves room for a wide flower bed and a strip of grass. The fence creates a backdrop from both sides as it gives structure to the garden. Plus it forms two smaller "rooms" that are nicely in scale with the house. Perhaps you don't want a fence cutting through your garden? You can add structure, or even divide your garden, with a hedge, a mix of shrubs or a few small trees.

There's a lot more to see in this garden. So check out the illustration below to see a layout of the garden, then turn the page and let's get started on our tour.

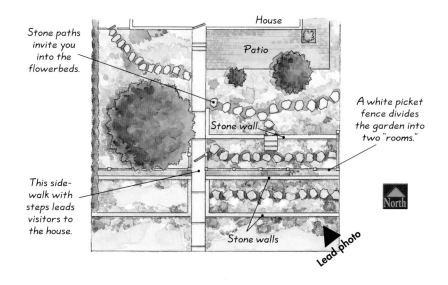

Stone paths invite you into the flowerbeds.

House

Patio

A white picket fence divides the garden into two "rooms."

Stone wall

This sidewalk with steps leads visitors to the house.

Stone walls

North

Lead photo

PHOTOS: © Charles Mann

(1) Dividing this front yard with low walls and stone paths makes it easier to maintain the individual narrow beds.

COLORFUL AND EASY

Botanical Names

Buffalo grass
Buchloe dactyloides
Catmint
Nepeta racemosa
Mullein
Verbascum bombyciferum

This garden is pretty. But there's more to it than that. Let me tell you about all of the smart design ideas it incorporates.

PLAN FOR BEAUTY *AND* EFFICIENCY You're meant to walk into this garden and enjoy it. The paths of large stone slabs in photo 2 are easy to stroll on in comfort. Irregular stones give a casual feel to the garden. These are large enough that you don't have to worry about stepping on the flowers that sprawl onto the edges. In the illustration below right you can see there are several of these paths to help you get into the beds easily.

You won't find big sweeps of one plant growing here; the placement is much more random. That helps keep a casual meadow look. Some perennials are individuals, like the purple catmint in photo 2, while others are in small groupings. But repeated plants and colors throughout the entire garden visually tie it all together.

Planting specimens like this also makes it easy to test new plants to see if they'll fit the low-care style. If a particular plant isn't happy, it's easy to replace, and visitors will never notice.

Since this garden is to be viewed from all angles, the majority of plants are less than 3 feet tall. The tallest are near the center of each bed, with height graduating down to the lowest plants along the edges and paths. Later in the season there are a few perennials, like grasses and the bold, gray-foliaged mulleins, that will spike up taller. Everything else is kept low to add to that feeling of standing in a colorful meadow. And they're also short since you don't want to block the view to or from the house. If you'd like more privacy, set taller plants near the center or along the fence area to form a leafy divider or screen.

CONSERVE YOUR RESOURCES There really isn't a steep grade in this garden. The low stone wall you see in photo 3 and the others shown in the illustrated plan to the far right aren't absolutely necessary. But these walls are as much a water conservation technique as they are decorative. Water runs off even a gentle slope, so the walls make the beds level. Now every drop of water that falls, from the sky or the hose, stays where it lands and has a chance to soak in.

SAVE TIME AND ENERGY Colorful flower borders like these are often crisply edged. But to encourage a casual, natural meadow feeling, the edge of the buffalo grass lawn you see in photo 3 has been left untrimmed. Perennials even bump out into the lawn to add to that informal look — a clean edge here just wouldn't look right. Plus it would be time-consuming to maintain because the garden is so big.

Buffalo grass makes a very low-maintenance lawn. It's best for areas with long, hot summers because it tolerates drought extremely well, needing only 2 inches of water per month to stay green. However, it does sprout runners, and can

(2) Stepping stones are large so when the plants around them begin to sprawl over the edges, there's still plenty of room for you to walk.

(3) Buffalo grass makes an easy-care lawn. It naturally stays short so if you don't mind a casual look like this, you rarely need to mow.

spread. Every year or two, dig some of it out along the edges — you don't want it traveling too far into the beds and choking out perennials.

Since this native grass only grows 4 or 5 inches tall, you don't have to mow in the summer heat if you don't mind a rough, native look. Before this grass greens up in late spring, one mowing is a good idea. That'll help remove some of the brown blades from last year.

You're seeing this garden at its peak time, in late spring to early summer. But there are many repeat bloomers that only need to be deadheaded or cut back after their first flowers fade to keep more flowers coming. Plus there are enough other perennials that bloom earlier and later, so once this garden starts in spring it never really stops until winter. On the next pages, I'll show you how to create long-blooming colorful combos like these in your own garden.

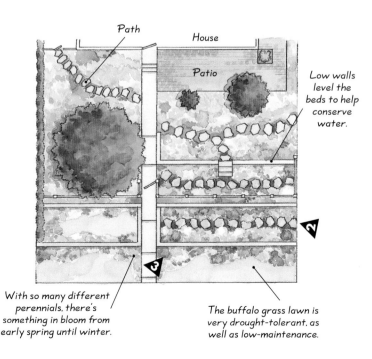

Path

House

Patio

Low walls level the beds to help conserve water.

With so many different perennials, there's something in bloom from early spring until winter.

The buffalo grass lawn is very drought-tolerant, as well as low-maintenance.

PLEASING **PLANT PARTNERS**

Grouping plants together, like the combinations you see in these photos, often takes some trial and error before you get just the look you like. But here are three easy-to-remember things to keep in mind as you plan any garden combo.

COLOR CORRECTIONS Start by picking a color scheme and then stick with it. In this garden, shades of pink and purple are the focus. Even some of the gray foliage has a definite blue hue so it blends well with purple tints. Gray also helps tie different colors together. Toss in a bit of contrasting yellow and you have a lively color scheme that's easy to work with.

FORM FOLLOWS TEXTURE It really does work to combine plants with different flower and leaf textures, like the ferny yarrow with coarse lamb's ears. Even the contrast of the overall shape of the plants adds interest — vertical sage and rounded yarrow create a pleasing combination.

CONSIDER CULTURAL CONDITIONS Since this garden is in a region where summers are dry, there's no point planting a water hog like a hibiscus in this drought-tolerant mix. All of these plants do best with lean, dry soil; they don't even want mulch. Plant something with them that requires lots of water and you'll have to baby it along, or replace it when it dies.

So take a closer look at these hard-working, drought-tolerant plants. Most of them are common cultivars you can find in catalogs or local nurseries. That'll make it easy for you to create your own custom combinations. □

— *Jim Childs*

Play up the foliage

You may notice flowers first, but foliage carries the scene when they fade. Here, coarse lamb's ear contrasts with the ferny foliage of early summer-blooming yarrow and Marguerite daisies. The plants I've identified here all bloom in early summer. Keep them going as long as possible by deadheading the spent flowers.

A Lamb's ear *Stachys byzantina*
Size 15 in. tall, 24 in. wide
Zones Cold: 3 to 8, Heat: 8 to 1

B Catmint *Nepeta racemosa* 'Walker's Low'
Size 15 in. tall, 24 in. wide
Zones Cold: 3 to 8, Heat: 8 to 1

C Common yarrow *Achillea* 'Moonshine'
Size 20 in. tall, 12 in. wide
Zones Cold: 3 to 8, Heat: 8 to 1

D Marguerite daisy *Anthemis* 'Blomit' (Susanna Mitchell)
Size 24 in. tall, 30 in. wide
Zones Cold: 3 to 7, Heat: 7 to 1

E Sage *Salvia xsylvestris* 'Blauhügel' (Blue Hill)
Size 20 in. tall, 18 in. wide
Zones Cold: 3 to 8, Heat: 8 to 1

Vary the heights

Notice the stepping stones that cut through this garden? The plants around and between the slabs are low so they won't brush against you as you stroll. But to keep the scene interesting from all angles, mix the heights up a bit further from the stones. And don't be afraid to tuck in a few bulbs and annuals, like these alliums and snapdragons, to keep the color coming. This group of spiky flowers adds height and punctuation.

A **Snapdragon** *Antirrhinum* x'Dulcinea's Heart'
Size 1 to 3 ft. tall, 12 in. wide
Zones Cold: 7 to 10, Heat: 12 to 1

B **Penstemon** *Penstemon barbatus* 'Elfin Pink'
Size 12 in. tall, 10 in. wide
Zones Cold: 3 to 8, Heat: 8 to 1

C **Golden garlic** *Allium moly*
Size 12 in. tall, 6 in. wide
Zones Cold: 3 to 9, Heat: 9 to 1

D **Betony** *Stachys macrantha*
Size 18 in. tall, 12 in. wide
Zones Cold: 3 to 8, Heat: 8 to 1

Let the plants weave

Like a tapestry woven in fabric, plants in this garden weave together. Many of them are set close enough that their colorful flowers blend into their neighbors. Here's a group of plants with varying heights. Grown together, sunlight reaches all of the plants to keep them healthy.

A **Salvia** *Salvia xsylvestris* 'Mainacht' (May Night)
Size 18 to 24 in. tall, 12 to 18 in. wide
Zones Cold: 4 to 8, Heat: 8 to 1

B **Common yarrow** *Achillea* 'Moonshine'
Size 20 in. tall, 12 in. wide
Zones Cold: 3 to 8, Heat: 8 to 1

C **Large penstemon** *Penstemon grandiflorus*
Size 2 to 4 ft. tall, 12 to 18 in. wide
Zones Cold: 3 to 9, Heat: 9 to 1

D **Rock soapwort** *Saponaria ocymoides*
Size 6 in. tall, 24 in. wide
Zones Cold: 3 to 7, Heat: 7 to 1

cindy combs
on beautiful curbside plantings

PHOTOS: Courtesy Cindy Combs

IN THE KNOW

CINDY'S TOP REASONS TO BEAUTIFY YOUR CURBSIDE

- Improve the curb appeal of your home
- Eliminate a struggling lawn
- And last but not least — you've run out of planting space elsewhere!

WEB extra

At-a-glance **guide** to even more drought-tolerant perennials.

Tree lawn. Curbside. Inferno strip. No matter what you call that area between the street and the sidewalk, it can be a difficult spot to make look good. To help you beautify yours, I got some tips from Cindy Combs, who is a popular garden lecturer on the topic of curbside plantings. On this page you'll learn how to choose the best plants for this tough spot. But before you start, be sure to contact your city and utility companies to find out what you can and can't do with this area.

MAKE YOUR SELECTIONS To help you choose plants, look at commercial gardens, such as office buildings, shopping malls and service stations. They're often designed with durable plants that look good with minimal care. And check out Cindy's list of "Tough, street-wise plants" below.

Aim for 80 percent of the plants to have winter interest to keep the garden looking good year round. The other 20 percent can embellish the garden with flowers and seasonal changes.

PLANT IN LAYERS Start your design with a few short shrubs or grasses that won't block visibility. Next, look for an evergreen ground cover to help squeeze out weeds. Now add the flowering bulbs, perennials and annuals. Choose varieties that don't need constant deadheading or dividing. For example, the black-eyed Susans and sedum in these photos will give you lots of color with almost no care. And euphorbia, Russian sage and purple coneflower all tolerate hot, dry conditions once they're established.

Before you grab your spade and start sticking plants into your curbside garden willy-nilly, check out a few design tips with the photos on the next page. For all the pleasure streetside gardens give daily, they're definitely worth the small amount of work they require. □
— *Jim Childs*

TOUGH, STREET-WISE PLANTS

Plant Name	Cold/Heat Zones	Height/Width	Comments
Flowering crabapple *Malus* 'Prairie Fire'	4-8/8-1	20 ft./10 ft.	Tree; vivid pink flowers in spring; persistent fruit
Lavender *Lavandula* spp.	5-8/8-1	18 in./18 in.	Perennial; fragrant foliage and flowers; blooms in summer
False holly *Osmanthus heterophyllus* 'Goshiki'	6-9/9-1	5 ft./4 ft.	Evergreen shrub; green, gold and cream mottled leaves
Rock rose *Cistus xpulverulentus* 'Sunset'	7-9/9-1	2-3 ft./2-3 ft.	Evergreen shrub; pink flowers in summer; tolerates poor soil
Rose *Rosa* 'Radrazz' (Knockout™)	5-9/9-1	4 ft./4 ft.	Shrub; everblooming cherry-red flowers; disease resistant
Wintercreeper *Euonymus fortunei* 'Emerald Gaiety'	5-8/8-1	3-5 ft./3-6 ft.	Evergreen shrub; green and white variegation; easily pruned

CREATE A "WALK THROUGH" GARDEN like this one by growing plants on both sides of the sidewalk. If you don't have a privacy fence along the walk, choose a few plants for your curbside garden that tie it to the rest of your front yard or foundation planting.

ACCIDENTS DO HAPPEN. It's inevitable that people and pets will step into the beds. Choose plants that can take some abuse, like this tall sedum, sometimes called "live-forever." If they get damaged, they'll quickly bounce back.

PEOPLE WILL ALWAYS TAKE THE MOST DIRECT ROUTE, so let them. Include several paths or narrow sidewalks so visitors can walk through the garden rather than having to go all the way around. And trim tree branches up high enough people won't need to duck.

DON'T BLOCK THE VIEW of drivers or pedestrians, especially near intersections. Drive your car along the area you want to design and look around. Then park, get out and walk along the sidewalk to determine how tall plants can be.

6 tips for traffic-stopping appeal

WHILE YOUR CAR IS PARKED along the curb, open the passenger door. That'll help you figure out how far to set plants back from the street so people getting out of cars won't have to step directly into your perennials. Usually the distance is at least a foot, but wider is better. A border of bricks or a few stepping stones like these help show visitors where to step.

PUT SEPARATE SOAKER HOSES in each bed so you don't have them stretched over paths where they can trip people. When you attach hoses from the house, clearly mark their locations over the sidewalk with a barricade so passersby won't trip. Cover the hoses in the beds with mulch so they don't show.

Find a look that fits your style with one of our three regional designs.

A Fabulous Foundation Garden

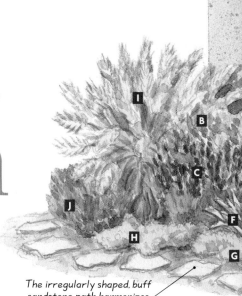

The irregularly shaped, buff sandstone path harmonizes with the house color and complements the informal style of the garden.

The situation

A 25-ft.-long bed in front of a south-facing urban or suburban home.

The homeowners want a colorful design that looks good in every season but is relatively low-maintenance.

WEB extra

Check out the complete **plans** for these three designs.

No matter what style your house is, a foundation garden is a terrific way to make your yard more welcoming. A great-looking foundation planting frames your house *and* blends it into your yard. And it needs to be easy care. When you've been out of town for three weekends in a row, you don't want to come home to a ratty looking garden that everyone else can see, too!

But all foundation plans certainly don't look alike. Travel around the country and you'll see as many different garden styles as you do house styles. And obviously we can't all grow the same plants.

That's why we asked garden designers from Colorado, Tennessee and Michigan to work up some gardens for you. All of the designs are based on the same footprint and general guidelines (see "The situation" at left). But as you can tell, each has its own regional flair and personal aesthetic.

For each garden, the designer chose the style of the home, plants that do well

in the region, and hardscaping of locally available materials. And though all three plans look good year round, we've shown each one in its peak season. As you look at the illustrations on the following pages, you'll see an explanation of the why and how for the design, the plant list and some specific tips on how to take care of the garden. You'll find the complete planting plan for each of these gardens on our Web extra.

Despite their very different looks, the plans use many plants that can be grown in several areas of the country. And the design ideas translate to many different regions and styles: Maybe you like Tom Peace's yuccas, Karen Petrey's wall fountain or Susan Martin's ranch update. So feel free to pick and choose plants and ideas from any of these plans, along with ones that reflect your personal taste, to create a special foundation design of your very own! □

— *Deborah Gruca*

Plant tips

Even drought-tolerant plants need consistent moisture until they're established.

For a more structured look, prune the blue rabbit brush, Russian sage and catmint in late spring for a dense, compact habit later in the year.

Space plants close enough that they'll knit together and look great. You'll minimize the need to weed and stake at the same time.

Code	Plant Name	No. to Plant	Type	Bloom Time	Bloom Color	Cold/Heat Zones	Height/ Width
A	Tall blue rabbit brush *Chrysothamnus nauseosus*	2	Perennial	Summer	Yellow	4-9/9-2	4 ft./4 ft.
B	Russian sage *Perovskia atriplicifolia*	3	Perennial	Late summer	Blue	4-9/9-1	3-4 ft./3 ft.
C	Tall pink hyssop *Agastache* 'Firebird'	7	Perennial	Summer-fall	Coral-pink	6-10/10-1	3-4 ft./2 ft.
D	Yellow coneflower *Echinacea* 'Sunrise' (Big Sky series)	6	Perennial	Summer	Yellow	4-10/10-1	2 ft./1 ft.
E	Variegated iris *Iris pallida* 'Aureo-Variegata'	7	Perennial	Spring	Blue	5-9/9-1	1 ft./1 ft.
F	Blue yucca *Yucca pallida*	2	Perennial	Spring	White	7-10/10-9	18 in./30 in.
G	Rock soapwort *Saponaria ocymoides*	11	Perennial	Spring	Pink	4-8/8-1	6-8 in./2 ft.
H	Yellow sunrose *Helianthemum* 'Wisley Primrose'	11	Perennial	Late spring	Yellow	6-8/8-6	6 in./2 ft.
I	Giant sacaton *Sporobolus wrightii*	1	Grass	Summer	Silver plumes	5-9/10-4	5 ft./4 ft.
J	Catmint *Nepeta racemosa* 'Walker's Low'	6	Perennial	Spring-fall	Blue	4-9/9-1	18-24 in./18 in.

TOUGH-AS-NAILS NATIVES

**Tom Peace,
Denver, Colorado**

This design reflects the relaxed attitude of this simple, buckskin-colored stucco bungalow. And in the arid mountain climate, it's important that every plant you choose is drought-tolerant and cold-hardy.

The tallest plant reaches to just 5 ft. — taller ones would be out of scale with the one-story house. For a two-story home, you'd want to include some larger shrubs and maybe even a small tree so the planting would have better proportions compared to the house.

You could do this plan with or without the path. As it is, it frames the bed, gives you a good spot to work from and helps the mail carrier move between houses. Get locally available stone (in this case sandstone) and don't worry about having it cut in regular shapes — this continues the casual look and will save money, too. If you wanted, you could even add more yellow sunrose and rock soapwort on the other side of the path so the path goes *through* the garden instead of bordering it.

This garden peaks in summer, which is what you see here. To blend the planting into the local landscape and to keep maintenance simple, Tom chose native plants that easily take the dry conditions of the area.

Most of these plants, such as the grass and the blue yucca, have a striking winter form whether the snow flies or not.

FLATTERING **FOUNDATIONS**

FRAGRANCE IN THE FALL

**K. Petrey Gardens,
Maryville, Tennessee**

Late summer and fall in this USDA zone 7 garden are awash with pastel colors and lots of texture contrasts. The straight lines of the bed and stone path reflect the style of this formal Federal-style brick home. A focal point — a traditional dolphin-head wall fountain — is reminiscent of Southern courtyards. It might seem odd that the stone path in front of the fountain doesn't lead

anywhere other than the wall. But it's acting more as a device to draw your eye to the fountain, and it gives the courtyard flavor to this garden without having an actual courtyard. If you wanted to, you could widen the path enough to make room for a small bench or a couple of chairs.

Although you don't want your plants to totally block the view out of your windows, it's a nice touch to have some of them poke up slightly above the bottom edge to help tie the house to the garden.

This garden is beautiful, but is designed with fragrance in mind, as well. Milder fall days are perfect for throwing open the

Plant tip

Though 'Fastigiata' boxwoods can reach 14 ft., they take pruning well. Clip them every year for the more formal look that's perfect for this setting.

windows, especially when the camellias' fragrance wafts into the room. Roses and lilies add their perfume earlier in the summer.

Code	Plant Name	No. to Plant	Type	Bloom Time	Bloom Color	Cold/Heat Zones	Height/ Width
A	Boxwood *Buxus sempervirens* 'Fastigiata'	2	Evergreen shrub	NA	NA	6-8/8-6	14 ft./6 ft.
B	Camellia *Camellia sinensis*	3	Shrub	Fall	White	7-9/8-7	4-6 ft./5 ft.
C	Japanese fatsia *Fatsia japonica*	2	Shrub	Fall	White	7-10/10-8	5-12 ft./5-12 ft.
D	Southern shield fern *Thelypteris kunthii*	4	Perennial	NA	NA	6-9/9-6	3-4 ft./3-4 ft.
E	Noisette rose *Rosa* 'Natchitoches Noisette'	1	Rose	Late spring-fall	Pink	7-10/10-6	3-5 ft./3-5 ft.
F	Siberian iris *Iris sibirica* 'Caesar's Brother'	10	Perennial	Late spring	Violet	3-9/9-1	2-3 ft./18-24 in.
G	Formosan lily *Lilium formosanum*	9	Perennial	Late summer	White	6-9/8-1	2-6 ft./1 ft.
H	Rosemary *Rosmarinus* 'Hill Hardy'	3	Perennial	Summer	Purple	7-10/12-8	2 ft./2 ft.
I	Hardy mum *Chrysanthemum* 'Country Girl'	8	Perennial	Fall	Pink	6-9/9-1	24-30 in./30 in.
J	Catmint *Nepeta racemosa* 'Walker's Low'	10	Perennial	Spring-fall	Blue	4-9/9-1	18-24 in./18 in.

Japanese fatsia trained up the wall and a stone path draw attention to the wall fountain.

Add in soft yellow pansies and lantanas to bridge the seasons.

To get berries on your female hollies, you'll need one male nearby.

Forever & Ever hydrangeas, which bloom on old and new wood, and weigelas wrap around the dogwood and enhance the curved line of the bed.

Code	Plant Name	No. to Plant	Type	Bloom Time	Bloom Color	Cold/Heat Zones	Height/ Width
A	Dwarf lilac *Syringa* Sugar Plum Fairy® ('Bailsugar')	3	Shrub	Spring	Lavender	3-7/7-5	4-5 ft./4-5 ft.
B	Holly *Ilex xmeserveae* 'Blue Boy'	1	Shrub	NA	NA	5-9/9-5	8-10 ft./6 ft.
C	Holly *Ilex xmeserveae* 'Blue Girl'	2	Shrub	NA	NA	5-9/9-5	8-10 ft./6 ft.
D	Weigela *Weigela florida* 'My Monet'™	5	Shrub	Late spring	Pink	4-9/9-1	12-18 in./18 in.
E	Kousa dogwood *Cornus kousa chinensis* 'Milky Way'	1	Shrub	Late spring	White	5-8/8-1	15-25 ft./15-25 ft.
F	Siberian iris *Iris sibirica* 'White Swirl'	6	Perennial	Late spring	White	3-9/9-1	32 in./18 in.
G	Lamb's ear *Stachys byzantina* 'Big Ears'	13	Perennial	Late spring	Lavender	4-8/8-1	8-10 in./spreads
H	Rose *Rosa* Pink Knock Out®	3	Rose	Late spring-fall	Pink	4-9/9-1	3-4 ft./3-4 ft.
I	Spurge *Euphorbia hypericifolia* Diamond Frost™ ('Inneuphe')	6	Annual	Spring-fall	White	10/9-1	8-12 in./10-12 in.
J	Hydrangea *Hydrangea macrophylla* Forever & Ever® ('Early Sensation')	5	Shrub	Summer-fall	Pink	4-9/9-1	3-5 ft./3-5 ft.

SHOWY SHRUBS IN SPRING

Susan M. Martin, Holland, Michigan

The bold, curving lines of this bed add interest to the foundation of this 1950s ranch. But the depth of the bed is less than half its length, so the garden doesn't overwhelm the single-story house.

A vase-shaped kousa dogwood at the corner of the house creates an instant focal point for this design, especially in spring. But the dramatic sweep of the bed's curved edge brings your eye toward the sidewalk and the front door, where most of the growing season, you'll get a burst of color from the three Knock Out roses. Lots of rounded shrubs repeat that curve, with some spiky foliage here and there to echo the vertical windows.

Gardeners make the most of the short growing season in northern Michigan, so this plan uses several shrubs to ensure that there is something of interest at all times. If you're planting in stages, start with these shrubs, even though it's tempting to put in the smaller perennials first. Beginning with the garden's "bones" will get you to a finished look more quickly.

Finally, when it comes to edging, save yourself some money — don't buy any. Instead, since this is a flat lawn, a trenched, or English, edge works just fine and won't distract from the house or garden. Want to know how to put in a trenched edge? We'll show you in "On The Cutting Edge" on p. 270.

Plant tips

Prune your holly and hydrangea to keep them compact. Do the holly at any time of year, but clip the hydrangea in early spring. And be sure to remove the faded hydrangea blooms throughout the summer to keep it flowering.

When you plant a young kousa dogwood, give it plenty of room. It'll look upright when it's young but will eventually branch out horizontally.

Instant Impact

4 ways containers make a splashy entrance

In spring, when the weather is nice and your energy is high, it's easy to come up with lots of new plans and projects for your garden. But hold on a minute. If the time you can spare to work in the garden is really limited to a few precious hours each week, you (and your garden) will be a lot happier when you know a few time-saving tips and shortcuts.

Want a big splash at your entry? Containers can do it almost instantly. It's true that they usually need to be watered throughout the summer, but there are ways you can maximize the impact of plants in pots while minimizing the effort. Let me show you how you can save time, work and money. □

— *Deborah Gruca*

You won't need to water bigger pots as often.

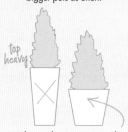

Wide, sturdy containers are less likely to tip on windy days.

Wider-mouthed pots are a lot easier to plant and empty.

1 THE RIGHT POTS = LESS WORK There are more choices than ever when it comes to containers. But don't be seduced by unusual shapes. Unique isn't always easier to take care of.

Although small plants look adorable in petite pots, fight the urge to use many of them. Most plants' roots soon fill any container, and with a small pot, it'll be close to impossible to keep the soil moist in warm weather.

A tall, upright plant, such as a shrub, has larger roots and will look (and grow) best in a large, upright pot. But make sure the pot isn't too top-heavy (especially if it's a lightweight material) or you'll be setting it back up at the end of every windy day.

Finally, think twice about planting in rounded containers that narrow at the opening. They can be a headache at the end of the season if you want to save any of the plants. You may actually have to cut up the root mass just to empty the pot. Even root-bound plants slide easily out of a straight-sided or wide-mouthed container.

2 QUICK FIX FOR CLAY If you live in a newer home, you may struggle to garden in heavy clay soil. You *can* amend the soil, but with clay, sometimes that's a never-ending battle — so why fight it? Growing in containers instead is a quick fix — no digging or amending necessary! Here, a dozen lush containers fill in beautifully around a few clay-tolerant shrubs such as barberries, spireas and Japanese tree lilac. The gravel mulch isn't great for most perennials and annuals in the ground, but works fine around trees and shrubs. It lasts forever and makes a stable base for your containers.

It's hard to tell exactly which plants are in containers!

3 SPRING FOR STRIKING CONTAINERS —BUT NOT TOO MANY Buy a few showy containers, like the large turquoise ones around this entry. Repeating this color creates a pulled-together look and gives season-long color. Planted with a large swaying grass and placed on the front stoop, one container draws attention and visitors right to the door. But too many of these would be overkill. Save money by using plastic or terra-cotta for plants that will cascade enough to hide their containers by early summer anyway.

4 CREATE SPECIAL EFFECTS Many plants will grow differently in containers than they do in the ground. With less elbow room in a pot, some vigorous annuals may spill over the sides and take on a trailing habit. Take advantage of this to get a full-sized "shrub" in just a month. By midsummer, a lush trailing ground cover like this red petunia can fill out and flow down the sides of its tall pot. It gives the effect of a flowering shrub, like a weigela or spirea, but in a fraction of the time. *And* it blooms and blooms all season long.

Follow our pointers for a perfect foundation planting — no matter which direction your house faces!

The Directional Challenge

Quick, what direction does the front of your house face? As a gardener, you need to know this because it influences which plants you'll be able to grow there. To me, there's nothing more frustrating than finding a plant I want and then discovering it won't grow where I want it to. For example, you really like the bright foliage of a golden privet and think it would look perfect with your burgundy front door. But your house faces north. In that heavy shade, the leaves will be green instead of the gold you fell in love with.

WHAT ARE THE DIRECTIONAL PROBLEMS? The number one consideration is usually the amount of sun that reaches the plants. But it could be combined with a moisture situation, either too much or too little. And wind — we all know how it can affect plants, especially if you live where winters are cold and dry. More problems arise when one end of the planting is different than the other. For example, on an eastern exposure the south corner gets much stronger sun than the north.

DESIGN LIKE A PRO Before we get into solving those design problems and helping you choose the best plants for each exposure, let me share a few basic tips. These will work for almost any foundation planting, no matter what direction it faces.

First, choose plants that have a long season of interest. Since these beds are usually narrow, there's not much room to hide something that isn't looking its best most of the time. And avoid lots of pyramidal-shaped plants like upright junipers or columnar pears. Their form is strong and they draw attention away from the architecture of the house. One or two strong verticals are OK, just don't overdo them.

Be sure to consider the eventual size of the plants you choose. You don't want to spend a lot of time trying to keep a 10-foot-tall shrub pruned to 4 feet so it won't block windows. But if plants are too small, they tend to get lost. This is especially true in front of a tall house.

And finally, here's a design tip that's easy to follow and makes your landscape look professionally done: To draw attention to your front door, set the tallest plants at the outside corners of your house. They should be about two thirds the height of the roof top or less. Then frame the door, the area you want visitors to spot first, with lower plants. Imagine drawing a line from the top of each corner plant to the top of the plants near your door. The lines should roughly form a "V." None of the plants between those two points should be taller than that imaginary line.

No matter where you live, whether it's a cold windswept area or a more temperate climate, the directional design solutions on the next pages will help you dress up your foundation in style. □

— *Jim Childs*

ILLUSTRATION: Mark Marturello

*Turn the page
to learn challenges
and solutions for
each direction.* ▶

A dense evergreen on the northwest corner, like this arborvitae, helps protect the rest of the plantings from sweeping winter wind.

North

NORTH SHADE

THE CHALLENGE This house is only one story high, but no matter what height yours is, it casts a triangle of shade on the north side. That means shade is deepest in the center, with some morning light creeping in from the east and strong afternoon sun from the west. A plant that works fine on one end may not be happy on the other — and probably neither will like the full shade of the center.

Moisture may not reach the north side if rains come from the south and west. But once this area does get wet, the soil can stay damp for a long time. And remember, you have to contend with cold blasts of winter wind, too.

THE SOLUTION Choose plants for the center that like full shade and, depending on your soil, tolerate moist or dry conditions. An asymmetric design will work best to let cool gentle sun from the east into the bed and block dry winter winds from the west. Use a tree or large shrub that will cast dappled shade on the east. On the west end, a dense evergreen solves the wind problem.

Code	Plant Name	No. to Plant	Blooms	Type	Cold/Heat Zones	Height/ Width	Special Features
A	**Common witchhazel** *Hamamelis virginiana*	1	Yellow-orange; fall	Shrub	3-8/8-1	15 ft./10 ft.	Large shade-tolerant shrub filters some sun from the east
B	**Five-leaf aralia** *Eleutherococcus sieboldianus* 'Variegatus'	1	Green-white; spring	Shrub	4-8/8-1	8 ft./5 ft.	Variegated foliage even in full shade; spines on stems; tolerates pollution
C	**Arborvitae** *Thuja occidentalis* 'Brabant'	1	NA	Evergreen shrub	2-7/7-1	12 ft./6 ft.	Soft, fragrant foliage; narrow form allows some late sun in and blocks winter wind
D	**Yew** *Taxus xmedia* 'Densiformis'	3	NA	Evergreen shrub	5-7/7-1	4 ft./4 ft.	Dark green shade-tolerant evergreen; good for year-round interest
E	**Rhododendron** *Rhododendron* 'Olga'	3	Pink; spring	Evergreen shrub	4-8/8-1	3 ft./3 ft.	Small evergreen leaves; may rebloom in fall; excellent spring color
F	**Hydrangea** *Hydrangea arborescens* 'Annabelle'	1	White; late summer	Shrub	4-9/9-1	4 ft./5 ft.	Long-lasting flowers change from white to papery brown and last into winter
G	**Japanese painted fern** *Athyrium niponicum pictum* 'Ursula's Red'	6	NA	Perennial	5-8/8-1	18 in./18 in.	Silvery foliage brightens up shaded north exposure; prefers moist soil
H	**Solomon's seal** *Polygonatum odoratum pluriflorum* 'Variegatum'	15	White; spring	Perennial	3-8/8-1	30 in./12 in.	Elegant arching stems with variegated leaves; spring, summer and fall interest
I	**Hosta** *Hosta lancifolia*	19	Lavender; late summer	Perennial	3-9/9-1	12 in./18 in.	Mass of clean green leaves help tie the design together

Code	Plant Name	No. to Plant	Blooms	Type	Cold/Heat Zones	Height/Width	Special Features
A	Burning bush *Euonymus alatus*	1	NA	Shrub	4-9/9-1	8 ft./8 ft.	Large shrub to filter morning sun and keep nearby plants in cool shade longer
B	Juniper *Juniperus chinensis* 'Hetzii Columnaris'	1	NA	Evergreen shrub	3-9/9-1	6 ft./3 ft.	Trained into a formal spiral shape, this evergreen draws attention to the door
C	Lilac *Syringa pubescens patula* 'Miss Kim'	3	Lavender-pink; late spring	Shrub	5-8/8-1	4 ft./4 ft.	Late-blooming lilac adds seasonal interest; can be clipped into a formal shape
D	Juniper *Juniperus procumbens* 'Nana'	3	NA	Evergreen shrub	3-9/9-1	10 in./24 in.	Low-spreading ground cover; very heat tolerant; good winter interest
E	Flowering crabapple *Malus* Red Jewel™	1	White; spring	Tree	4-8/8-1	15 ft./12 ft.	Small tree blocks hot afternoon sun; pink buds open white
F	Rose *Rosa* 'The Fairy'	14	Pale pink; summer	Shrub	4-9/9-1	2 ft./2 ft.	Lots of pink flower clusters for excellent summer color
G	Spirea *Spiraea japonica* 'Little Princess'	3	Rose pink; summer	Shrub	4-9/9-1	2 ft./3 ft.	Dense mound of small leaves; prune after flowers fade to keep the shrub tidy

SCORCHING SOUTH

THE CHALLENGE If there's no shade from a large tree nearby, scorching sun and reflected heat from the wall of the house are abusive, especially if you live where summers are hot. In an area with cold winters, this side can heat up on a sunny winter day. Plants think it's spring and try to resume growing. The end result can range from sunburn, especially on conifers, to damaged twigs, buds and stems. These dramatic fluctuations can even kill plants.

Rain reaches the south side easily, but it can evaporate fast, too. You'll probably need to do some extra watering during the summer.

THE SOLUTION Block hot afternoon sun with a small tree or large shrub, especially on the west end. Choose heat- and drought-tolerant plants and use mulch to conserve moisture and help reduce watering. Flower buds on early spring-blooming plants, like a star magnolia, can try to open on a warm, sunny winter day and end up *blasting*, drying up and not opening properly. Varieties that tend to bloom a bit later in spring work best on this exposure. If necessary, protect evergreen foliage and tender leaf and flower buds with a burlap screen or an antidesiccant spray.

Figure the ultimate diameter of the plants you choose and then set them away from the house. That way air can circulate and keep the plants cooler in summer.

South

With afternoon shade, you won't have problems with winter burn on evergreens on the east side of the house.

WEB
extra

Complete
planting plans
for all four gardens

THE GENTLE EAST

THE CHALLENGE Cool morning light, consistent moisture and no strong winds — sounds like the perfect growing spot, doesn't it? However, plants that need lots of sunlight won't be happy in this part shade area. And because of the lack of hot sun, moisture doesn't evaporate out of the soil very fast on an east exposure.

SOLUTION Even though the east side often looks like full sun, grow plants that do best in part shade. A small tree on the south corner keeps the shade consistent across the foundation. Problems with cold winter winds whipping around the northeast corner of your house? A dense evergreen placed there will help. And because the soil tends to stay damp, don't use plants that require very dry soil or you may have problems with rotting roots.

This is the side of the house where you can get away with shrubs that may be marginally hardy in your zone. The gentle sun, moist soil and lack of desiccating winds are easy on plants.

Code	Plant Name	No. to Plant	Blooms	Type	Cold/Heat Zones	Height/ Width	Special Features
A	Japanese maple *Acer palmatum* 'Bloodgood'	1	NA	Tree	5-8/8-1	12 ft./10 ft.	Red foliage holds color in part shade; one of the hardiest cultivars
B	Rhododendron *Rhododendron* 'Nova Zembla'	1	Red; spring	Evergreen shrub	5-8/8-1	5 ft./5 ft.	Evergreen leaves and large flower buds won't be damaged on an east exposure
C	Boxwood *Buxus* 'Green Mountain'	2	NA	Evergreen shrub	5-8/8-1	3 ft./3 ft.	Evergreen leaves will stay a bright green in part shade; pyramidal form
D	Hydrangea *Hydrangea macrophylla* 'Monred' (Red n' Pretty®)	3	Red; summer	Shrub	5-9/9-1	4 ft./3 ft.	Flower color holds well out of hot afternoon sun
E	Holly *Ilex cornuta* 'Burfordii'	1	White; spring	Evergreen shrub	6-9/9-1	10 ft./7 ft.	Dense evergreen with red berries for winter interest
F	Daphne *Daphne xburkwoodii* 'Carol Mackie'	2	Pink; spring	Shrub	4-7/7-1	3 ft./3 ft.	Semi evergreen; variegated foliage; fragrant flowers
G	Yew *Taxus xmedia* 'Geers' (Margarita™)	1	NA	Evergreen shrub	5-7/7-1	42 in./42 in.	Gold evergreen foliage won't burn on an east exposure
H	Hakonechloa *Hakonechloa macra* 'Aureola'	23	NA	Perennial	5-9/9-1	18 in./24 in.	Grass with gold foliage will like the cool moist soil on the east side
I	Hosta *Hosta* 'Halcyon'	5	Lavender; summer	Perennial	3-9/9-1	20 in./36 in.	Blue foliage cultivar does well in part to full shade

Code	Plant Name	No. to Plant	Blooms	Type	Cold/Heat Zones	Height/ Width	Special Features
A	**Viburnum** *Viburnum sargentii* 'Onondaga'	1	White; summer	Shrub	4-7/7-1	10 ft./10 ft.	Tough, durable shrub for a harsh exposure; ornamental red fruit
B	**Juniper** *Juniperus xpfitzeriana* 'Sea Green'	2	NA	Evergreen shrub	4-9/9-1	5 ft./5 ft.	Bright green foliage even in winter sun and dry winds; easy to shear for size
C	**Tree lilac** *Syringa reticulata* 'Ivory Silk'	1	Creamy white; summer	Tree	3-8/8-1	15 ft./10 ft.	Very hardy ornamental tree; blocks hot afternoon sun
D	**Maiden grass** *Miscanthus sinensis* 'Adagio'	1	Buff; late summer	Perennial	5-9/9-1	3 ft./3 ft.	Takes hot sun and harsh winds in stride; good winter interest
E	**Fountain grass** *Pennisetum alopecuroides* 'Hameln'	6	Buff; late summer	Perennial	5-9/9-1	2 ft./3 ft.	Airy filler plant is tough and durable for a west exposure
F	**Smokebush** *Cotinus coggygria* 'Velvet Cloak'	1	Burgundy; summer	Shrub	5-9/9-1	5 ft./4 ft.	Cut back to 1 ft. each spring to contain size; burgundy foliage adds summer color
G	**Deutzia** *Deutzia gracilis* 'Nikko'	5	White; early summer	Shrub	4-8/8-1	2 ft./3 ft.	Spring flowers and burgundy fall foliage; easily pruned if it grows too large
H	**Barberry** *Berberis thunbergii atropurpurea* 'Atropurpurea Nana' (Crimson Pygmy)	2	NA	Shrub	5-8/8-1	2 ft./3 ft.	Small dense shrub with burgundy leaves; tolerates almost any conditions

WEST SUNSHINE

THE CHALLENGE This side can fool even the most experienced gardener. Because it's in shade all morning, I used to think of it as part shade. But the afternoon sun is strong. It's better to treat a west exposure as a full sun spot. And the wind can be a problem here, in both summer and winter. Granted, the rain gets to the plants, but that hot afternoon sun and strong west wind suck it right back out of the leaves and soil again.

SOLUTION Stick to full sun plants only, and make sure they're tough ones. This is not the spot for temperamental or marginally hardy plants. On the south end, a large shrub or small tree will block some of the hot sun. And on the north corner, curb a bit of that strong winter wind with a dense, hardy plant like a viburnum.

On the north corner, keep the plantings dense, like this viburnum, to block winter winds.

West

Looking for some live entertainment?

Bring in the Birds!

ILLUSTRATION: Mavis Augustine Torke

Botanical Names

Cedar *Cedrus* spp.
Dogwood *Cornus* spp.
Hawthorn
    Crataegus spp.
Hemlock *Tsuga* spp.
Pine *Pinus* spp.
Serviceberry
    Amelanchier spp.
Spruce *Picea* spp.

Have you ever watched a robin splashing enthusiastically in a birdbath? Or witnessed a young bird step from a branch for its very first flight? If you have, you know what a joy watching our feathered neighbors can be. What you might not realize is that there are some simple things you can do to make your yard a more enticing place to all kinds of birds. By providing things birds need for food, water and shelter, you can make your place inviting to a surprising number of them.

Like other wild animals, birds are constantly on the lookout for food. So the easiest step is to put up feeders and keep them full. And to increase the number of different types of birds, add a constant source of water for drinking and bathing.

But only about 25 percent of wild birds will actually take advantage of bird feeders, so be sure to grow some of their favorite plants, as well. In addition to food, provide a place to take cover in storms and a safe place for raising a family.

Here, and on the next pages, I'll share tips to make your back yard into an enticing haven for lots of these feathered treasures.

Hang handfuls of nesting materials like string, yarn or lint on nails near feeders in early spring.

A pond will also attract dragonflies and other insects that birds will eat, as well as wildlife like frogs and bats.

FOOD

PROVIDE BERRIES OR SEEDS ALL YEAR
Because they fruit at different times, grow a couple different varieties of plants like serviceberry, hawthorn and dogwood to extend the berry season.

DOUBLE THE NUMBER OF YOUR FAVORITE BERRY PLANTS You'll insure that there's enough for both you and the birds. Plant fruit-bearing plants away from sidewalks, driveways and patio areas to reduce the mess.

FEED SEED, SUET AND FRUIT
Different birds have different tastes.

KEEP FOUR-LEGGED VISITORS OUT OF FEEDERS Use baffles below feeders or wrap posts in aluminum flashing to thwart furry looters. And don't grow plants close to feeders. (They can hide predators like cats!)

WATER

DON'T LET THE WATER RUN DRY
Keep birdbaths, ponds or bogs filled all season. Reliable sources of water, especially moving water, will attract more birds.

RINSE AND REFILL YOUR BIRDBATH OFTEN This will help prevent disease and mosquitoes. In winter, keep it ice-free with a heater, or empty ice and refill the birdbath every day.

FURNISH FIRM FOOTING Buy a birdbath with a rough or textured floor or add small stones to the bottom to prevent injury to birds.

PLACE YOUR POND IN THE OPEN
Avoid chemical runoff from surrounding lawn areas by building on level ground. Make an area of the pond 2 in. deep or less so birds won't drown.

SHELTER

PLANT EVERGREENS FOR NESTING
Spruce, hemlock, cedar and pine are great for nesting for cardinals, sparrows, towhees and other birds.

BLOCK WINTER WINDS WITH TALL TREES This will give birds a little relief from nasty winter storms that can sap their strength, thus helping them survive cold temperatures.

VARY HEIGHTS OF TREES, SHRUBS AND OTHER PLANTS You'll fill the needs of different birds who prefer to nest and feed in tree tops, shrubs or on the ground.

PROVIDE A SAFE PLACE TO PREEN
It's hard to fly with wet feathers. Grow shrubs within 10 ft. of ponds or bird-baths for safe places to dry off a bit before flying away.

Turn the page to learn about seven great back yard birds.

Lure squirrels away by giving them their own feeders far from your bird feeders.

To get rid of algae in your birdbath, add a half cup of bleach to the water, scrub with a stiff brush and rinse with clean water before refilling.

WEB extra

Make a *pinecone bird feeder.*

WORDS ON BIRDS

WHERE YOU'LL FIND THEM IN:

- Summer
- Winter
- Year-round

The kinds of birds you'll see visiting your yard depends on the area of the country where you live. City or country, woods or farmland also influence the types of birds. There are thousands of different birds that make their homes in the United States and Canada. Here are seven of my favorite birds that range over much of North America. Each is beautiful, unique and a joy to watch.

I'll share what makes them special, why you might want them around and some tips for attracting them to your back yard. So go ahead and lay out a tempting spread for your own favorites and create a haven to help them to feel right at home. I think you'll agree that it's pretty cheap admission for such great entertainment! □

— *Deborah Gruca*

BALTIMORE ORIOLE
Icterus galbula

The Baltimore oriole loves tall trees, where it searches for insect snacks among the leaves. But it will build its distinctive, hanging pouchlike nest in any available deciduous tree or shrub. A lovely call and bright-orange plumage make it an easy bird to spot. This bird is also a water-lover. Place a birdbath nearby so it can keep those beautiful feathers healthy.

Attract the oriole with fruit, especially oranges, or put up a nectar feeder. You'll often see it visiting mulberries for both insects and fruit.

TOP TIP Set out a small bowl of grape jelly next to your feeders to get orioles returning each year.

BLACK-CAPPED CHICKADEE
Parus atricapillus

Diminutive and active, this little insect- and nut-eater is very social — with humans, as well as other birds. Despite its size, it packs a loud whistle. Several species of chickadees live in a wide range across the United States and Canada. Though it will also feed on seeds, nuts, fruits and berries, its main food focus is insects found on mature trees, both conifers and deciduous. And because it feeds on the eggs as well as adults, it is excellent at keeping all kinds of trees safe from some very nasty bugs.

TOP TIP Grow royal or cinnamon ferns. Adults will use the fronds as a soft lining for their nests.

WHITE-BREASTED NUTHATCH
Sitta carolinensis

Forests are usually where you'll find the nuthatch, but it frequents back yard feeders where it finds them. You'll often see the nuthatch on the trunks of larger trees, probing the bark for insects. Clinging upside-down to the tree, it works from the top of the trunk, spiraling its way down to the ground.

The nuthatch loves seeds of conifers and oaks, as well as the insects that live on maples. Plant favorite foods like sunflowers.

TOP TIP A serving of mealworms (available from feed stores) in a tray feeder is a special treat.

DOWNY WOODPECKER
Picoides pubescens

This small member of the woodpecker family is easy to spot at the suet feeder or clinging to the bark of any tree. Insects make up most of its diet, but it also loves fruit, berries and nuts. Woodpeckers' acute hearing can pick up the sound of insect larvae and beetles boring under bark or even the wood in your siding. Having one hammering on your house may be a good sign you need to call the insect exterminator.

TOP TIP In summer months, offer a nectar feeder to satisfy this bird's craving for sweets.

NORTHERN CARDINAL
Cardinalis cardinalis

Possibly the most-easily recognized bird anywhere, the cardinal offers a melodious song, splashy red color and jaunty crest all year, since it does not migrate in winter. Females sport a subtler brown. Its heavy conical bill is good for cracking hard seed hulls but is also adept at eating soft fruits and insects like potato bugs and tomato hornworms.

Cardinals really enjoy birdbaths. A bit of clean water will provide you with lots of lively entertainment.

TOP TIP Cardinals and other birds love to eat salt. Put out a bowl of rock salt or set out a salt block (available at feed stores).

AMERICAN GOLDFINCH
Carduelis tristis

While some birds eat from a varied menu, the American goldfinch is chiefly a seed-eater. Niger seed offered in niger tube feeders is a surefire draw for this lively gold beauty. (Females are olive-green.) Millet and black oil sunflower seeds are also popular foods.

The goldfinch eats seeds from perennials, such as coneflower, annuals, such as cosmos, and even veggies, such as lettuce. And best of all? Dandelion and ragweed seeds, as well as those of other weeds, are special favorites!

TOP TIP Grow coneflowers and leave them standing for tasty seed snacks.

CEDAR WAXWING
Bombycilla cedrorum

Though this sleek bird's range includes nearly all of the United States, it rarely makes an appearance at your back yard feeder, instead, relishing the fruit from trees and shrubs. For most of the year it hangs out in small flocks of 12 to 20 birds. This bird is easy to attract, since the flock is always on the move, searching out a supply of ripe fruits and berries. Watch for its curious habit of passing berries or flowers back and forth between birds.

TOP TIP Any type of red berry will grab this bird's eye and get it to return to your yard year after year.

PHOTOS: © Jay Gilliam

the YEAR IN GARDENING **167**

Smart design ideas turn a small space into a showpiece

Simple Elegance

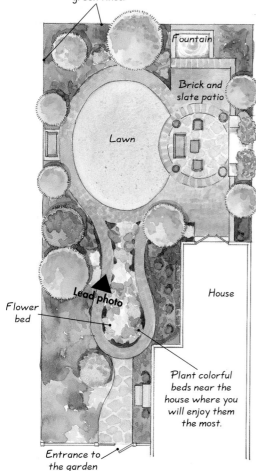

Soften the look of stark walls with dark green vines.

Fountain

Brick and slate patio

Lawn

Lead photo

House

Flower bed

Plant colorful beds near the house where you will enjoy them the most.

Entrance to the garden

North ▶ This symbol indicates the direction the photo was taken in the garden.

W hether you have a very large garden or a small one, you want to make every square foot count. First you want space to plant — after all, what's a garden without flowers and shrubs? Second, a bit of open space where you can stand back and look at the garden is always nice. And third, it should be easy to maintain. Gardening may be your passion, but you probably don't want it to monopolize all of your time.

ENTER THE WORLD OF ILLUSION As you step into the Cathcarts' South Carolina garden, you'll discover there are no grand vistas you could "borrow" to make the area look larger. But other techniques add the feeling of space.

The first thing that draws your attention is a flower bed set against a dark backdrop. Bright colors jump forward while the dark wall recedes to give an illusion of distance. Even at first glance, you'd guess this garden is larger than it really is.

In the photo, it's impossible to see the walls that enclose two sides of this roughly 40-foot-square back yard. They're covered with dense vines that help them blend into the garden. Check out the plan and you'll see there are also several trees in front of these walls. The light-colored crape myrtle trunks contrasts against leafy vines and break-up the flat vertical surface. To keep the walls from looking tall and imposing, limbs have been removed to create a canopy that covers top of

Open up the center and place the plants and structures around the edges if your small garden feels cramped.

the fence. And the foliage overhead adds to the romantic and intimate feel without wasting space underneath.

A small garden is often packed full of plants. But this one has a bigger visual impact because there's plenty of open space. The plantings are confined to the edges so the garden doesn't look cluttered.

RELAX IN CASUAL FORMALITY
When most people think of a formal garden, they think of straight lines. But the only straight edges you can find here are the garden walls, house and arbor. Yet the combination of gentle curves and crisp edges that define the beds definitely gives this garden a formal look and feel. A few classic materials and

structures, like old paving bricks and a white arbor, also add to the feeling of formality. So does limiting the plant pallet. Using fewer plants for your eyes to focus on lends a quiet, understated look to this garden.

On the next pages you'll discover more photos and lots more tips on how to keep a small garden looking great.

Botanical Names

Crape myrtle
Lagerstroemia indica

SMALL SPACE **DESIGN TIPS**

Botanical Names

Azalea
  Rhododendron hybrid
Daffodil
  Narcissus hybrid
Nemesia
  Nemesia hybrid
Pansy *Viola* hybrid
Stock
  Matthiola incana
Tulip *Tulipa* hybrid

Keeping a garden colorful, especially a small one, can be a challenge. There's no room for grand borders where you can plant enough variety that as one flowering plant begins to fade, another takes the spotlight. And if you live where summers bake, as they do in this South Carolina garden, it can be even harder. In the "3 garden tips for hot zones," on the next page, I'll share tips to keep your garden colorful. One of the best ways to make sure the color lasts in any size area is to plant a mass of annuals, like the ones in photo 2 below.

YOU STILL NEED A FOCAL POINT
Yes, every garden, including a small one, needs a focal point. In this one, the white arbor in photo 3 is sure to draw your attention. One white-painted element in a setting like this is enough. Too much white, just like too many plantings, would be confusing and overpowering in a small garden — you wouldn't know where to look. And since white tends to appear closer than it really is, it would make the garden feel smaller. But picking one item, like a structure, and painting it a bright color or white

gives it importance. Notice how the furniture and container are painted a dark green, almost black, so the emphasis is directed to the arbor.

To avoid a jumbled look, keep the number of different elements to a minimum in a small garden. Brick and slate are two classic garden materials that complement almost any style. In this garden, the brick forms a path that flows easily into an oval around a patch of lawn. The path leads you to a small, round seating area of slate. If the patio were brick, it would be fine. But

(2) Focus color where you'll spend the most time — in this case, the porch. This small bed of annuals and the billowing window boxes will be colorful for several months, long after the azaleas finish.

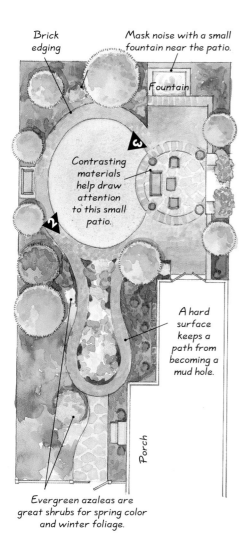

Brick edging

Mask noise with a small fountain near the patio.

Fountain

Contrasting materials help draw attention to this small patio.

A hard surface keeps a path from becoming a mud hole.

Porch

Evergreen azaleas are great shrubs for spring color and winter foliage.

▶ This symbol indicates the direction the photo was taken in the garden.

(3) Repetition helps create a put-together look. This arbor and furniture take their cue from the house and shutters, and the flower colors carry throughout the garden.

the contrast of the slate gives the patio more visual draw.

Hardscaping materials, like brick and slate, serve more than just a design purpose in any garden. But in a small garden, foot traffic is often concentrated into only a few areas. Lots of people walking in the same spot is hard on turf. Eventually you'll end up with muddy paths. But a solid, durable surface can stand up to lots of traffic and still look terrific. It may be more expensive than turf, but in the long run it's well worth the cost.

Along the paths you'll notice that bricks have been set on end, a couple of inches high, to make an edging. Because it matches the walkway material, this edge is barely noticeable. Yet it keeps the soil in the beds from washing out during torential downpours and making a mess on the path.

There's one final illusion I have to tell you about. Look again at the arbor in the photo above. Did you notice it's more than just a pretty focal point or a lovely spot to sit and smell the roses? Both sides have doors that open to reveal storage areas for tools. Perfect for a small garden where no space is wasted — and an idea you can use no matter what the size of your garden. □

— *Jim Childs*

3 GARDEN TIPS FOR HOT ZONES

Gardening where winters are cool, not cold, and summers are scorching requires some extra attention, especially when it comes to plants.

PRECHILL BULBS In USDA zone 7 and warmer, the soil doesn't get cold enough for tulips, daffodils and other spring bulbs. However, you can order prechilled bulbs and plant them in winter.

CHANGE OUT THE BEDS If you live where the soil never freezes, cool-season annuals, such as the stocks, pansies and nemesias in this garden, can be planted in autumn and will last through spring.

CONSIDER THE LOCATION Many plants that Northern gardeners place in full sun will probably do better in a bit of shade in a Southern garden. If in doubt, it's always best to find a spot out of the scorching afternoon sun.

A shady getaway that's beautiful all year long

Woodland Stroll

PHOTOS: © Charles Mann

Botanical Names

Azalea
Rhododendron spp.
Fothergilla
Fothergilla gardenii
Hemlock *Tsuga* spp.
Holly *Ilex* spp.
Japanese maple
Acer palmatum
Rhododendron
Rhododendron spp.
Trillium *Trillium* spp.
Witchhazel
Hamamelis spp.
Yew *Taxus* spp.

Who says shade gardens have to be bland? Not Steve and Joan Hoitink. They've used shade and the natural contours of their property to create this beautiful woodland garden in Spokane, Washington. And it's easy to grow and maintain, too!

Woodland gardens don't happen overnight; they evolve over a period of years. Steve and Joan have been working on their roughly 95-by-160-foot garden for about 40 years. And they still love how it constantly changes.

CHANGE WITH THE SEASONS Spring is the most flowery time. Trees' leaves are starting to unfurl. So the only shade is cast by a delicate web of branches and tiny foliage — perfect conditions for azaleas and rhododendrons to put on their show. Early perennials, like the white trillium in the center of the photo, also revel in the soft spring light.

Summer brings a textural garden, filled with ferns and other foliage perennials that do best in deep shade. Between the leafy canopy and garden floor are shrubs and small trees. Splashes of summer interest have been added by selecting plants with colorful foliage, like the red-leafed Japanese maple you see in the photo.

Fall brings shades of yellow, orange and red foliage. Witchhazels, fothergillas and even some of the ferns give the garden one last hurrah before the snow flies.

Winter's cold won't stop this garden. A few evergreen perennials, broadleaf shrubs, such as hollies, and some conifers, like yews and hemlock, look great against the bare branches of the deciduous plants. Most of the evergreens grow a bit looser in shade than they would out in the sun, but that just contributes to the casual, natural feel.

So where do you start when you want to create a garden like this? Well, what's the first thing that comes to mind when you think about taking a walk in the woods? If you said shade from large trees, I'd agree. They're the backbone of this garden. Many folks with lots of large trees have trouble dealing with all the shade. But that's just the ticket for this style of garden.

Join me as we continue our tour and learn some tips and techniques for making your own woodland garden.

A deck and small lawn area provide ideal places to relax and view the woodland garden.

Shade trees form the canopy for a woodland.

A natural-looking stream recirculates between this garden shed and the pond near the deck.

North

What more could you ask from a shade garden than to have loads of spring blooms, interesting summer textures and colorful fall foliage? Sprinkle in a few evergreens to make it look good in winter and you're set. It's not as difficult as you may think.

DESIGNING WITH NATURE

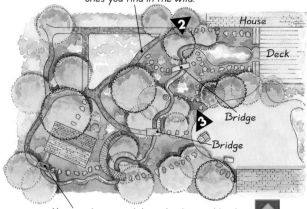

Use simple stone slabs as bridges to blend with the natural feel of the garden.

Botanical Names

Japanese maple
Acer palmatum

Simplicity is the word when it comes to a woodland-style garden. In photo 2 below, two slabs of stone make a simple bridge. Even though the stream is man-made, this rustic bridge gives it a more natural feel. On the garden plan to the right, you'll find a couple more bridges similar to this one crossing the stream before it falls into a pool near the deck.

Notice on the plan how the paths meander? They're really not designed to move you quickly through the garden. In a natural woodland, paths are often made by animals searching for food and water, so they may not be the shortest route to *your* destination. When you lay out paths in your garden, let them wander. Not only will they give you a place to walk, but they divide up the garden, making it easier to reach into each section when you work.

Keep the paths narrow like the ones in these photos so you interact with the garden. Plants brush against you as you walk, and the narrowness slows you down. But randomly placed flat stones are a good idea to keep you out of the mud and help define the paths. And don't worry about sweeping the path — a few scattered leaves add to the woodland feel.

Like any other garden style, a woodland has specific elements. To help you get started creating your own, I'll show you what those elements are on the next pages. □

— *Jim Childs*

(2) Moss-covered stone scattered along the edges and in the water make this manmade stream look natural. Let some of the woodland perennials grow right down to the water to disguise the edge.

(3) Once the spring flowers fade, a woodland garden becomes mostly about texture. To add some color for summer interest, use a few plants with colorful foliage, like this Japanese maple.

FIVE ELEMENTS OF A WOODLAND

Let's take a look at the elements of a woodland garden. That way you'll know exactly what you need to design a beautiful oasis like the one you've just toured. Think of the design in terms of layers. I'll start with the top layer you see in the illustration and work my way down to the ground.

Botanical Names

Birch *Betula* spp.
Crabapple *Malus* spp.
Japanese maple
   Acer palmatum
Mountain laurel
   Kalmia latifolia
Oak *Quercus* spp.
Pagoda dogwood
   Cornus alternifolia
Redbud *Cercis* spp.
Rhododendron
   Rhododendron spp.
Viburnum *Viburnum* spp.
Witchhazel
   Hamamelis spp.

1 USE OVERSTORY TREES FOR SHADE A woodland garden has to have shade — so that means trees. They don't have to be huge trees like mature oaks. But, like the ones in the illustration, they do have to be tall enough to form a canopy that you can plant several layers of plants under.

Below is a list of 6 shade trees with roots that won't compete for moisture and nutrients with plantings under them as much as shallow-rooted trees, such as maples will. However, you may find that because of the dense canopy of foliage, light rains don't reach the plants on the woodland floor. You'll need to do some extra watering until new plantings under them are completely established.

   Black tupelo *Nyssa sylvatica*
   Hickory *Carya* spp.
   Hornbeam *Carpinus* spp.
   Kentucky yellowwood
      Cladrastis kentukea
   Loblolly pine *Pinus taeda*
   Oak *Quercus* spp.

If you don't have room for mature overstory trees in your garden or time to wait for them to grow, you can start with the next layer, the understory. It'll form a similar canopy — just lower.

2 ADD THE UNDERSTORY Below the overstory trees, the next layer you see is called the understory. Here you'll find ornamental trees, large shrubs and tall climbing vines. They provide seasonal beauty at eye level and slightly above. Planting beneath tall trees means you'll need shade-loving understory trees. Pagoda dogwoods, Japanese maples and redbuds are all good. However, if you're only planting small trees as your overstory canopy, they'll have to be sun-lovers, like crabapples or birch.

3 TIE THE LAYERS TOGETHER WITH SHRUBS Shrubs blend the garden from just below the branches of the understory trees to near the ground. For variety, choose a mix of deciduous and evergreen shrubs. Witchhazels, viburnums, rhododendrons and mountain laurels are perfect for this layer. Notice how they're at eye level and below? You'll want these shrubs to have some attention-getting features. For example, flowers, foliage or unique branching habits are all things we like to look at as we walk in the woods.

4 MAKE THE WOODLAND FLOOR INTERESTING If you were walking on this path, chances are you would spend much of your time looking down. After all, you don't want to step in the wrong spot. So perennials, reseeding annuals and low shrubs make up the woodland floor. You want these plants to be interesting to look at up close. Unique flowers and foliage are always good choices.

Since they're under layers of leaf canopy, these plants must be tolerant of shade. But watch the shade patterns. There are often spots where you can grow things that like more sun. And soil, as in many gardens, is what really makes the woodland floor grow best. You can plant trees and shrubs in less-than-perfect soil and they'll survive. But most of these shorter plants like a moisture-holding humus-rich soil.

5 ADD A FEW DETAILS You have to have a way to walk through your garden without stepping on plants. But you don't want the walkway to look out of place. Paths can be hard-packed dirt, wood chips or a few well-placed stepping stones.

A water feature is nice to make soothing sounds that help mask noise from the outside world. Plus, water brings in wildlife to share your sanctuary.

And last but not least, every garden should have a spot where you can sit back and relax. It could be as simple as a large fallen log or a big boulder. But I prefer some rustic furniture where I can listen to the leaves rustling overhead and watch the sunlight dance over the woodland floor.

Mix and match the perfect combinations for *your* garden

Three-Season Border

Have you ever wanted to plant a new border but kept putting it off? You just didn't want to try to figure out what plants to grow in it. There are so many plants to consider, each with its own size, color and care needs — it's enough to make you give up before you even touch your trowel. Don't despair — help is here!

Take a look at this plan. It's designed to take the pain out of creating a border by giving you a starting point. What if the plants aren't right for your garden's soil or light, or you just don't like them? No problem. Turn the page for two more options for each plant with similar shapes, but different colors, zones, light needs or bloom times. You can pick and choose the perfect combination of plants for your taste and your garden situation.

If you're looking for year-round color, this plan has it. Spring-blooming black chokeberry and weigela start off the season, along with some of the smaller perennials. And the Jupiter's beard, monkshood and gas plant provide bright flowers in summer. But the border really peaks in late summer to fall when the brilliant red fall foliage of the black chokeberry catches your eye. Stiff, wheat-colored 'Karl Foerster' grass backs up the rich pink Joe-Pye weed blooms. And though they're done blooming, the weigelas still add a nice burgundy foliage accent in fall.

All these plants will appreciate good soil preparation with lots of compost tilled in. Make sure to give them a sunny location, with a little shade during the hottest part of the day. Or, if your garden is shady, take a look at some of the shade-tolerant choices on the next pages.

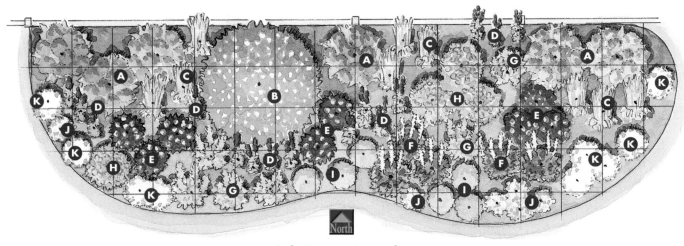

Scale: 1 square = 4 square feet

THE STARTING LINEUP

Code	Plant Name	No. to Plant	Blooms	Type	Cold/Heat Zones	Height/ Width	Special Features
A	Joe-Pye weed *Eupatorium dubium* 'Little Joe'	6	Pink; fall	Perennial	3-9/9-1	4 ft./3 ft.	Compact plant form; prefers moist soil; tolerates light shade; attracts butterflies
B	Black chokeberry *Aronia melanocarpa* 'Autumn Magic'	1	White; spring	Shrub	3-8/8-1	6 ft./6 ft.	Deep red fall color; large black fruit lasts long after leaves fall
C	Feather reed grass *Calamagrostis xacutiflora* 'Karl Foerster'	9	Pink-purple; early summer	Perennial	4-8/8-1	4-5 ft./2 ft.	Slender, upright plants stay in compact clumps; cut plants to ground in late winter
D	Monkshood *Aconitum carmichaelii* 'Arendsii'	15	Blue; summer	Perennial	3-8/8-1	4 ft./1 ft.	Spikes of rich blue flowers; prefers cool, moist soil; all plant parts are poisonous
E	Weigela *Weigela florida* 'Midnight Wine'	8	Red-pink; spring	Shrub	4-9/9-1	18-24 in./18-24 in.	Sometimes reblooms in summer to fall; tidy habit; best burgundy leaf color in full sun
F	Snakeroot *Actaea simplex* 'Brunette'	5	White; fall	Perennial	4-8/8-1	3-5 ft./2-3 ft.	White spikes rise above the plant; good cut flowers; afternoon shade in hot summers
G	Gas plant *Dictamnus albus purpureus*	6	Pink; summer	Perennial	3-8/8-1	2 ft./2 ft.	Flowers are followed by attractive seed pods good for drying; seldom needs dividing
H	Jupiter's beard *Centranthus ruber*	4	Pink; spring to fall	Perennial	5-8/8-1	2-3 ft./2-3 ft.	Self-seeds freely in ideal conditions; grows well in poor soil and stays more compact
I	Aster *Aster dumosus* 'Wood's Light Blue'	6	Blue; fall	Perennial	3-8/8-1	12-15 in./12-15 in.	Tidy, dwarf plant form; attracts butterflies; more mildew-resistant than most asters
J	Variegated strawberry *Fragaria vesca* 'Variegata'	6	White; spring	Perennial	5-8/8-1	8 in./12 in.	Prefers moist, humusy soil; rarely fruits; attractive red fall foliage
K	Candytuft *Iberis sempervirens* 'Alexander's White'	9	White; early summer	Perennial	3-8/8-1	8 in./12-18 in.	White flowers age to light pink; cut back plant by one-third after bloom to rejuvenate

MULTIPLE CHOICES

O K, you've seen the plants in the original plan. What if one or more of them won't grow in your zone? Don't like the pink of the Joe-Pye weed (A)? Swap it out for a fresh white phlox (A2). You get the idea. Maybe one or both of the alternate plants will be a better fit for you.

I've repeated the plan from the first spread here. For each plant, I've shown two options, along with their growing information. All three share the same letter. Notice that the alternate plants are similar in form to the original plants, but may be different colors or grow in different soils or zones. Simply pick the plants that suit you and your garden best. But have fun and remember that the sky's the limit, and all of the choices are completely up to you! □

— *Deborah Gruca*

A2

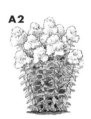

Phlox
Phlox paniculata
'David'
42 in. tall/36 in. wide
● 4-8   ● 8-1
Perennial; very resistant to powdery mildew; fragrant white blooms in summer; sun to part shade

A3

False indigo
Baptisia australis
4-5 ft. tall/3 ft. wide
● 3-9   ● 9-1
Perennial; blue flowers held above blue-green foliage in early summer; attractive seed pods; sun to part shade

B2

Colewort
Crambe cordifolia
4-6 ft. tall/4 ft. wide
● 5-9   ● 9-1
Perennial; 14-in. puckered leaves; white flowers early to midsummer; full sun

B3

Forsythia
Forsythia xintermedia
'Sunrise'
5 ft. tall/5 ft. wide
● 5-9   ● 9-1
Shrub; bright yellow flowers in late winter to early spring; sun to part shade

K2

Deadnettle
Lamium maculatum 'Beedham's White'
6 in. tall/2 ft. wide
● 3-8   ● 8-1
Perennial; white flowers in early summer; cut plant back to refresh foliage in late summer; part shade to shade

K3

Golden oregano
Origanum vulgare 'Aureum'
6-12 in. tall/18 in. wide
● 4-9   ● 10-1
Perennial; pink flowers in summer to fall; needs light afternoon shade in hot-summer areas; full sun

● United States Department of Agriculture (USDA) **cold-hardiness zones**

● American Horticultural Society (AHS) **heat-tolerance zones**

J2

Sea thrift
Armeria maritima
'Bloodstone'
8-10 in. tall/6-12 in. wide
● 4-9   ● 9-1
Perennial; pink globe-shaped flowers in early summer; prefers very well-drained soil; full sun

J3

Foamflower
Tiarella cordifolia 'Oakleaf'
8 in. tall/6 in. wide
● 3-7   ● 7-1
Perennial; delicate, airy pink flowers in late spring; needs consistent moisture; part shade to shade

I2

Lady's mantle
Alchemilla mollis
12-18 in. tall/12-18 in. wide
● 3-9   ● 9-1
Perennial; chartreuse flowers in early summer; appreciates afternoon shade in hotter zones; full sun

I3

Cushion spurge
Euphorbia polychroma
'Bonfire'
12 in. tall/18 in. wide
● 5-9   ● 9-1
Perennial; early green foliage turns to deep red for most of the season; bright green bracts in spring; full sun

C2

Switch grass
Panicum virgatum
'Heavy Metal'
3 ft. tall/2 ft. wide
● 5-9 ● 9-1
Perennial; blue-gray
foliage turns yellow
in fall; pink summer
flowers reach to 5 ft.;
sun to part shade

C3

Siberian iris
Iris sibirica
'Eric the Red'
3-4 ft. tall/2-3 ft. wide
● 3-8 ● 8-1
Perennial; wine-red
spring flowers; prefers
moist or boggy soil;
sun to part shade

D2

Delphinium
Delphinium
'Cliveden Beauty'
3-4 ft. tall/18 in. wide
● 3-7 ● 8-3
Perennial; pale blue
early summer flowers;
may need to stake;
full sun

D3

Mullein
Verbascum chaixii
'Album'
3 ft. tall/18 in. wide
● 5-9 ● 9-1
Perennial; white
flowers with mauve
centers in early to late
summer; prefers full
sun and poor soil

E2

Russian sage
Perovskia 'Blue Spire'
3 ft./3 ft.
● 4-9 ● 9-1
Perennial; silvergray
foliage; violet late-
summer flowers;
extremely heat and
drought-tolerant; full sun

E3

Deutzia
Deutzia gracilis
'Nikko'
1-2 ft. tall/2-5 ft. wide
● 5-8 ● 8-1
Shrub; deep-red fall
foliage; tiny white
flowers in spring;
sun to part shade

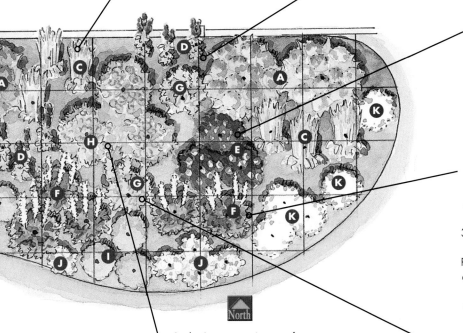

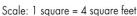

Scale: 1 square = 4 square feet

North

F2

Japanese anemone
*Anemone hupehensis
japonica* 'Pamina'
34 in. tall/18 in. wide
● 4-8 ● 8-1
Perennial; semi-double
dark pink flowers with
narrow petals in late
summer to fall; sun to
part shade

F3

Jacob's ladder
Polemonium caeruleum
3 ft. tall/14 in. wide
● 4-8 ● 8-2
Perennial; blue blooms
atop long stems in
spring; prefers moist
soil; part shade
to shade

H2

Caucasian comfrey
Symphytum caucasicum
2 ft. tall/2 ft. wide
● 3-9 ● 9-1
Perennial; blue flowers spring
to summer; deadhead to
prevent self-seeding; great for
dry shade areas; sun to
part shade

H3

Artemisia
Artemisia 'Powis Castle'
2-3 ft. tall/2 ft. wide
● 6-9 ● 12-1
Perennial; dense,
compact mound of lacy
silver-gray foliage;
tolerates humid
conditions; full sun

G2

Butterfly weed
Asclepias tuberosa
2-3 ft. tall/12-18 in. wide
● 4-9 ● 9-1
Perennial; orange flowers
in summer; tolerant of
drought and poor soil;
full sun

G3

Toad lily
Tricyrtis 'Empress'
2 ft. tall/2 ft. wide
● 5-9 ● 9-1
Perennial; white flowers
with purple spots in
summer to fall; prefers
humus-rich soil; part
shade to shade

Never mow again! Well-designed paths and easy plants make it possible.

Set in Stone

Botanical Names

Clematis
Clematis spp.
Creeping thyme
Thymus spp.
Hosta *Hosta* spp.
Lungwort
Pulmonaria spp.
Pinks *Dianthus* spp.
Rose *Rosa* spp.

Not every garden needs to be framed by lawn. Just ask Vern and Rochelle Eliason from Colorado. Their back yard is all garden, knit together with stone paths, like the one in this photo.

Most of the plants in this garden are easy-care, low-maintenance selections, such as the conifers you see here. Paths are made from large slabs of local stone, fit together and laid in a casual, random pattern. Ground covers, in this area creeping thyme, fill the cracks between the stones and soften the edges. The low plants also blend the path into the surrounding flower beds.

Climbing roses give a spectacular burst of color in late spring and early summer. Once they finish blooming, the foliage adds a clean backdrop for summer perennials. If you live in USDA zone 5 or colder, climbing roses may need to be laid down for the winter. If you're not into that much work, you could substitute a cold-hardy vine, such as clematis.

All of these perennials tolerate the heat that builds up from the stonework in this mostly full-sun garden. However, check out the small plan of the garden below left. Notice how there are a few large trees shading parts of the garden? Hostas, ferns and lungworts feel right at home in these shady areas.

But what really makes this garden beautiful is the careful attention to several landscape design principles. They've been teamed up with great plant selections for a well-designed garden. On the next pages I'll show you how to use these design tips in your own garden. And if you've ever shopped for stone, you know how overwhelming the choices are. I'll share information to help make your decision easier.

Climbing roses are tied to a heavy trellis along the privacy fence.

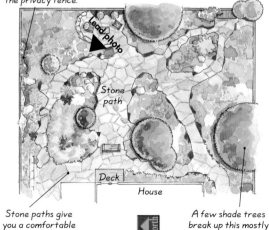

Lead photo

Stone path

Deck

House

North

Stone paths give you a comfortable surface to walk on.

A few shade trees break up this mostly sun garden.

(1) Creeping thyme is a great filler between slabs of stones and will give any path a softer appearance. Sprinkle in a few tiny pinks like these for some color.

PHOTO: © Charles Mann

4 DESIGN **MUST-KNOWS**

(2) A curving path creates curiosity about what might be around the bend. You step into the garden and move down the path as you seek an answer.

I've learned that the best way to show off plants is to grow them in a well-designed space. So, long before you think about choosing plants, here are four design principles to help you create your own beautiful garden.

SET A FOCAL POINT See the blue spruce in the background of photo 2? That's the focal point in this part of the garden. You notice it because it has a different color and form than the plants around it. As you look, you still notice all of the plants along the way, but the spruce is the most attention-grabbing. Once you're standing close to this focal point, you may spot a different one that'll pull your attention into another part of the garden.

ENCOURAGE MOVEMENT Next to the focal point in this photo is a curving path made of large stone slabs. The way it curves into the distance makes me wonder what's around the corner. How about you? That's move-ment — gently encouraging you, or even just your eye, to move through the garden. Movement is achieved with line, like this path, or subtle changes in color, size, form or texture.

Curving lines, such as this path, are meant to be traveled slowly. Straight lines move you, or your view, along faster.

ADD REPETITION Have you ever been in a garden with lots of dif-ferent colors or textures planted together? Because there's no obvious repetition, the confu-sion makes your eye jump from spot to spot.

But in photo 2, the repeated grassy texture of the sedges and daylilies with the tall maiden grass in the background really tie this garden scene together.

Randomly staggering clumps of plants with a similar texture creates an energetic feel. Their irregular placement also keeps the garden casual. If they were evenly repeated, it would instill a formal or subdued feeling.

KEEP YOUR BALANCE Balance gives a sense of equality to all parts of the garden. There are two types. With *symmetrical* balance, identical elements are opposite each other, as in a formal garden. If you drew a line through the center of the view, both sides would nearly match.

But in photo 3, the *asymmetrical* balance, where the halves don't match, achieves its goal by repetition of elements. This kind of balance uses masses that may look different, but carry the same visual weight. For example, the bed on the right is one large mass. On the other side of the path there are two beds. The areas are not exactly alike, but both contain similar plants, sizes, colors and quantities, so they balance.

One of the most striking features in this garden, after the beautiful plants, is the large slabs of stone. I'll show you three different types of stone on the next pages and explain some options you can use as you design your own patio and walkways.

A globe blue spruce makes an excellent focal point for this area.

An arbor-covered bench painted blue makes a focal point in this part of the garden.

Adjustments in size, shape, color and placement of the plants and hardscaping help you achieve an informal, or asymmetrical, balance.

Stone path

Deck

House

Curving paths encourage you to meander through the garden.

PHOTOS: © Charles Mann

Botanical Names

Daylily *Hemerocallis* hybrid
Globe blue spruce *Picea pungens* 'Globosa'
Maiden grass *Miscanthus* spp.
Sedge *Carex* spp.

(3) With the bench as a focal point, flower color, leaf texture and hardscaping elements give this view asymmetrical balance.

STONE ADDS PERSONALITY

When it comes to choosing natural stone, the choices can seem endless. Since there are so many kinds, I've chosen three widely available types. I'll share some basic information, as well as pros and cons, about each one.

SHOP WISELY First of all, did you know that shipping stone can add $10 or more per square foot to the retail price you pay? Check with local suppliers to determine what's available in your area before you set your heart on something and then learn it has to be shipped in.

Some retailers sell stone by the ton or by the pallet. Either way, you will need to ask how many square feet a ton or a pallet of *their* material will cover. Stone thickness can vary from ½ inch to more than 2 inches, and will affect the weight and coverage. Other retailers might sell stone, especially cut pieces, by the square foot.

Handling adds to the cost, so if you're on a budget, go with stone that hasn't been sorted. And pieces trimmed into even sizes and shapes will always be more expensive. You can save a little more by cutting your own. I'll show you basics in "Cutting stone" below right. To learn more, check out our Web extra.

MORTAR? Most stone patios and paths are fine laid on a bed of fast-draining sand and gravel. This technique allows you to make repairs or even adjust a design if you change your mind.

Mortar between the stones gives a more formal look to a patio or path. However, in areas that freeze, you'll need at least a 4-inch-thick concrete slab under the stone to prevent shifting and cracking with temperature fluctuations. Consult your supplier or a stone mason to determine how thick it needs to be in your area. Stones in mortar won't tip, and there's less sand to track into the house. However, it's tough to repair a crack or replace a broken stone. But no matter how you lay it, stone does make a perfect garden frame. □

— *Jim Childs*

LIMESTONE

You'll find some form of limestone in most regions of North America. When it's laid with gaps between the irregular edges, as you see in the left photo, the look is natural. However, limestone slabs can be cut to fit, for a slightly more structured landscape like the one below.

PROS Limestone's easy to cut and break. Fairly common, so it's one of the least expensive choices. Lots of color choices, from pale buff to rusty red.

CONS It's porous so it may absorb stains. Thickness and surface texture can vary from piece to piece, making it hard to lay an even, stable surface.

BLUESTONE

This dense material looks like and is often confused with slate, a harder and more expensive stone. If you think it only comes in dark blue-gray, like the stone in this photo, you'll be surprised to discover you can also find it in shades of red and green. Bluestone is most commonly found east of the Mississippi River, especially in the northeast United States and eastern Canada.

PROS Can be purchased in either natural rough-edged slabs or geometric shapes with uniform thickness, which are easier to lay.

CONS Usually more expensive than limestone, partly because of the cutting involved.

GRANITE

Granite is found in all areas, but it's most common in the upper half of North America. It can be polished smooth, but that makes it slick when it's wet. For garden applications, it's often rough cut into chunks like the ones you see in this photo. Since the pieces are usually small, they can be set in a wide variety of patterns to give you different looks.

PROS Will stand up to a lifetime of wear. Takes time to lay the small pieces, but they're easy for the do-it-yourselfer to handle, set and replace.

CONS Often expensive. Patio and path areas will be a bit rough or uneven and will need to be releveled if they sink over time. Granite can also be hard to cut.

CUTTING STONE

For a rustic edge, score a line in the stone by tapping it gently with a stone chisel and hammer. Once the mark is ⅛-in. deep, tap harder and the stone should break along the score. Cutting with an electric masonry saw gives a smooth edge. You can rent a saw at many stone retailers or rental stores. Sawing creates lots of dust and there will be flying chips with a hammer and chisel. Be sure to wear a dust mask, ear plugs and protective eyewear.

Score and break stone with a hammer and stone chisel if you want a natural edge.

Use a masonry saw with a diamond blade to get a straight, formal edge.

WEB extra

More detailed instructions and a step-by-step stone-cutting *video*.

5 Fabulous Foliage Combos

Get a beautiful garden all year.

Foliage often plays second fiddle to flowers in the garden. But have you ever thought about letting the leaves take center stage? They last longer than flowers and come in an infinite variety of shapes and sizes, as well as many colors.

There are no hard and fast rules when it comes to combining foliage. But these guidelines will help you get started. Using four design elements — color, texture, shape and size — foliage alone will keep your garden looking great. Let's start with color.

COLOR ISN'T JUST FOR FLOWERS You may think of leaves as green, but that's just the beginning. They come in a surprising number of other colors — yellow, red, purple, white and silver, to name a few. For combos with punch, combine contrasting colors like chartreuse and burgundy or silver and deep purple.

Remember, as the weather changes, so does leaf color. Gray-green in spring and summer, Koreanspice viburnum changes to the vibrant red you see in photo 1. The amount of light a plant gets can help determine the leaf color, too. You'll even notice differences within the same cultivar — for example, chartreuse hostas turn yellow in more sun. But the same hosta in shade stays chartreuse over the summer.

Even "plain old green" can be pretty exciting. There's a rainbow of greens to choose from in photo 2. Combine plants in several different shades of green and a variety of shapes and textures for an interesting monochromatic, or single-color, garden. And color isn't the only good thing about foliage. You'll find more fabulous design tips for foliage on the following pages.

2 MONOCHROMATIC ISN'T MONOTONOUS

A limited palette keeps its appeal with a variety of leaf shapes. Large hosta and ligularia leaves contrast nicely with the flowing foliage of the hakonechloa and the tiny honeysuckle. Some variation in color from the deep green ligularia and plain green fern adds depth and gives your eye a resting place.

A Hosta *Hosta* 'Paul's Glory'
B Hakonechloa *Hakonechloa macra* 'Aureola'
C Honeysuckle *Lonicera nitida* 'Baggesen's Gold'
D Sensitive fern *Onoclea sensibilis*
E Ligularia *Ligularia* 'The Rocket'

1 FANTASTIC FALL FOLIAGE

Viburnum's deep burgundy fall foliage, golden-yellow maiden grass and the red, yellow and violet of Labrador rose keep our test garden looking good right into fall. And when those autumn leaves disappear, the contrasting shapes of the grass, yucca and juniper really sing — even in winter.

A Maiden grass *Miscanthus sinensis*
B Koreanspice viburnum *Viburnum carlesii*
C Labrador rose *Rosa blanda*
D Yucca *Yucca filamentosa*
E Juniper *Juniperus horizontalis* 'Blue Chip'

GO FOR FOLIAGE!

Texture and leaf shape don't play quite such obvious roles as color does in the garden, but they're still crucial, especially when it comes to foliage.

TERRIFIC TEXTURE Touch fuzzy lamb's ear, a smooth rhododendron leaf or prickly sea holly and you've experienced texture. But there's a visual texture to leaves, too. It's often very subtle, as in the case of the fine-textured grasses or the deeply cut leaves of the Japanese maple in photo 3. On the other hand, there are times it can really make a statement, like the horned poppy in photo 4 does. Though these surfaces often have practical functions — lamb's ear's silver fuzz helps it beat the heat and retain water, for example — this tactile element also adds a lot of interest to the garden.

SHAPE AND SIZE Mixing different leaf shapes together keeps a garden interesting. The variety of shapes in photo 5 from comb-like to linear to rounded creates a sense of movement that really energizes this combo.

Pay close attention to the size of the leaves in your garden, too. If they're dramatically different, like a tiny thyme planted next to a large gunnera, it can look out of balance. Adding a few medium-sized leaves — an upright sedum, for example — creates a transition between the two extremes and helps you see the planting as a whole.

Don't let foliage in your garden sit in the background. Make it center stage and you'll have fabulous results. □

— *Sherri Ribbey*

3 KEEP IT INTERESTING This pair of pint-sized evergreens have similar textures and habits, but the different colors make them an interesting combination. Set against the warm-colored Japanese maple and grasses, these shrubs help create a visual tension that makes this a knockout garden.

A Mugo pine *Pinus mugo 'Aurea'*
B Blue globe spruce *Picea pungens 'Montgomery'*
C Maiden grass *Miscanthus sinensis*
D Little blue stem *Schizachyrium scoparium*
E Japanese maple *Acer palmatum dissectum 'Garnet'*

www.GardenGateMagazine.com

4 **SHARP CONTRAST** Deeply serrated blue-gray leaves of horned poppy are really dramatic, especially paired with the fine red leaves of the Japanese blood grass. The contrast of texture and color is what makes this combo work. The horned poppy can be hard to find. If you can't find it locally, try Digging Dog Nursery at www.diggingdog. com or 707-937-1130.

A **Horned poppy** *Glaucium flavum*
B **Japanese blood grass** *Imperata cylindrica* 'Rubra'

5 **DYNAMIC SHAPES FOR SUMMER** There are a lot of different leaf shapes in this planting, from the linear grass at the back to the comblike ferns and strappy purple heart climbing up from below. What ties them together and makes them shine is the contrast in shape and color with the rounded coleus in the middle.

A **Purple heart** *Tradescantia pallida* 'Purple Queen'
B **Australian sword fern** *Nephrolepis obliterata* 'African Queen'
C **Coleus** *Solenostemon* 'Black Velvet'
D **Coleus** *Solenostemon* 'Brilliancy'
E **Maiden grass** *Miscanthus sinensis* 'Variegatus'

Shady Retreat

Botanical Names

Astilbe
Astilbe hybrid
Hosta
Hosta hybrid

You have a large shady hillside covered with brush and poison ivy. At the bottom it ends with an eyesore of a ravine. What can you do? Why, turn it into a beautiful garden!

That's what Sandi Burdick and Tom Boyd from Tennessee did. The portion of their garden you see in the illustrations and photos on these pages is roughly 120 by 140 feet. That's pretty big for many of today's suburban gardens. But there are design ideas and plant choices here that you can adapt to any size space.

USE WHAT YOU FIND When Sandi and Tom started grading this overgrown hillside, they discovered large boulders and lots of smaller rocks just under the surface. Rather than dispose of the rocks, they set them aside to be used for the walls and paths throughout the entire garden.

Three of the largest boulders have been tucked back into the hillside after grading to create the waterfall you see here. Water recirculates from a lower pond to one above the waterfall. You can see its path in the illustration at left. If you don't have room for a water feature this size, don't worry. Even a small water feature can add sound to your garden. Plus, you'll be amazed at the birds that flock to water in both summer and winter.

PLANT POINTERS Another design idea used here is to mass plants in large groupings. That's great in a big area because it gives bold impact. Dots of individual plants in a garden this size would get lost. But you really notice these red and pink astilbes planted in clumps of three to five plants each.

And did you notice in the photo how the pink astilbes are repeated? That's a design tip to tie any size garden together. You don't need to repeat everything, just a few striking groupings or plants will be enough. After the astilbes finish, large, colorful hostas take over the repetition in this garden. Repeating a hardscaping material, in this case the native stone, unifies a garden design too, even where there are few plants.

Most of the plantings are low, especially in the center area. Sure, there are large trees overhead, but by keeping the shrubs and perennials short, you have lots of unobstructed views of the entire space. If you've ever visited a woodland glade, you'll notice that this hillside garden has a similar feeling, even though it's manmade.

Want to learn more great design ideas like these to use in your garden? Let's take a look on the next pages.

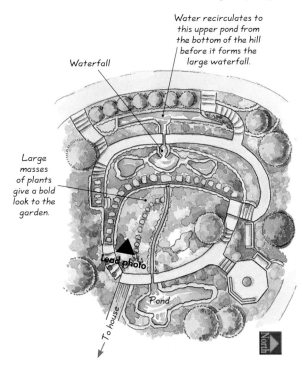

Water recirculates to this upper pond from the bottom of the hill before it forms the large waterfall.

Waterfall

Large masses of plants give a bold look to the garden.

Lead photo

Pond

To house

North

DESIGN THE GARDEN

Waterfall

Driveway

Steps help you keep the paths along the slope fairly level.

This terrace makes a great spot to sit and enjoy the hillside garden.

A cut in the path, rather than a bridge, lets water flow to the lower pond.

Pond

Firepit

To house

North

WEB extra

See a **slide show** of more photos from this garden.

Garden design always presents a set of challenges. For example, how do you cross the long stream between the pond and the waterfall? The obvious way would be a small bridge. But photo 2 shows you a much more creative solution. Interrupting the path, rather than bridging the stream, allows you to stop and dip your toes in the cool water on a hot summer day.

Here are more of the design situations that were addressed as work progressed on the garden.

LEVEL THE PATHS Getting from one area to another wasn't always easy on this hillside. The stone steps in photo 2 lead you from the lowest part of the garden up the hillside. There they con-nect to another path. And then more steps lead you to a gravel driveway at the top of the hill.

On the opposite side of the garden, there are more flights of steps. Any path, whether stone or mulch, can stay wet and become slippery. Steps like these mean you don't need to walk on inclines to reach the top. They keep all of the paths easy to navigate.

LEAVE ROOM TO GATHER Up on the hillside there's a large level area you see in photo 3. It's a spot where groups can gather. Setting it high gives visitors a view of the entire garden. To make a terrace more inviting during cool evenings, if you have room, a fire pit in the center is a great idea. And the bench that goes around the edge is the perfect spot to sit and relax with friends. It also creates an unobtrusive railing to keep visitors from accidentally stepping off the terrace and tumbling down the hill.

RELAX WITH SOOTHING COLOR Sandi wanted a calming color palette. Muted shades of pink and blue in photo 4 are the main colors, with a bit of white sprinkled in. If you spend evenings in your garden, pastels help brighten up the shade and seem to illuminate the area. Plant pale-colored

(2) Stones set in mortar help ensure solid, secure footing. These steps and paths were created from rocks excavated during grading.

or white flowers near paths to help guide you in low light.

You may want to add a little zip to a pastel color scheme so it's restful but not boring. A few touches of bright yellow and chartreuse add life to any garden. In photo 4, gold hostas brighten up this shaded area. Foliage is a great way to get long-lasting color in the shade. But if you're gardening in a sunny spot, use gold foliage carefully and in small quantities. The color seems to intensify in bright light and can be distracting or overpowering.

See the birdhouse in photo 4? It's really not for birds — it hides the electric controls for the lights and water pumps.

Like most gardens, there are several distinct growing conditions within this one. Choosing the right plants makes all the difference. If you have dry or damp shade, I have plant help for you on the next pages.

(3) The large terrace partway up the hillside gives visitors a full view of the garden. A low railing around it also serves as a sturdy bench.

(4) Foliage *and* flowers add up to a zippy color scheme. Groups of pale-pink astilbes really stand out when they're set among clumps of bright gold and blue-green hostas.

FOCUS ON PLANTINGS

I bet no matter what the size of your garden, you have at least two different kinds of conditions. It's definitely true in this shade garden. The hillside is dry, yet the level bottom is moist, even wet at times. Plus, after grading, there were pockets of good soil, as well as areas that are not so good. So a better soil mix and lots of compost had to be brought in to fill planting areas, especially between the stones. With a goal of having color all year round, it still took some doing to find just the right plants to fit the different areas. Let's take a look at some great plant choices.

PLANTING A DRY SLOPE Many spring-flowering bulbs, like daffodils, actually like dry conditions, especially when they're dormant. And most bloom weeks before the trees overhead sprout leaves, so shade is not a problem.

For the biggest impact, plant bulbs in large masses. And plant hostas between the drifts of bulbs. Their leaves make a great cover-up to keep the garden tidy.

Hostas alone are OK, but you can make the garden more interesting with texture combinations. Barrenworts, hellebores and ferns are right at home under the shady canopy of oak branches and add lots of summer foliage texture. Most of these perennials spread on their own, eventually establishing fairly large colonies. That's important in a big garden, especially if you're working with a budget. Buy a few plants and let them grow into colonies. Or you can lift and divide them occasionally to spread them around.

In any area, no matter what time of year, potted plants are a great way to add quick color. They're especially handy to highlight areas like the steps in photo 5. Guests will spot these bright pink hydrangeas and can easily locate and navigate the steps, even in low light. Their blooms should last several weeks, even a couple of months. When the flower color fades, you can quickly swap them with something new.

Fall means foliage color. Even in shaded areas Japanese maples and dogwoods will turn orange and red. And a few shade-loving dwarf conifers, mixed with the textured bark of paperbark maple, will keep any garden from looking lifeless in winter.

GROWING THIRSTY PLANTS At the bottom of the hill, the moisture level rises. Because it stays wet much of the time, most spring bulbs are not happy here. That means the brightest early spring color is on the hillside. But see the clumps of pink astilbes and the grassy foliage of the Japanese and Louisiana iris toward the back of photo 6? They're right at home in these damp conditions. So is the calla lily, which happens to be hardy in this garden. If it won't survive the winter in your zone, you can dig and store the tubers each fall. Cannas and caladiums like the same damp conditions and can be dug and stored, too.

(5) Need quick color? Pots of bright pink hydrangeas are a great way to highlight an interesting spot in your garden, like these steps.

(6) Gardens with lots of one plant don't need to be boring. Just mix different leaf colors and bloom times, like these clumps of hosta and astilbe.

Tuck in a few tropical plants for a burst of summer texture and foliage color. Many will tolerate the shade as well as the moist soil. Hardy perennial monkshood and turtlehead add purple and pink flowers from late summer into autumn. Their colors blend well with the bold tropical foliage that always seems to look best just before cold weather arrives.

As you've seen, any area has gardening possibilities. Big or small, you can use these same design tips in any moist or dry shady garden to create your own garden hideaway. □

— *Jim Childs*

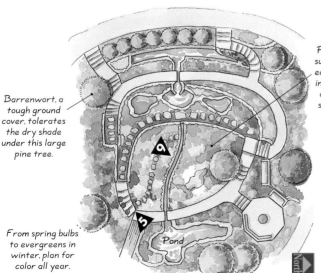

Barrenwort, a tough ground cover, tolerates the dry shade under this large pine tree.

Plant tropicals, such as elephant ears and cannas, in the low, moist area for late-season texture and color.

From spring bulbs to evergreens in winter, plan for color all year.

Pond

North

10 MUST-HAVE SHADE PLANTS

Do you have moist shade, or is your soil on the dry side? This garden has both. Choosing plants for these areas involved careful consideration of the growing conditions. Here are 10 selections Sandi finds grow well in her garden.

DRY SHADE

Barrenwort *Epimedium* spp.
Perennial; various colors of early spring flowers; semi-evergreen foliage; 6 to 12 in. tall, spreading; cold-hardy in USDA zones 4 to 8; heat-tolerant in AHS zones 8 to 1

Bloodroot *Sanguinaria canadensis*
Perennial; white flowers in early spring; 6 in. tall and 12 in. wide; cold-hardy in USDA zones 3 to 9; heat-tolerant in AHS zones 9 to 1

Christmas fern *Polystichum acrostichoides*
Perennial; evergreen; 2 ft. tall and 2 ft. wide; cold-hardy in USDA zones 3 to 9; heat-tolerant in AHS zones 9 to 1

Hellebore *Helleborus* spp.
Perennial; evergreen, flowers in late winter; 12 to 36 in. tall and wide; cold-hardy in USDA zones 5 to 8; heat-tolerant in AHS zones 8 to 1

Trillium *Trillium grandiflorum*
Perennial; white flowers in early spring; 2 ft. tall and wide; cold-hardy in USDA zones 4 to 9; heat-tolerant in AHS zones 9 to 1

MOIST SHADE

Astilbe *Astilbe* spp. and hybrids
Perennial; pink, red or white flowers in summer; 6 to 48 in. tall and 24 in. wide; cold-hardy in USDA zones 4 to 8; heat-tolerant in AHS zones 8 to 1

Calla lily *Zantedeschia aethiopica*
Tuber; white flowers in early summer; 2 to 3 ft. tall and 2 ft. wide; cold-hardy in USDA zones 8 to 12; heat-tolerant in AHS zones 12 to 1

Canna *Canna* hybrids
Tuber; red, orange or yellow flowers in late summer; 1 to 5 ft. tall and 2 ft. wide; cold-hardy in USDA zones 8 to 12; heat-tolerant in AHS zones 12 to 1

Elephant ears *Alocasia* spp.
Tender tuber; 3 to 5 ft. tall and 2 to 4 ft. wide; cold-hardy in USDA zones 9 to 12; heat-tolerant in AHS zones 12 to 1

Monkshood *Aconitum* spp.
Perennial; blue flowers in midsummer; 3 to 4 ft. tall and 18 in. wide; cold-hardy in USDA zones 4 to 8; heat-tolerant in AHS zones 8 to 1

Try tropicals for a dramatic fall look.

Going Out With Style

Botanical Names

Banana *Musa* spp.
Brugmansia
   Brugmansia spp.
Cordyline
   Cordyline spp.
Elephant ears
   Colocasia esculenta
Ginger *Alpinia* spp.
Japanese aralia
   Fatsia japonica
Sweet potato vine
   Ipomoea batatus

Tropicals are hot! Elephant ears, bananas and brugmansias are just a few of the tender plants you'll find at the garden center these days. And although I usually think of tropicals as summer garden staples, they often are at their big, blooming peaks in fall. That's when this photo was taken in Andrew Bunting's Pennsylvania garden. See how big the giant banana leaves are?

Bold plants need bold design ideas. It takes some planning to keep tropicals from looking out-of-place in a temperate garden setting. Because they often have unique forms and shapes, they make great focal points. But they always seem to look most natural if you can use more than just one tropical in your garden. This keeps them from looking stuck in.

As you can see in photo 1, bananas and a Japanese aralia with a yellow-flowered brugmansia under it make great companions. Here they're grouped together for a striking background to lots of other foliage plants.

Many annuals could be considered tropical plants, too. Use low-growing annuals or vines, like these sweet potatoes, to make a lush, colorful ground cover. Set smaller plants like these in groups to balance the size of the tropicals. In other words, *one* would just get lost in a scene like this.

Tropicals aren't shy, and neither is the red chair tucked under them. This garden scene would be fine without the chair, but it becomes much more dramatic with that splash of red. And an object, rather than a plant, makes an ideal focal point that can remain the same even after the tender plants are gone for the winter.

A word of advice as we talk about design: Set large-leafed tropicals in areas that aren't subject to abusive wind. Bananas, and other plants with large leaves, can shred easily.

On the next pages I'll share more information on design techniques that will help your tropicals look right at home. And later I'll have tips on winter care so you can enjoy them for many years to come. Let's find out more about designing tropicals into any landscape.

(1) Tropical plants reach their peak in late summer. The banana on the left and the yellow brugmansia tucked under a Japanese aralia make great companions to annuals, which also tend to look best late in the season.

A grouping of tropicals gives the biggest impact.

Shed   Garage

Patio

Lead photo

Lawn

Pond

House

North

Potted tropicals add color and texture to this patio area.

DESIGNING WITH TROPICAL PLANTS

Botanical Names

Agave *Agave* spp.
Banana *Musa* spp.
Boxwood
Buxus spp.
Brugmansia
Brugmansia spp.
Chinese
forget-me-not
Cynoglossum
amabile
Cordyline
Cordyline spp.
Dogwood
Cornus florida
Elephant ear
Colocasia
esculenta
Flowering maple
Abutilon spp.
Fountain grass
Pennisetum
setaceum
Japanese hydrangea
Schizophragma
hydrangeoides
Juniper
Juniperus spp.
Oriental poppy
Papaver orientale
Peony
Paeonia hybrid
Salvia
Salvia splendens
Sweet potato vine
Ipomoea batatas
Yew *Taxus xmedia*
Yucca *Yucca* spp.

Rather than just sticking a pot of brugmansia in where something has died, assess your needs and plan ahead. Do you need height or bright colors in an area? Perhaps a bold texture or form would add some punch. Planning in advance will give any garden a bigger impact, especially with tropicals. Here are some tips to help you design yours.

INCLUDE SHRUBS, VINES AND BULBS Tropical plants don't really come into their own until late. So you'll want some interest the rest of the year. A striking hardy vine, like the Japanese hydrangea in photo 2, makes a statement no matter what the season. Evergreens, such as boxwoods, junipers and yews, play starring roles in winter. And beds where the tropicals will be set are great places for spring bulbs.

Tough, early perennials, like peonies or Oriental poppies, are ideal spring fillers until the tender tubers and plants get growing. And annuals are great as easy-care ground covers under tall plants like bananas. Sow seeds of hardy annuals, like Chinese forget-me-nots, and let them reseed every year.

PLAN A COLOR THEME Color is a great way to tie any garden together. In photo 3, pots of cordylines on a wall behind bright salvias and 'Rubrum' fountain grass set a rich red color scheme. Behind, a hardy dogwood tree with the blushing red foliage and red fruit you see in the inset continues the red. And in photo 4, rusty-red 'Sweet Caroline Bronze' sweet potato vines and the large banana plant with a red-brown center rib keeps the theme going.

(2) Hardscaping details, like this arbor and gate, give a garden structure any time of year.

Dogwood foliage and fruit

If you use a lot of red, you may want to keep it from looking dark and depressing. Intersperse flashes of bright gold and pale green flowers and foliage throughout the garden, like the flowering maple under the banana in photo 4.

ENERGIZE WITH TEXTURE CONTRAST Tropicals offer textures you just can't find in your usual garden options. And texture contrast can really energize a garden. Just look at the combinations in photo 4. Banana leaves above small-leafed flowering maple, sweet potato vine, spiky yucca and agave make your eyes travel across the whole scene. And the very large elephant ears down the line make a strong contrast to the boxwood in front of them.

MAKE IT EASY ON YOURSELF It's hard to tell from these photos, but some of the tropicals, like the bananas, are planted directly in the garden. Others, such as the brugmansias, have been set into the ground in large containers. Both techniques will help keep your tropicals standing better than if they're in pots above ground. And they require less watering this way, too.

On the next pages I'll share tips on ways to care for tender plants over the cold winter months.

(3) Color unifies a diverse group. Tropical cordylines, annual salvia and a dogwood tree work together because of their red foliage, flowers and fruit.

(4) Texture contrasts make a garden. Large banana leaves seem even bigger next to spiky yucca and the small leaves of a bronze sweet potato vine.

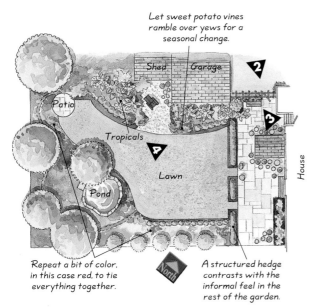

Let sweet potato vines ramble over yews for a seasonal change.

Shed   Garage

2

Patio

Tropicals

4

Lawn

Pond

House

3

Repeat a bit of color, in this case red, to tie everything together.

North

A structured hedge contrasts with the informal feel in the rest of the garden.

TROPICAL CARE AND SURVIVAL

As you've seen, tropicals can have great impact in every garden. It simply takes some advance planning. But before you try to construct a rainforest in your back yard with lots of tender plants, you need to consider some care issues. For example, how do you take care of them over the winter if you live where temperatures drop well below freezing?

In the information on these pages you'll discover most of these plants are really quite easy to store for the winter. Next spring, pot them up or bring them back outside when temperatures regularly stay above 50 degrees, especially at night, and give them the summer to grow. □

— *Jim Childs*

New leaves sprout just below the spot where this brugmansia was pruned last fall.

LEAVE THEM IN THEIR POTS Some tropicals do best staying in pots all summer *and* winter. Move them indoors before night temperatures drop to 40 degrees. If they've grown too big to fit in your house, prune now. Just like the brugmansia in this photo, new foliage will sprout next spring and fill in by summer. You can remove a few inches up to a few feet on the plants in the list below, except cordylines, which don't really need pruning.

Don't worry about bright light while the plant is resting. Just set it in filtered light, such as a north window, or under lights in your basement. Many will drop some of their leaves during storage, but don't be alarmed. Over the winter, keep the soil barely moist and don't add any fertilizer to stimulate growth. A few weeks before it's time to move the pot back outdoors, resume fertilizing and regular watering and move the plant into bright light, as you see in this photo. If you need to move the plant to a larger container, do it now.

TROPICALS THAT CAN STAY IN POTS
Brugmansia *Brugmansia* hybrid
Cordyline *Cordyline* spp.
Flowering maple *Abutilon* hybrid
Ginger *Alpinia zerumbet*
Hibiscus *Hibiscus rosa-sinensis*
Japanese aralia *Fatsia japonica*

OVERWINTER BANANAS Most bananas grow largest planted directly in the soil rather than in a pot. However, many of these tender plants won't survive north of USDA zone 8 or 9. You'll need to dig them before frost and shake off most of the soil. Cut off all the leaves except the top one and set the trunk in a dark area that stays around 50 degrees. Spritz the roots with water as you wrap them loosely in a plastic bag. Some air needs to circulate around them or they'll rot. Pull back the bag to check the roots occasionally, as I've done below. If they're dry, add water and rewrap them.

Spoiled area

Dusting sulfur

TUBERS OR BULBS YOU CAN STORE

Calla lily *Zantedeschia* spp.
Caladium *Caladium* hybrid
Canna *Canna* spp.
Elephant ear *Colocasia esculenta*
Giant elephant ear *Xanthosoma* hybrid
Taro *Alocasia* hybrid

STORE THE TUBERS Lift tender tubers before frost — most of these tropical plants don't survive freezing temperatures. Cut off the leaves, leaving just the tuber, and let it dry in a warm, shaded area for a few days. When stalk ends and roots have withered and are thoroughly dry, wrap the tubers loosely in sheets of newspaper and lay them in a basket or box as you see in the photo above. Store them in a spot that stays dark and around 45 to 50 degrees — too much light and warmth and the tubers may try to grow.

In the basket above, I've unwrapped a few bulbs to check the tubers for soft spots during storage. Squeeze them, and if you discover soft mushy spots, don't panic. You may not have to throw the tuber away. Simply cut out the spoiled area to prevent it from spreading. The inside of an elephant ear tuber should be solid and white like a potato, but as you see in the top inset at left, this one isn't. In the bottom photo I've cut out all of the rotten parts, and I'm sprinkling dusting sulfur, a fungicide, into the wound to prevent more decay. I'll let the cut dry for a few days, wrap the tuber in fresh paper and put it back in storage. As long as you leave a portion of the root area and the growing tip, the tuber will grow fine when you plant it in your garden next spring.

Wilbur D. Jones Jr.

on accessible gardening

PHOTOS: Courtesy of Wilbur D. Jones Jr.

IN THE KNOW

FAVORITE TOOL A "grabber" lets you reach into beds to groom plants, or pick up bits of trash without stooping. With practice, you can pull weeds or bend flower stems closer for picking and deadheading. Look for a grabber that's sturdy but lightweight with rubberized tips so it grips better. You can find them at medical equipment and supply stores or some larger drugstores.

WEB extra

Our *list* of great accessible gardening aids.

None of us are getting any younger — it's a fact of life. And continuing some of our life passions, like gardening, means we often have to adapt the way we work. Last year I received a letter and these photos from a reader, Wilbur D. Jones Jr., of Ohio. As you can see, Wilbur's garden is colorful and beautifully maintained. Yet he'd been through heart surgery, a stroke and several heart attacks. He wasn't able to get around as easily as he used to and needed a motorized scooter much of the time. I spoke with him about how he kept up his garden. These tips will help keep you gardening whether you need to use a walker or a wheelchair, have arthritis or just a broken ankle.

BE PREPARED The last thing you want to do is waste precious energy and gardening time making trips back and forth to the garage or garden shed. Always carry pruners, a trowel and other small tools with you in a basket, like the one on the front of Wilbur's scooter. And on a scooter, you can take along a couple of gallon jugs filled with water or mixed fertilizer. Set them in the basket or on the floor boards as you head out to the garden.

Plan to garden during the cool of the day. Hot sun and humidity can quickly sap your strength. Always be sure to carry a bottle of water for yourself when you head outdoors.

BRING THE GARDEN TO YOU
Getting down on the ground, or even just bending over, can be difficult. (Actually, getting *down* isn't hard — getting *up* can be!) But if your health requires you to use a wheelchair, motorized scooter or even a cane or walker, it's nearly impossible. Here's where raised beds and containers are great. See the impatiens behind Wilbur's scooter? Notice how they're raised a bit with an edge of concrete blocks? Just a few inches like this can make a big difference when it comes to working from a seated position.

You can also plant in large pots that are tall enough to work in while you're sitting, like the ones in photo 1. Flower-filled pots are a great substitute for bedding plants in the ground. They give lots of color without the work of getting up and down to plant, weed and cultivate.

Pots between 15 and 20 inches tall are about right. If you need the pots higher, raise them up with a few bricks or concrete blocks. Check to see that the pots are stable and won't tip over while you're working on them. Make sure to set the pots where you can easily walk or roll up to them when you need to work.

Once set, large pots can stay in the same place all winter if they're made from a material that won't freeze and crack. Otherwise, ask for help lifting and storing them each fall.

Shrub borders are easier to get into and maintain than densely planted flower beds.

Replace bedding annuals with large flower-filled pots. They're easy to plant and care for.

(1) Perennials that can get by with attention about once a year, like the day-lilies in the foreground, make it easier for gardeners with physical challenges to grow flowers. Small shrubs are also good because you don't usually have to bend over to maintain them.

Either way, dump or scoop out at least some of the soil and replace it each spring.

Other tasks, like pushing a mower or cleaning the pond, can seem daunting. Don't hesitate to ask friends and family to help. In return, find ways to assist them with their gardens, perhaps sharing a few plants they've admired.

RAMP IT UP Garages or tool sheds and gardens are rarely on the same level. A ramp like the one in photo 2 is a necessity if you're in a wheelchair. Ramps make it easy for folks on wheels to get from one area to another. They should be sturdy and securely fastened in place to avoid accidents.

Handles on the door frame will give you a bit of extra pull and balance if you're able to stand up from your chair or scooter and walk. Do you have more strength in your legs or arms? If your legs are stronger, you can place the handles low, a bit above shoulder height and lift using your legs. Weak legs but strong arms? You'll need the handles higher, as you see on Wilbur's garage, so you can pull yourself up with your arms. To get the best placement, roll up to the door, extend your arms towards the frame, grip it and stand. When you find the spot where it's easiest to get up, have someone mark the height. That's where you'll want to screw the handles securely in place.

During work on this article, Wilbur passed away. Here at *Garden Gate*, we admired his gardening stamina, as well as his philosophy: "Stay active as long as you can." Even if all you can do is get your hands dirty, get out there and do it! □
— *Jim Childs*

A textured surface helps prevent slips.

(2) A ramp is a necessity if you can no longer walk. Even if you can, but your legs are stiff or weak, a ramp can make a step into your tool shed easier to navigate.

Lee Reich
on fantastic fruit for any back yard

Botanical Names

Clove currant
  Ribes odoratum
Cornelian cherry
  Cornus mas
Jujube
  Ziziphus jujuba
Lingonberry
  Vaccinium vitis-idaea
Maypop
  Passiflora incarnata
Medlar
  Mespilus germanica
Pawpaw *Asimina triloba*
Serviceberry
  Amelanchier spp.
Strawberry
  Fragaria spp.
  and hybrids

Nothing beats the taste of fresh fruit you pick yourself. But most of us don't have much room for fruit trees and shrubs in our gardens. Or do we? I spoke with Lee Reich, author of "Uncommon Fruits for Every Garden," about ways all of us can design a few "edibles" into our landscape. His book focuses on unique fruit you won't find at your local supermarket, but is beautiful, tasty and easy to grow. Here's what Lee shared with me:

3 REASONS TO PLANT FRUIT
First, we all want trees and shrubs that look great in the garden. All of the uncommon fruit plants we'll talk about bloom and then bear colorful fruit. Some of them change color for fall and several have interesting bark or structure to add winter interest.

Second, bragging rights. Be honest — most gardeners relish growing something out of the ordinary. You could plant a plain old apple tree, but

wouldn't you love to be the first in your neighborhood to grow a medlar or a jujube?

And last but not least, it's just plain satisfying to grow and share something others can enjoy. What's better than a bowl or basket of beautiful — and unusual — fruit?

So how do you work these great plants into your garden?

GROW VERTICAL Stuck with a blank wall or an ugly privacy fence? Put up a trellis or two, as we've done with the patio in the illustration, and grow a maypop or a kiwi vine. Or train vines onto a sturdy pergola or arbor for some shade.

SCREEN A VIEW Who doesn't have something they would like to block from sight? Or maybe it's stiff winds you'd like to buffer? Asian pears grouped in the back yard screen a view from the neighbor's second story windows and filter wind on the patio. Serviceberries, pawpaws and Cornelian cherries are other trees less than 25 feet tall that do a great job in both situations.

PLANT HEDGES AND ACCENTS Short or tall, shrubs make great hedges to direct traffic or give you privacy. In the illustration, red currants define the edge of a patio and give some enclosure to the area. Plus you have easy access to harvest ripe fruit.

Plant a few fruiting shrubs among your perennials as accent plants. Clove currant grows less than 6 feet tall and adds multi-season interest in

a flower border. The fragrant yellow flowers, appearing about the time tulips bloom in spring, are followed by colorful, edible fruit in late summer. And the bright green leaves turn shades of red and purple for autumn.

COVER THE GROUND WITH FRESH FRUIT Can you imagine picking fruit from your ground cover? You can with the low-bush blueberries in our garden design. Several other edible plants, such as lingonberries and strawberries, also make dense ground covers as they spread by rhizomes or runners.

ENJOY LIVE ENTERTAINMENT Many of these edible plants also attract birds and other wildlife. They'll enjoy the harvest almost as much as you do. On established plants there's often enough produce to go around. (If you want to protect the fruit, a few shiny objects hanging from the branches help to scare away hungry birds.)

You may have a bit of mess left behind by the birds, but you'll forget all about it when you enjoy the tasty fruit. Speaking of mess, plant trees with fruit that may drop, such as pears, away from patios and sidewalks.

On the next page, in the lower right-hand corner, you'll discover a couple of mail-order sources. They carry these uncommon fruits, and many more, to help you get started on your edible landscape. □

— *Jim Childs*

Asian pear *Pyrus pyrifolia*
- 10 to 12 ft. tall and wide
- White spring flowers
- Fruit ripens in early autumn
- Plant two or more for pollination
- Cold-hardy in USDA zone 4 to 9
- Heat-tolerant in AHS zones 9 to 1

Arctic kiwi *Actinidia kolomitka*
- 15 ft. tall, 5 ft. wide
- Pink-splashed foliage
- 1-in.-long fruit
- Need both male and female plants
- Cold-hardy in USDA zone 5 to 8
- Heat-tolerant in AHS zones 8 to 1

Lowbush blueberry
Vaccinium angustifolium
- 4 to 24 in. tall, 36 in. wide
- White flowers in spring
- Sky blue berries in fall
- Prefers acid soil and part shade
- Drought tolerant once established
- Cold-hardy in USDA zone 2 to 8
- Heat-tolerant in AHS zones 8 to 1

Red currant *Ribes rubrum*
- 3 to 5 ft. tall and wide
- Harvest fruit from July to September
- Plant in full sun or part shade
- Cold-hardy in USDA zones 3 to 5
- Heat-tolerant in AHS zones 5 to 1

Mail-order sources

One Green World
www.onegreenworld.com
877-353-4028. *Catalog free*

Raintree Nursery
www.raintreenursery.com
360-496-6400. *Catalog free*

PHOTOS: Courtesy Lee Reich (portrait); © Neil Soderstrom (red currant); © Joseph G. Strauch Jr. (lowbush blueberry); © Jerry Pavia (Asian pear); © Ken Meyer (Arctic kiwi)

did you know...

Slip the wet foam and plastic bag into the paper sack.

Tie a ribbon around the center of the sack.

Disposable vase
Julia Moon, Tennessee

Julia loves to share vases full of flowers from her garden. To avoid the hassle of returning the vase, she makes one that can be tossed along with the spent blooms.

She uses the plastic bag her newspaper comes in, a narrow paper sack, a block of florist's foam (Oasis® is a popular brand) and some ribbon to make her disposable vase.

Cut the foam to fit the bag, then allow the block to sit in a bucket of water until it's saturated. Then slide the foam into the plastic bag, and the plastic bag into the paper sack, as you can see above.

Poke the cut ends of the flowers into the foam. Tie a ribbon around the center of the bag, and your beautiful bouquet is ready to share with a friend.

Hose saucer
Iris Martin, Washington

Flat soaker hoses make it easy to water plants, but, like most hoses, they're not always easy to store in winter. Long and loose, they slip off hooks or trip up an unwary gardener. Iris saves space by storing her hose in a plastic pot saucer. She starts with the sealed end at the outside edge of the saucer and winds the hose in toward the center. Her 50-foot hose fits nicely inside a 25-inch saucer, and the whole thing stores neatly on a shelf until she needs it. If you use more than one hose, store it in another saucer and stack it on top of the first one.

in the news

Cut flowers make you happy

Science has proven what gardeners have known for years — flowers make you happy. A recent study by Dr. Nancy Etcoff of Harvard Medical School and sponsored by the Society of American Florists and the Flower Promotion Council found that as long as people have a bouquet of flowers in their home, they have elevated moods. In contrast to others in the study who received a candle, people with flowers felt more compassionate, less worried and less depressed. So go ahead and buy a bouquet or bring in some flowers from the garden.

How to site a greenhouse
Tammy Geary, Montana

Q *I bought a small portable greenhouse for my spring seedlings. Where is the best spot for it and when can the seedlings go in it?*

A Since you're using your greenhouse for seedlings, put it in part shade to help avoid heat buildup (see illustration below.) In this case, the direction it faces isn't a concern.

Move your seedlings into the greenhouse when they have their second set of leaves, and daytime temperatures reach at least 40 degrees.

If you were going to use your greenhouse for growing plants to maturity, you'd want to make sure it received at least 6 hours of direct sun every day and that the ends faced east and west.

The amount of sun your greenhouse should get depends on how you're using it.

Trees, shrubs and fences protect a greenhouse from heavy rain or strong winds.

A greenhouse for mature plants needs full sun and east-west orientation.

A seed-starting greenhouse needs part shade and easy access.

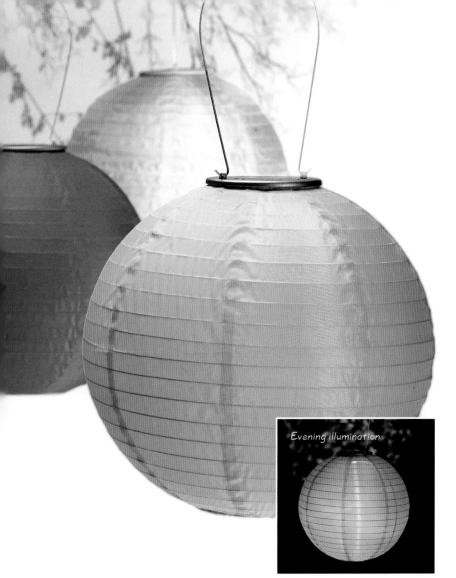

product pick
Soji Solar Lantern

This new product takes solar lights to a whole new level — eye level. Soji Solar Lanterns are easy to hang from a low tree branch or shepherd's hook. Just one day in the sun charges the battery enough for six to eight hours of light. They won't give you enough light to read by, but these charming 10-inch globes are a great evening accent for the garden. Lanterns come in five festive colors: orange, blue, white, red and green.

Bottom line: With no electrical cords to worry about, you can hang these lanterns wherever you like to enjoy them!
Source: www.allsopgarden.com or www.GardenGateStore.com
Price: $15.99 each

Evening illumination

product pick

The Life Cycles of Butterflies

That beautiful butterfly flitting from zinnia to zinnia in your garden wasn't always so delicate and graceful. You can find out how these "ugly ducklings" transform in *The Life Cycles of Butterflies*. Step-by-step photographs show the stages from tiny egg to hungry caterpillar to chrysalis and finally to colorful butterfly. Additional information includes range maps, size, nectar and host plants and time of year you can expect to see these visitors.

Bottom line: This is a book both kids and adults will love.
Source: Local or online bookstores or www. GardenGateStore.com
Price: $16.95 paperback; 152 pages

did you know... (CONTINUED)

Save your back
Debbie Heaton, Georgia
Tired of straining her back while laying a path, Debbie came up with a better idea. Instead of re-laying the large, heavy rocks over and over to get the right fit, she lays the stone down where she wants it. Then she paints the ground around the rock with bright orange spray paint. When she lifts the rock back up, she knows exactly where to dig the hole. Only one more move and her rock is in the hole. Any spray paint that gets on the surface is hidden in the soil.

Easy plant hangers
Patricia Di Nieri, New York
Decorative plant hangers can add such a nice touch to the garden. Here's how you can make your own using metal coat hangers. Cut off the top of a hanger with wire cutters. Then simply use pliers to twist the hanger into any design you like; the more curves and curls, the fancier the hanger. Patricia uses hers to hang plants, feeders, bird houses and wind chimes. (Test to be sure that it will hold the weight of the object first.)

Round off any sharp points on the ends of the hanger with sand paper.

product pick

Copper fire bowl

Enjoy your patio even on cool fall evenings with this beautiful fire pit. The bowl is hand-hammered copper set in a wrought-iron stand. We like the large, heavy-duty bowl that allows you to build a bigger fire that burns longer. A mesh cover (included), along with the deep sides, keeps the sparks contained. And the package includes a protective vinyl cover so the fire pit doesn't turn into a pond on rainy days.

Bottom line: Heavy duty and beautiful, it's a stylish addition to any outdoor living area.
Source: Gardener's Edge at 888-556-5676 or www.gardenersedge.com
Price: $289.99; 12 inches tall, 30 inches wide and 8 inches deep

Sow leaf lettuce among young carrots.

Start kale in the shade of mature tomatoes.

Plant several crops of bush beans in one area.

Finding room to grow
Diane Decker, Missouri

Q *I know late summer is a good time to plant cool-season vegetables. But how do I find space in my garden for them?*

A Here are some tips, as you can see above, for making the most of your available garden space.

Grow in the shade — Plant short-season, shade-tolerant plants in the shade of mature summer plants. The shady space next to mature tomato plants is great for starting lettuce, spinach, kale or peas.

A little extra water and a layer of mulch will conserve the moisture and get the young plants off to a good start.

Double up — Sow quick-growing plants with shallow roots, like lettuce or radishes, around slower-growing root crops, like carrots or onions. (Sow the greens around the individual carrots after they've been thinned.) The leafy veggies will be harvested quickly and won't get in the way of the developing carrots and onions.

Reuse the same space — Make several plantings of the same plant every two weeks from spring to midsummer. As the older plants fade, tear them out and plant new ones in the same space. This works well with bush beans. Pull any weeds and work in a little compost before each new planting.

in the news

Rain gardens to the rescue
Did you know that 50 percent of the rain water that falls in cities flows into storm sewers? The pollutants that wash away with each downpour end up in nearby waterways and can cause real problems for wildlife and even people. Researchers have found that rain gardens can be a big help. A two-year study at the University of Connecticut found that rain gardens trap and retain up to 99 percent of common pollutants, such as nitrates, ammonias and phosphorus. That means cleaner rivers and streams for everyone. If you'd like to learn more about constructing a rain garden in your yard or community, check out www.nemo.uconn.edu/tools/publications.htm or contact your local extension agency for information.

design
challenge
and drawing board
plans to solve *your* most challenging garden situations

HOW'D YOU DO THAT? is what most folks want to know when they see a gorgeous garden. Let us give you the solutions for six common situations gardeners face. From tips you can apply to your yard to specific planting plans for great-looking beds, it's all here!

Year-round Curb Appeal

Many older homes, like this one in Richmond, Virginia, were built close to the street, on narrow lots. That's wonderful for chatting to the neighbors in the evening, but not so good for gardening.

It's always a challenge to figure out what to plant in a small space. The owner, Joyce Hart, wants a garden that looks good all year, as well as plenty of flowers for color. And it all needs to fit in an east-facing bed that's approximately 9 feet deep and 16 feet long.

Not only is this space small, but one end (on the left) is heavily shaded by a big tree, while the small strip to the right of the steps gets a lot more sun. And that makes it hard to keep the two sides looking like they belong together. This area also has a slope down to the sidewalk, so it can be difficult to get plants started.

Dark brick walls are set off by crisp white trim, but the house still seems big and dark, almost looming over the street.

We'd like to plant shrubs and a small tree for year-round appeal, with perennials and a space for annuals to give lots of color. Let's see how we can combine them to bring some excitement to this small, shaded garden-to-be.

PHOTO: Courtesy of Joyce Hart

Peace and quiet

A porch should be a peaceful place to relax. But when the house is this close to the street (and on a corner, as well), you may feel like your porch is on permanent display. This planting area is small, but don't be afraid to include one or two small trees or large shrubs (in this case, the Japanese maple), to provide a leafy screen between you and the sidewalk.

Careful choices

When you're trying to achieve year-round interest in a small space, choose plants with care. The bright-green Japanese maple stands out against the dark brick of the house. Even when the leaves fall, the beautiful branch structure will look great in winter. Two varieties of boxwood add a touch of formal elegance. And their glossy green foliage looks great summer and winter. Boxwood tolerates both sun and shade, so you can repeat them on either side of the steps to make the sunny little strip to the right fit in with the rest of the garden. Also, the horizontal row of boxwoods and the weeping branches of the maple draw your eye across the narrow, vertical front of the house, making the garden seem wider.

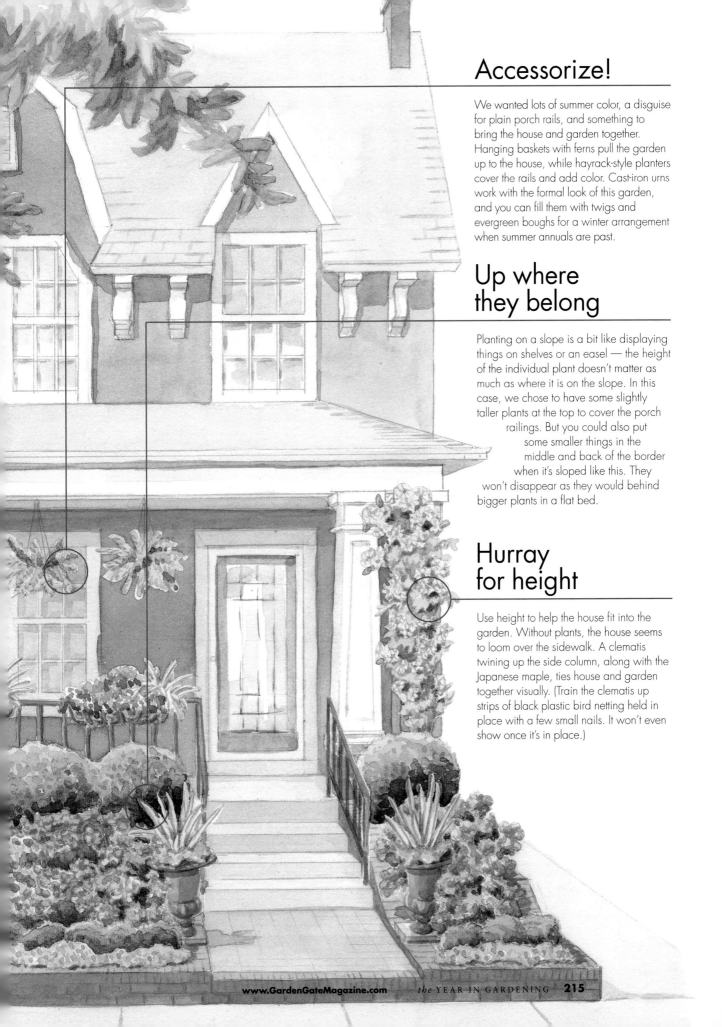

Accessorize!

We wanted lots of summer color, a disguise for plain porch rails, and something to bring the house and garden together. Hanging baskets with ferns pull the garden up to the house, while hayrack-style planters cover the rails and add color. Cast-iron urns work with the formal look of this garden, and you can fill them with twigs and evergreen boughs for a winter arrangement when summer annuals are past.

Up where they belong

Planting on a slope is a bit like displaying things on shelves or an easel — the height of the individual plant doesn't matter as much as where it is on the slope. In this case, we chose to have some slightly taller plants at the top to cover the porch railings. But you could also put some smaller things in the middle and back of the border when it's sloped like this. They won't disappear as they would behind bigger plants in a flat bed.

Hurray for height

Use height to help the house fit into the garden. Without plants, the house seems to loom over the sidewalk. A clematis twining up the side column, along with the Japanese maple, ties house and garden together visually. (Train the clematis up strips of black plastic bird netting held in place with a few small nails. It won't even show once it's in place.)

A Small Garden That Thinks Big

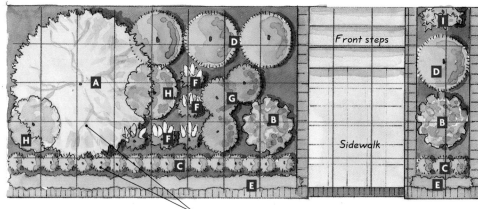

Front steps

Sidewalk

Spray boxwoods and Japanese maple twigs with an antidesiccant spray in late fall to protect them from drying winter winds.

Scale: 1 square = 4 square feet

A tiny strip of land, a bit of slope, shade…it might not sound like the best conditions for a garden. But you'd be surprised by what you can do with the right combination of plants. On the previous pages I showed you what this garden looks like in summer. Here, you see it in the spring — it truly has multi-season appeal.

In a small garden, it's best to stick to a limited color palette and plant selection. That way, you'll have room to plant several of each plant, which gives a lot more impact than scattered ones and twos. Pinks and whites will show up against the dark brick of this house and light up the shady spot under the tree. For color, astilbe and geraniums join a rose that blooms better in a bit of shade than most roses do. (Although we took care to keep the roses closer to the sunny end.) An unusual reblooming azalea, great for this Southern garden, adds a burst of bloom in the spring, and then flowers again from midsummer to fall.

Leave space around the Japanese maple for annuals and bulbs. You can change what you plant every year for a different look. And the hanging baskets, hayrack planters and urns offer flexibility from year to year, or even from season to season. Spring bulbs in the planters and tucked around the perennials make the season start early.

PLANNING TO PLANT

Sometimes, a tough planting site calls for some special measures. On even a mild slope, there's going to be erosion until the plant roots are established and can hold the soil in place. You may be tempted to use landscaping fabric, but don't. It doesn't break down, and that can limit your perennials as they spread to their full size. Instead, pin burlap in place with landscaping pins. It'll rot eventually, but for the first couple of years, it will hold the soil on the slope. Cover the burlap with a fibrous mulch, like shredded bark (not bark chunks, because they'll float away).

You'll probably need to create planting "pockets" for moist-soil-loving plants like astilbe. For each plant, dig out a hole about 18 inches wide and 12 inches deep and line it with plastic. Poke a few holes in the plastic for drainage, then refill the hole until it's the right size for planting.

Now you're all ready to start beautifying a small, shady garden area of your own. This might not be the huge 2-acre garden that every gardener dreams about, but by the time everything's planted and blooming its heart out, you may decide it's all the garden you need! □

— *Stephanie Polsley Bruner*

THE SHADY SIDE OF THE STREET

Code	Plant Name	No. to Plant	Blooms	Type	Cold/Heat Zones	Height/ Width	Special features
A	**Japanese maple** *Acer palmatum dissectum* 'Waterfall'	1	NA	Tree	6-9/8-2	7 ft./8 ft.	Fine, lacy green leaves turn yellow-orange in fall; strongly weeping shape
B	**Rose** *Rosa* 'The Fairy'	2	Pale pink; early summer to fall	Shrub	5-9/9-1	3 ft./3 ft.	Tolerates shade better than many roses; flowers in small clusters
C	**Boxwood** *Buxus microphylla japonica* 'Morris Midget'	20	NA	Shrub	5-9/9-1	12 in./14 in.	Grows slowly; can be sheared to maintain shape and size
D	**Boxwood** Southern *Buxus* 'Green Velvet'	4	NA	Shrub	5-8/9-1	3 ft./3 ft.	Prefers part shade, especially in hot climates; shear to maintain shape and size
E	**Plumbago** *Ceratostigma plumbaginoides*	20	Bright blue; midsummer to frost	Perennial	5-9/9-1	9 in./12 in.	Slow to emerge in spring; foliage turns red in fall
F	**Astilbe** *Astilbe xarendsii* 'Weisse Gloria' ('White Gloria')	5	White; midsummer	Perennial	4-8/8-1	18 in./16 in.	Needs consistently moist soil for best foliage and flowers
G	**Geranium** *Geranium* 'Patricia'	3	Magenta-pink; late spring to summer	Perennial	5-8/8-1	2 ft./2 ft.	Cut foliage back if it starts to flop open in midsummer; will regrow new, clean foliage
H	**Autumn Chiffon™ azalea** *Azalea* x 'Robled'	2	Pale pink; early spring	Shrub	7-9/9-4	30 in./36 in.	Reblooms in midsummer to fall; evergreen foliage
I	**Clematis** *Clematis* 'Nelly Moser'	1	Mauve; late spring/late summer	Vine	5-8/8-1	10 ft.	Mauve petals have pink stripes; clematis pruning group B or 2

QUICK TIP

Tuck in a few bulbs for a burst of early spring color. We chose several clumps of pink tulips and yellow daffodils. But be careful where you plant them — they won't like the damp-soil pockets you create for astilbe, so plant them closer to trees and shrubs.

From House to Home

It's a classic "builder's land-scape" — a few evergreens too close to the house and a couple of hostas in too much sun. The uninspired planting above just doesn't do much to show off the house, does it? But the right plantings can help make your new house seem warm and wel-coming right away.

Eric and Cristi Flynn aren't sure they want the same things in a planting. He'd like flowers and foliage, and she'd like something neat and trim. But they definitely agree that their Iowa garden needs dressing up.

Bold curves, stone edging and careful selection of plants do just that, creating a welcoming front entry that balances out the tall house. There's plenty of col-orful foliage and bright flowers, but it's fairly low maintenance — no need to spend hours keeping it clipped and tidy. And including shrubs, a couple small trees and some well-defined edges means this garden looks great all year.

Let's take a look at how we made this front yard inviting.

Shape and shade

This big house seems to loom out of the empty yard. You'll have to wait a while for large shade trees to mature. But in the meantime, smaller ornamental trees will make the house feel more sheltered and connected to the landscape. This white fringetree shelters the front door, providing a little late-afternoon shade for the plantings next to the southwest-facing house. On the right, an ornamental pear has a narrow, upright shape that echoes the peak of the roof.

Two ideas, one garden

Compromise can be a win-win situation. What do you do when one owner wants a loose, "fluffy" garden with lots of foliage and flowers, while the other prefers a tidy look? First, start out with bold bed edges, like the stone edging around this bed. That'll make the area look crisp and defined. Next, choose plants that stay neat without much trimming, like this ornamental pear. You won't have to spend a lot of time snipping them into shape. (If you've steered clear of ornamental pears in the past, 'Chanticleer' is less prone to breakage than older varieties.)

Welcome home

The front door is the most important part of any entry or foundation planting. This entire planting is focused on the door, with bright roses leading your eye toward the house. Two clumps of graceful maiden grass, one on either side, mark the front steps. An extra touch: Some ornamental low-voltage lights along the path will create a warm welcome for evening guests. (Learn more about the front-door planting on the next page.)

Plenty of room

Think big when you're planning a foundation or entry planting. How deep you make your planting will depend on your house (and how much room you have in the front yard). But a skimpy planting won't set off the house, and it'll also tempt you to put trees or shrubs too close to the foundation. This bed is almost 15 ft. deep at the right side of the house — plenty of room for a small tree and some midsized shrubs — and big enough to balance a tall house.

Simple Solution for a Tough Site

Y ou want your entryway to say, "Come on in!" But sometimes an entry needs a little work before it extends a warm welcome to anyone.

ONE TOUGH SITE Up against the house, little rain reaches the ground, and the lawn irrigation system doesn't extend that far. But it's close to an outdoor faucet, so providing some extra water will be easy.

The sun exposure is a challenge, too. This house faces southwest, and by early afternoon, this area is very hot and sunny. But it's in shade until then, and that dramatic change to hot afternoon sun is hard on plants. It's crucial to choose tough plants that'll tolerate these conditions. A white fringetree (see the previous page) casts a little late afternoon shade for smaller plants near the house.

SAY HELLO TO STYLE A blank wall to the left of the door is a bit stark, but what a great place to showcase your garden taste! Three containers of annuals on pedestals add height and interest. But you could also use trellises or garden art to show off your own flair. Lights on either side of the door coordinate with the low-voltage lights along the sidewalk and help break up those walls, as well.

In the garden, pale-pink roses bloom from late spring until fall. The rest of the plants offer plenty of interest without depending on flowers for color. Sweetspire forms a light-green backdrop most of the summer, but the white spring flowers and red fall leaves are great bonuses. Burgundy sedum and coral bells add color all season, while silvery lamb's ear ties the whole planting together. Finally, graceful, upright maiden grass highlights the front step. It'll look great through the winter, too.

Even the toughest entry can be blooming and beautiful. Try these tips, and see how wonderful it can look. □

— *Stephanie Polsley Bruner*

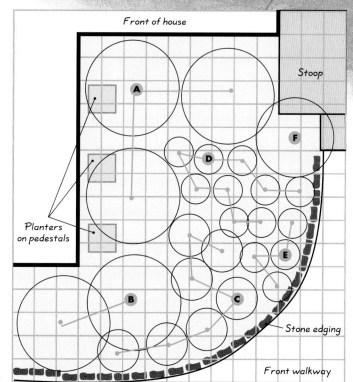

Scale: 1 square = 1 square foot

SERIOUSLY SUNNY

Code	Plant Name	No. to Plant	Blooms	Type	Cold/Heat Zones	Height/Width	Special Features
A	Sweetspire *Itea virginica* 'Henry's Garnet'	3	White; spring	Shrub	5-9/9-1	3-4 ft./4-5 ft.	Fragrant flowers; glowing red fall foliage
B	Rose *Rosa* Blushing Knock Out™	2	Pink; late spring to fall	Shrub	5-9/9-1	3-4 ft./4 ft.	Shell-pink flowers; glossy, disease-resistant foliage; deadhead to keep plant tidy
C	Sedum *Sedum telephium* 'Black Jack'	7	Rose-pink; late summer to fall	Perennial	3-9/9-1	2 ft./2 ft.	Dark purple-black foliage; late-summer flowers attract butterflies
D	Coral bells *Heuchera* 'Purple Petticoats'	9	Green-white; summer (insignificant)	Perennial	4-9/9-1	18 in./18 in.	Grown for frilly burgundy foliage; can cut back flowers if desired
E	Lamb's ear *Stachys byzantina* 'Big Ears'	4	Purple; summer	Perennial	4-9/9-1	6-12 in./12-24 in.	Attractive ground cover with fuzzy silver-green leaves; purple flowers seldom occur
F	Maiden grass *Miscanthus sinensis* 'Morning Light'	1	Silver plumes; late summer	Perennial	5-9/9-1	4-6 ft./3-5 ft.	Narrow green leaves with cream variegation look silvery; seedheads persist into winter

A Total Turnaround

Wow! A 40-by-50-foot oval. That's bigger than a lot of back yards. Think of all the great planting you could do there — if you could figure out where to start.

Some spaces are just hard to handle. Take this circular driveway in Mary Miller-Schulte's Wisconsin yard. It's flat and, other than the birch trees in the center, has no features to suggest planting ideas. Mary considered raised beds, but she didn't think they'd look quite right.

But berms, or mounded banks of soil, would add shape to the bed, as well as some height and privacy. They give the same effect as raised beds, without the need to build walls.

Let's see how these berms and plantings work together to create privacy and four-season color and interest. And we'll discuss how to plant a garden that looks great whether you're coming into the driveway, looking out the front door or strolling in the garden itself.

PHOTO: Courtesy of Mary Miller-Schulte

Stick with a theme

Whenever you add a new bed, make sure it echoes the other plantings around the house. This bed is so large that it could easily take on a life of its own. But a wild, meadow-style garden would look out of place against the tidy house and garden in the background. Plants with neat, controlled outlines, like umbrella-shaped crabapples and soft, upright willows, keep this garden from looking messy. On the other hand, you don't want it to look too stiff and formal, so include a few plants with looser habits, like vase-shaped serviceberries and billowing roses.

Draw a line

Where a gravel drive meets grass, there's often a weedy area that's not quite lawn, not quite flower bed, not quite driveway. A poured (or extruded) concrete edge creates a crisp line. It's a less-expensive, less time-consuming alternative for a big bed than brick or stone would be, and you can have the concrete tinted or stamped with a pattern, as we've done here. That way, you get the look of a brick edge without as much cost or labor. Check with your local landscaper or concrete company.

Manage the view

This driveway planting is essentially a big island bed, which means you can view it from more than one direction. A path leading through the bed gives access and creates an inviting view from all sides. Some larger trees and shrubs create a privacy planting for the house, without completely blocking the line of sight down the driveway. These taller plants, with the added height of the berm, also give the inner seating area plenty of privacy. Last but not least, shrubs and grasses, combined with the peeling bark of the original river birches in the center, add a bit of winter interest.

Raise your expectations

Most of the outer beds in this planting are bermed. An 18-in.-high berm adds height and interest to the garden, and it also creates a small, private seating area inside the turnaround. (We'll show you more about the seating area on the next page.) When you build a berm, make it higher than the desired final height. Then allow it to stand for a year before you plant trees or shrubs in it, or you risk exposing their roots as the soil settles. Depending on the type of soil you use, a berm can settle as much as one-third to one-half of its newly built height.

Hiding in Plain Sight

Imagine suddenly "discovering" a 40-by-50-foot space in your garden that you haven't already packed with plants! In our Design Challenge on p. 222, we showed you how to make the most of this flat, featureless oval. But the real surprise? A hidden garden getaway tucked into the center, with just enough room for a couple of chairs.

This driveway garden is big enough that you probably don't want to plant every square inch of it. You won't be able to see all of it anyway — unless you include a path and a seating area, as we have here, so you can view it from the "inside." Grass paths are inexpensive, and in this low-traffic area, grass will hold up just fine.

A serviceberry planted on the berm, combined with river birches that were already in the area, creates a shady spot to relax in. All these trees cast light, dappled shade, so many perennials will bloom well underneath them. (Shade gardens aren't all about hostas!) And the taller trees are on the west side, so there's plenty of morning sun. Ornamental grasses and trees and shrubs with strong shapes or colorful bark give this area some four-season interest, too.

Winter interest is important in this garden in USDA zone 4, where winters are long and cold. When you garden in zone 5 or colder, buy perennials, trees and shrubs that are grown in your zone or a colder area. They'll have a better chance of making it through the winters without difficulty. (Ask your local garden center where their plants come from.) □

— *Stephanie Polsley Bruner*

QUICK TIP

Let a newly built berm settle for a year before you plant trees and shrubs in it. And you can break the perennial planting into a couple of stages so it's not so overwhelming. Fill in with annuals for summer color until all the perennials are in place. You may decide to leave some spaces to tuck in annuals in the future, too.

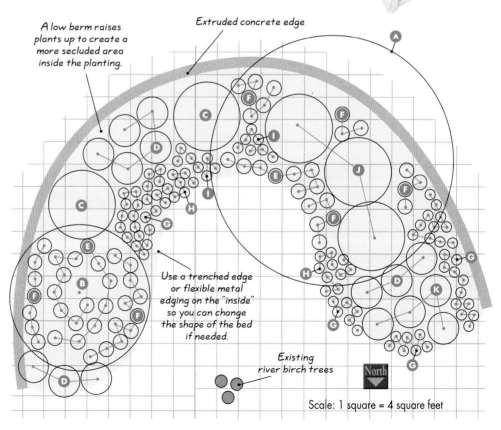

A low berm raises plants up to create a more secluded area inside the planting.

Extruded concrete edge

Use a trenched edge or flexible metal edging on the "inside" so you can change the shape of the bed if needed.

Existing river birch trees

North

Scale: 1 square = 4 square feet

COOL AND SHADY

Code	Plant Name	No. to Plant	Blooms	Type	Cold/Heat Zones	Height/ Width	Special Features
A	**Serviceberry** *Amelanchier laevis*	1	White; spring	Tree	4-8/9-1	15-30 ft./15-30 ft.	Edible purple berries in summer; red fall foliage
B	**Crabapple** *Malus* 'Coralburst'	1	Coral-pink; spring	Tree	4-7/8-1	10-12 ft./12-15 ft.	Few, small fruit that won't drop and make a mess
C	**Compact redtwig dogwood** *Cornus alba* 'Alleman's Compact'	2	White; spring	Shrub	2-8/8-1	4-8 ft./4-8 ft.	Red twigs in winter; new growth has brightest color so cut back oldest stems every spring
D	**Rose** *Rosa* 'Morden Centennial'	11	Pink; summer	Shrub	3-7/7-1	3-4 ft./3-4 ft.	Deadhead to keep blooming, but stop midsummer to allow rose hips to form
E	**Fern** *Athyrium* 'Ghost'	22	NA	Perennial	4-9/9-1	24 in./18 in.	Upright, silver-gray foliage; more tolerant of dry soil than many ferns
F	**Foamflower** *Tiarella* 'Spring Symphony'	36	Pink and white; spring	Perennial	4-9/8-1	10 in./18 in.	Deeply divided leaves with black splotch in the center
G	**Veronica** *Veronica* 'Goodness Grows'	56	Blue-purple; summer	Perennial	4-7/7-1	12 in./12 in.	Deadhead to keep plants reblooming
H	**Bellflower** *Campanula carpatica* 'Blaue Clips' (Blue Clips)	19	Blue; summer	Perennial	4-8/7-1	8 in./9-12 in.	May rebloom into fall in cooler climates
I	**Martagon lily** *Lilium martagon* 'Pink Attraction'	14	Pink; early to midsummer	Bulb	3-7/7-1	4 ft./1 ft.	Slow to establish; one of the few lilies to bloom in part shade
J	**Hydrangea** *Hydrangea arborescens* 'Annabelle'	3	White; midsummer to fall	Shrub	3-9/8-1	3-5 ft./4-6 ft.	Prune back to 4 or 5 in. above the ground in early spring
K	**Blue oat grass** *Helictotrichon sempervirens*	4	NA	Perennial	4-9/9-1	24-36 in./24-30 in.	Semi-evergreen; clean out dead stems or cut back as needed

Reclaim Your Privacy

Grow a screen

Columnar evergreens, such as these Leyland cypress, make a good screen. Buy the largest ones you can afford for a fast cover. But before you buy, determine the number you'll need. Figure the eventual diameter of each plant and then plan to set them a foot or two closer. That way they'll grow together and block the view. No point buying more plants than you need, or worse, ending up with gaps in the screen.

Noise. You may live on a busy street with lots of traffic. Maybe there's a barking dog next door. Lynn Christie has a new condominium complex behind her Arkansas home. It has a patio where folks like to sit and talk on their cell phones while she's trying to relax on her porch or work in her vegetable garden. As you can see in the photo, there's a board fence between the properties, but it simply isn't enough. She needs help, with both the visual and the sound problem.

We came up with several ways for Lynn to take back the privacy she misses. Have a look!

PHOTO: Courtesy of Lynn Christie

Plant in layers to absorb noise

Dense planting is a very good way to block noise. Granted, the cypress hedge helps, and so does the board fence behind it. But plant some vines, such as honeysuckle or clematis, on the fence and you'll make it more effective at deadening noise. Add a few broadleaf trees and shrubs, like hollies and crape myrtles, in front of the evergreens to block even more noise. Their flat leaves make excellent sound baffles. The more layers of foliage you can make in the space you have, the quieter your garden will be.

Make the view interesting

As you sit on the porch and look toward the back yard, a tall hedge could look pretty imposing in a small garden. But ornamental trees trimmed up high and with multiple trunks help break up this vertical wall. Another way to draw attention away from the green wall is to plant a colorful perennial and shrub border in front. It'll draw your eye down and away from the hedge, as well as the windows that peek above it. This bed is built on a berm. The mound of soil will absorb noise and the plants growing on it will deflect it. And because the berm makes the bed sit a bit higher than the lawn, the flowers show better from a distance.

Choose the best trees

GROW FAST AND THEN PRUNE Fast-growing plants, like the Leyland cypress, can grow larger than you expected very quickly. It's easy to shear them to the size you want using hedge clippers. But don't risk your safety trying to prune shrubs that are taller than you can safely reach from the ground, especially near power lines. It's a good idea to hire a professional for a task like that.

BUT LEAVE THE CRAPE MYRTLES ALONE We don't want to reduce the height of the crape myrtles in front of the hedge. So only the lower branches have been removed to show off the beautiful bark, and to make more planting area underneath.

PLAN FOR SUNSHINE Shade trees, along with large shrubs, are the backbone of any garden. But be careful where you place them. Here we want sun to reach the back border and the vegetable garden to keep them blooming and healthy. Small trees, like the ones in this garden, help block the view and cast some cooling shade. But they won't grow so large that they block out too much sunlight.

Beautify the vegetables

To make the vegetable garden handier to the back door, we moved it from the far back area to the side yard. It's in a very visible spot so we've suggested ways to make it ornamental, starting with a curving edge at the front. Since we don't need to block sound or the view to the north, an open trellis provides a place for vines. And to keep this spot from looking like a traditional vegetable garden, we've also included lots of flowers for cutting. You'll find a detailed plan for this area on the next page.

Surround the porch

A fringetree blocks the view into the porch from the condos' second story windows. Yet it's not so dense that people on the porch can't see out into the garden. And the open branching still lets cooling breezes in. The small, gurgling water fountain beneath it and a set of windchimes on the overhang cover more noise, plus their sound is very relaxing.

Feast for the Senses

Vegetables are good for you, so why not grow a few of your own in your garden? There's nothing better than picking a ripe tomato and serving it still warm and juicy from the heat of the day. With this flowery veggie garden you can do that, and cut a bouquet to dress up your table at the same time.

This is not a garden that'll give you lots of vegetables for the freezer, but it will keep your table filled. A tomato plant on a wooden obelisk makes a striking focal point, especially as the fruit ripens. Okra is a dramatic ornamental plant with its pods pointing straight up. Climbing beans, especially the ones with purple pods, make a lovely backdrop for the rest of the garden. I've left a narrow path next to

them so you'll have room to stand as you harvest.

All the flowers are easy to grow from seed, bulbs or starts you buy at the store. And some, like the nasturtiums and marigolds, are even edible. Many of these annuals, like the zinnias and cosmos, are not only very good cut flowers, but are attractive to butterflies, too.

I've specifically chosen only annual flowers and vegetables for this garden. To me, there's nothing better than heading out to the garden each spring with my spade to work up the soil. Turning over the earth is almost as satisfying to me as the veggies and flowers that my labor will produce later in the season. □

— *Jim Childs*

Pole beans will probably grow taller than the fence, so let them twine along the top.

A wood chip path will keep you out of the mud when you harvest beans.

Scale: 1 square = 1 square ft.

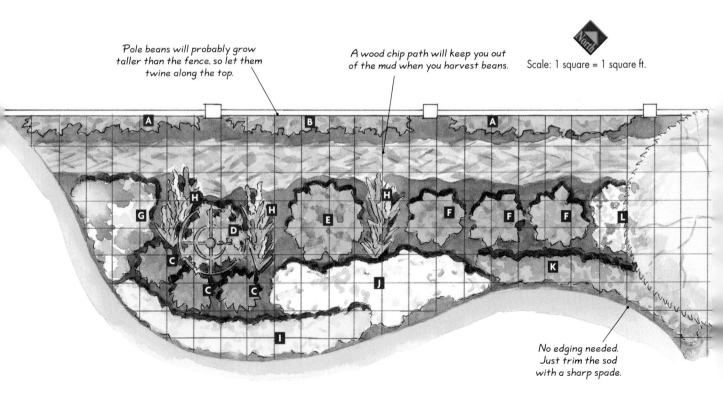

No edging needed. Just trim the sod with a sharp spade.

WHAT'S ON THE MENU?

VEGETABLES

Code	Plant Name	No. to Plant	Days to Maturity	Height/Width	Growing Tips
A	Lima bean *Phaseolus limensis* 'Big Mama'	Seed	80	10 ft./vine	Thin seedlings to stand 8 in. apart; 8-in.-long pods packed with sweet beans
B	Pole snap bean *Phaseolus vulgaris* 'Purple King'	Seed	75	8 ft./vine	Thin seedlings to stand 8 in. apart; 5- to-6-in.-long purple pods
C	Bell pepper *Capsicum annuum* 'Karma Hybrid'	3	85	2-3 ft./2 ft.	6-by-4-in. sweet peppers turn red; thick walled; excellent for stuffing; disease-resistant
D	Tomato *Lycopersicon* 'Brandywine'	1	80	4 ft./vine	Heirloom; large fruit; excellent flavor; indeterminate cultivar
E	Cucumber *Cucumis sativus* 'Salad Bush Hybrid'	Seed	57	18 in./3 ft.	Plant three to five seeds in a hill; 8-in.-long fruit with smooth skin; disease-resistant
F	Okra *Abelmoschus esculentus* 'Clemson Spineless	3	56	4-5 ft./2 ft.	Harvest pods when 3 in. long; straight pods with no spines

ANNUALS

Code	Plant Name	No. to Plant	Blooms	Height/Width	Growing Tips
G	Zinnia *Zinnia elegans* 'Cut and Come Again'	Seed	Mixed colors; summer	24 in./12 in.	Thin seedlings to stand 12 in. apart; 2½-in.-diameter flowers on long stems; deadhead for rebloom
H	Gladiolus *Gladiolus* hybrid	18	Mixed colors; summer	30 in./6 in.	Space corms 4 in. apart; plant a few every 2 weeks for a good supply of cut flowers
I	Marigold *Tagetes patula* 'Janie Primrose'	Seed	Yellow; summer	8 in./6 in.	Thin seedlings to stand 6 in. apart; blooms 6 weeks after sown; attracts butterflies
J	Petunia *Petunia* hybrid 'Frillytunia White'	9	White; summer	12 in./18 in.	3-in. blooms with ruffled edges; compact plants; long-blooming
K	Nasturtium *Tropaeolum majus* 'Peach Melba'	Seed	Peach-yellow; summer	12 in./12 in.	Thin seedlings to stand 6 in. apart; flowers have maroon spots; compact habit; blue-green foliage
L	Cosmos *Cosmos bipinnatus* 'Sonata Mix'	Seed	Pink and white; summer	24 in./15 in.	Thin seedlings to stand 10 in. apart; shades of pink and white flowers; ferny foliage

Make a Splash!

What could be better than spending a hot afternoon by the pool? Spending a hot afternoon by the pool, surrounded by beautiful plantings!

John and Betty Pilato of New York enjoy their pool, but they'd like to dress it up. Of course, it's important to enclose a pool, both for safety and privacy. But this back yard seems to have miles of privacy fence. And since the deck of the pool is concrete, there's just not a lot of planting space. (See our plan for a raised bed over concrete on p. 232.)

Maybe you don't have a pool, but you have lots of concrete or pavers, or little planting space around a patio or courtyard. These design tips can help you, too. Put them to use anywhere that needs to be brightened up but doesn't have room for a "traditional" garden.

Strategic uses of containers, trellises and furniture can make any space a favorite summer retreat. We'll even show you a plan for a colorful summer container, at right.

DESIGN: Kerry Mendez, Perennially Yours, Ballston Spa, New York; PHOTO: Betty Pilato

Trim the tree

A large spruce offers a little shade without the mess of falling leaves. Although most experts don't recommend limbing up evergreens because it changes their natural shape, this one had already been pruned to keep it away from the fence. So we removed a couple more of the lower limbs to give more clearance. They were right at eye level, and in this limited walking space, that can be hazardous. There's not much space around the trunk for planting, but a few hostas will soften the bare trunk.

Contain those plants

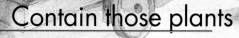

Around a pool, on a patio, or even in an unused driveway, containers are the way to go. We put these containers on wheels so they're easy to move. Group them near the patio for a dinner party, or roll them out of the way if you need to do some pool maintenance. You can purchase plant caddies or stands with wheels in most home improvement stores or garden centers. Choose one with a locking wheel so the container can't be moved by a gust of wind.

Face up to a fence

Privacy fences can be boring. Here, custom-made trellises break up the horizontal line. (You only see one, but we repeated them along the fence for impact.) The trellises' tapered shape echoes architectural features of the Craftsman-style house. If you have space, use planters at the base of the trellises to grow annual vines. But here there's only about 3 ft. between the fence and the pool's edge, so trellises with a strong shape can be a decorative element even without plants. Baskets mounted on the fence posts add an extra splash of color to the fence, too.

BIG, BRIGHT, BOLD

This colorful container could wake up any garden. Strong colors and a bold, tropical feel make this planting a perfect accent near a pool. Flowering annuals combine with striking foliage plants to create a summer-long display. And it's all set off by the teal-blue glazed container. At 24 in. across the top, it's big enough to hold a lot of plants!

A **Canna**
   Canna 'Phaison' (Tropicanna™)   **1**

B **Browallia**
   Browallia Endless™ Illumination   **3**

C **Tuberous begonia**
   Begonia Illumination® Orange   **2**

D **Morning glory**
   Ipomoea tricolor 'Heavenly Blue'   **2**

E **Bacopa** *Bacopa*
   Snowstorm® Giant Snowflake   **3**

F **Creeping Jenny**
   Lysimachia nummularia 'Aurea'   **2**

Choose flexible furniture

You want to be comfortable when you sit in your garden. We chose matching, lightweight wooden chairs to replace the built-in benches and miscellaneous poolside furniture. These chairs can be moved around, grouped for conversation or set out of the way. For an extra pop of color, paint your furniture to make it stand out even more. And don't forget the cushions — these bright prints play up the tropical feel, and there are lots of great new easy-care, waterproof, fade-resistant fabrics available.

How to Garden on Concrete

It's hard to garden when you don't really have any soil! In this case, it's a poolside planting, but you might face this same situation if you have a paved patio or courtyard. Just because you have a lot of concrete or pavers doesn't mean you can't garden!

There's not much planting space inside this fenced-in area. But a simple solution, a raised bed, comes to the rescue. It's filled with plants timed to look their best in June, July and August, just when you're spending time by the pool or relaxing outside. (Of course, if you have room, this plan would look nice planted directly in the ground, too.)

This corner bed, tucked in next to a patio, is actually built over concrete. If you're concerned about piling soil against a fence, as here, continue the raised bed edge all the way around the back of the bed. Be sure that the deck of the pool slopes down toward the fence — you don't want muddy water flowing into the pool. What you use for bed edges depends on the look you want — this one is actually built of recycled concrete chunks, and filled with a mixture of topsoil and compost.

How deep do you need to make a raised bed? It depends on the plants you want to use. This bed was originally only about 8 inches high, but we suggested that the homeowners make it 14 to 18 inches high. That'll give more room for roots. You'll need to choose plants with shallow, fibrous root systems (even the pagoda dogwood has a shallow root system), instead of taproots. But you could put bigger plants, like shrubs or small trees, in containers and set them on top of the raised bed (Just roll them into the garage for the winter if you live where it freezes.)

Plants with chartreuse foliage light up this partly shaded corner. Repetition is a good design idea in any garden. But this small planting will have the most impact if you choose just a few species and plant several of each. That'll give your garden a more unified look than planting one or two of many different kinds of plants.

These plants do best with consistently moist soil. Topdress with a couple inches of compost every spring to keep the soil in good shape and add some nutrients.

Whether you're planting on a patio or near a pool, this garden is the perfect way to dress up a corner! □

— *Stephanie Polsley Bruner*

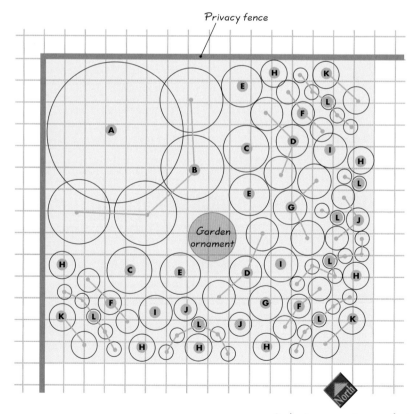

Privacy fence

Garden ornament

Scale: 1 square = 1 square foot

THE GARDEN'S PALETTE

Code	Plant Name	No. to Plant	Blooms	Type	Cold/Heat Zones	Height/Width	Special Features
A	**Pagoda dogwood** *Cornus alternifolia* 'Golden Shadows'	1	White; spring	Small tree	3-7/7-1	8-10 ft./ 6-8 ft.	Green leaves with gold edges; fragrant flowers followed by dark-purple berries that attract birds
B	**Hosta** *Hosta sieboldiana elegans*	4	White; early summer	Perennial	3-9/9-1	30 in./ 36 in.	Heavy, puckered blue-gray leaves; may reach as much as 5 ft. across if left undisturbed
C	**Bleeding heart** *Dicentra spectabilis* 'Gold Heart'	2	Pink; spring	Perennial	5-9/9-1	36 in./ 24 in.	Red stems and pink flowers stand out against bright chartreuse-yellow foliage; may die back later in summer
D	**Astilbe** *Astilbe simplicifolia* 'Pink Lightning'	6	Pink; summer	Perennial	4-9/9-1	18 in./ 18-24 in.	Rose-pink flowers are lightly fragrant; blooms mid- to late summer
E	**Astilbe** *Astilbe chinensis* 'Purpurkerze' (Purple Candles)	3	Purple; summer	Perennial	4-8/8-1	36-40 in./ 18-24 in.	Upright, purple blooms; flowers in early summer; can leave seedheads for late-season interest
F	**Coral bells** *Heuchera* 'Plum Pudding'	9	White; summer	Perennial	4-9/9-1	12 in./ 12 in.	Shiny plum-purple leaves with silver overlay; grown for foliage so can cut back flowers if desired
G	**Masterwort** *Astrantia major* 'Claret'	4	Maroon; early to midsummer	Perennial	4-7/7-1	22 in./ 18 in.	Needs uniformly moist soil; papery flowers remain attractive for a long time after bloom
H	**Deadnettle** *Lamium maculatum* 'Pink Chablis'	7	Pink; summer	Perennial	3-8/8-1	8 in./ 12-18 in.	Prefers moist soil; shear back in midsummer if needed to refresh foliage
I	**Jacob's ladder** *Polemonium reptans* 'Stairway to Heaven'	3	Blue; early to midsummer	Perennial	3-7/7-1	12-24 in./ 18 in.	White leaf margins edged with pink; deadhead for possible late-summer rebloom
J	**Fernleaf bleeding heart** *Dicentra* 'Ivory Hearts'	5	White; early to midsummer	Perennial	3-8/8-1	8-10 in./ 12 in.	Keep soil moist for healthy foliage all summer; may bloom continuously in cool summers or will rebloom in fall
K	**Creeping Jenny** *Lysimachia nummularia* 'Aurea'	6	Yellow; spring	Perennial	3-9/9-1	3-6 in./ 12-18 in.	Quick-growing ground cover; chartreuse foliage maintains best color in part sun
L	**Browallia** *Browallia* 'Endless™ Illumination'	31	Blue; spring to fall	Annual	NA	8-10 in./ 6-8 in.	Pinch back for a more compact plant

A Standout in the Shade

W hen you think of a garden, you probably think of a bed with plants in it, maybe a path or an arbor, a birdbath or a garden ornament. It's easy to forget about the surrounding spaces, whether it's buildings, natural features or other plantings. And what's around a garden can play just as big a role in how it eventually looks as any of the things you intend to plant in it.

Marie Wagner found that to be true. A wooded lot provided a nice backdrop of trees for her Michigan garden, but they did cast a lot of shade. It was hard to get plants started, and even when they got a little bigger, they disappeared against the leafy background.

So let's take a look at this space. With the right plants and the right hardscaping, we can figure out some ways to create a beautiful garden that works with the surroundings. And it'll be something that looks good from the first month it's planted, too!

Create a transition

You might think there are enough trees around already, but including a small tree in this bed actually helps link the garden with the surroundings. This dense-foliaged star magnolia is bold enough to stand out against the leafy, wispy background, and it's the right size to tie the taller trees and the shorter garden plants together. Some bold-textured shrubs, like the oakleaf hydrangeas at the far right, are also great backdrop plants for smaller perennials. Trees and shrubs add a little winter interest in a garden, too.

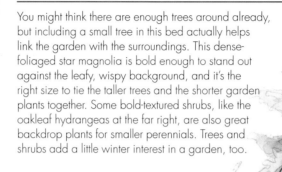

PHOTO: Courtesy of Marie Wagner

Add instant "oomph"

For immediate impact, we turned to hardscaping instead of waiting for the trees and shrubs to grow. Three 6-ft.-tall custom-made screens, painted turquoise, add instant height and color. They also create a visual "stop," keeping your eyes focused on the bed in front of them, instead of the trees behind. And they're just tall enough to peep over the top of the shrubs at their full-grown height. Two groupings of glossy purple containers planted with annuals also help make the garden look established quickly. (We'll give you some more ideas for a quick fix in a new garden on the next page.)

Plant in drifts

We've talked about how this garden needs to stand out against the busy background. Most perennials just aren't bulky enough. But use the tried-and-true landscaping tip of planting them in drifts. They'll have a lot more impact that way, especially in a setting like this, where one or two plants would get lost, but a clump of eight or 10 will really make a statement. Be sure to choose the right plants, too — before you plant, spend some time to find out exactly how much sun your garden gets. Sun perennials and ornamental grasses will get too lanky and stretched out in this bed. But shade-lovers, like astilbe and hosta, will perform just fine.

Make the bed

An island bed is one of the most flexible garden designs around. You can start small and make it bigger as plants grow or as you have more time or ideas. We stuck with the original curving bed shape and size because it has a laid-back, casual feel that looks just right with the wooded area around it. It's about 28 ft. long and 15 ft. wide, so it's plenty big enough for some good-sized plants. As a rule, a bed with a small tree in it should be at least as wide as the tree is high to look in scale. (Here, the star magnolia gets about 15 ft. tall, so this bed is just the right size already.)

Grow a Lush Garden From Year One

Digging in compost, hauling water and spreading mulch are the *easy* parts of putting in a new garden. The hard part? Waiting for it to grow.

How do you plan so your new garden isn't a disappointment the first couple of years? Three things: Phased planting, annuals and hardscaping. Let me show you how to use these techniques to make any garden look great from the beginning.

PHASED PLANTING When you have a garden all planned, it's tempting to buy all the shrubs and perennials at once. But you'll be happier with your new bed in the short term if you don't. All those little plants will look sparse and spotty.

Instead, plant the trees and shrubs and some of the perennials first. Give this initial planting a few years to get established, then plant the rest of the perennials.

ANNUALS Just think of annuals as quick plants to fill in and add color around a new perennial planting. You'll plant them in the spaces you're leaving for more perennials in a year or two.

Choose annuals that don't sprawl — you don't want them to smother the tiny perennials around them. Here, we tucked in impatiens and caladiums for color. In the back, elephant ears add much-needed height while the shrubs are small.

HARDSCAPING Whether it's a pergola, an obelisk for annual vines or screens like these, hardscaping makes something happen in the garden right away. These screens are painted turquoise so your eye will be drawn to them, instead of to the just-getting-started plantings.

Containers are another quick fix. Group them together for maximum impact and fill them with annuals for an eye-catching focal point.

Here, we've shown you a two-step plan for a shady garden that looks great from the beginning. The first plan, on this page, incorporates shrubs, a few perennials and some annuals. Turn the page and we'll show you how to take the next step.

Enjoy your new planting as it grows and changes. Before you know it, it'll be all grown up! □

— *Stephanie Polsley Bruner*

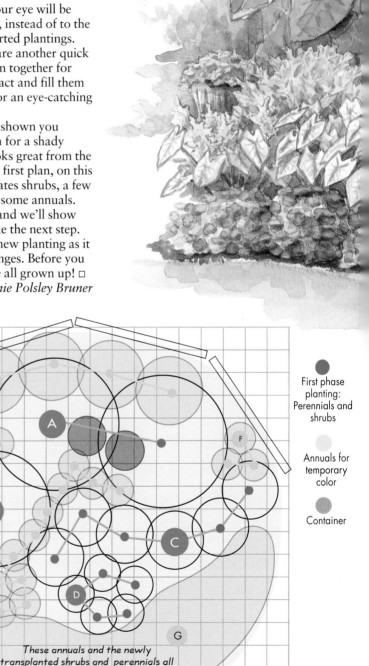

First phase planting: Perennials and shrubs

Annuals for temporary color

Container

These annuals and the newly transplanted shrubs and perennials all need plenty of water to thrive.

North

Scale: 1 square = 1 square foot

QUICK TIP

Replant new elephant's ears or caladiums every year, or overwinter the bulbs. Shake off the soil and store them in dry peat moss or wood shavings at about 65 degrees F.

THE FIRST YEAR'S PLANTING

Code	Plant Name	No. to Plant	Blooms	Type	Cold/Heat Zones	Height/ Width	Special features
A	Oakleaf hydrangea *Hydrangea quercifolia* 'Flemygea' (Snow Queen)	2	White; early to midsummer	Shrub	5-9/9-3	5 ft./6 ft.	White blooms fade to pink, last until fall; burgundy-red fall foliage
B	Itea *Itea virginica* 'Henry's Garnet'	1	White; spring	Shrub	5-9/9-1	3 ft./5 ft.	Glowing red fall foliage
C	Hosta *Hosta* 'Halcyon'	6	Lavender; late summer	Perennial	3-8/8-1	24 in./30 in.	Heavily puckered, blue-green leaves
D	Astilbe *Astilbe xrosea* 'Peach Blossom'	7	Pink; early to midsummer	Perennial	4-9/9-1	24 in./18 in.	Keep soil moist for healthy foliage all summer

Plant these tender bulbs and annuals for instant impact!

Code	Plant Name	No. to Plant	Blooms	Type	Cold/Heat Zones	Height/ Width	Special features
E	Elephant's ear *Colocasia esculenta*	4	N/A	Tender bulb*	8-10/12-1	4 ft./3 ft.	Best in afternoon shade, out of strong wind; do not allow soil to dry out
F	Caladium *Caladium* 'White Queen'	17	N/A	Tender bulb*	9-10/12-1	18 in./18 in.	Grown for showy foliage; best in afternoon shade, out of strong winds
G	Impatiens *Impatiens* Super Elfin® Paradise mix	3 flats	Mixed colors	Annual	Annual/12-1	10 in./12 in.	Blooms all summer; very sensitive to even the lightest frost

* Treat as an annual or overwinter bulbs indoors.

There aren't any hard-and-fast rules about when you plant what in a new bed. You can adapt the time frame we used here to your own garden and schedule. If you're in a hurry, you could purchase bigger-sized new plants to speed things up.

But here, we gave the original plantings three years to get established and put on some growth, filling in with annuals in the meantime. The fourth spring, we planted the four perennials listed in "The second phase," below, instead of annuals.

This plan is geared toward spring, but if you want more blooms in fall, read the list at the bottom of the page. It offers summer- and fall-blooming alternatives. Or pick a couple plants from both lists for a long-blooming, beautiful bed. □

— *Stephanie Polsley Bruner*

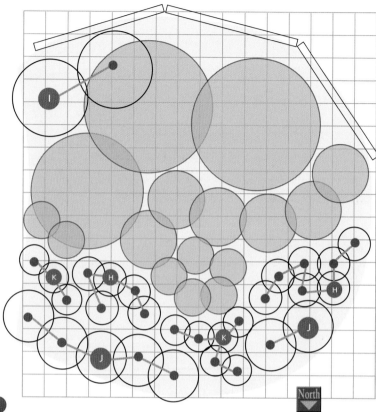

Existing perennials and shrubs   Second-phase perennials

North

Scale: 1 square = 1 square foot

THE SECOND PHASE

Code	Plant Name	No. to Plant	Blooms	Type	Cold/Heat Zones	Height/Width	Special features
H	Fringed bleeding heart *Dicentra* 'Luxuriant'	12	Pink; midspring	Perennial	3-9/9-1	18 in./18 in.	Foliage holds up in all but the hottest weather; some summer rebloom
I	Goatsbeard *Aruncus dioicus*	2	White; midspring to early summer	Perennial	4-8/8-1	5 ft./3 ft.	Prefers moist soil
J	Lungwort *Pulmonaria saccharata* 'Mrs. Moon'	7	Pink and blue; early spring	Perennial	3-8/8-1	12 in./28 in.	Flowers open pink, fade to blue; narrow, dark-green leaves have silvery spots
K	Coral bells *Heuchera* 'Plum Pudding'	9	White; early summer	Perennial	4-9/9-1	18 in./15 in.	Grown for ruffled, plum-purple leaves with silver markings

WANT MORE BLOOMS IN FALL?

Switch out a couple (or all!) of these perennials for the ones listed above. Adjust the number to plant as needed.

Code	Plant Name	No. to Plant	Blooms	Type	Cold/Heat Zones	Height/Width	Special features
H	Japanese anemone *Anemone hupehensis japonica* 'Pamina'	8	Pink; late summer	Perennial	5-8/8-1	2 ft./2 ft.	Double pink flowers; compact plant
I	Bugbane *Actaea simplex* (Atropurpurea Group) 'Hillside Black Beauty'	2	White; late summer to early fall	Perennial	4-8/8-1	30 in./4 ft.	Purple foliage; 4- to 6-ft. flower spikes in fall
J	Toad lily *Tricyrtis formosana* 'Gilt Edge'	7	White with purple spots; late summer to fall	Perennial	5-8/8-1	1 ft./2 ft.	Leaves have irregular chartreuse variegation; prefers consistently moist soil
K	Corydalis *Corydalis lutea*	9	Yellow; early summer to fall	Perennial	5-7/8-1	18 in./18 in.	May reseed; if foliage gets tattered, cut back hard to refresh

« Most gardens incorporate several of these design building blocks. In the photo at left, the LINE of the path leads your eye to the FOCAL POINT of the arbor. Clumps of plants are REPEATED along the path. The petals of the poppy below have a silky TEXTURE and the purple and orange are a great color CONTRAST.

building blocks of design

As you read *The Year in Gardening*, you'll notice design terms like "line," "shape," and so on. These are the building blocks of good design, whether you're planting a garden, painting a picture or decorating a room. Below, find out how to put these tools to work in your own garden.

COLOR Everyone has different taste in color. But keep in mind that warm colors (browns, oranges, reds and yellows) can feel either energetic or cozy, and warm-colored flowers or objects often seem closer. Cool colors (blues, greens, lavenders, purples) are serene and soothing, and they usually recede, making a cool-colored object seem farther away. There can be some overlap; for instance, a pink flower might be a warm pink with undertones of salmon and orange, or it might be a cool pink with a touch of lavender or blue.

CONTRAST Contrast happens when two dissimilar objects are compared. That's the textbook definition, but what does it really mean? Pair a fuzzy-leafed plant with a plant that has smooth, glossy leaves, or plant bright-red flowers next to bright-blue ones — that's

contrast. A black iron bench blends in against a dark-green yew hedge, but a white bench stands out because of the color contrast. Use contrast to call attention to a special plant or ornament and to keep the garden exciting and interesting.

FOCAL POINT A focal point is where your eye goes first when you look at a scene, like a bold shape against a finer-textured background or a bright splash of color that draws your eye. If part of your garden looks bleak at a certain time of the year, place something bright in a different part of the garden. Your eyes will go to the bright spot without noticing the less-attractive area.

LINE A line can be straight, curving, vertical or horizontal. Edging, a sidewalk or a row of plants can create a line. Use lines to direct people's eyes to a certain

view (for instance, position a statue at the end of a straight pathway; your eyes will follow the path directly to the statue). Lines also define shapes, as a well-defined edge (the line) shows off a bed shape.

REPETITION Repetition is exactly what it sounds like: A garden element that's repeated over and over. It might be clumps of one type of plant scattered through the garden, or it could be the same bricks used in a patio, in a path and as edging. Repetition makes your design look planned and deliberate, so all the small, separate areas are clearly part of one garden. (Think of it as having your shoes and your belt match — everything just looks more pulled together.)

SHAPE Flower shapes (like spikes or daisies) can create a mood or feeling in the garden. A planting with a lot of spiky, upright flowers has lots of energy, while round or daisy-shaped flowers look cheerful and serene. Bed shapes are important too. Simple geometric shapes like circles and rectangles look at home in a formal garden, while curving, irregularly shaped beds are more casual.

TEXTURE Texture is the surface quality of an object. A leaf might be furry or smooth. A pea gravel path has a finer texture than a flagstone path, while a tree with large, bold twigs has a coarser texture than a tree with fine, wispy twigs. If you want to show off a specimen tree or shrub, it's best to set it in front of a group of fine-textured plants, which blend together to create a backdrop that won't distract.

all about
containers

grow the *best containers* on the block!

IF YOU WANT INSTANT IMPACT, growing container gardens is one of the best ways to get it. Want to punch up your entry this weekend? Plant a container! Tired of your deck's color scheme? Do a quick switch of your pots. Here you'll find gorgeous container plans for every season as well as some great advice on how to buy potting soil and a project that takes old black nursery pots and turns them into charming faux stone planters. Now get growing!

Tips for care

- To help retain moisture, line the box with plastic with a few holes cut into it
- Add water-retaining crystals to the soilless mix before planting
- Full sun to part shade
- Fertilize every time you water with ¼-strength liquid fertilizer

This billowy window box practically sings "spring" with lush flowers in mostly yellows and purples. Touches of orange add accents and soft, airy white blooms tie everything together. An added bonus in this design? Throw open the window on a nice spring morning and enjoy the lovely fragrance!

Nemesias provide three of the colors of this cool-weather combo — lavender, white and yellow. When this fragrant, free-flowering annual is young, pinch it back by about half so it'll grow bushier.

Pansies add to the yellow-and-purple color scheme. They bloom profusely in cool spring or fall weather. Look for strong, stocky plants with few blooms and lots of buds at the garden center.

As you might guess from its name, sweet alyssum gives off a delicate honey-like fragrance that's popular with the bees and butterflies. Cut back the first flush of flowers to encourage more blooms.

Window boxes tend to dry out quickly. Check the moisture often, especially in very hot weather. □

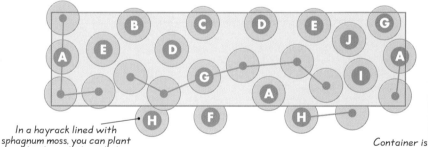

In a hayrack lined with sphagnum moss, you can plant right through the sides!

Container is 30 in. long by 7½ in. wide

SUNNY SPRING WINDOWSCAPE

Code	Plant Name	No. to Plant
A	**Nemesia** *Nemesia hybrids*	7
B	**Pot marigold** *Calendula officinalis*	1
C	**Asparagus fern** *Asparagus spp.*	1
D	**Cape daisy** *Osteospermum hybrid*	2
E	**Cosmos** *Cosmos bipinnatus*	2
F	**Calibrachoa** *Calibrachoa hybrid*	1
G	**Pansy** *Viola hybrid*	7
H	**Sweet alyssum** *Lobularia maritima*	3
I	**Brachyscome** *Brachyscome hybrid*	1
J	**Snapdragon** *Antirrhinum majus*	1

The best advice I ever got is, "Keep it simple." One look at this plant combination proves that it also applies when designing containers.

A simple soft-pink theme draws your eye to this gorgeous design. But did you notice that this cloud of pink is actually made of two different plants? The taller nemesia, with its fragrant flowers at the tips of its stems, closely matches the pink of the shorter verbenas.

But as any gardener knows, you *can* have too much of a good thing. That's where the yellow daisy-shaped flowers of the 'Topmix' dahlia come in. Its larger, slightly shiny leaves give your eyes a little rest from all that pink. Unlike the other plants in this pot, the dahlia won't grow much larger during the season. Place it where it won't get covered up and pinch back its more-vigorous neighbors so the dahlia can have its share of the spotlight.

Trailing purple calibrachoas also help to break the pink theme. To keep them full, use a little ¼-strength acidic fertilizer like Miracid® in the soil immediately around them once a month.

You may enjoy this colorful show for a while before you notice the subtle black pot it's planted in. (Make sure the container gets afternoon shade, so it doesn't get too hot.) With its sleek simple look, it simply stands back and lets the plants be the stars in this performance. □

Tips for care

- Full sun, afternoon shade
- Moist, well-drained soil
- Feed with a balanced water-soluble fertilizer twice a month

Container is 12 inches in diameter.

THINK PINK

Code	Plant Name	No. to Plant
A	Nemesia *Nemesia* hybrid	2
B	Dahlia *Dahlia* 'Topmix'	2
C	Verbena *Verbena* hybrid	1
D	Calibrachoa *Calibrachoa* hybrid	2

Stunning containers start with great soil.

How to Buy Potting Mix

You're at the garden center to buy potting mix. Some bags are less than a dollar, while some are more expensive. These bags say that there's fertilizer added. Those bags say there's compost in the mix. You just want to pot up some plants and have them grow well. This should be easy, but all these choices are confusing.

Let me help you. I'll answer your questions on potting mix so the next time you need to stock up on a bag or two, you'll know what you're buying. And I'll give you a few tips on getting the most out of it once it's in your containers, too.

HOW CAN I TELL IF I'M BUYING GOOD POTTING MIX?

First, read the bag. For most uses, you want a soilless mix — that means it doesn't have any actual topsoil in it. A soilless mix is lightweight, with plenty of room for air and moisture around plant roots. It also won't carry soilborne diseases. These mixes contain peat moss, finely shredded bark, perlite, sand and sometimes compost.

Unfortunately, reading the bag doesn't always tell the whole story. Most brands say what the ingredients are, but few of them tell you percentages of ingredients.

But you can tell quite a bit about potting mix even without a detailed label. Lift the bag, then squeeze the mix inside. If the bag is lightweight and the consistency inside is springy, that's a good sign. Steer clear of a bag that's very heavy, or if the mix inside squeezes into a shape and stays that way.

IS IT WORTH IT TO BUY THOSE MIXES WITH FERTILIZER AND MOISTURE-HOLDING CRYSTALS?

Most of those products are good potting mixes. They're a little more expensive than plain old potting mix, but they're so common now that sometimes it's hard to find a mix without extra ingredients. Water-holding crystals do help keep soil moist, but if you find a good mix without them, you can always add them yourself.

The fertilizer in these mixes is in slow-release pellets. It provides some nutrients over several months, but it's not enough to last your containers all summer.

I like to control how much fertilizer plants are getting, so I usually purchase a mix without any extras. Garden centers often sell their own special mix without fertilizer or crystals, or look for mixes labelled "organic" or "professional." Usually, although not always, these mixes have just the basic ingredients.

MY CONTAINERS DRY OUT SO FAST THAT I CAN'T KEEP THEM MOIST. WHAT CAN I DO?

A potting mix with moisture-holding crystals may still dry out quickly. Add more crystals in a layer about halfway down the container, or try this tip: I mix one part compost with three parts potting mix before I put it in my hanging baskets, which tend to dry out quickly. The added compost helps the mix hold moisture better.

WHEN I WATERED MY CONTAINERS AFTER PLANTING, THE MIX JUST "FLOATED" UP OUT OF THE POT. WHAT'S WRONG?

You need to moisten potting mix before you put it in containers. Peat moss, the main ingredient, holds water well once it's wet, but it can be hard to get it wet in the first place. I always put dry potting mix in a tub, pour water on it, and work the mix with my hands until it's damp. (Pour water into the bag if you don't have a tub handy.) Premoistened mix won't float the first time you water, and you'll be sure you're getting enough potting mix. Planting in dry mix will leave your plant roots exposed because the mix will compress when it gets wet.

GOOD VS. BAD

Here's a simple test for potting mix. Get it wet and squeeze a handful of it. Below left, you'll notice that the potting mix crumbled, with lots of loose pieces still sticking to my hand. A good, lightweight soilless mix will look like this.

In my other hand, on the right, is a very different sample. This bag was labeled "potting soil," but you're going to be disappointed if you use it for potting. It actually has soil in it, and there's a lot of clay in this mix. Squeezed hard, the lump holds together in a firm ball. It won't work well in containers because it'll be too heavy and roots won't have any air space. So is this bag no good? If you find yourself with a mix like this, use it to fill holes in your garden, or stir it into your compost.

Good potting mix crumbles when you squeeze it.

Plant roots would have a hard time growing in this.

MY CONTAINERS GOT TOO DRY, AND NOW I CAN'T GET THE POTTING MIX WET AGAIN. WHAT SHOULD I DO?

Once potting mix dries completely, it shrinks and is hard to rewet. Put a couple inches of water in a tub, set your container in the tub and let the mix soak up water from the bottom. It'll take a couple hours, but eventually the mix will absorb the moisture. Or poke holes in the top of the mix with a pencil and press the mix down against the edges of the container, then water slowly from the top. Wait a few minutes, then water again. Check by lifting the pot — when it's heavy again, all the potting mix is damp. □

— *Stephanie Polsley Bruner*

Quick-Switch Window Box

If you like to grow plants in window boxes, here's an idea to make it even easier and more versatile: When you put plants in the box, leave them in their pots. This allows you to switch out plants when they start to fade with ones that are just hitting their peak. If you use similar size containers every time, swap-outs are a breeze.

I've come up with the simple plan you see here to help get you started. You can use lots of different plants in the three 1-gallon containers (A) and the four 4-inch containers (B). Putting leaves, stems or cut flowers into the four vases (C) adds extra impact. For a fuller look, tuck in even more vases.

Be sure to pick a window box that's roomy enough. Ours measures 10x10x36 inches. Here are three different looks I designed with this plan along with the plant lists for each design.

Since the plants are all in individual pots, you may need to water them every day. Top the containers with a layer of decorative mulch, such as Spanish moss, to help them stay moist and to give the whole box a nice finishing touch. □

— *Deborah Gruca*

Small vase

Window box is 10x10x36 in. 1-gal. 4 in.

FRESH & FLOWERY

Nothing says spring like a window box full of beautiful blooms! We've used a cool collection of purple pansies, lavender Persian violets and lavender and purple Dutch iris for this arrangement.

Pansies are easy to find at the garden center in both spring and fall. The mounded masses of tiny Persian violets will look fresh in full sun in cooler seasons, but if you use them in hotter months the colors will stay brighter in a little shade.

A	Persian violet *Exacum affine*	3
B	Pansy *Viola* hybrid	4
C	Dutch iris *Iris* hybrid	12

TROPICAL FLAIR

Here's proof that you don't need a lot of flowers to get a lively look. The pink starflowers inject a lot of zip into this window box, but even without their bright blooms, those gorgeous caladium leaves will continue to provide the focal point for this design. Clip a few airy fountain grass plumes for the vases to add movement to this vibrant combination.

A Caladium *Caladium* spp.   1
   Starflower *Pentas lanceolata*   2
B Licorice vine
   Helichrysum petiolare   4
C Fountain grass *Pennisetum alopecuroides*   4
                                  bunches

FORMAL ATTIRE

Three lightly trimmed boxwoods are the anchor plants in this combination. White-splotched, long-blooming deadnettle trails happily down the front of the box. You can plant those and the boxwood in your garden later. And to keep this box from looking stodgy, try this tip for the vases: Layer two fresh hosta leaves, offsetting them slightly, and wrap them around a single calla stem. Keep all three together with a couple straight pins pushed through the stems.

A Boxwood *Buxus* spp.   3
B Spotted deadnettle
   Lamium maculatum   4
C Calla lilies
   Zantedeschia spp.   4
   wrapped in
   Hosta leaves *Hosta* spp.   8

Want to heat up a little spot in the shade? This design emits warmth, starting with the container itself, right up through the foliage of all four of its colorful plants.

The hot chartreuse leaves of 'JoDonna' coleus, with their deep-red-splashed centers, virtually erupt from the center of this container. A tidy plant habit means it doesn't need a lot of pinching to keep it from elbowing out its companions. And the color of the leaves deepens with age and more light.

Vying for its share of the limelight, 'Vancouver Centennial' geranium shines with colors similar to the coleus, but on maple-leaf-shaped foliage. The small, red-orange flowers almost feel like an afterthought when compared to the lively leaves. I sometimes remove the flower buds so they don't distract from the rest of the plant.

Trailing down the front of the pot is a plant you may not be familiar with. In the full sun it prefers, erect seaberry displays a deeper bronze. When grown in part shade, it shines with the chartreuse hue you see here. And despite its name, it can be trained to a cascading habit with a few well-placed weights. Check out the inset for one option for a decorative anchor.

Every pretty picture requires a good background. And that's where the orange sedge comes in. Once it's planted, this is one of those rare plants that requires zero care. Feathery foliage, emerging green and aging to bronze-orange, catches the slightest breeze. It's flexible about moisture and light conditions — it'll take on a brighter orange the more sun it gets — a perfect complement to this glowing grouping! □

Tips for care

- Part shade
- Soilless potting mix
- Fertilize at each watering with ¼-strength all-purpose fertilizer
- Pinch back the coleus and geranium to keep them compact

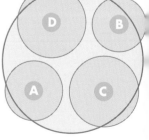

Small weights — like this stone wrapped in copper wire — on the ends of erect seaberry stems encourage a trailing habit.

MELLOW YELLOW

Code	Plant Name	No. to Plant
A	**Geranium** *Pelargonium* 'Vancouver Centennial'	1
B	**Orange sedge** *Carex testacea* 'Prairie Fire'	1
C	**Erect seaberry** *Haloragis erecta* 'Wellington Bronze'	1
D	**Coleus** *Solenostemon* 'JoDonna'	1

Container is 16 inches in diameter

The fascinating flowers of glory bower open in summer.

Here's a container for the casual gardener. These plants don't require a lot of fussing to keep looking their best. Once they're planted, about all you need to do is a little watering and feeding. Even the heat of summer doesn't make these plants skip a beat.

This gorgeous recipe is as easy to look at as it is to care for, but its best feature may be how long it will last. If you garden in a frost-free zone, it'll thrive outdoors all year. In a colder zone, you can easily cut these tender perennials back, overwinter them indoors and bring them back out in spring. Most of the plants in this container are more than two years old — and have been in the same pot the whole time! After about three years you'll need to replace the soil and replant. Here's how to keep a container like this going until then.

Start with a large pot with rich, well-drained potting mix — you won't need to add moisture crystals for these plants. When frost nips the plants in fall, cut back the dead foliage, place the pot by a bright window in a cool room and water it sparingly through winter.

Step up watering in spring and roll the pot outdoors when temperatures stay above 50 degrees F. Give it a shot of fertilizer and protection in the event of a cold snap and this container is raring to go into spring and right through another colorful summer! □

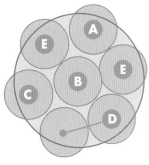

Container is 24 inches in diameter.

SNAPPY COMEBACK

Code	Plant Name	No. to Plant
A	**Glory bower** *Clerodendrum thomsoniae*	1
B	**Common dragon tree** *Dracaena marginata* 'Tricolor'	1
C	**Variegated plectranthus** *Plectranthus* 'Limelight'	1
D	**Variegated kalanchoe** *Kalanchoe fedtschenkoi* 'Aurora Borealis'	2
E	**Geranium** *Pelargonium* 'Maverick Orange'	2

Tips for care

- Full sun
- Moist, well-drained soil
- Spot feed with a balanced time-released granular fertilizer around the geranium

Container Makeover

I had great hopes for the container in the "before" photo. When I planted it in early spring, I thought this combination would look fantastic. But by June, it was clear that it wasn't going anywhere. Fortunately, it wasn't too late. With a little midseason shopping, I was able to remodel and create the colorful container you see in the "after" photo.

Originally, this container was all about texture. The bristly foxtail fern, fuzzy white velvet, and rounded bugleweed leaves should have looked great. But the smaller plants didn't fill in and there wasn't enough color or interest. I didn't want to dump the whole thing, though. It's a nice container and the fern has great architectural form.

SHOP CREATIVELY You may find it a little harder to get nice plants in midsummer, but it can be done. I found most of these at local garden centers. Look for bigger plants because they'll give you instant impact. Don't be afraid to "shop" in your own garden, too. This Swedish ivy came from a container where it was crowding its companions.

TEST NEW LOOKS To see if a grouping works, set the plants you've brought home in the container, then step back for a look. Keep at it until you find an arrangement you like. It took me several tries before settling on the combination you see in the large photo. In this case, tall showy plants like hibiscus overshadowed the fern while smaller plants with subtler color made it shine. These peachy orange begonia flowers are bright, but not so intense that they overwhelm, and the coleus foliage is a nice link between the flowers and the variegated ivy. The dark leaves of the coral bells add depth and contrast to the bright green leaves.

BRING IT ALL TOGETHER When you move plants, water the container thoroughly the day before. This helps minimize root damage, which can stall plant growth. Moist soil breaks apart easier and roots won't stick to the side of the pot. Remove the unwanted plants from the original container with a trowel and replant them in the garden or throw them away if they're too far gone. The Swedish ivy took the move from one container to another without missing a beat. Using a trowel with a serrated edge or a soil knife makes it easier to carve out a large soil mass if plants have a lot of roots in their original container.

Once you have the plants you want all together, fill any empty spaces around the root balls with potting soil. Give the container a good drink to remove air pockets in the soil. Fertilize your container with a 12-4-8 liquid formula like Miracle Gro® every 10 days.

If the ivy or coleus get too big or leggy, snip them back. Both respond well to pinching by producing more branches and making a fuller plant.

As the season comes to an end, lift the perennial coral bell and plant it in your garden. Do this a couple of weeks before a hard frost to give the plant time to get established. Apply 3 to 4 inches of mulch after a hard freeze to avoid frost heaving.

Next time you have a disappointing container, don't be afraid to make some improvements. It's a lot easier than remodeling your kitchen! □

— *Sherri Ribbey*

Botanical Names

Bugleweed
Ajuga reptans
Hibiscus
Hibiscus moscheutos
Foxtail fern
Asparagus densiflorus 'Myersii'
White velvet
Tradescantia sillamontana

PHOTO: Brent Isenberger (before)

Container is 22 inches in diameter.

FROM FAILING TO FABULOUS

Code	Plant Name	No. to Plant
A	**Foxtail fern** *Asparagus densiflorus* 'Myersii'	1
B	**Coral bells** *Heuchera* Dolce™ Licorice	1
C	**Swedish ivy** *Plectranthus madagascariensis*	1
D	**Coleus** *Solenstemon* 'Royal Glissade'	1
E	**Tuberous begonia** *Begonia xtuberhybrida* Nonstop® Rose	1

Fishing line tied around the fern keeps the arching stems more upright.

Prop begonia stems up with thin green bamboo stakes so the flowers stay up where you can see them.

I kept the fern and built a new planting around it.

Before

Plant the coral bells in your garden in fall.

From Drab to Fab

Quick, easy and inexpensive faux stone pots

Do you have a stack of plastic nursery pots in your garage? Too many to ignore, too ugly to use, too good to throw away. What do you do with them? Even if you have a place to recycle plastic pots, I thought it'd be great to be able to use them somehow. So I came up with an idea for making them look good enough for the garden without spending a lot of time or a small fortune. The rolled-edge, stone-look containers in the big photo are nursery pots that have been dressed up, for about $10 each and a trip to the hardware store. Check out the photos and "Materials and tools" at right to see how it's done.

Paint makers are offering lots of new formulas that look just like stone, metal or other materials. A can of spray or brush-on paint may be a bit pricey, but each can holds enough to coat lots of pots. And the process is so quick and easy, you can make a bunch of containers for yourself and your friends in just a few hours. With some foam pipe insulation and a little glue — voilà! That homely plastic pot is ready for the garden. □

— *Deborah Gruca*

PHOTOS: Craig Anderson (images on p. 252)

POT MAKEOVER

STEP ONE This technique works best on sturdy pots with rims. First wash the pot well and dry it completely so the paint will stick to the plastic. Also, sand the pot lightly with fine sandpaper to scuff up the surface. The pipe insulation comes with a lengthwise slit in it. Pull the insulation apart along this slit and slide it onto the rim of the pot to see how long a piece you need to fit around the top edge. With scissors, cut the insulation to the right length, then remove it.

STEP TWO Apply a bead of construction adhesive, such as Liquid Nails®, to the top edge of the lip of the pot. Replace the insulation on the lip and place a piece of duct tape over the insulation where the two ends meet. The tape will hold it onto the pot and hide the gap, as well. You'll be painting over the tape, so smooth it down to make it blend into the rim.

Glue foam pipe insulation on the rim for a rolled edge.

STEP THREE Place the pot on a couple bricks or a piece of scrap wood outdoors so you can paint all the way to the bottom edge. Spray the outside of the pot and the insulation with paint, as well as the top 2 in. of the inside. The number of coats you'll

You can paint the duct tape hiding the ends of the pipe insulation.

need depends on the color of your plastic pot. I liked the look of the black plastic showing through the paint, so I used a single coat. If you want to completely hide the underlying color, wait the time recommended on the can and apply a second coat.

After the paint is dry, spray or brush on a clear coat of sealer to protect the finish and give the pot a nice glazed look. A water-based urethane, like Varathane® Outdoor Spar Urethane, is good to use because it won't yellow when exposed to sunlight.

That's all there is to creating a pot like this. Check out our Web extra for more tips and creative effects you can get with paint — the possibilities are almost endless!

Materials and tools

Plastic nursery pot, 2-gal. or larger
Pre-slit flexible pipe insulation,
   1½-in. outside diameter for
   smaller pots, 2-in. outside
   diameter for larger ones
Liquid Nails construction adhesive
Scissors

Duct tape
Sandpaper
Spray paint (we used Rust-
   Oleum® American Accents
   Stone, Mineral Brown)
Varathane Outdoor
   Spar Urethane

WEB
extra

Check out *tips* on
using paints for
special effects.

Instant Fall Color

For pots with pizzazz, use plants that look great right now!

COOL & CLASSIC

The cool hues of this eye-catching container make a real splash, while looking right at home in an autumn setting.

Jazz up a combination of plants with similar colors by throwing in different textures and plant forms. Long, arching stems of butterfly bush contrast well with the bunchy asters, round flowering kale and the ivy trailing over the edges of the urn. And the blocky kale and asters keep it all from looking messy.

Code	Plant Name	No. to Plant	Pot Size
A	**Butterfly bush** *Buddleja davidii* 'Attraction'	1	2-gal.
B	**New York aster** *Aster novi-belgii* 'Purple Viking'	3	6-in.
C	**Variegated ivy** *Hedera helix* 'Variegata'	4	2-in.
D	**Flowering kale** *Brassica oleracea* 'Color-up Purple'	3	4-in.

O K, the days are growing shorter and the weather's getting cooler. But that doesn't mean you have to throw in the trowel for the year. In fact, cooler weather, fewer bugs and fresh plants arriving at garden centers make fall the best time for container gardens!

Designing a container in fall is different from doing it at other times of the year. The big reason, of course, is that there's just a short time left in the growing season. That means you can use the biggest and best-looking plants you can find for instant impact, and care is easier since they won't be in the container for very long. This really opens up the kinds of plants you can use to anything that looks good right now.

PLANTS PLUS Pillage plants from your beds, like annuals that are perking up in the cooler weather or sections of divided perennials. Rescue vigorous plants from your played-out containers and pick up fresh, colorful fall annuals from the nursery. While you're there, take advantage of year-end sales on good-sized plants. Look for fall-blooming perennials like asters, and shrubs with great autumn color or flowers, like butterfly bush. You'll still have time to plant them in your garden later. Go even farther and include branches, colorful berries and dried flowers. And tuck in some grasses with fall color, like feather reed grass or prairie dropseed — either cut stems or whole plants.

FALL CONTAINER CARE The beauty of fall containers is, because the weather's cooler, plants don't grow as fast or need as much moisture. So you can pack them in tighter than you normally would. And since the season's winding down and the plants won't be in the container that long anyway, you don't need to fertilize.

To get you started, I put together two fall containers with different looks. Follow these recipes or use your imagination to create your own instant fall color! □

— *Deborah Gruca*

WARM & WONDERFUL

A blanket flower with a sunny personality is the star of this container. I love how the yellows and oranges of the coreopsis and blanket flower keep a warm summer feeling going right into fall. You can't miss the red accents of the peppers and the pansies. Even the metal tub adds its coppery glow to the combination. I've added a single fountain grass to give the planting a vertical dash.

At this point in the season, don't worry about feeding the container. But good-sized plants like this need moisture, so be sure to water them before the soil gets completely dry.

Code	Plant Name	No. to Plant	Pot Size
A	Pansy *Viola Tequila Mix*	2	6-packs
B	**Blanket flower** *Gaillardia 'Fanfare'*	1	1-gal.
C	**Coreopsis** *Coreopsis verticillata 'Zagreb'*	1	1-gal.
D	**Fountain grass** *Pennisetum alopecuroides 'Hameln'*	1	6-in.
E	**Ornamental pepper** *Capsicum annuum*	2	4-in.

What makes window boxes so popular? Could it be the way they tie your house to the rest of your garden? Or maybe it's how they instantly turn even a drab house into a colorful, cheery place? Whatever the reason, window boxes are a great finishing touch you can give your home.

Want a good tip for designing a great window box? Stuff it! To get a full, lush look like this, pack your container with plants, and then add a few more. After all, once they get going, you can always do some judicious snipping.

The other part of the secret is to pamper the plants. Keep moisture even — an overly dry plant is a stressed plant.

These heliotropes and fuchsias, in particular, need even moisture. Mix in a few inches of compost to the potting mix before you plant to help hold moisture. And feed your plants every week to ten days for the best growth and most flowers. (Pinch the growing tips of the petunia and sweet potato vine regularly so they won't take over.)

One more tip: Pick plants for your situation. These thrive in this part-shade, southern exposure. You can't choose which direction your window faces, but with the right plants and a little TLC, you can have a colorful container to beautify your house, as well as the rest of your garden! □

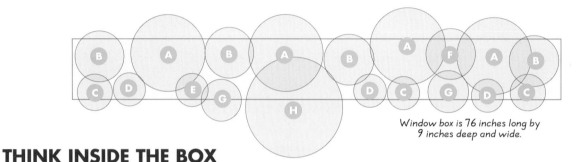

Window box is 76 inches long by 9 inches deep and wide.

THINK INSIDE THE BOX

Code	Plant Name	No. of Plants
A	**Heliotrope** *Heliotropium arborescens* 'Marine'	4
B	**Geranium** *Pelargonium* hybrid	4
C	**Sedum** *Sedum rupestre* 'Angelina'	3
D	**Purple heart** *Tradescantia pallida*	3

Code	Plant Name	No. of Plants
E	**Fuchsia** *Fuchsia* 'Autumnale'	1
F	**Fuchsia** *Fuchsia* 'Gartenmeister Bonstedt'	1
G	**Sweet potato vine** *Ipomoea batatas* 'Margarita'	2
H	**Petunia** *Petunia* Wave™ Purple	1

Tips for care

- Full sun to part shade
- Feed every 7 to 10 days with balanced water-soluble fertilizer
- Spacers behind the box prevent moisture damage to the house

**Tips
for care**

- Barely moist, well-drained potting mix
- Mist plants if weather is dry
- Spray with antidesiccant; protect from wind

Cold weather in northern zones doesn't have to mean the end of gorgeous gardens. Take this container, for example. Tough but beautiful, these plants combine to make a lovely entry container that takes frosty temperatures in stride.

Two kinds of cypress — one green and one gold — anchor this window box. Alternate them to set off the different colors; then put small edible cabbage seedlings in around them. The large, pale-green leaves contrast nicely with the fine-textured cypress and the pink heather blooms. Pinecones and red wintergreen berries provide accents among all the greens.

When I planted, I left everything but the cabbage in its 4-inch pot. I boosted plants to the right height by filling the box halfway with mulch, then added the containers and tucked a little more mulch around and on top to hide the edges. Next I tucked the cabbage seedlings into the mulch.

These small plants won't overwinter in their pots in zones colder than about 6 or 7. Either treat them as annuals or in December move the plants into pre-dug holes in the garden and mulch them well until spring. □

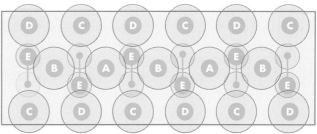

Container is 10 by 10 by 36 inches.

COLD-WEATHER COLOR

Code	Plant Name	No. of Plants
A	**Gold cypress** *Chamaecyparis lawsoniana* 'Ellwood's Gold'	2
B	**Cypress** *Chamaecyparis lawsoniana* 'Elwoodii'	3
C	**Wintergreen** *Gaultheria procumbens*	6
D	**Heather** *Calluna vulgaris*	6
E	**Cabbage** *Brassica oleracea*	12

did you know...

Let soil flow from the bag to fill the pot.

just say "om"

Looking for inner peace?

Head out to your garden. Just taking a few moments to sit and look at a garden has been shown to increase feelings of health and well-being. For even more relaxation, spend some time putting together a few containers. That gentle exercise releases a flood of endorphins, hormones associated with happiness. With benefits like these, gardening may just be the new yoga!

Soil faucet
Mary Ann Broderson, Florida

Scooping potting soil from bag to pot can be messy, and those bags are heavy! Mary Ann saves energy and potting mix by keeping the bag on her potting bench. She cuts the corner off the bag with a pair of scissors. That way the soil can "flow" into the pot below, as you can see in the illustration. As the bag empties, scoot it forward so more soil will fall out of the bag. When the pot is full, roll up the corner of the plastic bag and close it with a clothes pin. Larger pots can be moved into place with a two-wheeled dolly.

Once Mary Ann has lifted the bag into place, she doesn't have to lug it around any more. And she cuts down on mess and waste because she doesn't spill her potting soil.

Water hanging baskets less
Marge Opacki, Pennsylvania

Marge found a way to keep hanging baskets from the garden center looking great *and* cut down on watering. All she needs — a pencil and a jar of water-absorbing crystals.

She uses the pencil to poke at least six holes 3 to 4 inches deep around the edge of the basket. They're usually about 3 inches apart. By keeping the holes close to the perimeter, she avoids damaging the roots.

Next, Marge checks the label on the water crystals for the correct amount. (Different brands have different application rates.) She measures out the right amount for the size of her basket and divides the crystals up so an equal amount goes in each hole.

Once that's done, she refills the holes with potting soil, gives the basket a good drink and it's ready to go.

Super-sized plant tray
Laura McCue, Massachusetts

Laura found that an inexpensive boot tray helps her water her house plants and protect her floor. Normally reserved for muddy shoes, this rectangular plastic tray has an edge to contain the water that drains from the pots. In winter, the water in the tray adds a little humidity to the air, which helps plants hold on to their leaves.

product pick

The Pot Lifter

How do you move a large container without renting a backhoe or wrenching your back? Try the Pot Lifter. Sturdy, self-cinching straps fit around any pot (or even a rock) up to 6 feet in circumference. It can hold up to 200 pounds if you and your partner can. We found it made easy work of moving this potted lemon tree to just the right spot in the garden. The handles are plastic and easy to grip. We found it's a good idea for each person to snug the straps up tight on his or her side before lifting, especially with those smooth ceramic pots. That way, there's no chance of slipping when you pick up the pot.

Bottom Line: For a heavy job you need a heavy-duty tool like this one.
Source: Gardener's Supply Company at www.gardeners.com or call 888-833-1412
Price: $29.95

product pick

Potlevel

Keeping containers upright on a slope, whether it's steep or slight, can be a challenge. This simple tool has two circular discs of polymer that rotate to varying heights to match the grade of your slope. The Potlevel is 12 inches across and has a 7-inch hole in the middle that makes changing the height of the Potlevel easier. It helps water drain from the pot, too.

Bottom Line: This clever device keeps your containers on the level and looking good.
Source: Kinsman Company at www.kinsmangarden.com or 800-733-4146
Price: $16.95

With a 500-pound capacity, the Potlevel can hold just about any container.

did you know... (CONTINUED)

product pick

Cumberland Square Planters

The first thing our staff said when they saw these containers was, "Ooooh!" When they found out they could pick one up, they said, "Wow!" Lead-Lite® containers are made from a special material that's up to 80 percent lighter than its metal counterparts. The Cumberland Square Planter at left is just one of several styles and sizes. They're so convincing that even a close look won't reveal your secret. And don't worry about the elements wearing your containers down — they're UV- and frost-resistant.

Bottom line: You can't beat lightweight containers that are strong and beautiful.
Source: Independent garden centers or go to www.campaniainternational.com to find a retailer near you.
Price: Campania's Cumberland Square Planter comes in four sizes and ranges in price from $32 to $286.

Blazin' Rose iresine
(new in 2006)

Accent™ Pink Picotee
impatiens (new in 2006)

Accent™ Carmine impatiens

Fanfare® Bright Coral
spreadingimpatiens
(new in 2006)

Homemade Potting Mix
1 part prepackaged soil
1 part perlite
1 part peat moss
— Mix Together

Houseplant soil recipe
Alison Thorpe, Wisconsin

Q *I'd like to make my own potting mix for my indoor plants. Can you suggest a recipe?*

A There are lots of different recipes that you can use to make your own potting mix, but the index card above shows a good basic one. Just be sure to buy pasteurized soil for your mix to ensure your plants' health. You should be able to find all of the ingredients at your local garden center.

Lighten up containers
Beth Riedman, Indiana

You see a lot of those big ceramic containers in gardens these days. They're beautiful, but so heavy.

Beth's tip lightens the load, saves on potting mix and gets a jump start on compost.

In spring, she rakes up the leaves from last fall. Then she runs them through her blower-vac to shred them and fills her pots one-third to half full, packing the leaves in tight.

Beth says you don't have to shred the leaves, but they break down faster if you do. Once planted, the containers look good all summer.

At the end of the season, just dump the contents of the container into the compost pile.

Most of what's in the bottom of the pot is well on its way to being compost that can nourish the garden next spring.

2x4 board

4x4 post

Use rust-proof coated deck screws to attach pieces.

Scrappy pedestal

Jeanne Vaver, Illinois

Thanks to some lumber scraps, Jeanne was able to expand the gardening space on her small deck.

As you see in the illustration, she screwed a 2x4 board to each side of a 4x4 post to make a sturdy pedestal. Going vertical got things up off the floor of the deck, leaving room for more containers. With pedestals of different heights, Jeanne can easily show off several containers at once.

Since Jeanne used cedar scraps, there was no need to finish the pedestals. She's been using them for six years and they're still going strong.

in the news

Potted plants fight pollution

You've probably heard that indoor plants filter toxins from the air we breathe. A recent study by researchers in South Korea and at the University of Georgia showed that English ivy (*Hedera helix*) is the best plant for filtering benzene and toluene, fumes found in gasoline. Peace lily (*Spathiphyllum wallisii*) and arrowhead philodendron (*Syngonium podophyllum*) ran a close second. So if you have an attached garage, you might want to pick up a few of these fume-filtering house plants the next time you're out.

product picks

SoilSponge™

Want to spend less time watering your containers? Add SoilSponge to your potting mix. It's a soil supplement made mostly of coconut coir (the coarse fiber from coconut husks), which holds moisture just as well as, if not better than, traditional peat moss. In our test, containers with SoilSponge stayed moist several days longer than those without it. SoilSponge works in the garden, too. Just work it into the top 6 to 9 inches of soil or add it to the bottom of a planting hole to encourage roots to go deep.

Bottom line: Less watering saves you time.
Source: Local Menards stores or www.GardenGateStore.com
Price: $9.99 for a 16.5 ounce bag

Mix one part SoilSponge with six parts potting mix to extend the time between waterings.

P. Allen Smith's Container Gardens

The hard part about container gardening is knowing which plants look good and grow well together. "P. Allen Smith's Container Gardens" has 60 of his best "recipes" to make things easier. Arranged in a season-by-season format, each container has a full-page photo next to a page with design insights, a planting plan and tips for growing the plants. In the back of the book you'll find general planting instructions, a plant dictionary, tips for selecting the right container and helpful techniques to keep your containers in blue-ribbon condition.

Bottom Line: From casual to formal, sun to shade, terra-cotta to wicker — you name it — this book has a container for anyone's style.
Source: Local or online bookstores or www.GardenGateStore.com
Price: $32.50; hardcover; 224 pages

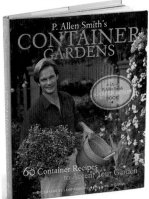

gardening
basics

how to *grow* the garden you've always wanted

GETTING YOUR HANDS DIRTY is one of the best parts of gardening, right? Want to know how to get the most out of your gardening efforts? You've come to the right place. For everything from fertilizing, watering, amending your soil and pruning, you'll find it here. Plus we've added a couple of weekend projects that are easy to build *and* on the eyes!

From Six-pack to Impact

Cut the plant back to right above a leaf or pair of leaves.

Gently pull apart the roots to help stimulate new growth.

Botanical Names

Coleus
Solenostemon hybrids
Impatiens
Impatiens walleriana
Petunia
Petunia xhybrida

There they are, those little plants in their six-pack. Cute, aren't they? Now imagine them as full-grown, traffic-stopping beauties. Let me show you how I take my annuals from six-pack to high impact every single year. The secret's in the fertilizer. Watch how my technique and timing affects a single plant through the summer in "What's happening above and below the soil?" at right.

Of course, great soil can only help your plants' roots live up to their potential. So start your containers with a soilless potting mix and your beds with plenty of compost. Are you ready to plant?

Getting started I know I said fertilizing is the key to great annuals, but some prep work at planting helps, too. When you bring them home, make sure plants' soil stays moist, especially right before you plant.

That way when you pull them out of the cells, the fine hair roots won't stick and get pulled off or damaged.

Be ready to show some tough love. See how the little plant at right is more than twice the height of its root ball? Cut the stem back by half. This will encourage more branching, deeper roots and more blooms.

If the plants are root-bound with almost no soil showing, tease the roots apart to stimulate them to grow outward.

In containers, be sure to premoisten the potting mix so settling doesn't expose the roots when you water. After you plant, water gently. Then I like to spread up to 2 inches of mulch around my annuals. Layer mulch around short plants less thickly until they grow.

Here's the first fertilizer hint: Don't fertilize at all when you plant. You'll get to that later.

Week 2 After a week, you should see new growth above ground. Below ground, the roots are stretching. It's time to fertilize with an organic, sea-based fertilizer like Neptune's Harvest at the rate recommended on the package. Organic liquid fertilizers attach themselves to soil particles better than inorganic ones. So they stay in the soil longer and are available to the plants' roots as needed. Do this watering in the morning — foliage can burn when fertilizer is heated by the sun. And wet leaves at night encourage fungal diseases.

Water (in the mornings) when the top inch of the soil is dry.

ILLUSTRATION: Mavis Augustine Torke

Week 4 It's hard to believe, but two weeks after that first fertilizer, you may not even recognize your plants. The roots will have doubled in size at this point, and the plants are putting on a lot of growth, too. Now give them another dose of that organic, sea-based fertilizer solution at full strength. Then put it away for a while.

But keep on watering regularly. Water until you see it run from the bottom of the container. If the plants are in the ground, a good rule is to water an area to the count of 10. This makes sure the water soaks in deeply, and the roots will follow the water down — right where you want them to go.

Week 6 Now your plants are blooming and looking great above and below ground. The healthy root system you've been encouraging is paying off and has probably tripled in size. This is your opportunity to help plants like impatiens, coleus and even petunias develop a bushier habit and more flowers. Pinch out the growing tip on all the stems at this point. With all this feeding, they're going to grow by leaps and bounds.

Buy a package of balanced water-soluble fertilizer, such as Miracle-Gro™, and use it at the recommended strength. Now that the plants are robust enough, they can handle a big burst of fertilizer, and if they're not already blooming like crazy, they will be after this.

Of course, continue to water. And keep an eye out for pest problems and treat them as soon as you see them.

Week 8 and beyond

Start fertilizing every time you water with that same balanced liquid fertilizer. But don't use it at full strength — this could burn your plants. Mix it up at quarter strength in your watering can or hose-end sprayer. There is a trick to this, though: Water first, then follow it up with the fertilizer solution. This will ensure that the fertilizer stays in the soil where the roots need it. It's like your plants' daily vitamins. By this time, your plants are huge and gorgeous, and if you keep doing this through fall, they'll stay that way! □

— *Marcia Leeper*

What's happening above and below the soil?

In the early days of feeding your plants, there's more happening than you can see above ground. Have a look!

WEEK 2

For the first couple of weeks, you might see a little bit of new growth above ground, but the roots are settling in and starting to grow.

After about a month, your plant's root ball should have doubled in size.

WEEK 4

Pinch the growing tips on the stems now to encourage a fuller habit.

WEEK 6

At this point, the root ball has probably tripled in size. This translates into big, blooming annuals.

Make More Plants...It's Easy!

I admit, I have a hard time letting go. I can't just throw out the gorgeous 'Angel Earrings' fuchsia at right in fall. That's why my back room is full of plants all winter. So here's the system I use for overwintering tender plants. It gives me big, lush tropicals year after year *and* as many new plants as I want! I'll show you how well this process works for my fuchsia, and it's a great way to propagate plenty of other plants, too. Check out a starter list of other tropicals that you can propagate this way in "Easy cuttings" at right.

Before night temperatures are regularly in the low 50s, bring your tropicals into a cool, light room. Trim the plants down by a third and water just enough to keep the soil moist. In late winter or early spring, take cuttings. You can do this in the fall, but then you have to babysit them all winter. Save work, and wait until spring!

Let me show you how I propagated my fuchsia last year and how you can do it, too. □

— *Marcia Leeper*

GET STARTED

FILL A 4-IN. POT WITH SOIL-FREE POTTING MIX Go soil-free because it's lighter and roots grow better there than in true soil. Premoisten the mix to ensure that it doesn't compress with the first watering.

MAKE THE CUTTING. To start, look on the mother plant for a healthy green branch with leaves. Clip it near the soil line. The branches I used were about 14 in. long. See the leaf in the cutting below? I already stripped the one below it off and am cutting the stem about an inch below the bulge the leaf left. This will be the end that goes in the mix. Next I'll trim off the stem right above the leaf you see (about where my thumb is). The piece that's left will be the new plant. I should be able to do this several times with a stem.

Make sure rooting hormone covers a leaf junction.

GIVE IT A BOOST

DIP YOUR CUTTING INTO ROOTING HORMONE to cover the bottom leaf junction. This powder gives your plants a faster start. To avoid spoilage, don't dip the cutting straight into the bottle. Pour a little bit into a small disposable drink cup and dip your cuttings in that. Then throw the excess powder out. Poke the cutting into your potting mix, making sure to bury the bottom leaf junction in it. This leaf junction is where the roots will emerge.

'Angel Earrings'— I love this fuchsia!

HELP IT GROW

KEEP YOUR CUTTING WARM AND MOIST under plastic wrap or a dome and a fluorescent light. Hang the light 6 to 8 in. above the new plants. Set a timer for 12 hours of light each day. You *can* place cuttings in a window, but I've had better luck when I keep the temperature and light more consistent. Water just enough to keep the mix moist, but never wet. Mist with water once a week if the soil looks dry.

SEE IT TAKE ROOT

YOUR CUTTINGS SHOULD TAKE ABOUT SEVEN DAYS TO ROOT. If you gently tug on a cutting and it resists, it's grown some roots. See how the roots are coming right out of the leaf junction above? That's about a week after I took the cuttings. About two weeks after you take the cuttings, you can remove the plastic dome. This is the time to start feeding your new plants with a half-strength 10-10-10 liquid fertilizer once a month. Keep the soil uniformly moist (bottom watering is the best way to protect from fungal diseases). Don't put them outside until after all danger of frost is past. Hurrah! More fuchsias to stop people in their tracks.

Easy-Mix Soil

Two no-fail recipes for a great garden

Have you ever noticed that gardening and cooking both require a bit of skill to turn out something enjoyable? You just need different ingredients. Mixing one or more of the six soil amendments shown in the photos below with the soil you already have is the key. That'll help you create the soil, and the *garden*, you've always dreamed about.

The first recipe on the next page improves sandy soil that drains much too quickly, leaving plants dry and underfed. Using organic ingredients, you can turn sand into soil that holds moisture and nutrients. You'll want the second recipe if you have clay. Dense clay doesn't let oxygen get to the roots, so your plants suffocate. In both cases, what you're aiming for is called "loam," not too dense yet not too fast draining.

If you're not sure if you have clay, sand or loam, check out "Know your soil" at right. I'll share a simple test to help you determine your soil type.

Amending the top 6 inches will help you grow great plants. But to get even deeper root growth, remove the amended layer and spread more ingredients in the trench. Till them in and then replace the first layer.

Follow these recipes for better soil and soon you'll be enjoying a healthy, and beautiful, garden. □

— *Jim Childs*

ORGANIC INGREDIENTS

Bark chips Sometimes used as a mulch, these are small pieces, 5 to 15 millimeters in diameter. Don't use large pieces; they take too long to break down. Reapply every two or three years.

PROS Take a long time to completely decompose.

CONS Wood draws nitrogen from the soil as it decomposes. Sprinkle some nitrogen fertilizer, according to package directions, when you first add bark chips to your soil. As the chips decompose they will release the nitrogen back into the soil.

Compost The best compost is simply decomposed plant material and/or animal waste. To get the longest-lasting benefit, work it in when the pieces are only partially broken down.

PROS It's free if you make your own. Many municipalities offer it for a small fee.

CONS There really aren't any.

Peat moss All peat moss is not the same. The best for adjusting soil texture is milled sphagnum. It's fairly coarse so it holds the most moisture between the sandy particles. Finer peats are more decomposed so they break down faster and you'll need to add them often.

PROS Easy to find and till into the soil.

CONS Can be expensive.

INORGANIC INGREDIENTS

Sand River sand is best for amending soil because the rounded particles can't pack together like sharp builders' sand. Choose a particle size around a millimeter or slightly larger so it won't immediately stick to the clay particles and form concrete.

PROS Inexpensive and easy to find.

CONS Heavy to transport.

Perlite When you see crunchy white particles in potting mix, odds are it's perlite. It's a volcanic glass that's been expanded by heat and steam.

PROS Lightweight and holds some moisture and nutrients. Good for small areas and spot amending.

CONS Expensive for large garden beds.

Vermiculite While it can be used as insulation, this shiny brown material, rather square in shape, also resists soil compaction. It's mica, a rock, that's been expanded by heat.

PROS Lightweight and holds some moisture and nutrients.

CONS Expensive if you're amending a large garden.

Bark chips

Compost

Peat moss

Sand

Perlite

Vermiculite

PHOTOS: Craig Anderson ILLUSTRATIONS: Mavis Augustine Torke

Moisture-holding sand

Sandy soil
3 to 6 in. of organic ingredients

INSTRUCTIONS Start with soil that won't hold together with a ribbon test as in "Know your soil" at right. Spread one or more of the organic ingredients from the photos. Work the ingredients into the sandy soil to a depth of at least 6 in. You can use either a spade or tiller to incorporate all of the ingredients. Either way, you may need to go over the area several times to make sure everything is thoroughly mixed to a 6-in. depth.

MAINTENANCE Organic material breaks down over time so every year or two you'll want to add more. You can spread a 2- to 3-in. layer of any of the ingredients as mulch. But after a couple more years, it also begins to break down. Before you add another layer in spring, scratch or hoe the old layer several inches into the soil. And whenever you divide or plant in the area, dig generous holes and work lots more of any of the organic ingredients into the new hole.

Organic ingredients

Existing sandy soil

Improved clay

Clay soil
3 to 4 in. of inorganic ingredients
3 to 6 in. of organic ingredients

INSTRUCTIONS Loosen the surface of the clay with a tiller or spade. Spread a layer of inorganic materials and a layer of organic materials. With a spade or tiller, work them into the clay to a depth of at least 6 in. That's deep enough for most flower beds or vegetable gardens. But if you can go deeper, by all means do it. Keep in mind you can adjust the mix to "taste." Just don't be skimpy with the organic stuff — too little and you end up with concrete.

MAINTENANCE The inorganic materials won't break down, so you probably don't need to add them again. But adding more organic material will be an ongoing process. These particles gradually disappear and the soil becomes heavy again. So, spread a 2- or 3-in.-thick layer over the surface every year or two as mulch. And as you lift and divide perennials, work more into the hole and surrounding area as you dig. Just remember that peat moss begins to acidify soil if you use it year after year. So eventually you'll want to do a soil test to make sure you're not lowering pH below what your plants can tolerate.

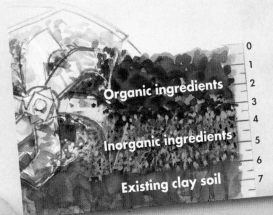

Organic ingredients

Inorganic ingredients

Existing clay soil

KNOW YOUR SOIL

Grab a handful of wet soil and knead it into a tight ball. Rubbing your thumb against your index finger, pinch the soil to form it into a ribbon. If you can make a ribbon, but it's less than 1 to 2 in. long, you have loam soil.

SAND When you try to form very sandy soil into a ball it just won't hold together, even when it's wet. So there's no chance it'll form a ribbon. That's sandy soil in my hand above. If your soil forms a ribbon less than an inch long, you'll want to treat it like sand and add amendments.

CLAY If your soil forms a ribbon 2 in. long or longer, you have clay. Unless you have plants that like clay, they won't be healthy.

On the Cutting Edge

WEB extra

Watch how to create a trenched edge in our step-by-step *video*.

Check out the photo at the top of the next page. See how this clean, crisp edge shows off the garden? I always think a nice edge puts the finishing touches on a garden's great lines. My favorite style is a trenched, or English, edge. Why? No plastic or metal strips heave out of the ground and it's easy to change the bed's shape. Plus, it's free! I admit that cutting one of these in takes some legwork, but once it's there, it doesn't take much to maintain in the long run.

Sometimes you see these trenches as much as 10 inches deep, but in my experience, all you really need is about 4 inches — just the depth of a half-moon lawn edger. Getting one of these edges is time-consuming the first year, but it's a repetitive task that gives you time to dream about your garden's possibilities. It's also a great time to look closely for damage, insects or disease.

Let me walk you through the steps for digging and maintaining your own trenched edge. I'll show you the easiest way to approach it and give you some tips for maintaining it, too. The steps you see here are for an existing bed. In our Web extra, you can watch a video of the process and I'll also show you the technique to use when you're creating a new bed. □

— *Marcia Leeper*

1

2

STEP ONE — LAY OUT YOUR NEW BED EDGE

Get out the garden hose and use it as a guide for the shape of your garden's edge. Without turning your lawn mower on, run it along the hose to see if the machine will track the edge in one smooth mowing pass. If it won't, adjust the curve until it will. Leave the hose in place to guide you as you cut your edge. Line up the half-moon edger at the edge of the hose, push the tool into the ground and step on it. If you angle the handle toward yourself slightly, the next step, prying the sod out, will be a lot easier to do.

STEP TWO — CUT AND LOOSEN THE SOD

Pull the handle toward you until the sod breaks loose. Move the edger along so it overlaps the end of the cut you just made, and repeat.

A crisp trenched edge is easy to maintain — just pull the mulch back into the bed a few inches and freshen the edge with your half-moon tool every year. Remove any trimmings and push the mulch back in the trench.

③

④

STEP THREE — REMOVE THE STRIP OF SOD

Grab the end of the sod strip you just cut and pull it out of the trench. Add the sod to your compost pile or use pieces to patch your existing lawn.

Push any loose soil up evenly toward the plantings as you take out the sod. This will make a smooth mound from the plants down to the bottom of the trench.

STEP FOUR — TOP WITH 3 INCHES OF MULCH

Spread your mulch on the bed and put extra into the trench up to the grass, as I'm doing here. The mulch should be level with your lawn so you can run the lawn mower's wheel just on the mulch, making a clean cut every time you mow.

Invisible Staking
Well...almost!

Are your liatris leaning? Do your digitalis droop? If you're like me, you never think about staking your garden until it's too late. By summer I'm out there hugging my asters and heliopsis, trying to make them stand up straight. We all want our perennials to look natural without any strings, stakes or wires showing, but it seems to take a magician to pull off this trick.

It can be done. First, you have to do it when the plant is still young. Once the stems flop, it's hard to stake them so they look natural. Second, learn the habit of the plant you're staking. It'll help you decide which method will work best. And last, keep the stakes about two-thirds the ultimate height of the plant, so they won't stick out the top.

In these illustrations I'll show you four staking techniques. One of them is sure to work for almost any perennial.

Let the magic begin! □

— *Jim Childs*

USE A MAGIC WAND

WHAT KIND OF PLANTS? Loops are like magic wands when it comes to staking flowers with tall stems and heavy heads.

HOW TO DO IT Stick the loop in the ground near the stem as the flower buds begin to swell and then wind the stalk into it. Even though it'll show a bit, a loop is quick and much easier than tying a stem to a bamboo stake. And after the flowers finish, simply pull the loop out again and put it away — it'll last forever. Plus loops let stems lean a bit and even move in the breeze so they look more natural, not bound stiffly to a stake.

USE IT ON THESE PLANTS

Hybrid lily *Lilium* hybrid
Delphinium *Delphinium elatum*
Hollyhock *Alcea rosea*
Foxglove *Digitalis purpurea*
Spike blazing star *Liatris* spp.

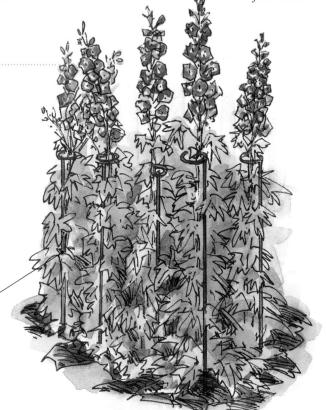

Metal loops, painted green, are sturdy and won't show much.

ILLUSTRATIONS: Mavis Augustine Torke

WEB OF ILLUSION

WHAT KIND OF PLANTS? Bind medium to tall bushy perennials securely and, unlike a good magician, they can't escape.

HOW TO DO IT Figure the ultimate height of the perennial and then select four or more bamboo stakes that length. Push about a third of the stake into the soil. An inch or two above the young plant, weave string or light twine (green will show the least) in a random pattern between and around the stakes. You can add as many grids as you like, but keep the top grid lower than the ultimate height of the plant so it won't show.

If the stakes end up being a bit too tall, you can easily snip them off with shears.

USE IT ON THESE PLANTS

Yarrow *Achillea* spp.
Marguerite daisy *Anthemis tinctoria*
Tickseed *Coreopsis* spp.
Tall sedum *Sedum spectabile*
False sunflower *Heliopsis helianthoides*

As the plant grows, add another layer of string, keeping it lower than the ultimate height of the plant.

VANISHING RINGS

WHAT KIND OF PLANTS? Metal hoops will disappear on tall bushy perennials that only need gentle support.

HOW TO DO IT Push hoops into the ground early and they'll soon be covered by foliage. The stems still move around a bit and the natural form of the plant remains. Just make sure the rings are tall enough to hold the stems upright. If the hoop is too short, the flowers will flop over the top ring and might snap off.

USE IT ON THESE PLANTS

Peony *Paeonia* hybrid
Russian sage *Perovskia atriplicifolia*
Whirling butterflies *Gaura lindheimeri*
Baby's breath *Gypsophila paniculata*

Need a bit more support? You can always weave some twine between the rings.

DISAPPEARING TWIGS

WHAT KIND OF PLANTS? Shrub clippings are perfect when performing a disappearing act on low plants.

HOW TO DO IT Insert three or more pieces of brush, often called "pea stakes," around the perennial. Bend the "fingers" together and hook them into themselves, forming a twiggy dome. Stems are supported as they push up through the woven twigs. If some of the fingers still poke through the mature perennial, I simply snip them off.

USE IT ON THESE PLANTS

Catmint *Nepeta* (Faassenii Group)
Aster *Aster* spp.
Threadleaf coreopsis *Coreopsis verticillata*
Perennial geranium *Geranium* spp.

Gather pieces of brush that are about 18 in. tall and trim them to size as you work.

THE WEEKEND Garden Smarter GARDENER

4 secrets to soaker hose success

Water Less!

Nothing breaks my heart faster than watching my beautiful perennial border struggle and turn brown in the heat of late summer. At about the same time, the dry weather can make watering the garden an endless chore.

Whether you've tried soaker hoses or not, it's time to give them another look. Once you set it in the garden, the soaker slowly trickles water through tiny holes along its length. It works with the faucet turned on just enough so the entire hose is weeping, but not spraying. The great thing about soakers is that they'll use a lot less water — up to 70 percent less — than wands or sprinklers do. And none of the water is wasted since it's directed right into the soil near the roots where it's needed. You can leave these hoses in place all season and, if that's not enough to convince you, the leaves of your plants stay dry, so you'll cut down on foliage problems, too!

Sometimes it takes a little practice to know how long to let your soakers run. Experiment in your garden by running the soaker for an hour with the faucet on a quarter turn. The next day see if the soil is still moist at least 2 inches down. If the soil's dry, water again and this time let the soaker run longer or turn the faucet up a bit.

Here are four soaker secrets that'll make using this time-saving tool even easier, and, if you can believe it, save even more water! □

— *Deborah Gruca*

1 Faucet fittings

Soakers, many made from recycled tires, come in ½- and ⅝-in. sizes in 25-, 50- and 100-ft. lengths and start around $10. They'll all work well for you, but the more heavy-duty ones will last longer. You'll find hoses, fixtures and accessories at many hardware stores and home centers.

To keep from contaminating your drinking water, use a backflow preventer (A) on your faucet when using any type of garden hose. Some communities actually require you to use them. A good one costs less than $10.

If you'd like, attach a timer (B) so you don't have to remember to turn the faucet on or off. You'll find timers that range from inexpensive models to programmable battery-operated ones that can be set to water every day to once a week. This timer sells for around $40.

Then add a pressure regulator (C) — at about $10 — to get the water pressure down to 10 to 12 PSI (so the hose won't burst!). Hook up a regular garden hose that's long enough to reach the bed you want to water and connect the soaker hose to the end of that hose.

2 On the level

Flower beds, vegetable gardens and shrub borders that are relatively flat are ideal places to use soaker hoses. Laying them on inclines causes the water to weep unevenly, so use other watering methods, such as sprinklers, drip or underground irrigation systems, for hillside or sloping gardens.

3 Go the distance

Soakers work best when they're not too long. If your hose is more than 100 ft. long, you'll have some pretty thirsty plants at the end. Buy a soaker hose long enough to wind around the plants in your bed. If you need more than 100 ft. of soaker, attach a splitter to the faucet. Then you can hook up and run more hoses at the same time.

4 The right place

After laying your soaker hose in the sun until it's warm and pliable, zigzag it through your plants. Place the hose within an inch of young plants when they're small to make sure they get enough moisture. (Be sure to cover at least half the root zone.) Once they're bigger, keep it at least 2 in. away from the crown of the plants.

Your plants will grow quickly and cover the hose. But if you want, top it with a couple inches of mulch to help hide it until plants grow larger. The mulch will keep the sun from damaging the hose, as well as keep the soil moist, saving you even more water.

You can expect your soaker to last several years. (After all, it'll still work even if it springs a leak!) To make it last longer, empty and bring it in for winter in colder climates. And remember to check where the hose is before digging into your bed!

TIP: If you're having trouble keeping a hose in place, pin it down. Bend 7-in.-long pieces of coat hanger wire around the female end of a hose. Then use the pins to fasten the hose down.

Wrap wire around hose end

When You Need Shade in a Hurry

Have you ever had a storm blow through and knock down a big limb or even a tree? If you have, you know what happens to a shade garden suddenly thrust into the unforgiving sunlight. Brown, crispy leaf edges, droopy, wilting plants. It's heartbreaking. But you can keep your plants from going through this kind of trauma, even if you lose a tree limb in July. Let me show you how.

First, you have to deal with the situation at hand: Your yard is a mess! Move your most prized plants to a more protected location while you tackle the cleanup. But it's simply not practical to move an entire bed in one weekend. So what can you do to save these shady characters until a new tree grows or the old one fills in? Create shade!

FLOATING ROW COVER If you grow vegetables, you've probably used this product before. It's a gauzy spun fabric that you lay over plants to keep beetles off your broccoli and rabbits from your radishes, among other things. But in a pinch, it makes great sun protection, too. It's so light that you can just throw it over your plants like a sheet, and it'll give them a little break from the sun. This is only a very temporary solution,

(1) Upright screens are perfect when you need to shade a plant from the afternoon sun but not all day long.

Instant shade

Not long ago, I came across this Sudden Shade Cooling Kit. It includes shade cloth (either 6x12 ft. or 12x12 ft.) that you can cut to any size with ordinary scissors or a knife. Rope and easy-to-use plastic clips make it easy to tie down with no special tools. And it's reusable. I know it's something I'm going to keep in my garden shed from now on. If you'd like to buy a kit for yourself, visit www.GardenGateStore.com.

(2) Overhead screens are what you need to protect plants that do best in full shade, such as these hostas.

though. After all, you probably don't want to cover your garden with a sheet all summer, right?

SIMPLE SCREENS Next, let's look at simple screens. These are great for hot spots and plants that need some special attention. A downed branch may have opened up a small area to direct sun or you may have a new plant that needs temporary shade to get it going. In photo 1, a small screen on the west side of the hostas protects their foliage from the afternoon sun. Or you may need to put in some overhead protection like the horizontal screens in photo 2 if you need all-day protection.

These two screening options are both wood frames with shade cloth stapled to them. For an easy-to-assemble ver-

sion of either one of these, buy a wooden screen door frame at your local hardware store and staple the shade cloth to it.

These two screens are relatively sturdy and built to last at least a few years. But say you're transplanting something in July and run into these heat and sunburn issues. I'll show you a solution that I often use in "Shade tent" below.

Shade cloth comes in black or green and is categorized by the amount of light it lets through (30 to 90 percent). A 60-percent shade cloth is a good all-purpose one that simulates the shade cast by a deciduous tree with medium foliage density. You often have to special-order it in specific sizes from commercial greenhouse suppliers and decide if you want it to have grommets for tie-downs. But I recently found a shade cloth kit perfect for just this use. Find

(3) A large pergola is the way to go when you've lost a shade tree and you need quite a bit of protection quickly.

out more about it in "Instant shade" above.

LARGE SHADE STRUCTURES The solutions I've shown you so far work well on a small scale, but if you lose a big shade tree, you'll be needing a larger-scale solution. That's where a pergola comes in. It might take just a week to build the structure in photo 3. But it can give you the same amount of shade as a tree that's taken years to grow.

With lattice on the top and some additional shade cloth if you need it, you can cool the area beneath the pergola several degrees. You may want to add a seating area there, too, while you're at it! □

— *Marcia Leeper*

Shade tent

I know it's not ideal, but every once in a while, I do divide and move plants in the middle of summer. And here's a great way to protect those tender transplants for a few weeks while I baby them along: Lash two bamboo stakes to either side of a couple of old aluminum window screens with zip ties. Place the screens together in a tent over your plants and push the bamboo stakes into the ground. Then connect the screens at the top.

Poke a hole in the screen and zip tie it to the bamboo pole.

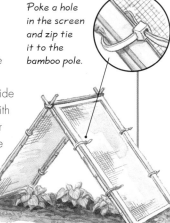

Prune Any Shrub

Sharp tools and 4 simple techniques are all you need

Pinching evergreens

Taking off the tips of needled evergreens will keep the plant more compact and full.

Remove ⅓ to ½ of the new growth when it looks like this, before the new needles stretch.

I wish I could come over to your garden and show you how to prune each of your shrubs, but that's just not possible. So, the next best thing is to show you the pruning methods you'll need to know before you tackle most any of them. Then I'll let you know which methods work on *your* shrubs in the "Plant-by-plant guide" below.

Keep in mind that if three options are checked, it's best to start with the least drastic technique. For example, you *can* rejuvenate a shrub, but try thinning or heading back first.

PINCHING EVERGREENS First, let's start small and easy. Pinching is the way to go if you want to keep most needled conifers, like mugo or Swiss stone pines and globe spruce, dense and compact. This technique doesn't involve any tools, although you can use scissors if you want to.

In spring, as soon as the new growth has stretched and the needles are about to start growing, it's time to pinch. As you see in the illustration, remove the top ⅓ to ½ of the new growth. Grasp the tip in your fingers and snap the tip off.

PLANT-BY-PLANT GUIDE

Plant name	Best time to prune	Blooms on	Pinch	Head back	Thin	Rejuvenate	Tips
Abelia, glossy *Abelia xgrandiflora*	Winter	New wood	☐	☑	☑	☑	Head back to control size; thin out the oldest stems to the ground each winter to keep this shrub blooming its best
Almond, dwarf flowering *Prunus glandulosa*	Late spring	Old wood	☐	☐	☑	☑	Prune each year to prevent a leggy, misshapen appearance
Azalea *Rhododendron* hybrid	Late spring to early summer	Old wood	☐	☑	☐	☑	Prune for size and shape; slow to recover from heavy pruning; may retard blooming for a year or two
Barberry *Berberis* spp.	Late spring or early summer	Old wood	☐	☑	☑	☑	Same for deciduous and evergreen types; thorny, so wear gloves; will tolerate pruning at other times of the year
Bayberry *Myrica pensylvanica*	Early summer	Old wood	☐	☑	☑	☑	Maintain natural, informal shape and size with light pruning; rarely needs rejuvenation
Beautyberry *Callicarpa japonica*	Winter to very early spring	New wood	☐	☐	☑	☑	Prune each year to get the heaviest berry production
Burning bush *Euonymus alatus*	Anytime	NA	☐	☑	☑	☑	Prune before new growth for a more casual look or after new growth for a tighter, more formal appearance
Camellia, Japanese *Camellia japonica*	Late spring	Old wood	☐	☑	☑	☑	Slow to recover from rejuvenation pruning so try to keep it in shape with heading back
Carolina allspice *Calycanthus floridus*	Spring or late summer	Old and new wood	☐	☑	☑	☑	Lightly head back or thin to maintain form
Chastetree *Vitex agnus-castus*	Late winter	Old wood	☐	☑	☑	☑	Shrubs can be headed back, thinned or rejuvenated; only thin or head back tree-form specimens
Cotoneaster *Cotoneaster* spp.	Winter	Old wood	☐	☑	☑	☑	Prone to fireblight so prune well below infected areas and sterilize shears between cuts with bleach solution

*If more than one method is checked, it's safest to try the least drastic first.

The plant won't look dramatically different when you're finished, but pinching will stimulate more side branches to grow. After a couple of years of pinching, your shrub will be more dense.

Before I get into the next techniques, you need to know two terms. If you read that a shrub blooms on *old wood*, you have to leave the growth that grew last year or you won't get any flowers. If it blooms on *new wood*, you can prune while the plant is dormant, when it's often easiest to see the branching structure, and it'll flower later in the season.

HEADING BACK This technique is for deciduous shrubs, such as azaleas, that have grown too large or too leggy and sparse. Check out the two illustrations at right and you'll see that you remove only the ends of the branches back to a side bud or another branch.

Heading back

This technique removes the tips of branches so the shrub stays dense and compact with a nautral form.

Cutting to an outward-facing sidebud or branch helps keep an open center so air circulates better.

Sidebud

Another branch

Heading back a shrub while it's dormant makes it easy to see the structure. Just make sure your shrub blooms on new wood or you'll be cutting off the flower buds.

Plant name	Best time to prune	Blooms on	Pinch	Head back	Thin	Rejuvenate	Tips
Deutzia *Deutzia* spp.	Early summer	Old wood	☐	☑	☑	☑	Blooms better with annual pruning
Dogwood, red twig *Cornus alba*	Winter or early spring	New wood	☐	☑	☑	☑	Head back for size, but heavy thinning or rejuvenation produces the most colorful stems for winter interest
Firethorn *Pyracantha coccinea*	Summer	Old wood	☐	☑	☑	☑	Thorny, so wear gloves; sterilize shears between cuts to prevent spreading fireblight
Forsythia *Forsythia* hybrid	Spring	Old wood	☐	☑	☑	☐	Prune every year after blooming to keep this fast-growing shrub under control
Fothergilla *Fothergilla gardenii*	Early summer	Old wood	☐	☑	☑	☑	Open habit and small size; rarely needs thinning or rejuvenation
Heavenly bamboo *Nandina domestica*	Spring	NA	☐	☑	☑	☐	Head back tips to maintain size; thin out four or five of the oldest stems each year to keep this shrub looking good
Honeysuckle *Lonicera* spp.	Summer	Old wood	☐	☑	☑	☑	Tolerant of almost any type of pruning; quick to recover from rejuvenation
Hydrangea, smooth *Hydrangea arborescens*	Late winter	New wood	☐	☑	☑	☑	Heading back will allow the plant to grow tallest; rejuvenation will give you fewer, but larger, flowers
Kerria *Kerria japonica*	Early summer	Old wood	☐	☑	☑	☑	Thinning promotes heavier flowering and more bright green stems for winter interest
Leucothoe *Leucothoe fontanesiana*	Early summer	New wood	☐	☐	☑	☑	Blooming is improved with heavy thinning; quick to regrow and reflower after rejuvenation
Lilac, common *Syringa vulgaris*	Late spring	Old wood	☐	☑	☑	☑	Head back or thin regularly to control size; only rejuvenate when overgrown — takes several years to resume blooming

THINNING AND REJUVENATING

Thinning

Cutting out branches lets in air and sunlight to make the shrub healthier and more resistant to wind and storm damage.

Remove the oldest or largest stems from the center of the shrub first.

Cut away branches that point toward the center to allow better air circulation and prevent rubbing stems.

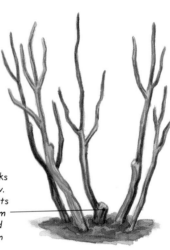

This shrub looks very thin now, but new sprouts will grow from the base and begin to fill in the center.

THINNING Do you need to open up a dense deciduous shrub, such as a forsythia, so air can circulate better? Thinning lets in sunlight and air, so the shrub has better foliage and more flowers. And thinning allows the wind to filter through the branches so the shrub is resistant to storm damage. Just like heading back, thinning is a spring task and will maintain a natural-looking form.

On an old shrub, take out some of the oldest or largest stems from the center. On a young shrub, your objective is to prune out branches pointing inward that will make the plant too dense. Thinning cuts are not arbitrary, though. Just as in heading back, you make each cut directly above a larger branch or outward facing bud, usually low on the plant, to help maintain an open center.

REJUVENATING Brace yourself. This is a drastic form of pruning. And before I start, I should tell you that not all shrubs will react the same way. In fact, some won't tolerate it. If in doubt, don't try rejuvenation pruning.

Depending on the shrub, rejuvenating may be a task you do every year, or only rarely. For example, Japanese spirea, which blooms on

Plant name	Best time to prune	Blooms on	Pinch	Head back	Thin	Rejuvenate	Tips
Lilac, dwarf Korean *Syringa meyeri*	Early summer	Old wood	☐	☑	☑	☑	Rarely needs much pruning to stay dense and compact
Maple, Amur *Acer ginnala*	Midsummer	NA	☐	☑	☑	☑	Wounds bleed sap if cut in winter or early spring
Mockorange *Philadelphus* hybrid	Late spring	Old wood	☐	☑	☑	☑	Remove oldest stems from the center to keep this shrub blooming its best; only rejuvenate when overgrown
Mountain-laurel *Kalmia latifolia*	Early summer	Old wood	☐	☑	☑	☐	Perfoms well with minimal pruning; deadhead spent flowers to stimulate more side branches
Pine, mugo *Pinus mugo*	Late spring	NA	☑	☐	☑	☐	Pinch as new growth stretches but before needles grow; thin to give the shrub a more natural appearance
Pine, Swiss stone *Pinus cembra*	Late spring	NA	☑	☐	☑	☐	Pinch as new growth stretches but before needles grow; thin to give the shrub a more natural appearance
Potentilla *Potentilla fruticosa*	Winter or early spring	New wood	☐	☐	☐	☑	Blooms better and looks neater with rejuvenation every year
Privet *Ligustrum* spp.	Early spring	New wood	☐	☑	☐	☑	Do heavy pruning in early spring, but can be lightly trimmed at any time during the year
Pussywillow *Salix caprea*	Late spring to summer	Old wood	☐	☑	☑	☑	Heading back or thinning will produce long, straight stems for cutting; quick to recover from rejuvenation
Quince, flowering *Chaenomeles japonica*	Late spring to summer	Old wood	☐	☑	☑	☑	Wear gloves and long sleeves, flowering spurs are similar to thorns
Rose-of-Sharon *Hibiscus syriacus*	Early spring	New wood	☐	☑	☑	☑	Train to a tree form, allow to become a large shrub or keep small with regular pruning

*If more than one method is checked, it's safest to try the least drastic first.

Rejuvenating
Cutting all of the stems near the ground will encourage a more compact habit and better flowering.

Don't worry about looking for a bud or outward-facing branch when you cut.

There's no need to be afraid of cutting many shrubs back to 1 ft. or less — they'll grow back.

the new or current season's wood, may grow back to its normal size and flowering schedule the first year. However, a large shrub, or one that blooms on old wood, like a lilac, may take three years or more to recover and start blooming normally.

Rejuvenation is often better than ripping out an overgrown shrub and starting over. Why? A shrub with established roots will regrow faster than a new one will grow. New shrubs need time to establish before growing. And once you rejuvenate your plant, it'll bloom better and have a better form, too.

Just before the leaf buds break in the spring is the time to rejuvenate. Cut all of the stems down to within a foot of the ground. But unlike heading back or thinning, don't worry about where you make the cuts, it won't matter. New growth will sprout from the ground and dormant buds that you can't see, low on the stems.

Now you know how to prune. In the chart below I've listed 44 common shrubs with the methods of pruning that work best for them, when to do it and tips to help you have the best-pruned shrubs in your neighborhood. □
— *Jim Childs*

Plant name	Best time to prune	Blooms on	Pinch	Head back	Thin	Rejuvenate	Tips
Siberian peashrub *Caragana arborescens*	Late spring	New wood	☐	☑	☑	☑	Rarely needs pruning except to control size; only head back or thin plants trained into tree-form
Smoke tree *Cotinus coggygria*	Winter	New wood	☐	☑	☑	☑	Train into a treelike specimen or cut to the ground each winter to maintain a small shrub; new growth has the best foliage
Spirea, Japanese *Spiraea japonica*	Late winter	New wood	☐	☑	☐	☑	Rejuvenate each year for dense growth and more flowers; trim lightly after flowering for a possible rebloom
Spirea, Van Houtte *Spiraea xvanhouttei*	Late spring or early summer	Old wood	☐	☑	☑	☑	Recovers quickly from rejuvenation; best form and flowering with regular pruning
Spruce, globe *Picea pungens 'Globosa'*	Late spring	NA	☑	☐	☑	☐	Rarely needs pruning; only pinch to keep it from growing too large
Viburnum, arrowwood *Viburnum dentatum*	Late spring	Old wood	☐	☑	☑	☑	You'll lose the fall fruit with spring pruning, but this shrub will flower normally next spring
Virginia sweetspire *Itea virginica*	Summer	Old wood	☐	☑	☑	☑	Pruning will keep this shrub from growing loose and floppy; rarely needs rejuvenation
Weigela *Weigela florida*	Summer	Old wood	☐	☑	☑	☑	Head back or thin to promote the best flowering; recovers quickly from rejuvenation
Winterberry *Ilex verticillata*	Late winter	New wood	☐	☑	☑	☑	Head back to control size; regular thinning will result in more colorful fruit; slow to recover from rejuvenation
Witchhazel *Hamamelis* spp.	Late spring to summer	Old wood	☐	☑	☑	☑	Open branching habit rarely needs much pruning; head back to control size
Yew *Taxus* spp.	Late winter	NA	☐	☑	☑	☑	Late winter for heavy pruning; can be trimmed anytime trimmed anytime

Bedding Down Your Bargains

In the fall, you see a plant you've always wanted at a great price. You get it home…and what do you do with it? There isn't time to dig that new bed you're planning. Don't let your bargain plant go to waste — here's how I hold plants in the test garden until I'm ready for them in the spring.

Fall sale plants may have tattered foliage and twigs, but that's OK. They're about to go dormant anyway. Just steer clear of trees with big wounds on the trunk or plants with obvious disease symptoms. Those aren't bargains at any price.

KNOW WHEN TO HOLD 'EM

Many perennials can be saved over the winter with the method I've described on this page. But some perennials have problems with crown rot in wet conditions, so it's best to buy and plant those in spring. These lists will help you be sure you're not throwing money away in the fall.

STORE WELL OVER THE WINTER
Astilbe *Astilbe* spp.
Black-eyed Susan *Rudbeckia* hybrids
Coneflower *Echinacea* hybrids
Daisy *Leucanthemum* hybrids
Daylily *Hemerocallis* hybrids
Hosta *Hosta* hybrids
Salvia *Salvia* spp.
Tall garden phlox *Phlox paniculata*
Veronica *Veronica* spp.

BUY AND PLANT IN SPRING
Baby's breath *Gypsophila paniculata*
Bellflower *Campanula* spp.
Columbine *Aquilegia* spp.
Coral bells *Heuchera* hybrids
Delphinium *Delphinium* hybrids
Hellebore *Helleborus* hybrids
Lavender *Lavandula* spp.
Pinks *Dianthus* spp.
Sedum *Sedum* spp.

SAVE THE TREES Of course, early to midfall is a good time to plant trees and shrubs. But if it's too late, or you just aren't ready to plant them yet, hold them over the winter. In USDA zones 7 and warmer, you can just set most trees and shrubs in a protected corner, but where it gets colder, there's a little (but not much!) more effort involved.

I like to create a temporary berm over the plants. I do this in the vegetable garden, because it's already cleaned off and there's no grass to damage. But you could build the berm behind the garage, or locate it where you're planning to put a new bed next spring anyway. Starting from the bottom, the illustration at right shows you how to layer the plants with materials that protect and insulate them for the winter.

This method of overwintering works best with small, young trees and shrubs, so the containers aren't too big and the branches don't stick out much. Wait for all the foliage to fall off the plants before you tuck them in. Don't use this technique with broadleaf or needled evergreens — it's too easy for foliage to be damaged or to rot. Water the pots thoroughly before you tip them on their sides.

THINK SMALL You can save perennials over the winter with this technique as well. Sink 6-inch or 1-gallon pots around the edge of the landscaping fabric, and mound the compost over them, too. ("Know when to hold 'em," at left, lists perennials that hold well this way, and those that often don't make it.)

When I find 3- or 4-inch pots of perennials on sale, I plant them in the ground wherever I have room. (Tease the roots out a little so they're not circling.) I'll transplant them in spring, but they're small so I won't have to dig much. My secret technique? Mulch them as soon as you plant, even though the ground hasn't frozen yet. It'll give them extra time to establish roots. When the soil freezes, add 3 or 4 more inches of mulch to keep them from heaving out of the ground.

Last but not least, if you find bagged mulch, potting mix or fertilizer on sale in the fall, go ahead and buy it. Store the bags in a dry garage or shed so the plastic won't break down. Layer a few mothballs between the bags to keep rodents from making a winter home in the mulch.

Happy bargain hunting! □

— *Marcia Leeper*

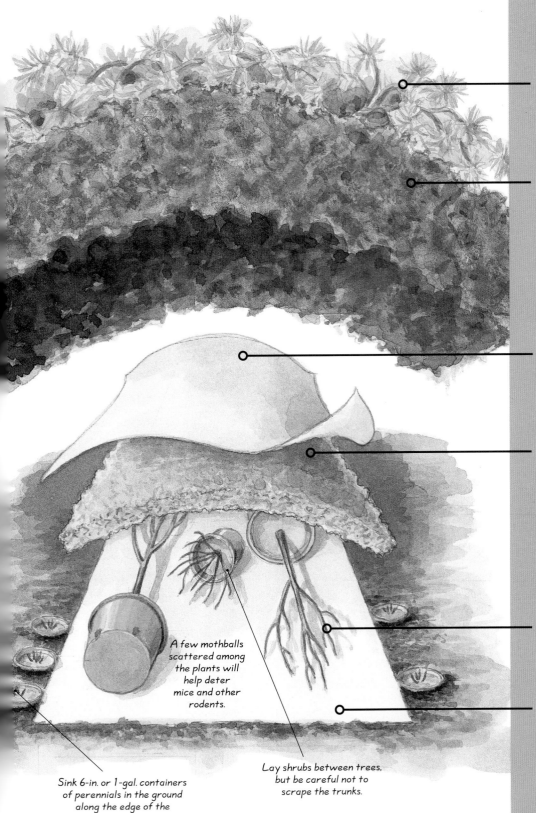

EVERGREEN BRANCHES Lay these on top to hold the compost in place. They'll also help you remember where you piled your plants so you're less likely to walk across them.

24 TO 30 IN. OF COMPOST AND CHOPPED LEAVES Mix compost with chopped leaves (about a 50:50 mix). This sounds like a lot, but it will settle quickly. You can use the compost on the garden in spring.

ANOTHER LAYER OF LAND-SCAPING FABRIC The fabric holds the chopped leaves in place. It'll also hold the compost, above, away from the plants, making it easier to lift them in spring without tearing or damaging branches.

5 TO 6 IN. CHOPPED LEAVES Chopped or shredded leaves can sift down around the branches to insulate the plants better than whole leaves. I like to use oak leaves because they're firm and crisp, but any kind will work if you run your lawn mower over them. Just be sure the leaves are dry — your stored plants will be healthier that way.

TREES AND SHRUBS Lay the trees and shrubs flat, turning them in opposite directions so they'll take up the least amount of space.

LANDSCAPING FABRIC It's not crucial, but putting landscaping fabric on the ground under the plants makes it easier to clean up the pile in spring.

A few mothballs scattered among the plants will help deter mice and other rodents.

Sink 6-in. or 1-gal. containers of perennials in the ground along the edge of the landscaping fabric.

Lay shrubs between trees, but be careful not to scrape the trunks.

Fountain in a Weekend

If you've admired stone or concrete water features, but not their hefty prices, you're going to love this charming fountain. Not only is our design *not* pricey, but you can make it yourself in just a weekend! And you'll find many of the items you'll need to build it right in your own kitchen.

GET READY First, find a level place to work outdoors. A piece of plywood on a pair of sawhorses makes a good work surface. Place a layer of newspaper on top of the wood to protect your plasticware from scratches. Then gather the materials and tools listed below. You'll need a plastic cereal bowl and the lid of a plastic cake keeper as molds for the fountain and a 2½-quart plastic deli container for the base.

You'll form the hollowed-out area on top of the fountain by placing the cereal bowl upside-down in the larger mold. (See small illustration at right.) To make the bowl easy to remove later, wrap it with plastic wrap before you add the concrete mix.

MIX CONCRETE Now you're ready to start mixing, so put on your rubber gloves. Fill your cake keeper to the top with dry cement to measure out the approximate amount. Then pour

MATERIALS AND TOOLS

For the fountain:
(not including the reservoir)

6-in. x 12-in. plastic cake keeper lid
Plastic cereal bowl
2½-qt. plastic deli container
10-ft. x ½-in. (inside dia.) PVC pipe
  (cut into 2 10-in. lengths plus one piece
  long enough to go from the pump to the
  top of the fountain)
Gallon of water
60-lb. bag of cement (gravel mix)
Cooking spray
Plastic wrap
Liquid concrete dye (optional)
Thick rubber gloves
Large plastic tub for mixing concrete
Rolling pin

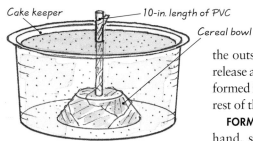

Cake keeper — 10-in. length of PVC

Cereal bowl

the cement into your plastic mixing tub, add about a third of the water, and mix it by kneading the ingredients together with your hands. (If you're using liquid concrete dye, mix it into the water before you add it to the dry cement.) Keep adding water and kneading until the concrete is the consistency of thick brownie dough.

PACK INTO MOLDS Next, spray the inside surface of the cake keeper lid and the deli container with cooking spray. Place the cereal bowl upside-down into the lid and, while holding it in place with one hand, use the other to pack several handfuls of concrete mix around and on the bowl until it stays put. Then continue filling with more concrete until the lid is about half full. Use the rolling pin to tap

the outside of the lid a few times to release any air bubbles that may have formed in the concrete. Fill the lid the rest of the way and tap it again.

FORM THE CONCRETE Using your hand, smooth the top of the concrete and remove any excess so the surface is nice and even. Then insert the wrapped 10-inch piece of PVC vertically into the concrete. Get it as centered and straight as possible.

Now repeat these steps with the 2½-quart deli container for the base, except leave out the bowl. Set both the cake keeper lid and the container aside to dry. In the meantime, dig a hole and set up the reservoir as you see in the cutaway illustration below. If you'd like step-by-step instructions on setting up the reservoir, go to our Web extra or send a SASE to Fountain Plan, *Garden Gate* magazine, 2200 Grand Ave., Des Moines, IA 50312.

UNMOLD THE FOUNTAIN After the concrete is set — about 5 to 6 hours — twist the PVC pipes a few times and pull them out. The concrete isn't completely hard yet so turn it over carefully and remove the lid, the bowl and the container. If you like the smooth finish, let the concrete dry overnight. To get the texture in the photo, replace the pipes and set the concrete where you can give it a good hard spray with the garden hose. This washes away a little of the cement and reveals more gravel. Spray it a little at a time until you get just the amount of texture you want. Then let it dry. Make sure the concrete has cured for 24 hours before using the fountain continuously.

ASSEMBLE THE FOUNTAIN Once the concrete is dry, assemble everything as you see in the illustration below and start enjoying the beauty and the soothing sounds of a fountain you made yourself! □

— *Deborah Gruca*

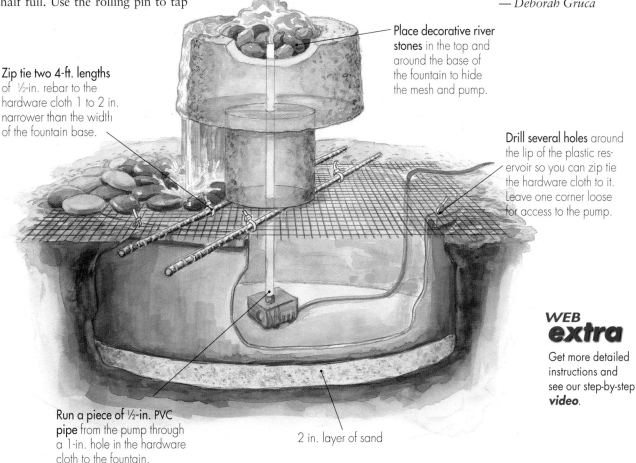

Zip tie two 4-ft. lengths of ½-in. rebar to the hardware cloth 1 to 2 in. narrower than the width of the fountain base.

Place decorative river stones in the top and around the base of the fountain to hide the mesh and pump.

Drill several holes around the lip of the plastic reservoir so you can zip tie the hardware cloth to it. Leave one corner loose for access to the pump.

Run a piece of ½-in. PVC pipe from the pump through a 1-in. hole in the hardware cloth to the fountain.

2 in. layer of sand

WEB extra

Get more detailed instructions and see our step-by-step *video*.

**WEB
extra**
More detailed
instructions and
tips on modifying
this gate.

Easy
Weekend
Gate

Create a high-style garden entry

Would you believe that this beautiful gate can be built in a couple of days with a few simple tools? It's true. And it only costs around $200, too. You might expect to pay something closer to $500 for a project like this, right?

Though it may not look like it, this gate is pretty simple to make. On the next pages, I'll show you how to build the four parts — the ladders, the frame, the grills and the handles — and put them together.

I'll include a few tips to make it easier and to save you some time. For even more detailed instructions, check out our Web extra — you'll also find some tips on how to modify the size of this gate.

BUY THE MATERIALS The first place you can save yourself some time and work is at the home center when you get the materials. Take the materials list at right with you and pick up the copper pipe, oak dowels and the straightest pieces of cedar you can find. (We're using cedar because it's rot-resistant and looks beautiful as it weathers outdoors.) Then have the staff at the home center cut the cedar and copper pipe to length for you. These stores usually allow you a set number of cuts free and then charge a minimal fee after that. Be sure to keep all the scrap pieces, too, in case you need to replace a part.

Many home centers won't cut wood into pieces shorter than 12 inches, so you may end up cutting the dowels and the smaller pieces yourself. If the store doesn't cut copper pipe, pick up a copper pipe cutter while you're there, too. It's not hard to use.

CUT THE SMALL PIECES When you get home, cut everything not already cut to length and label all the parts with a pencil (you can sand the marks off later) to make building easier and faster. OK, now we're ready. Turn the page and let's get started!

TOOLS

Miter box and handsaw
Clamp (opens to at least 7 in.)
Copper pipe cutter
Hammer or mallet
Electric drill and ¾-in. and
   ⅞-in. spade bits, 1/16-in. drill bit
   and phillips screwdriver bit
Masking tape
Tape measure
Square
Pencil

MATERIALS

8 8-ft. cedar 2x2
1 12-ft. cedar 1x6
1 8-ft. cedar 2x4
1 8-ft. cedar 2x6
9 ¾-in. oak dowels 36 in. long
1 ¾-in. copper pipe 10 ft. long
1 box of 100 2½-in. deck screws
1 box of 100 3½-in. deck screws
Polyurethane glue

CUT YOUR MATERIAL INTO THE FOLLOWING LENGTHS:

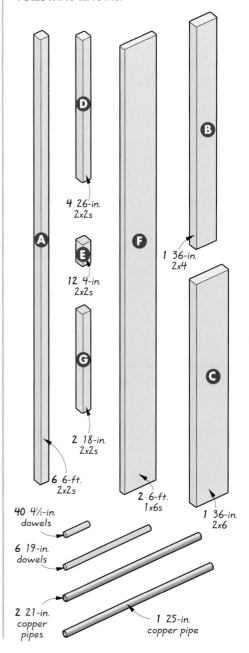

A
D 4 26-in. 2x2s
E 12 4-in. 2x2s
G 2 18-in. 2x2s
6 6-ft. 2x2s
B 1 36-in. 2x4
F 2 6-ft. 1x6s
C 1 36-in. 2x6
40 4½-in. dowels
6 19-in. dowels
2 21-in. copper pipes
1 25-in. copper pipe

ASSEMBLY **MADE EASY**

With all the pieces cut to length and labeled, all you have to do is drill some holes and put the parts together. I've broken this gate into four basic parts: the ladders, the frame, the upper and lower grills and the handles. Refer to the illustrations and photo as you go. □

— *Deborah Gruca*

1 Build the ladders

PARTS YOU'LL NEED:

4 **A** — uprights
40 4½-in. oak dowels
Polyurethane glue

DRILL HOLES FOR THE RUNGS You've already cut the 40 4½-in. dowels for the rungs. Now mark and drill holes in the upright pieces (A) to hold these rungs. Starting 6½ in. from the top, mark off every 3 in. until you have 20 marks.

Next, line all four uprights up side by side and clamp them together. Make sure the ends are even and, with a square, draw a line across all four at each mark. You might also find it helpful to use a

chalk line to mark the vertical center of each of the pieces. Holding the drill straight up and down, drill a ½-in.-deep hole at the center of each line. I'll show you how to make sure your holes are exactly the right depth in the tip below.

ASSEMBLE THE LADDERS Dribble polyurethane glue into the holes in the uprights and insert the rungs into the holes of one of them. Lay the upright with the rungs on the floor and, bracing the upright with your foot, use a rubber mallet or hammer to pound the other upright over the ends of the dowels so the uprights are 3½ in. apart. (If you use a hammer, place a scrap piece of wood over the upright first to protect it.)

TIP: With a piece of masking tape, mark the spot on your ¾-in. spade bit ½ in. from the "spur" of the bit. This will show you when you've drilled the hole to the correct depth.

When assembling uprights, start at one end of the ladder and work toward the other end.

2 Assemble the frame

PARTS YOU'LL NEED:

2 **A** — uprights
1 **B** — top
1 **C** — bottom
4 **E** — fillers
2 **F** — boards
40 ● — 2½-in. deck screws
The two ladders

DRILL HOLES IN THE TOP AND BOTTOM
Before you assemble the frame, drill three ½-in.-deep holes with your ¾-in. spade bit in one edge of the top (B) and the bottom (C). Use the spacing shown on the illustration at left. The longer dowels will slide into these holes later when you assemble the grills.

ASSEMBLE THE FRAME Now, lay the top and bottom pieces down. Make sure the edges with the holes are facing each other. Spread these two pieces far enough apart that you can lay the two ladders on top to form the frame. Attach ladders to the top and bottom with four 2½-in. screws at each end of the two ladders. Predrill all holes for screws first with a ¹⁄₁₆-in. straight bit to prevent splitting the wood.

Next, butt the four fillers (E) up against the ladders, and then the two remaining uprights (A). Attach all the pieces with two screws each. Finally, set the 1x6 boards (F) in place and attach by screwing them to the fillers. (Carefully place the screws so they don't hit those in the fillers underneath.)

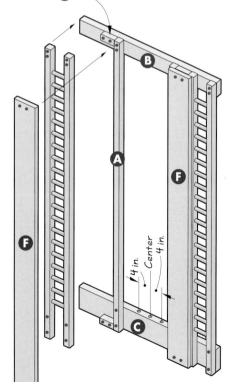

3 Add the grills

PARTS YOU'LL NEED:

- 4 **D** — crosspieces
- 8 **E** — fillers
- 8 ● — 2½-in. deck screws
- 16 ● — 3½-in. deck screws
- 6 19-in. dowels

DRILL THE FOUR CROSSPIECES Place a crosspiece (D) on a scrap piece of wood and, using the spacing shown at right, drill three ¾-in. holes all the way through the piece. Next, use this piece as a guide to drill another crosspiece just like it. Then replace the tape as shown in the tip below and repeat with the last two crosspieces, but drill the holes only ½ in. deep. The top and bottom grills each need one piece with through-holes and one with ½-in.-deep holes.

ASSEMBLE THE GRILLS Flip the gate over so you're looking at the back side. Insert three of the 19-in.-long dowels into the holes in the top of the frame. You won't need to glue the dowels into these holes. Slide a crosspiece (with the through-holes) over the dowels and then place another one (with ½-in. deep holes) onto the ends of the dowels. Tuck one filler under each end of each crosspiece. These help the longer screws to keep the vertical boards from cupping or bowing. Put two 3½-in. screws at each end of the crosspieces, through the crosspieces and the fillers into the frame. Now repeat these steps for the grill at the bottom of the gate.

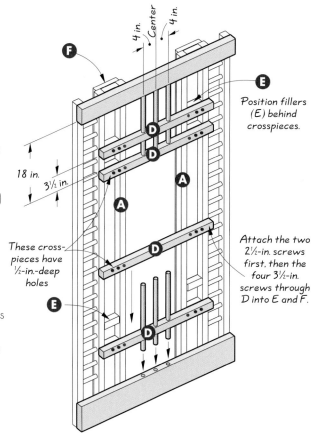

Position fillers (E) behind crosspieces.

18 in.

3½ in.

These cross-pieces have ½-in.-deep holes

Attach the two 2½-in. screws first, then the four 3½-in. screws through D into E and F.

4 in. Center 4 in.

TIP: Use your first drilled crosspiece (D) as a guide. Clamp it to each of the other three crosspieces and drill remaining holes.

½ in.   2 in.

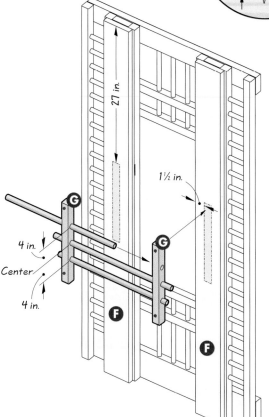

27 in.

1½ in.

4 in.
Center
4 in.

4 Attach the handles

PARTS YOU'LL NEED:

- 2 **G** — handles
- 4 ● — 2½-in deck screws
- 2 21-in. copper pipe
- 1 25-in. copper pipe

DRILL THE TWO HANDLES Change to a ⅞-in. spade bit in your drill and drill three holes all the way through the two handles (G) using the measurements at left. The three copper pipe pieces will run horizontally through these holes.

ATTACH THE TWO HANDLES Flip the gate over again, so you're looking at the front. Center the handles on the boards (F), 1½ in. from the inside edges. Attach each handle in place with one 2½-in. deck screw at each end. Slide the three lengths of copper pipe through the holes in the handles, the long one in the center holes and the two shorter ones through the top and bottom holes. If it's a tight fit, tap the ends with the rubber mallet.

FINISH UP Coat your gate with an exterior finish, such as Penofin® Penetrating Oil Finish, or leave it to weather naturally to a nice silver gray.

This 6-ft.-by-3-ft. gate is hefty, so I mounted it with three heavy-duty hinges and a matching latch. You can find them at hardware stores or the home center where you got all of the other materials.

did you know...

Not an ant in sight

Dennis Boren, Washington

Tired of seeing an army of ants picnicking at his hummingbird feeder, Dennis created an ant moat with a few simple household items.

To get started, Dennis opened the end of an eyebolt to form a hook. This makes a nice deep U-shape so the feeder won't slip off, and it's easier to hang without spilling, too. Then he drilled a hole the same diameter as the eyebolt in the bottom of a tuna can. Assembling the moat is easy. Just follow the illustration below and place the hardware in the order it's shown. When you tighten the last nut, make sure the rubber washer fits snugly against the bottom of the can. That's what forms the watertight seal.

Once his invention was finished, Dennis hung it above the feeder and filled the tuna can with water. If the ants try to cross the water, they'll drown. Now the hummingbirds don't have to share their meal with the ants. During hot weather, he checks it every couple of days to make sure the water hasn't evaporated. Otherwise, he fills it about once a week.

Hang the feeder about 5 feet from the ground to keep cats from making a meal of your hummers.

Ant invasion

Karen Jones, New Hampshire

Q*My yard's been taken over by ants. What can I use to get rid of them that's safe to use near pets?*

A There are a couple products, organic diatomaceous earth and BUGS 'R' DONE™, that veterinarians say are safe to use around pets.

Diatomaceous earth (DE) is an organic powder with a texture like ground glass. It cuts the bodies of insects that crawl across it, killing them. But it's non-toxic and won't harm pets if they eat it. Be careful not to inhale the dust as you apply it around the anthills — it can irritate your lungs. And make sure you use the natural-grade DE made for gardening, not the product used for swimming pools.

If you'd rather not deal with the dust, try BUGS 'R' DONE. It's a spray made of orange-peel oil that kills ants by damaging their breathing passages. With a sweeping motion, spray ants and their anthills.

For other pet-safe products, check out the Colorado State Home Pesticide Use Database at http://wsprod.colo state.edu/cwis487/.

Chipmunks, beware!

Inez Klimist, Michigan

Inez knows that when chipmunks are in the garden, no plant or bulb is safe. These voracious pests don't think twice about nibbling on fruit, vegetables, seedlings, flowers or bulbs. But Inez found that spreading dog hair around the plants she wants to protect seems to keep the chipmunks from returning to dine again.

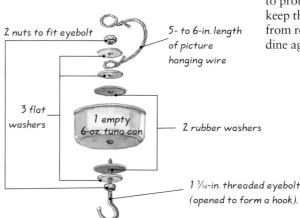

2 nuts to fit eyebolt

5- to 6-in. length of picture hanging wire

3 flat washers

1 empty 6-oz. tuna can

2 rubber washers

1 ³⁄₁₆-in. threaded eyebolt (opened to form a hook).

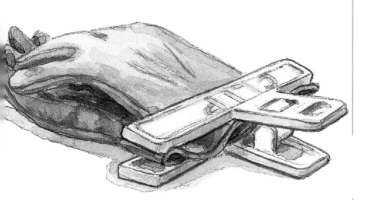

in the news

Free pesticide booklet

Nobody likes pests, and everyone likes a freebie, so this deal from the Environmental Protection Agency is a win-win situation. It's a free booklet on how to use both organic and chemical solutions to get rid of pests in your house or garden. Visit www.epa.gov/OPPTpubs/Cit_Guide/citguide.pdf to download your copy of the 54-page *Citizen's Guide to Pest Control and Pesticide Safety*.

Spiders, keep out!

Patricia Haas, Illinois

Patricia likes to leave her garden gloves out in her tool shed where they're needed. But she worried that spiders, especially poisonous ones like the brown recluse, would take up residence while the gloves weren't in use.

To save herself some worry, or a bite, Patricia now clips a potato chip clip over the open ends of her gloves when she's done gardening. The heavy spring keeps the gloves closed so there's no entry, even for small spiders.

Tomato fake-out

Clark Camp, Texas

Do birds get to sample your tomatoes before you do? Clark was having that problem, too. When he came across a box of light bulbs in his garage, a light bulb went on in his head!

Since the bulbs are about the same size as his tomatoes, he thought he could make a disappointing substitute for those hungry birds. To provide the fragile light bulb with a hard coating, he mixed up some thin concrete and dipped each bulb in it. If your mixing container's too shallow, Clark says you can pat the concrete on the bulb, too. When it was dry, he applied a coat of red paint.

A piece of copper wire wrapped around the ridged end of the bulb several times served as a "stem" so he could attach the decoy to the cage or plant.

Clark hangs three or four fake tomatoes on each plant right before the real tomatoes start to turn red. The birds, thinking they're in for a treat, find that these tomatoes aren't such easy pickings. They soon lose interest and look for an easier meal somewhere else.

product pick

Rabbit Repellent

If you're tired of finding tiny nibbled nubs when you go out to look over your perennials, try Rabbit Repellent. We found this easy-to-apply spray a big help in our test garden. One of the best things about it is that it lasts up to 30 days without washing off in the rain. Rabbit Repellent smells and tastes bad to rabbits but to humans, it actually has a pleasant peppermint fragrance. And it's organic, too, so it's safe to apply to edibles. This repellent is good but don't expect miracles. It always helps to rotate tactics with critters since they'll eat just about anything if they're hungry enough.

Bottom line: Rabbit Repellent is a good addition to your pest-control arsenal.
Source: Messina Wildlife at www.messinawildlife.com or call 888-411-3337
Price: $14.99 for a 35.2 oz. pump sprayer; $24.99 for a 1-gallon refill

product picks

Garden Bag

Keep all your garden stuff in one place with this new garden bag. The tough nylon fabric stays upright without any help and it's easy to clean — just rinse it off with a hose, both inside and out. The hefty rubber bottom keeps whatever's inside dry even when the bag is sitting on soggy ground. With plenty of pockets, it's easy to get pruners, gloves, hand tools, twine and other garden necessities all in one trip. There's even a mesh pocket with a cinch closure on each end that's perfect for keeping a water bottle handy on hot days. Bags are 13½ inches wide by 14½ inches tall and 7⅜ inches deep.

Bottom Line: Tough and roomy, this bag makes it easier to tote what you need.
Source: Duluth Trading Company at www.duluthtrading.com or 800-505-8888
Price: $29.50

Comfort hand tools from Corona® aren't new but they are indeed comfortable. You can find them at most local Ace Hardware stores or online at www.acehardware.com.

GardenGrips garden clogs

If you've been searching for a garden clog that's mo than cute, try GardenGrips™. Other clogs we've tri were colorful and fun to wear but a little hard on th feet. These new clogs have cushioned insoles and a supports so you can stay in the garden all afternoo And with the stiff shank, it's easy to give the shovel a good hard push while edging a bed. The specially designed sole is similar to soccer shoes so there's no slipping and sliding on wet grass. On top, there's a rubber toe and stain-resistant leather in three color — moss, shale or indigo (shown).

Bottom Line: These sturdy clogs will keep your feet good shape.
Source: GardenGrips at www.gardengrips.com or 877-447-4771
Price: $69.95, available in whole and half women's sizes 6 through 12

Leave toxic plants like datura out of the compost bin.

in the news

Promising paper compost

You may have heard of a study at the University of Warwick in the United Kingdom that found mixing 20 percent green compost (the kind made from yard debris) with peat suppresses some plant diseases by as much as 72 percent. This is a great way to reduce the amount of peat moss being used and help preserve peat bogs. Recently, these same scientists found that compost made from waste paper (like the tons produced in homes and offices daily) is just as effective at suppressing disease. Though further research is needed, this may open up new and promising uses for recycled paper.

What *not* to compost

Preston Rook, Kansas

Q *I know that datura plants (Datura spp.) are poisonous. Can I compost them at the end of the growing season?*

A The short answer: It's probably safest to leave them out.

First, compost piles tend to attract animals and insects. If any of them ingest enough of the datura toxins, it could be fatal. Plus, the bacteria that work to break down the organic matter are the lifeblood of your compost pile. The toxins could destroy these beneficial organisms, as well.

Second, if you use the compost in your vegetable garden, the toxins could be absorbed into the produce from that garden. Ideally, your compost pile will make enough heat to destroy the toxins. But since you can never be 100 percent sure that your compost is getting hot enough, it's probably best not to add any toxic plants.

Better later than never

Sheri Normand, Michigan

Q *It's hard for me to find time to water my plants in the morning. Is it harmful to water in the evening?*

A It depends on how you water. If you use a soaker hose or direct water below the foliage with a watering wand, you won't be wetting the leaves. In those cases it makes no difference when you water.

If you overhead water or use a sprinkler, the best time is early morning. Since it's usually cooler then, you'll lose less water to evaporation, so more will soak into the ground and get to the roots. The plants get a good supply of water to face the heat later in the day.

No time to water early in the morning? Later on is fine as well — just be sure to do it early enough that the leaves will dry before dark. If the leaves stay wet overnight, the plants will be more likely to get fungal diseases.

Labels that rock!

Mary Trenerry, Nebraska

With a garden tour on the horizon, Mary found a creative way to label her plants — river rocks! Clean the rocks with dish soap and water then let them dry overnight. Then write the name on the rock using a paint marker containing xylene. (These are available at craft stores.) Some of Mary's labels have lasted more than seven years.

did you know... (CONTINUED)

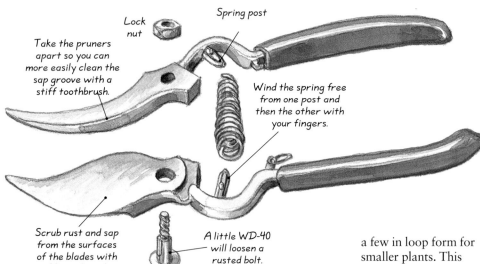

Take the pruners apart so you can more easily clean the sap groove with a stiff toothbrush.

Lock nut

Spring post

Wind the spring free from one post and then the other with your fingers.

Scrub rust and sap from the surfaces of the blades with 00 steel wool and oil.

A little WD-40 will loosen a rusted bolt.

WEB extra

Our **video** of sharpening and oiling a pruner.

How to clean bypass pruners
Lois Holmes, Pennsylvania

Q *I want to know how to clean my Corona® bypass pruners. They're dirty and a bit pitted and don't make a clean cut anymore.*

A Loosen the lock nut of your pruners. If it's stuck, spray it with a little WD-40® first. Twist the spring off one post and then the other. Remove the nut and pull the pieces apart. You can see how many pieces you should have above. To clean the buildup of dirt, rust and sap off the blades, spray them liberally with more WD-40. Soak them for a few minutes and scrub with 00 steel wool and more lubricant. Next, wipe the parts with a clean rag, reassemble them and add two drops of 3-in-One® oil to lubricate the blades.

As long as the blades are sharp and clean, a little pitting won't hurt anything. But if you have a big problem with the blades pitting, use cleaners like Lysol® or Listerine® to sterilize the blades. They're much less corrosive.

Quick cuts
Marsha Alesi, Missouri

Using old nylons to tie up wayward stems is a great way to keep plants in place and recycle, too. Gardeners often cut long thin strips, but Marsha found she saves time by making cuts across the leg about 1 inch apart. Then she gathers the loops together, and with one quick snip, she has plenty of nylon ties to keep her plants in place. Because the hose leg tapers, the strips come in a variety of lengths, so there's one for every job. You can even keep a few in loop form for smaller plants. This soft, durable fabric lasts all season and won't damage your plants' stems

Shoot for better pruning
Josephine Borut, New York

Josephine prunes the easy way — with her digital camera! After the leaves are gone, she photographs trees or shrubs that need pruning, taking care to get shots from several directions. It's easier to see which branches need to be removed when there's no foliage. Different vantage points give her a good idea of the overall shape of the plant. Once the photos are printed, Josephine marks any branches that need to be removed on the photo with a marker. At the appropriate time for pruning each plant, Josephine goes to work with her photo and her saw.

Give your cuttings a lift
Donna Saverino, Michigan

Make sure coleus cuttings get off to a good start with Donna's vase, made from a 12-ounce plastic water bottle. A few notches cut into the edge support the leaves so they don't fall into the water and rot. And when the stem is held off the bottom of the vase, it can take up water more easily. To make the vase, cut off the top of the bottle where it starts to curve in to the neck as you see in the small illustration at right. Then cut a few V-shaped notches, like those in the illustration below, for the leaf stems to catch on. As soon as a few roots appear, Donna's coleus are ready to pot up.

Cut the bo top off with a par scissor

There's room for sev notches around the to multiple cuttings

No-stick mower trick

Bill Eyermann, Missouri

Mowing the lawn is a big enough job without the added work of scraping grass clippings off the inside of your mower. Bill found a way to save time and energy with WD-40®. Every time he mows, he first gives the under-side of the mower deck a spray. The grass doesn't stick, and he doesn't have to worry about another chore to do later.

Ouch!

Sharon Kremnitzer, Wisconsin

Sometimes while gardening, Sharon gets a small prickle in her finger that's just too tiny to remove with twee-zers. Now she pulls the prickles out with ease, using one of those wax strips for removing unwanted facial hair. These strips are available at phar-macies or discount stores and there are several in each box, so you should have plenty for the season. Warm a strip between your hands to make the wax supple. Then apply it to the spot where the prickle is. Press it down to make con-tact, give it a quick pull and the prickle is gone. You might need two or three tries with the strip to get the job done.

in the news

Gardening = strong bones

Researchers at the University of Arkansas recently found that gardening is good for your bones. Women age 50 and over who gardened at least once a week had higher bone densities than did those who jogged, swam, walked or did aerobics. It's probably the combination of hard work — digging, pulling and pushing — and being outside in the sun. Sunlight boosts vitamin D production, which helps the body absorb calcium. So get out there and pull weeds — it's good for you!

product pick
Leatherman Hybrid™

You'll always be prepared with this tool in your pocket or on your belt. The Hybrid is a stainless steel bypass pruner with handles that fold over the blades, as you can see in the small photo. It works perfectly for deadheading and light pruning. When you're done, slip it into the nylon sheath that attaches to your belt or in your pocket. The coolest thing about this pruner is the collection of five little gadgets packed into the handle. There are two pint-sized screw-drivers (Phillips and flat head), a weed remover, a saw and a grafting knife. We liked that you could easily switch from, say, pruning raspberry canes to sawing out a woody grapevine without car-rying around an arsenal of tools.

Bottom line: Pocket-sized tools aren't usually this sturdy — this is the one to get.
Source: A.M. Leonard's Gardener's Edge at www.gardenersedge.com or call 888-556-5676
Price: $59.95

Use the center adjustment screw to disassemble your pruners and sharpen the stainless steel blade.

Nonslip handles are comfortable and secure.

Fold the mini-tools neatly back into the handle and they stay out of the way while you use the pruners.

Easy seed planting chart
Jan Krass, Iowa

Planting season is always hectic, so before it's even warm enough to sow the first seed, Jan spends an evening on the couch getting organized for her annual cutting garden.

Jan plants in rows, by height, for easy care and harvest. To make planting time go smoothly, she's created a chart that lists the seeds in height order along with other important information, such as plant spacing and depth. When the weather warms and it's time to get out and plant, a quick glance at her chart tells her which seed to start with and what comes next. There's no need to juggle seed packets and try to find the information in small type on the back. A little winter time prep saves Jan valuable time during the busy planting season.

Beaded planting guide
Cindy Sawyer, Massachusetts

Cindy takes advantage of downtime in winter to make spring vegetable planting a kid-friendly experience. She fashions a planting guide like the one in the illustration at right from mason's line, pony beads and waterproof glue, such as Gorilla Glue®. Mason's line is a nylon twine you can find at the hardware store.

To start, Cindy measures enough line so it's a couple feet longer than her garden row. That

Loop the mason's line around and through the hole to keep your pony bead in place.

way, there's enough to loop around and through each bead as the small illustration at left shows. She also makes a loop at each end to anchor the line.

Stringing all those beads is a big job, but once it's done, the guide lasts for years. Since mason's line is slippery, put a drop of glue inside each bead as you go to keep it in place. By alternating red and white beads 4 inches apart, Cindy can use one line for two different plantings. It's easier for the kids that way, too. They plant the first row of onions beside every bead, 4 inches apart. Then they move the guide to the next row, and plant a potato beside the red beads, 8 inches apart.

With this handy guide, the vegetables get planted and the kids enjoy knowing that what they plant now they can eat later.

Have your bulb planter do double duty. Use it to dig the holes for your annuals!

Find out how deep you've pushed the planter down (up to 4 in.) with the measuring guide.

product pick

Quick-Release Bulb Planter

Bulb planters aren't always worth the trouble — with most of them the soil sticks inside the cone. The Quick-Release Bulb Planter solves this problem. When it's time to empty the soil, give the lever under the cushy handle a pull and the "jaws" that form the cone open up to drop the soil out. You may find it difficult to squeeze the hand lever over and over if you have a small hand or don't have a lot of hand strength. Otherwise, this is a great way to plant bulbs or even annuals.

Bottom line: The sturdy construction of this tool means you'll be planting bulbs and annuals with it for years.
Source: Oxo International, Ltd. at www.oxo.com or call 800-545-4411
Price: $12.99

Ready-made raised bed

Judy Gums, North Carolina

Inspired by her grandson's plastic swimming pool, Judy decided to build a raised bed to avoid the quack grass that kept invading her garden. But instead of a child's pool, she got a preformed pond liner.

If you take a close look at the bottom of the liner in the illustration at right, you can see that Judy drilled several holes for drainage. She laid out a circle of bricks under the liner to keep it off the ground so there was no way outside roots could work their way into her new bed. (For larger pools you may need to run bricks across the center for support.) That done, Judy placed the liner on its "foundation," filled it with a good quality bagged top soil and added some plants.

Mounded soil hides the bare sides. Another row of bricks holds the soil in place and is easy to mow around.

Hose solution

Penny Griffin, Georgia

Gardeners with large yards know what a "drag" it can be to get the hose to the back of the yard when it's time to water. To deal with this problem, Penny runs an extension hose from the area near the faucet on her house, along her property line, to the back of her yard. She leaves it in place all year and hides it behind shrubs or underneath mulch. During the

summer, another hose is attached to the far end of the extension hose and left rolled up at the back of the yard until it's needed. When it's time to water, Penny simply attaches a third hose from the faucet on the house to the nearest end of her handy extension hose.

A spot of tea

Carleen Bailey, Oregon

Carleen has found a recipe for growing beautiful roses: She makes a tea by putting alfalfa pellets in water, and letting it sit overnight. Every three months, she makes a new batch and waters it into the soil around her roses.

A word of caution: Alfalfa mixes can be smelly. You can get similar results by applying a handful of pellets around each rose bush and working them in well.

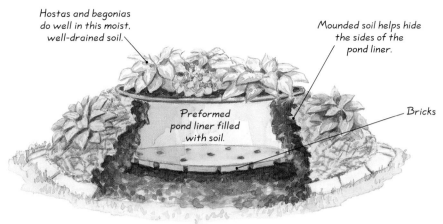

Hostas and begonias do well in this moist, well-drained soil.

Mounded soil helps hide the sides of the pond liner.

Preformed pond liner filled with soil.

Bricks

in the news

From disease to cure

Scientists at the University of Florida have found a way to make a virus work *for* a plant instead of *against* it. A genetically modified form of tobacco mosaic virus is effective against a broad range of pests and is harmless to humans, pets and most plants. It works by blocking insects' digestive system so after they eat treated leaves, they starve. Though one application of this virus lasts all season, it does need to be reapplied every year. An added bonus is that treated leaves can be harvested, dried and ground into a powder for use in sprays and baits for mosquitoes. More testing is needed on this new insecticide but scientists hope a home garden version will be available in the future.

product pick

Terracycle™ plant food

Worm castings are well-known for providing a rich supply of micronutrients to plants. This new liquid form doesn't disappoint. The newest formulas feed your tomatoes and other veggies or your lawn — one package covers 5,000 square feet.

You may notice that all the bottles aren't quite the same. Terracycle packs all its products in recycled soda bottles. The company invites groups to participate in its Bottle Brigade — earn 5 cents for every bottle you send in. Visit www.terracycle.net to find out how to get your organization involved.

Bottom line: It's great to have good-looking plants and help the environment at the same time.
Source: Home Depot and other local retailers
Price: Lawn fertilizer $14.92 for two 1-liter bottles; tomato food $8.99 for a 2-liter bottle

Overlapping the ends of the duct tape holds the grass securely.

Moss confusion
Sandi Trent, Washington

Q *What are the differences between peat moss, sphagnum peat and sphagnum moss?*

A They're basically different forms of the same thing — sphagnum or other mosses. But they each have different traits that make them good for certain situations.

Peat moss and sphagnum peat are both acidic (pH 3 to 7), lightweight soil amendments. (Peat moss is made from decomposed mosses, sphagnum peat from only decomposed sphagnum moss.) They both hold up to 15 times their dry weight.

Sphagnum moss is a long-fiber plant that's sold green or dried, but not decomposed.

Check out "What's the difference?" below for more information on how to use each of them in your garden.

Mulch mold
Linda Huser, Indiana

Q *I was raking and noticed mold growing on the mulch around my plants. What should I do?*

A Wood mulch decomposes over time. The mold, which isn't harmful, is actually feeding on the bacteria on the wood and will normally disappear on its own.

You probably won't be able to get rid of all of the mold. But if you want to minimize it, stir up the mulch with a rake to help it dry out. If it really bothers you, replace the wood mulch with rocks — this mold can't grow on stone.

A cooler potting bench
Kelly Austin, Pennsylvania
During the summer, Kelly uses her 70-quart insulated cooler for picnics like most of us do.

But once picnic season is over, she uses it to store her potting soil, gloves and a few tools. It saves space and keeps the soil from freezing in her unheated garage. In winter, when she's ready to pot up an amaryllis or start seeds, she brings the whole thing inside, unpacks it and uses it as an indoor potting bench. By holding pots over the open cooler as she fills them, she keeps the mess to a minimum. When the planting is done, the cooler goes back in the garage. Next spring, Kelly cleans and disinfects the cooler so it's ready for picnic duty again.

Simplify grass cleanup
Sonia Sugarman, New York
Cutting back ornamental grasses during spring cleanup can be a real pain — especially with big clumps. The blades whip you in the face and arms and fall over, making a big mess to clean up later. Sonia's duct tape came to the rescue.

She wraps a length of tape (or two, depending on how tall the grass is) around her clump of grass before cutting.

Make sure to overlap the ends of the tape since the adhesive doesn't actually stick to the grass. With the tape wrapped around the middle, Sonia had an instant bundle that's easy to carry to the compost pile or stick in a yard waste bag.

And since the tape doesn't stick to the grass, it's easy to cut it off. When we tried this, we discovered you'll need a helper on larger specimens to keep the tape from tangling.

Free mulch
Sara Tanis, Kansas
To save money and help the environment, Sara has found some unique sources for mulch. She calls recycling centers, tree removal companies or her local road commission. These groups cut down trees and chip them into mulch, which is often available to the public free or at a much lower cost than mulches purchased at garden centers.

For sources in your area, ask friends or neighbors or look in the yellow pages. It should only take a call or two to locate a company that is happy to get rid of its excess wood chips!

What's the difference?

	Peat moss/ Sphagnum peat	Sphagnum moss
What it is	Also called moss peat, decomposed sphagnum and/or other mosses	Living or dried sphagnum moss plants
Looks like	Dark brown; fine texture like soil, but not as heavy; mixes easily with soil	Long green or brown fibers
Used for	Soil amendment, pots, starting medium for seeds and cuttings	Lining hanging baskets, wreaths, indoor plant mulch, growing medium for orchids and air layering
Sold in	Bags or bales	Bags or bales

Color code your glads

Jan Krass, Iowa

Jan loves the rainbow of colors gladiolas provide in her cutting garden. For a succession of bloom, she plants them at three different times, two weeks apart. Her labeling technique ensures that she has a good mix of colors in each group.

It just takes a few clothespins spray-painted to match the flower colors. When the flowers bloom, she attaches the appropriately colored clothespin low on the foliage where it's not noticeable. She leaves it there for the rest of the season.

After a light frost, Jan digs the glads and cuts the foliage down, making sure to reattach the clothespin to the stub. Then she lets the bulbs dry for about 10 days. Once that's done, she sorts the bulbs by color, wraps them in newspaper and places them in mesh bags (like those that onions come in). Last of all, she closes the bags with the right color of clothespin so she'll know which color of glad she's planting next spring.

in the news

Clean mulch

Make sure your bagged mulch is free of chromated copper arsenate (CCA) this spring by looking for the label at right. CCA is a pesticide that's high in arsenic and, until 2003, was used to preserve wood. The Mulch & Soil Council has developed a nationwide certification program to make sure wood saturated with this chemical isn't added to shredded mulch. When you see this label, you'll know the council is monitoring not only CCA, but also mulch quality and volume accuracy. Find out more at www.mulchand-soilcouncil.org.

CERTIFIED PRODUCT	
	Premium Potting Soil
	Standard Potting Soil
	Landscape Soil & Soil Amendment
	Specialty Soils
✓	Mulch

This product has been registered and tested for conformance to the standards of the Mulch & Soil Council for the indicated product category for pesticides, and this certification mark does not apply to pesticide claims. For more information, refer to the MSC website at www.mulchandsoilcouncil.org.

product pick
Wide-brim braided hat

The sun is wonderful for plants but hard on a gardener's skin. Add an extra layer of protection (after you apply your sunscreen, of course) with this wide-brimmed hat. Made of twisted paper and cotton, it's soft and comfortable but has a tight weave so it's durable, too. Not only that, it looks good! An independent lab gave this hat a UPF rating of 50+, which is the highest rating available. You can get one in light brown (shown) or dark brown and it has a leather strap to keep it in place even on windy days.

Bottom line: Keep your skin safe from sunburn with this sturdy and stylish hat.
Source: www.GardenGateStore.com (light brown) or www.sloggerstore.com
Price: $24.99; comes in one size (medium); 23 inches around inside of crown

Push prongs into the soil to hold the umbrella in place.

When the bottom has worn away. put the basket over your favorite perennial for a decorative touch.

Readers' best staking ideas

We asked you to send us some of the most unusual methods you use to stake your plants. Here are a few of our favorites.

Charlotte Yearwood, Wisconsin

Charlotte's old umbrellas get a new life as garden stakes. She cuts the fabric off of the umbrellas and uses the handle and spines as a stake for her unruly plants.

Linda Lindgren, Montana

Linda's favorite method of supporting floppy plants is to use old wire-framed lamp shades. She removes the material from the shade and places the frame over her plants.

Marianne Gordon, Washington

Marianne lives near a state wildlife area. After hunting season, she collects lost arrows to use as plant stakes. They are strong and easy to camouflage in the garden, and the pointed ends make it easy to push them into the ground.

Steve Carroll, Missouri

While in a second-hand store, Steve had an inspiration for an unusual plant stake — aluminum knitting needles. They come in many lengths and diameters and are attractive and durable. You can also pick them up at yard sales for little cost.

Weed baskets

Darene Martin, Michigan

As Darene walks through her garden, she always finds herself stopping to pull weeds. To help with this chore, Darene tucks decorative baskets in different places around the garden. Then when she spots a weed, she can pull it and drop it in a basket instead of carrying it with her. Since the baskets are outside, the bottoms eventually rot away, but that's no problem. She just sets the baskets over perennials in spring while plants are young. As the plants grow, they create a basket full of flowers to enjoy for the rest of the season.

Crossing the needles helps keep potted plants upright.

Creative staking
Rose Wingert, Ohio

Looking for something a little different to keep your plants upright? Rose found just the ticket on sale at her local antique store: A fireplace screen. She placed it in her garden like the illustration at right shows. Bending back the "wings" on each side kept it upright. But she added a wooden stake where the panels meet for added stability. The plants in front cover the stakes. Now Rose's false sunflowers stay upright and don't smother the roses.

Holiday hold-up
Kathleen Wyatt, California

Wind is a real problem in Kathleen's garden. So instead of looking for mall bargains after the holidays, she keeps an eye out for wreaths put on the curb for recycling. She puts them to good use as stakes in her garden.

When she gets home, she discards any wire or decorations and runs the greens through the chipper. They make great compost.

In spring, Kathleen lays the frames on the ground around young plants like Iceland poppies and papyrus that need support later. Getting a head start prevents broken stems.

As plants grow, she adds three or four bamboo or metal stakes as "legs" to the frame.

Two wooden 2x4s help stabilize the screen.

Secure the frame to the legs with twist ties.

product pick

The Essential Garden Maintenance Workbook

Puzzled over what to do once you've planned and planted your new garden? Or maybe you've inherited a neglected plot of flowers with your new house. It's hard to know where to begin. *The Essential Garden Maintenance Workbook* can get you started. We especially liked the chapter called "Caring for Plants" that has all kinds of information including how to take cuttings, an A to Z of common pests and diseases and even a short botany course so you know how your plants grow. Simple line drawings and photographs illustrate the tips and how-tos.

Bottom Line: Keep your garden in tip-top shape with this thorough book.
Source: Local or online bookstores or www.GardenGateStore.com
Price: $34.95 softcover; 384 pages

Back-saving garden

Mary Favicchio, New York

Mary loves gardening, but back trouble makes it difficult for her to bend. Fortunately, she came up with an idea that helps her continue with her favorite hobby. She had her husband, Jon, build her a garden on legs. The base is made of an old metal table top supported on concrete-block "legs." Jon drilled some holes in the table top for drainage. Then he used 1x12 cedar lumber to build a frame, set it on the table and filled it with compost and soil.

In fall, Mary plants cool-season crops like arugula and lettuce, then covers the bed with a couple of old storm windows to convert it to a cold frame. Some years these tasty veggies have even lasted into December.

Freezing temperatures have never caused any problems for Mary. But in more exposed areas with cold winters, pack bags of leaves or straw bales under the table to help insulate the bottom.

Mary has been gardening this way for 10 years and enjoys it so much she now has two more raised beds.

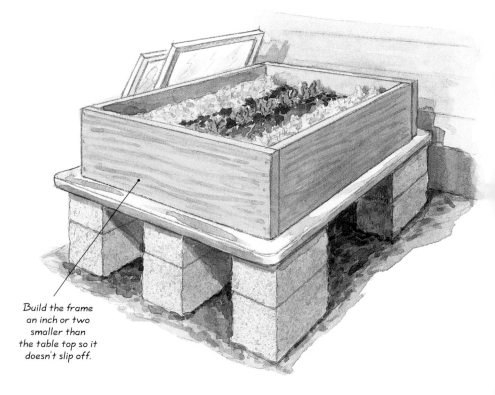

Build the frame an inch or two smaller than the table top so it doesn't slip off.

No more mystery plants!

Mary Wager, Louisiana

Mini blinds make great labels, but the ink often fades in a season or two. To make sure she doesn't end up with unidentified plants, Mary writes the name of the plant on both ends of the mini blind with permanent marker. She found that even if the name above the soil fades, the ink in the soil still looks as fresh as when it was written — even after a couple years.

Using wood ash on lawns

Richard Stover, Pennsylvania

Q *We burn wood to heat our home and live in an area with acid soil. Is it all right to spread the wood ashes on our lawn?*

A Wood ash does contain lime and potassium, which would help to raise the pH of your acid soil. But because the powder clumps so badly, it can be tricky to spread evenly on lawns. It might be better to save it to use in a flower or vegetable garden instead. If you haven't tested your soil, it's always good idea to do that before add any amendmen your garden.

Spring bulb especially appre a light applicati (less than ½ inc ash in early spr as it contains tr elements they r But don't sprea near broad-lea evergreens like leas — these pl prefer acid soil And don't spre ash heavily (m than 2 inches c or apply it on l every year, or y make your soi alkaline.

Stretching your storage space
Michelle Simon, Ohio

Michelle has a simple way to store plant stakes over the winter. With bungee cords and some metal screw hooks, she created a handy storage area between two studs of her garage wall.

Starting 3 or 4 inches from the floor, she screws a hook on the inside of the stud. Then she measures up 12 inches and puts in a second hook, and so on. The highest hook is about 3 feet above the garage floor.

Michelle puts hooks on the opposite stud, too, centering them between the ones on the first stud. Finally, she stretches bungee cords from hook to hook, creating the zig-zag pattern you see above. Now Michelle's stakes are out of the way and out of the elements.

Instant plant tag
Marilyn Ferlita, Nebraska

Spring is such a busy time. Getting new plants tagged and their locations recorded in your garden journal can be difficult. Marilyn found a quick and easy solution for her roses. Many nursery pots that roses (and some perennials) come in now have a label attached to the pot with a small metal ring. Marilyn cuts a large V-shaped wedge, like the dotted line in the illustration, from the nursery pot. The metal ring in the center still holds the tag while the pointed "V" slips easily into the ground. Because everything is plastic and meant to hold up outside anyway, it stands up to wind and weather easily. When things slow down, she records the location in her garden journal and replaces the plastic label with one that's permanent. Marilyn says that now there's "no more losing rose names because life interfered while I was planting."

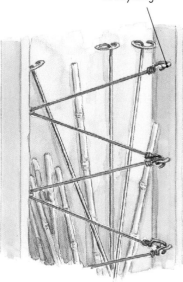

Face screw hooks in toward the wall so they don't catch on anything.

save your fingers

Growing plants brings beauty to your yard, but not every plant is entirely benign. After all, who hasn't been pricked by a rose thorn? So protect your hands with a sturdy pair of gloves. They'll save you from painful scrapes and blisters, and protect you from irritating plant sap and more sinister soil-borne diseases.

When you're choosing gloves, look for a sturdy pair made of leather or a stretchable, breathable fabric, with reinforcements in the palm and thumb (where gloves typically get the most wear and tear) and protection for your wrist. The pair should be flexible and washable, and should feel snug without being difficult to slip on or off. But most important, they should be comfortable enough that you want to wear them. (Pallina gloves, *below*, are available through www.GardenGateStore.com.)

Gloves with long gauntlets protect your wrists and forearms from cuts and scrapes.

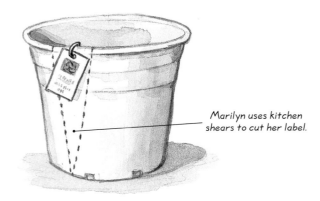

Marilyn uses kitchen shears to cut her label.

beneficials you should know

Big-eyed bug
Geocoris spp.

IDENTIFICATION These insects may not be pretty, but they're good to have around. The appropriately named big-eyed bug is a predator other bugs steer clear of.

There are 19 different species of big-eyed bug in North America, all with similar habits and life cycles. One of the most common, *Geocoris punctipes*, is shown below.

Adults are about 3/16 in. long with transparent wings and a broad head as wide as the oval-shaped body. They have piercing-sucking mouthparts that they use to stab prey.

Big-eyed bugs usually eat whiteflies, aphids, mites, small caterpillars and insect eggs. A single nymph can eat 151 tobacco budworm eggs and an adult, up to 80 mites per day! They'll occasionally

Actual size: 3/16 in.

feed on plants when prey is scarce, but damage is minimal.

LIFE CYCLE Big-eyed bugs only live about 30 days. They emerge in spring to hunt and lay eggs. These eggs hatch in about a week into tiny juveniles that look just like the mature bugs. What makes this insect so helpful is that males, females and all stages of juveniles eat insects — mostly those you don't want around. Late-season adults spend the winter in leaf litter, turf thatch, under loose bark or any place they can find. Insects like big-eyed bugs that overwinter as adults have a chemical in their system to prevent ice from forming. Once the body temperature reaches 55 degrees F in spring, they start waking up.

Big-eyed bugs are so abundant you don't have to do anything to attract them to the garden. But to encourage more of these hungry predators, avoid spraying insecticides.

Fiery searcher
Calosoma scrutator

Actual size 1 to 1½ in.

You may not see them; you may not even know they're there. But they are. Quietly going about the business of hunting insects, especially caterpillars, fiery searchers are helpful predators to have in the garden.

NICE TO HAVE AROUND Found throughout North America, this ground beetle hides in leaf litter, under rocks or in decaying logs during the day and emerges at night to find a meal. One of the larger beetles, the fiery searcher grows 1 to 1½ in. long and has large mandibles for grabbing prey. It's especially fond of tent caterpillars and gypsy moth larvae and will even climb trees to find a midnight snack.

EASY TO RECOGNIZE Fiery searchers are colorful, with brilliant green ridged wing covers ringed in red. Its legs, abdomen, head and pronatum (the area behind the head) are shiny blue-black. Even though the fiery searcher has wings, it rarely uses them. It's more likely to run for cover on its long legs than fly if it sees you coming near.

Be careful if you handle this beautiful beetle. When startled, it releases a foul odor as protection against predators, such as raccoons, frogs, birds, squirrels and other animals.

PUT OUT THE WELCOME MAT You'll notice beetles emerging from their winter hiding places in spring to feed and mate. Eggs are laid singly in the soil and hatch into long, slender larvae with short front legs. It takes about a year for the beetle to mature. Juvenile beetles inhabit the soil and feed on a variety of insects, including, you guessed it, caterpillars. Long-lived for an insect, the fiery searcher can reach the ripe old age of three or even four years.

You can't buy these helpful insects, but you can encourage them by providing hiding places such as stepping stones, a compost pile or a rotten log. Also, avoid spraying insecticides whenever possible, since the chemicals will kill these beneficial insects along with the pests.

Toads *Bufo* spp.

You don't need to kiss them to turn them into the princes of your garden. While toads aren't handsome creatures, they do provide a wonderful service. After all, you can invite them to dinner and they'll gobble up most of the garden pests that you want to get rid of.

Toads are nocturnal — they sleep during the day and feed at night. One toad can eat 50 to 100 insects at a time. That's as many as 3,000 bugs per month! A toad's diet includes mosquitoes and their larvae, flies, slugs and cutworms.

IDENTIFICATION All toads are frogs, but not all frogs are toads. Toads are known by their dry, warty skin and swollen bumps on their heads. These bumps are called "paratoid glands" and they contain an irritating substance used to ward off predators — it isn't harmful to humans.

LIFE CYCLE Although they live on land, female toads return to the water in the spring and lay thousands of eggs in gelatin-like strings up to four feet long. Tadpoles hatch from the eggs and live in the water until they develop legs and move onto land. Toads can live 4 to 15 years and sometimes longer.

To encourage toads to take up residence in your garden, all you need to do is provide them with a little shelter and water and avoid using chemical pesticides whenever possible. The pesticides reduce their food supply and can be toxic to them.

You can create a toad haven using things you have around your house. Broken clay pots make great homes. Put a clay saucer or other shallow container filled with water on the ground nearby. Toads drink through their skin, so the container should be low enough for the toad to hop into.

pests to watch for

Sooty mold coverage is often spotty like this, but in severe cases can coat the entire leaf.

Fungus gnat *Bradysia* spp.

IDENTIFICATION If you've noticed tiny flies that take flight from your house plants when you water, they may be fungus gnats. Fungus gnats are actually small dark gray flies about ⅛ in. long. They thrive with plenty of moisture and decaying organic matter.

These small flies live only three to four weeks. Most of their lives are spent as larvae feeding below the soil surface on decaying organic matter and plant roots. After pupating, adults emerge and live seven to 10 days. In that time, females can lay up to 300 eggs.

DAMAGE Adult fungus gnats are generally only considered a nuisance. But the larvae, in large enough numbers, can be a real problem. They feed on root hairs and small feeder roots, which causes stunted growth, off-color leaves or, in cases of severe infestation, leaf drop.

CONTROL There are several simple ways to prevent fungus gnats from taking over. Avoid overwatering, use a sterile potting mix to keep from passing larvae along and remove plant debris from the soil's surface.

If you do see these winged visitors hovering around your plants, push a potato cube into the soil of each plant to attract the larvae. Remove the potato piece after a few days and discard in the trash. Add another potato if you still see gnats around. For severe infestations, try Gnatrol®. It's a special strain of Bt bacteria (*Bacillus thuringiensis*), which is safe for home use. Ask for it at your local garden center.

Actual size ⅛ in.

Sooty mold

WHAT IS IT? Have you noticed a coating that looks like chimney soot on your plants, trees or even the deck or sidewalk? You can rub it off and it doesn't seem to harm anything but it sure looks bad. More than likely, it's sooty mold. This harmless fungus is actually a by-product of insects infesting nearby plants. Sooty mold grows on honeydew, a clear, sticky substance secreted by sucking insects, such as aphids, scale, mealy bugs and whiteflies.

WHAT DOES IT DO? While most of the damage caused by sooty mold is purely cosmetic, a thick layer on leaves or evergreen needles can reduce a plant's ability to perform photosynthesis, or feed itself. This weakens the plant, making it more susceptible to other diseases or insects. It's a particular problem for shade or understory plants, such as rhododendrons, hostas or hydrangeas, which already grow in low light.

HOW TO FIX IT To keep sooty mold from coming back, you'll need to eliminate the insects producing the honeydew. Take a good look above the area where you see sooty mold. The most common sap-sucking culprits you'll find are aphids and scale. Aphids are easily dislodged with a good strong spray from your hose. Use horticultural oil on scale insects to suffocate them. Also, some plants are sensitive to these oils, so be sure to check the label before you spray. Once the insects and the honeydew they produce are gone, the mold will gradually wear away from leaf and stem surfaces. To remove stubborn spots on hardscaping, a little scrubbing with soapy water does the trick.

Aphid *Aphid* spp.

IDENTIFICATION Just about every gardener has come across a colony of aphids at some point.

There are 250 species of these soft-bodied insects and they've been known to dine on almost anything. Most aphids are black or brown but some are green, red, gray, orange, yellow or even pink. Depending on the species, weather conditions and environmental stresses like overcrowding, some aphids will have wings and some won't.

Only living about a month, most aphids are females that give birth to several live nymphs each day. The last generation of the season lays eggs on various host plants, where they overwinter and hatch in spring.

DAMAGE With their sucking mouthparts, aphids draw sap from leaves, stems, branches, fruit, flowers and even roots. Look for twisted or curled leaves or stems, discolored leaves, galls or stunted growth. Plants can often survive the physical damage aphids do, but these pests also spread a lot of plant diseases. The cotton aphid, for example, can transmit more than 50 plant viruses and the peach aphid more than 100.

CONTROL The simplest way to get rid of aphids is to spray the affected plant with a jet of water from the hose. You can also snip off any affected leaves or stems and dispose of them in the trash. If that doesn't help, try horticultural oil (available from local garden centers). It's safe to use around people and pets and has little effect on beneficial insects. It also helps inhibit the spread of the viruses aphids carry. Spray the leaves' top and bottom. Some plants and trees are sensitive to these oils, so check the label directions first.

Actual size: 1/16 to 1/8 in.

6 weeds to know

Common burdock
Arctium minus

IDENTIFICATION If you've ever walked through a patch of weeds and come out with brown spiky balls stuck to your clothing, you know why you want to get rid of burdock.

This biennial spreads by seed. The first year it makes a low rosette of coarse, pale green leaves. In spring of the second year, the center of the rosette begins to stretch, and by summer, the branched flowering stalk can be 5 ft. tall. Near the base, this stalk and its side branches are often tinted pink or burgundy.

Rosy purple flowers bloom in summer and early fall. As they fade, the flowers change into ¾-in. fuzzy brown seed clusters, or *burrs*.

FAVORITE CONDITIONS Found across much of the United States and well into Canada, this weed is very adaptable. Full sun or shade, rich soil or poor, will suit it fine. Since it takes two years to produce seed, common burdock likes areas that are undisturbed. You'll find it in shrub borders or along fences. Occasionally it sprouts in thin spots in your lawn, but mowing will usually keep it short with no seeds.

CONTROL Cultivating will kill common burdock seedlings. If you don't get rid of first-year sprouts, your objective is to prevent seeds on second-year plants. Pulling can be difficult — this weed has a long, fleshy tap root. Instead, as you spot flower stems starting to stretch, cut the plant off with a sharp spade at the base. However, root pieces in the soil will grow back, so repeat this process until the plant dies. If flower heads have started to turn brown, they've set seeds. Cut them off and send these plants away in the trash.

And as with many pesky weeds, you can use a herbicide. In lawns, a broadleaf herbicide containing 2,4-D, is effective but won't harm the grass. Nonselective weed killers, such as Round-up®, are fine where you don't mind getting rid of everything.

First-year rosette

Burrs

Second-year flowering plant

White campion
Silene latifolia alba

IDENTIFICATION If this biennial or short-lived perennial weed didn't get out of hand so quickly, you might want it in your flower border. From June until August the white to pale-pink flowers open in the evening to release their sweet fragrance.

After being pollinated by night-flying insects, one female white campion plant can produce 24,000 seeds. That can spell trouble in your garden for years to come if you don't get rid of this pest before it drops seeds.

White campion reaches 1 to 3 ft. tall and is often confused with night-flowering catchfly, another pesky weed. But catchfly is covered with a sticky substance and white campion isn't.

FAVORITE CONDITIONS White campion grows in the upper three quarters of the United States and well into Canada. You'll find it in dry areas that have been disturbed, but are not cultivated regularly. Perennial, ground cover and shrub beds, as well as fence rows and hedges, are all spots where you'll find it making itself at home.

CONTROL Since this is a short-lived pest that produces huge quantities of seed, your objective is to prevent those seeds from forming. Cutting off plants as soon as you spot the flowers, or before, is a good control. So is hoeing or cultivating the area. And if you have a large stand of white campion where you can't till, use a non-selective herbicide, such as Roundup®.

Prostrate vervain
Verbena bracteata

IDENTIFICATION This sprawling annual or short-lived perennial often grows in colonies or dense mats. Start pulling individual plants and you'll find each one is 6 to 12 in. tall and between 6 and 18 in. wide with a single taproot. The branches all radiate from one central point.

Tiny blue to pale-purple clusters of flowers start opening in summer and continue to bloom well into fall.

FAVORITE CONDITIONS You'll find this pest spreading in shrub borders or among your perennials and ground covers, as well as out into your lawn. Rarely will you find it in areas that are regularly cultivated.

Prostrate vervain thrives with full sun in poor, dry conditions. During extreme drought the fuzzy leaves in the center of the plant will turn brown, but it'll keep on flowering. This is a weed that tolerates gravel areas and grows just fine in the cracks of a sidewalk.

CONTROL Since prostrate vervain spreads by seed, hoeing or pulling the seedlings before they bloom is a good way to get it under control. In your lawn, you'll need to apply a selective broadleaf herbicide, such as 2,4-D or dicamba, so you don't kill the grass.

Wild garlic
Allium vineale

IDENTIFICATION If you smell garlic when you pull a handful of weeds or walk across your lawn, you've probably encountered wild garlic. All parts of this perennial have a garlic odor.

The grassy leaves are hollow waxy tubes, up to 2 ft. long. There's a groove along the side that faces the flowering stem in the center. In mid- to late summer, some wild garlic plants will have clusters of pale green, lavender or pink flowers atop 3-ft. stems. In among the tiny flowers will be *aerial bulbils*, tiny bulblets that develop above ground. Some wild garlic plants will have clusters of bulbils without any flowers.

Dig and you'll discover a small, onionlike bulb with a papery covering. Next to the main bulb will often be several smaller bulblets.

FAVORITE CONDITIONS Wild garlic grows in cultivated gardens as well as lawns, prefers heavy fertile soil and will tolerate wet conditions. It's found throughout much of the United States and southern Canada, especially in areas where summers are hot and moist.

CONTROL Dig in late spring and make sure to get rid of even the tiniest bulblets for an effective control. Repeated tilling will also rid your garden of this weed, but it may take several years. Herbicides, such as 2,4-D or glyphosate, will kill wild garlic. Always read the label for specific instructions. Mowing or cutting the stems back so the plant can't set seeds or produce aerial bulbils is always a good idea to prevent the spread of this pesky weed.

Common ragweed
Ambrosia artemisiifolia

IDENTIFICATION If you have pollen allergies, often called "hay fever," you'll certainly know when the spiky green ragweed flowers open. Common ragweed is found over most of North America except the very coldest regions of Canada and the United States. This 3-ft.-tall annual is a prolific bloomer, releasing large quantities of pollen before it sets seeds. And it has a couple of equally prolific relatives.

Giant ragweed, another annual, grows in much of North America except the far west coast and desert areas. It can grow up to 15 ft. tall with large, coarse leaves and stems you might mistake for tree saplings.

Western ragweed grows 3 ft. tall and spreads by underground roots or by seeds. It's perennial but often acts as an annual in very cold winter areas and then only spreads by seed. You'll find it in much of North America, except for the southeastern United States and far west Canada.

Common ragweed
Ambrosia artemisiifolia

Giant ragweed
Ambrosia trifida

Western ragweed
Ambrosia psilostachya

FAVORITE CONDITIONS All three ragweeds need full sun and grow quickly in poor, dry soil. But you'll find them in your nice, compost-enriched, regularly watered vegetable gardens and flower borders, too. They prefer spots that are cultivated or disturbed once or twice in spring or summer and then ignored the rest of the season.

CONTROL All of the species are easy to pull or hoe out before they set seeds. However, since western ragweed is a perennial, make sure you remove all of the roots. Large patches of ragweed can be repeatedly cut down to keep them from setting seed. Or use a broadleaf or a nonselective herbicide to kill it in areas where you can't pull or keep it mowed.

Honeyvine milkweed
Cynanchum laeve

IDENTIFICATION From early summer to fall, if you peek under the heart-shaped leaves of this vine, you'll find clusters of tiny white flowers. Often the vines are mistaken for morning glories or bindweeds, but the insignificant flowers are the easiest way to tell the difference.

Once you spot the distinctive 3- to 6-in.-long seed pods in late summer, you'll know this is a member of the milkweed family. And like a common milkweed, the pod splits open in fall to release lots of brown seeds with long silky white hairs. Once open, that tuft of hair helps the seed drift on the wind.

FAVORITE CONDITIONS Found over much of the eastern two-thirds of North America, honeyvine milkweed grows lush in full sun and fertile, moist soil. Usually you'll spot this pest winding its way up into

shrubs, tall perennials or fences. However, it can also spread across the ground or even drape over a wall. You'll also find it grows in both cultivated and undisturbed areas.

CONTROL This perennial spreads by seeds and underground rhizomes. Keep stems cut short to prevent seeds from forming. If you spot hanging pods in late summer, pick them and send them away in the trash.

When you try to pull or dig these vines, you'll find a deep taproot with many side shoots. The roots are also brittle and break easily. Any pieces left behind in the soil will grow a new vine. The best control is a systemic herbicide, such as Roundup®, that will kill roots and all.

3- to 6-in.-long pods are filled with seeds.

Rhizomes are brittle and hard to pull out.

know YOUR zone

WHAT'S A ZONE AND WHY DOES IT MATTER?

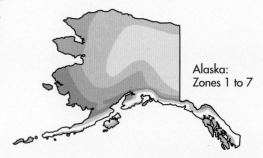

Alaska:
Zones 1 to 7

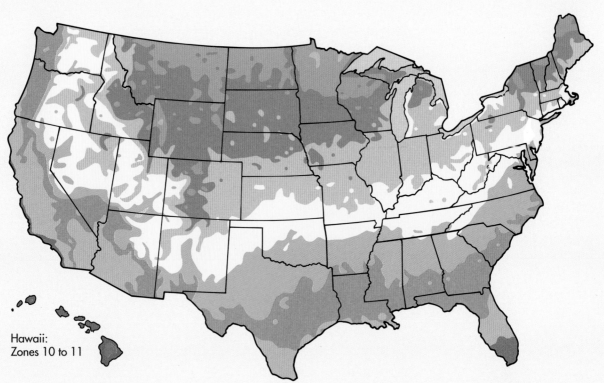

Hawaii:
Zones 10 to 11

COLD Hardiness

The USDA cold-hardiness map has long been the authority to help gardeners pick plants that will survive through the winter. It creates zones based on coldest average annual temperatures throughout the United States. A plant's cold-hardiness zone rating indicates where it's likely to survive the winter.

NOTE: For zones in Canada and Mexico, visit www.usna.usda.gov/Hardzone/ushzmap.html.

AVERAGE LOW TEMPERATURE			ZONE
Below -45			1
-40	to	-45	2
-30	to	-40	3
-20	to	-30	4
-10	to	-20	5
0	to	-10	6

AVERAGE LOW TEMPERATURE			ZONE
10	to	0	7
20	to	10	8
30	to	20	9
40	to	30	10
Above 40			11

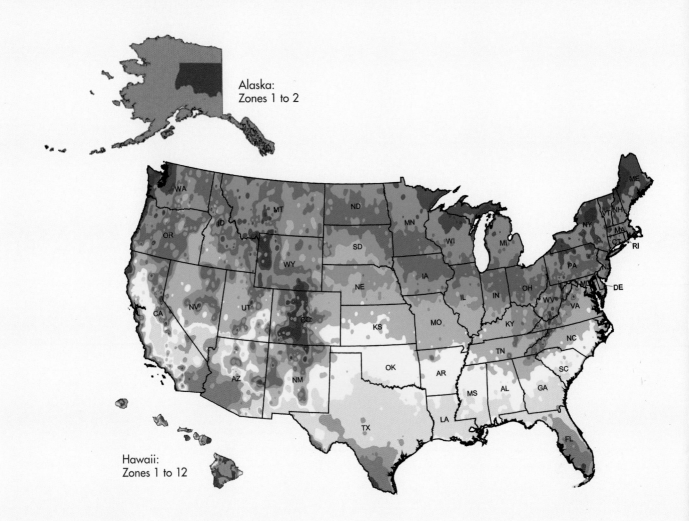

Alaska:
Zones 1 to 2

Hawaii:
Zones 1 to 12

DAYS ABOVE 86°	ZONE		DAYS ABOVE 86°	ZONE
Fewer than 1	1		60 to 90	7
1 to 7	2		90 to 120	8
7 to 14	3		120 to 150	9
14 to 30	4		150 to 180	10
30 to 45	5		180 to 210	11
45 to 60	6		More than 210	12

HEAT Tolerance

The American Horticultural Society's heat-zone map can help you determine how plants will cope with heat.

This map of the country is divided into 12 zones to indicate the average number of days in a year when the temperature goes above 86 degrees F. This is the temperature at which plants begin suffering and are unable to process water fast enough to maintain normal functions. Zone 1, the coldest zone, has less than one day. Zone 12, the hottest zone, has more than 210 days above 86 per year.

did you know...

Arbor Day Foundation changes zones

The National Arbor Day Foundation (NADF) has updated its hardiness zone map. Starting with the USDA zone map as a base, researchers examined 15 years of temperature information from the National Oceanic and Atmospheric Administration's 5,000 climatic data centers across the country. When everything was tabulated, the NADF decided to make some changes. Many areas of the country have moved up a full zone because of temperature changes over this time period. Check out www.arborday.org for the new cold-hardiness zone recommendations.

The YEAR IN GARDENING Volume 13 INDEX

How to use your index

The index is divided by main topics with specific references following. All plants are referred to by botanical name.

For example, if you are looking for information about burning bush, the entry will look like this:

  burning bush *see Euonymus*

Then turn to the reference for *Euonymus*, which looks like this:

Main topic (in this case, genus name)

Euonymus ——— Species reference

  alatus (burning bush)   Specific reference
    pruning, p. 278 ◄——— to topic
    for south-facing foundation, p. 160

You also might come across a topic that gives you specific references as well as an idea of other places in the index to look for similar information. For example:

  containers
    see also garden plans; hanging baskets
    buying potting soil for, p. 244
    for entries, p. 156

ILLUSTRATIONS: Mavis Augustine Torke

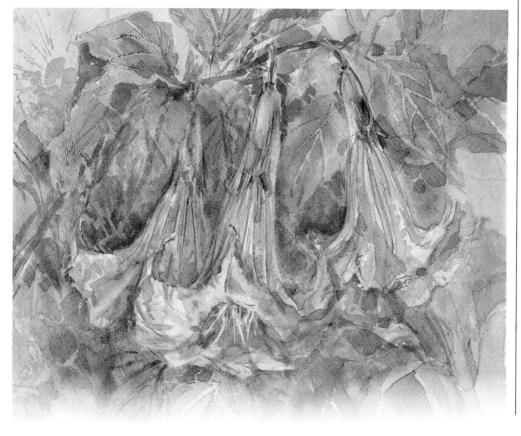

Want helpful garden advice delivered EVERY WEEK?

Then you'll LOVE our weekly e-notes. They're filled with:

- At-a-glance plant guides
- Pests and weeds to watch (and how to eliminate them)
- How-to videos and projects
- Practical tips that make gardening easier

Visit **www.GardenGateMagazine.com** to become a member today!

Garden Gate *e-notes*
From our garden to your desktop

For more great gardening, visit... GardenGateMagazine.com I GardenGateStore.com

a twist in time trains vines

If you ever wanted to train a vine up a brick wall without having to drill into it to install a trellis or hooks, try this technique.

Use clear silicone adhesive sealant (available in small tubes at hardware stores) and plastic-coated twist-ties to secure the vine. Dab a small amount of the sealant onto the wall. Then bend the twist-tie into a "U" shape and put the center of the "U" into the blob of sealant. Let the sealant set for a day, then gently bend the vine over and fasten the twist-tie around it.

Try to use green or black twist-ties and clear sealant because they're nearly invisible once the vine is tied up. Twist-ties attached like this will last for years, but peel off easily with a small scraper (without damaging the surface underneath) if you need to remove them.

This method works well for almost any type of vine, including those that need to be pruned hard every year. It's easy to unfasten the twist-tie and take down the mass of cut-back stems.

favorite tools

Pruner sharpener FREE $10.99 value

Pruning Gift Set

Felco pruners and sheath, The Pruner's Bible and a sharpener — the perfect gift for the gardener in your life...

Simplicity
is the
ultimate
Sophistication

— *Leonardo da Vinci*